LANGUAGE USE AND SOCIAL CHANGE

LANGUAGE USE AND SOCIAL CHANGE

Problems of Multilingualism with Special Reference to Eastern Africa

Studies presented and discussed at the ninth International African Seminar at University College, Dar es Salaam, December 1968

Edited with an Introduction by

W. H. WHITELEY

Foreword by

DARYLL FORDE

Director, International African Institute

Published for the

INTERNATIONAL AFRICAN INSTITUTE

by

OXFORD UNIVERSITY PRESS

1971

Oxford University Press, Ely House, London W.1

GLASGOW NEW YORK TORONTO MELBOURNE WELLINGTON
CAPE TOWN SALISBURY IBADAN NAIROBI DAR ES SALAAM LUSAKA ADDIS ABABA
BOMBAY CALCUTTA MADRAS KARACHI LAHORE DACCA
KUALA LUMPUR SINGAPORE HONG KONG TOKYO

SBN 19 724183 2

Printed in Great Britain by Richard Clay (The Chaucer Press), Ltd., Bungay, Suffolk

Contents

B. EMPIRICAL STUDIES WITHIN AFRICA

(i) *The Implications and Results of Particular Language Policies*

(ii) *Education and Language Policies*

(iii) *Language Modernization*

Foreword

The papers prepared for and discussed at the Ninth International African Seminar, which was held at University College, Dar es Salaam in December 1968, under the Chairmanship of Professor W. H. Whiteley, are presented in this volume. Several of them have been revised in the light of arguments and further material that emerged during the week of very active and constructive debate.

The Seminar had been arranged to coincide with a three-day Regional Conference sponsored by the Survey of Language Use and Language Teaching in Eastern Africa, which is conducting field studies in five countries in the region. Most of the field research workers on this project participated in the Seminar, and a number of others attending the conference took part in some of the Seminar sessions. The Institute was happy to have the opportunity of co-operating with the Survey project in this way and wishes to express its thanks to the then Director, Professor Clifford H. Prator. It enabled participants in the Seminar to meet and have most useful discussions with a number of other linguists and with teachers and administrators concerned with language studies in East Africa.

The twenty-two papers presented here are somewhat different in scope from those published in earlier volumes recording the work of the International African Seminars. In the first place the theme of the Seminar was focused on one region—Eastern Africa—and did not attempt to review problems relating to Africa as a whole. Furthermore, the subject discussed—the social implications of multilingualism—is one on which relatively little research had so far been undertaken in Africa. We therefore invited the participation of several scholars who could make relevant contributions concerning theoretical problems and methods in socio-linguistic studies although their own work had lain mainly outside Africa.

The Introduction by the Chairman outlines and comments

on several fields of inquiry that were discussed during the Seminar. The papers have been grouped in two sections: the first includes general and theoretical studies, and the second empirical studies of various aspects of multilingualism in Africa. Among the former are papers on national languages and languages of wider communication in developing nations; the communication roles of languages in multilingual societies; the social and cognitive aspects of bilingualism; the study of restricted codes in sociolinguistics; and the interrelationships and utility of alternative measures of bilingualism. The studies on particular socio-linguistic problems in Eastern Africa are relevant to several larger themes: the objectives and effects of national language policies; language policies in education; language modernization; language use in the urban milieu; multilingualism and multiculturism. They contribute to a fuller understanding of a number of practical and often urgent questions, such as the language policies of Uganda and Tanzania; the differing and changing roles of Swahili and English; the problems of education in a foreign language; the use of broadcasting in the adaptation of a language for modern uses; methods for language elaboration as illustrated by work on basic Wolof; the study of loan words as exemplified in Luganda.

The Institute is greatly indebted to the participants in the Seminar for the time and thought they gave to the preparation of their papers, and especially to Professor Whiteley for his most capable chairmanship and for editing the volume. It wishes to thank the Principal of University College, Dar es Salaam, Dr. W. K. Chagula, for the welcome and hospitality given to the Seminar and his staff for their assistance in organizing the meetings. It also gratefully acknowledges the continued and generous financial support of the Ford Foundation, which enabled us to organize and conduct this Seminar and to publish this volume.

January 1970

DARYLL FORDE
Director

Introduction

PREAMBLE

It is perhaps no more than trite to suggest that multilingualism has been a fact of social life in Africa for a very long time, but facts lack significance until they are brought within an ordered frame of reference, and for many years both linguist and social anthropologist were more concerned with uniformity than with diversity, with a holistic rather than an atomistic view. In social anthropology this was due in part to a legacy of Malinowskian functionalism with an emphasis on units like that of the tribe, worked out in conditions very different from the African setting.[1] It also derived in part, I think, from the development of techniques for the intensive study of small communities over long periods: if such study were to form a viable basis for extrapolation to the tribe or tribal group,[2] then there must be some presumption of uniformity. Characteristically, concern for language in such studies was pragmatic: one learned the language of one's people and believed intuitively in an entity labelled 'their language'. In some cases language featured specifically in the definition of tribe,[3] but more usually it constituted simply one of a number of distinctive features. Occasionally this was questioned, thus, 'If the Nupe tribe is thus not a local group in the strict sense of the word, it is not a linguistic

[1] 'The illusion of tribe', A. W. Southall, *Journal of Asian and African Studies*, 5, 1/2, 1970. See also *Tradition and Transition in East Africa*, ed. P. H. Gulliver, Routledge, 1969, esp. the Introduction.

[2] This is not to deny that the initial choice of segment may have been made with careful regard for a number of variables. See in this connection, 'On quantification in social anthropology', J. C. Mitchell in *The Craft of Social Anthropology*, ed. A. L. Epstein, Social Science Paperbacks, 1967, pp. 17–45.

[3] Thus, Radcliffe-Brown using the Australian aborigines as an example, 'A number of clans had the same language, and had similar customs; they therefore formed a linguistic community, which is referred to as a *tribe*.' 'Social Structure' in *Method in Social Anthropology*, selected essays by A. R. Radcliffe-Brown, ed. M. N. Srinivas, University of Chicago Press, 1958, p. 171.

unit either',[1] but Nadel was certainly one of the few people at the time to appreciate the social significance of language and language variation, though in his Saussurean distinction between the operational and structural aspects of languages he misses completely the significance of the operational aspects for linguists.[2] Linguists, for their part, eschewed the situational view of language stressed by Malinowski, and concentrated on making extremely detailed descriptions of a limited corpus of material obtained from one or more informants. This is not to question the value of the single-informant technique as a procedural imperative in the face of linguistic complexity, but to ignore the fact that 'even a single individual comprises a range of styles and a span of history',[3] and to use the material as a sample from which to extrapolate to the point where one could say that it constituted a grammar of language X seems to me much more questionable.

Where previously, however, there was a presumption of uniformity, present awareness is of diversity: ethnic boundaries are recognized as being essentially blurred, and not only because wider, more inclusive, groupings have been established. Increased social mobility has resulted in the development of ethnically heterogeneous communities, even in rural areas; towns have swollen enormously in size and are increasingly permanent places of residence. Yet if the concept of tribe is no longer a useful tool, and positive anathema to the politician, one may note in passing with what passion tribal identities are being fought for by those for whom supra-tribal affiliations do not yet evoke comparable loyalties. Linguists, for their part, have recognized anew the truth of Firth's dictum 'there is no such thing as *une language une* and there never has been',[4] and have discovered such phenomena as 'diglossia' and 'register'.[5]

[1] *A Black Byzantium*, S. F. Nadel, Oxford, 1942, p. 13.

[2] See, for example, Chapter V (esp. p. 88) in *The Foundations of Social Anthropology*, S. F. Nadel, Cohen and West, 1951.

[3] 'Creole language areas considered as multilingual communities', David DeCamp, *Symposium on Multilingualism*, CSA/CCTA, 1964, p. 229.

[4] 'The Technique of Semantics', reprinted in *Papers in Linguistics, 1934–51*, J. R. Firth, Oxford, 1957, p. 29.

[5] The term 'diglossia' was originally introduced by Ferguson for a more or less stable situation in which 'two or more varieties of the same language are used by some speakers under different conditions' ('Diglossia', *Word*, 15, 1959, p. 325), with the result that one tends to acquire a 'high' status and the other a 'low' status,

Ferguson's work followed on from the earlier studies on language contact by such scholars as Haugen and Weinreich and has itself stimulated much further work in the fields of bilingualism and multilingualism. The term 'register', elaborated by Halliday, stressed what had long been ignored, namely, that languages vary according to use as well as according to user and that such varieties are co-variant with 'fields of discourse' or social setting. It may turn out that the concept of register is as elusive to describe as its illuminating predecessor 'the context of situation' has turned out to be, but of its existence there can be no reasonable doubt. Though linguists were first sensitized to linguistic diversity by the study of language contact, this was, for some years, conceived in terms of a twilight zone of interference between two undifferentiated entities; a situation which was difficult to describe in unistructural terms, and one which had, moreover, an air of the marginal about it. The recognition that the entities were themselves highly differentiated, and that even in the so-called monolingual communities speakers had at their disposal a number of functional variants or registers[1] facilitated important changes in outlook. It has forced linguists to recognize language variety as a matter of central concern to linguistics, but perhaps more importantly, it has made possible

---

e.g. the Katharévousa and Standard Demotic varieties of Greek. Later writers have expanded its use: thus Fishman, 'In the diglossia situation a single society recognizes two or more languages as its own, with each having its own *functionally exclusive* domains' ('Nationality-Nationalism and Nation-Nationism', in *Language Problems of Developing Nations*, eds. J. A. Fishman, C. A. Ferguson, J. Das Gupta, Wiley, 1968, p. 45). Fishman also makes the point that while bilingualism is a feature at the level of individual behaviour, 'diglossia' operates at the institutional level.

To the extent that a 'register' is also a functional variant of a language (*The Linguistic Sciences and Language Teaching*' M. A. K. Halliday, A. McIntosh, P. Strevens, Longmans, 1964, esp. Ch. 4) one might also regard the two varieties of Greek as registers, but generally speaking, this term is used of more restricted varieties, i.e. of the myriad, discrete codes which a speaker/writer may have at his disposal in participating in social roles. Thus one can talk about the registers of football, the courts, medicine, advertising, etc., provided that they are marked off significantly from one another by grammar and lexis. In this they display affinities with the 'codes' of Bernstein (see below and p. 13, fn. 1).

[1] See, for example, the early article of B. Bernstein, 'Language and social class', *British Journal of Sociology*, 11, 1960, and the discussion of Bernstein's ideas in Denis Lawton, *Social Class, Language and Education*, Routledge, 1968. Also, W. Labov's *The Social Stratification of English in New York City*, Center for Applied Linguistics, 1966.

a reintegration of linguistic and sociological studies. New questions are now being asked: how do particular language varieties pattern in respect to the social roles, situations, transactions, networks, and domains of the sociological and social anthropological literature?[1] Yet it is not simply a question of establishing the congruence or otherwise or sociological and linguistic categories set up originally for intra-disciplinary purposes but rather of devising new techniques on an interdisciplinary basis in order to achieve a sociolinguistic description. This is now being done.[2]

Africa presents many challenges of a sociolinguistic kind: some, at the national level, have already received a good deal of attention; others, at community level, have so far been comparatively neglected. At the national level many states are preoccupied with problems of accommodating their multi-ethnic and multilingual components within a single political framework. One aspect of this preoccupation is the formulation of specific language policies which attempt to reconcile the importance acquired by a metropolitan language during the period of Colonial rule with post-independence aspirations. Among the most powerful devices for implementing a language policy is the educational system, particularly if the most widely desirable rewards are given to those who pass through it. Where additionally the system may be represented by a very steep-sided pyramid, there is a good chance that the language skills of those who, say, complete only primary education will not only be different from but in some sense opposed to those who continue right through the system. Some of the more accessible—as well as the more important—sociolinguistic

[1] There is a considerable literature on social roles to which I will not refer in detail here, but it is worth noting how sparse are the references to the contribution of language in the general studies of role analysis. For expositions of the other technical terms see J. van Velsen 'The extended-case method and situational analysis', in Epstein, op. cit., pp. 129–49; F. Barth, *Models of Social Organization*, Occ. Paper 27, RAI, 1966; J. A. Fishman 'Language maintenance and language shift as a field of enquiry', *Linguistics*, 9, Nov. 1964, 32–70 and also 'The relationship between micro- and macro-sociolinguistics in the study of who speaks what language to whom and when?' to appear in *Directions in Sociolinguistics: the Ethnography of Communication*, eds. Dell Hymes and J. J. Gumperz, Holt Rinehart, 1970.

[2] One approach has been sketched out by Dell Hymes in his 'Models of the interaction of language and social setting', *Journal of Social Issues*, XXIII/2, 1967, 8–28. Another view has been put forward by J. A. Fishman in 'Sociolinguistic perspective on the study of bilingualism', *Linguistics*, 39, May 1968, 21–49.

problems of multilingualism are exemplified by the educational system, and scholars have not been slow to take advantage of the fact. Such problems as the aptitudes of bilinguals, attitude formation in culturally heterogeneous communities, and the teaching of a second or third language to children of differing first languages have attracted the attention of psychologists, social psychologists, and educationists. The educational interest was particularly in evidence at the colloquium on multilingualism held at Brazzaville in 1962[1] under the auspices of the Scientific Council for Africa, where two-fifths of the papers dealt with educational implications of multilingualism. The remainder dealt with descriptive studies of contact situations and problems of Creoles and Pidgins, and it is not surprising that Creolists have been among the first to recognize the limitations of unistructural assumptions in linguistic analysis.[2] Since then the focus of interest has widened to include the study of national language policies,[3] the urban milieu of multilingualism, and a variety of situations marked by diglossia. The papers in the present volume, therefore, prepared for the Ninth International African Seminar held at the University College, Dar es Salaam, in December 1968, cover a wide range of topics. If they, and the discussion carried on over the six days of the Seminar, throw into relief lacunae in our present knowledge they also point the way to fruitful areas for further research.

It has not been easy to arrive at a satisfactory ordering of the papers, since both in subject matter and approach they represent a series of antitheses or perhaps complementarities. There is, for example, a group of six papers dealing with general or theoretical issues that are based on material derived from work done largely outside Africa but which provide hypotheses for testing in the African context. The rest of the papers, by contrast, are concerned to describe empirical studies either in progress or recently completed. As an alternative one could view one group of papers as being primarily concerned with the implementation or outcome of present or past language policies,

[1] *Multilingualism*, CSA/CCTA, No. 87, 1964.

[2] See, for example, the articles by J. Berry and David DeCamp in the publication cited above.

[3] A good example of this is J. A. Fishman, C. A. Ferguson, and J. Das Gupta, op. cit., and the forthcoming *Can Language Use be Planned?*, eds. J. Rubin and B. Jernudd, East–West Centre, 1970 (?).

where the choice has already been made, as distinct from another set which is concerned mainly with describing particular multilingual situations so as to clarify the factors which need to be taken into consideration when future choices are made. Running through many of the papers, and throughout much of the discussion, there was also a thread of concern for research techniques which occasionally polarized into the advocacy either of survey-type techniques developed in social psychology and sociology or of intensive studies of situations or small communities along the lines developed by social anthropology. The sequence which I have adopted, while it violates the order in which the papers were presented at Dar es Salaam, does nevertheless, I feel, make for as great a sense of continuity as is compatible with their very diverse contents. One of the pleasures of discussions at which specialists from other disciplines and regions are present is the opportunity provided for absorbing and testing new hypotheses. I should like, therefore, to return to three of the more general topics discussed at length during the Seminar with a view to providing some additional exemplificatory African data and to assessing the problems this entails.

THE TYPOLOGY OF NATIONAL LANGUAGE POLICIES

So much material is accumulating on language policies throughout the world that it is now possible to mark the advance of our knowledge by setting up a typology of language policies and decisions relating to them. Joshua Fishman has now done this in the present volume, and I should like to carry the process a stage further by considering the extent to which the language policies of Kenya and Tanzania can be said to fall within the Types A and B as proposed by him, thereby making good, to some extent, the loss of information suffered in the process of abstraction, and assessing whether the simplification inherent in the process of idealization has also distorted the picture. Fishman stresses, and this seems to me to be particularly important, that the new states must reach a synthesis between the old or indigenous and the modern or foreign. The prevailing pattern can be seen in the relative importance accorded to decisions relating to 'nationism', the search for operational efficiency, as against those relating to 'nationalism', the search for authenticity. In the schema proposed by Fishman, Type A policies are, among other things, characterized by the former, and Type B policies by the latter. In the present context of Tanzania and Kenya, it seems to me arguable that decisions characteristic of both Type A and Type B policies are operated simultaneously within a single state in just such an attempt to synthesize the conflicting demands made upon it. Fishman recognizes the problem by allocating Tanzania to an intermediate position between Type A and B, but whereas he appears to regard this as a transitional phase, I see no reason why a 'steady state' should not be achieved over a fairly long period by judicious balancing of elements from each. On the face of it Kenya would appear to fall into Type A. There is no 'Great Tradition' in Redfield's sense of the term. A Language of Wider Communication, English, is extensively used as an official language, and this selection appears to serve the needs of 'nationism'. There are, in consequence, few problems of language planning other than at a pedagogic level. On the other hand, there is also a considerable body of *élite* opinion in the country that is more concerned with authenticity, that argues that Swahili provides some kind of a Great Tradition, and that it could and should replace English as soon as possible and in as wide a range of contexts as possible. In so far as any bilingualism or bicultural goals are formulated, they would appear to be closer to Type C than to either A or B. The result of this situation is that while English is used in many official contexts, the claims of nationalism require that local languages be used on the Radio, in Primary education, and in the African cultural revival which is advocated from time to time. A combination of these and other factors, such as the repudiation of tribalism, requires that Swahili be used as the language of the Provincial and District administration. It is interesting to note that President Kenyatta has recently pledged Swahili as the country's official language in terms which unequivocally stress the object of authenticity, 'We have got to be proud and use our own language', and he declared that, 'We are soon going to use Swahili in Parliament, whether people like it or not.'[1] It is characteristic that announcements relating to authenticity should be made in the context of large, public rallies, while

[1] Reported in the *Daily Nation*, 1 September 1969.

those relating to modernity should be made in small committees or not at all. The publicity given to the former ensures a spate of comment in the Press and reiteration of the main points in smaller meetings during the succeeding weeks. The latter, when pressed, stress the importance of internationalism and efficiency, 'If we were to introduce Swahili as an official language, what should I do in drafting legislation?'[1] Tanzania, by contrast, would appear to fall into Type B, rather than intermediately. An indigenous language, but certainly also an inter-regional lingua franca, Swahili, is officially the national language and is demonstrably capable of serving an integrative function at nationwide level (see also Abdulaziz, pp. 168 ff). Any 'Great Tradition' has very little historical depth, but such a tradition which, it is claimed, Swahili is uniquely able to express and maintain, is rapidly being built up by the current ruling *élite*. It would be true, I think, to say that Tanzanians already possess 'a strong national identity but must seek to render it more functional for the purposes of national well-being in the modern world' (one of the characteristics of Type B policies). The role of English is diminishing and is essentially one of expediency; modernization of the national language is being undertaken by agencies such as the National Swahili Council. On the other hand, objectively, in terms of its Great Tradition, or lack of it, Tanzania would appear to be closer to the Type A pattern, and it is certainly true that English is being retained at critical points in the system out of considerations for operational efficiency. It is also true that in terms of policies towards local languages Tanzania is much closer to those of Type A than to Type B.

In both Kenya and Tanzania it seems to me that some decisions conforming to a Type A pattern co-exist with others related to a Type B pattern, and that the particular flavour of a country's language policy at a given moment in time is dependent on whether modernity or authenticity require stressing—and these are essentially political decisions. While Tanzania is primarily concerned with authenticity at the present moment, Kenya is largely committed to modernity, but the recent debate in Parliament preceding the President's announcement suggests

[1] The Attorney General, Mr. Charles Njonjo, as reported in the *East African Standard*, 26 July 1969.

that an authenticity-seeking period may be imminent. Other countries present similar patterns: Malawi, for example, appears to conform very closely to that suggested for Type A policies, but the recent decision to elevate Chewa to the status of an official language alongside English, and the consequent implications of this for education, the Radio, the Press, and for administration generally suggest that here, too, there is a need to stress authenticity. Fishman suggests that in Type B policies there will be a need for extensive language-planning, since it is the indigenous/indigenized language which performs the crucial integrative role. In suggesting that decisions characteristic of both Type A and B policies are likely to co-occur, it is clear that unless the planning processes as applied to African languages are maintained at a fairly constant level there is likely to be a good deal of wasted effort. This is particularly important in relatively 'poor' countries, where, during periods in which modernity is at a premium, scarce resources may be switched from language-planning activities. The essentially cyclic character of language-planning activities in Turkey, and perhaps also in the Irish Republic and Norway,[1] provide interesting examples of the kind of situation that may develop in eastern Africa. On the other hand, there are other authenticating and modernizing devices than language, so that it is possible that the role of official/national languages may be drastically altered in the future.

ELABORATED AND RESTRICTED CODES

There is no gainsaying the fact that the ideas of Bernstein and his colleagues engender an excitement which is by no means all dispelled by the difficulties attendant upon their validation and application. While discoverable linguistic differences are postulated between the two ideal codes, 'elaborated' and 'restricted', the major difference between the two appears to be that they 'are generated by a particular form of social relation. Indeed they are likely to be a realisation of different social structures'.[2] Elsewhere in the article quoted Bernstein talks of the codes as

[1] See, in particular, the articles by C. Gallagher and J. Macnamara in the volume edited by Rubin and Jernudd, op. cit.

[2] 'A socio-linguistic approach to socialization: with some reference to educability', B. Bernstein in *Directions in Sociolinguistics: the Ethnography of Communication*, eds. Dell Hymes and J. J. Gumperz, Holt Rinehart, 1970.

'realizing' particular social roles. The elaborated code occurs in roles where information is sought or offered about either the physical or social world, and in Britain 'the middle class are socialized into the attitudes, knowledge and skills which constitute this code' (Robinson, p. 78). The restricted code occurs where role definitions are sought or reaffirmed, in personal relations, and again, in Britain 'for the working class, especially the lower working class, language is not a medium of special significance. Speech has the primary function of defining the nature of such immediate role relations as mother, mate or boss' (Robinson, p. 78). The differences between the two may be summed up as follows, 'In terms of what is transmitted verbally, an elaborated code encourages the speaker to focus upon the experience of others, as different from his own. In the case of a restricted code, what is transmitted verbally usually refers to the other person in terms of common group or status membership. . . . Thus restricted codes could be considered status or positional codes whereas elaborated codes are oriented to persons.'[1] However, if the codes are in some sense realizations of roles it is not clear why at the present time restricted codes should tend to be generated particularly by 'low-status' groups (Robinson, p. 88); presumably role relations need to be defined at all levels of social class. What is more, it seems probable that roles are defined differently at different social levels, and that some provision ought to be made for these differences to be recognized in the codes. There seem to be two important problems here: the first concerns the linguistic differences between the codes and their possible relationship to such language varieties as registers. The second problem concerns the extent to which the codes are role-expounding or role-defining. If they have the former function, and if only two codes are postulated, then each code will presumably express a plurality of roles, and subsume several varieties of language; if the latter, then it would seem that a plurality of codes must be postulated. Bernstein himself does not make this point very clearly: in the article cited above there is an emphasis on the role-expounding function of the code, but in an earlier article he refers to the fact that, 'The code defines the form of the social relationship . . . these codes are induced by the social relation, they express it *and* regulate

[1] Bernstein, op. cit.

it.'[1] The issue is, however, an important one when considering the possible relevance that Bernstein's work may have in a multilingual setting. There has, so far, been no systematic attempt to test his findings in East Africa. This is partly, I think, from ignorance of them, but partly also because his general thesis is already accepted. In a superficially monolingual society like Britain a functional analysis of language linked to social stratification strikes an original note and carries serious implications for the educational system as a whole. In a multilingual country, such as Kenya, for example, there is widespread acceptance of the fact that particular codes are role-linked, and also of the fact that many of the most prestigious roles in current society require the ability to speak English, whether this fulfils the requirements of an elaborated code or not. A corollary to this is the awareness that a large section of the community is being deprived by not having access to English, so that one response, practised over a number of years, is to introduce study of the language progressively lower down the educational system. The possibility that there might come a time when there were more English-speakers than prestigious—or indeed any—jobs to offer them is only slowly being recognized. Such generalities, however, give little indication of the complexity of the situation, and some illustrations are called for. In a rural Kenya homestead which is ethnically homogeneous, inter-personal roles across generations, and even within the younger generation, are likely to be expounded in the local language whatever the actual choices available to an individual member. Such settings, like those in the rites of passage described for Kampala by Parkin (p. 359), may be described as language-fixed. Language-free settings, in which participants are not constrained to make particular selections, are much less common, and may be restricted to *élite* groups, though in some areas witnesses in court cases are free to speak in whatever language they like, it being incumbent upon the officers of the court to provide interpreters. Settings in which the participants are ethnically heterogeneous, whether these are inter-personal or not, are also language-fixed, but the actual choice of language will be determined by what is common to the group as a whole, or by what

[1] 'Elaborated and restricted codes: an outline', B. Bernstein, in *Explorations in Sociolinguistics*, ed. Stanley Lieberson, Mouton, 1966, pp. 128–9.

is laid down procedurally or by the nature of the inter-personal relationship and the roles which it entails. In rural Kenya this language will usually be Swahili. Now it is certainly true that there are many cases where the criteria for an elaborated code as set out by Bernstein will be met by Swahili, 'An elaborated code, where prediction is much less possible at the syntactic level, is likely to arise in that social relationship which raises the tension in its members to select a *verbal* arrangement from their linguistic resources which closely fits specific referents. This situation will arise where the intent of the other person cannot be taken for granted, having the consequence that meanings will have to be expanded and raised to the level of *verbal* explicitness.'[1] But it is also true that many inter-personal relationships are also expounded by Swahili, where the code would appear to be restricted. Similarly, there are settings, such as court cases, where a local language serves as an elaborated code. The position may be more complex in towns. Parkin (pp. 351 ff) has given three examples of language use in Kampala. In the first case, X used Swahili to a neighbour, a fellow Kenyan and a co-eval, for a short informal conversation, but switched to Luganda and then to English for a more formal conversation with a more senior Ugandan neighbour, from whom he was hoping to solicit a job. In the second case, of a meeting of the local tenants' association, Swahili was laid down as the normal language of business and the use of English by a member was criticized as improper. Finally, he cites the case of a group of friends from three ethnic groups who used English during an evening's conversation in a bar, but relapsed into their local languages when tempers became frayed. If one is thinking simply in terms of role-expression, then it would seem that the variety of Swahili constituted a restricted code in the first example, but an elaborated code in the second. The use of English in the first example constituted an elaborated code but probably a restricted one in the third. The question of language switching is more difficult: does one assume that in the first example the switch from Luganda to English marked a switch in roles, from that of friend to supplicant? This seems plausible, but there are many other cases where switching does not seem to mark such a switch in roles. In a multilingual situation it

[1] Op. cit. (1966), p. 128.

seems that, still in terms of role-expression, each language must, at the very least, be accounted capable of occurring in both restricted and elaborated codes, and that since particular settings impose restrictions on the actual choice of language, one language may act as a restricted code in one setting and as an elaborated code in another. As was noted in the previous section, however, present-day values in Kenya tend to polarize along the axes of modernity and authenticity, and the linguistic exponents of these are English and the local language respectively, with Swahili occupying an intermediate position, offering something of authenticity and something of modernity. In this sense the languages have acquired some of the attributes of the elaborated and restricted codes as worked out for the British context. Both in Kenya and in Britain, however, it seems to me that the important thing for the individual is to maximize his role and code competence. It is role and code versatility that is rewarding, and role and code limitation which impoverishes.

THE MEASUREMENT AND EXTENT OF MULTILINGUALISM

At the 1962 Colloquium on multilingualism one of the recommendations called for inventories of important multilingual areas, not only for their intrinsic interest but also for their relevance to language planning. Surveys of language use and/or teaching have been or are being carried out in Ethiopia, Uganda, Tanzania, Kenya, Zambia, Ghana, and Senegal, with particular reference to urban areas. Some of these surveys are more ambitious than others, but all are concerned to establish basic facts relating to who speaks what languages to whom, in what situation, and for what purpose. They aim to raise the level of our knowledge of multilingual areas from the present state of impressionism, by which we make inferences from such facts as relate to their general degree of linguistic heterogeneity. Beyond the establishment of basic facts there is at present great interest in problems relating to language attitudes, to the incidence and pattern of code-switching,[1] to the development or

[1] It is important to recognize that the term 'code' is used in at least two widely differing senses. In Bernstein's use it corresponds to some extent with Halliday's register, and perhaps also to Gumperz's 'sub-code' and 'style'. Gumperz, however,

recession of ethnicity, and to the recognition and description of different varieties of particular languages. One of the most controversial issues in such survey work has been that of methodology: social psychologists and sociologists have brought to the scene a battery of survey techniques and a host of sophisticated experimental procedures (see Lambert, pp. 95 ff, Fishman and Cooper, pp. 126 ff), while social anthropologists have contributed their experience of studying small groups intensively over a long period. Most recently linguists have begun to develop exciting new techniques for handling variation in language.[1] Certainly some items of information relating to language behaviour are likely to be more easily detachable from the setting than others; new problems are likely to require new methods, and these can best be worked out in an inter-disciplinary context where the limitations of individual specializations can be appreciated. One solution, being adopted by the Madina survey in Ghana (see Berry, pp. 318 ff), is to regard the initial survey as a device for establishing what kinds of problems will require intensive study in the second phase: Parkin, in his current work in Nairobi, started at the other end and used a prolonged period of study of some urban housing estates as a means of refining the extensive survey techniques which he developed subsequently. An illustration of the kinds of difficulty that such a survey may encounter is provided by some recent work in Northern Kenya. Turkana in the vicinity of Lodwar claimed to speak Swahili when they went to the District Office in Lodwar or to the local trading centre, and this appeared to be borne out by relatively superficial observation. On the other hand, they also reported that this contact was effected only at infrequent intervals, so that any assessment of the importance of Swahili for these speakers seemed to require that frequency of usage, plus the

---

reserves 'code' for 'genetically distinct languages' ('Types of linguistic communities' *Anthrop. Linguistics*, 4, 1962, reprinted in *Readings in the Sociology of Language*, ed. J. A. Fishman, Mouton, 1968, p. 464). Dell Hymes follows him in this, thus 'By choice of *code* is understood a choice at the level of distinct language' (op. cit., (1967), p. 24). Among linguists, therefore, code-switching is generally understood to mean a shift in language rather than a shift in register or style, and it is in this sense that I shall use it here.

[1] See, for example, 'The Study of Language in its Social Context', W. Labov, *Studium Generale*, XXIII, 1, 1970, 30–87.

comparative importance to them of the occasions on which it was used, should be taken into account. Yet further discussion revealed that from visits to the trading centre for buying and selling, the outsider or Government official could infer surplus resources, and at a time when the non-payment of the Graduated Personal Tax was causing Government concern it was evident that this would act powerfully against the surveyor being able to obtain accurate information on frequency of visits. Here at least was some justification for a period of preliminary acclimatization to refine one's techniques.

Apart from gross differences regarding methodology, which can easily degenerate into sterile affirmations of entrenched positions, there are numerous problems relating to the efficacy of particular research techniques or to modifications of standard techniques which may need to be effected in special settings. What type, for example, of sampling procedures should be adopted when the universe from which the sample is to be drawn is extremely ill-defined—as in urban housing estates? To what extent can responses to questions on language attitudes be quantified? How important are supplementary interviews in depth? In what language(s) should questionnaires or interviews be carried out? To what extent can test situations be validly set up without prior knowledge of the local cultural setting? How can the degree of code-switching be measured?

In Kenya code-switching is particularly common between a local language and English, or between Swahili and English—more rarely between all three—in semi-formal or informal styles of speech between co-evals of the younger generation who have received some secondary schooling or who have, for some other reason, acquired proficiency in the languages concerned. Its locale includes bars, telephone conversations, intra-office discussions, tea-parties given by *élite* wives and a wide range of inter-personal, semi-formal relationships. It is an urban or semi-urban (small towns, trading centres) rather than a rural phenomenon. In form it varies very widely, from the interpolation of stock markers (lexical items or phrases such as 'I say', 'of course', 'so', etc.) to the juxtaposition of long stretches of each language. While switching is essentially a phenomenon of the bilingual speaker, the widespread availability of stock markers makes it possible, even for monolinguals, to give an impression of bilingualism. Switching will often provide linguistic evidence for a change of role, but the converse is less common, since the number of available language variants is likely to be smaller than the number of roles available to an individual, so that each variant is likely to occur in several roles. Another dimension of switching has been introduced by Gumperz[1] with the terms 'transactional' and 'personal' switching. He notes that there are some social settings which are marked by transactional interaction, settings that is, in which the individuality of the participant is suspended and the form of the interaction stereotyped, e.g. buying and selling, visiting a doctor, bank, etc. In settings marked by personal interaction, on the other hand, the individual is given full freedom to express himself. Switching which occurs within transactional interaction appears to correlate with alterations in the formal character of the setting, e.g. the arrival of an additional participant, while switching which occurs within personal interaction is associated with differences in topic. In his Indian material Hindi and a regional variant of Hindi occur in transactional switching, while two variants of the vernacular mark personal switching. At this point it is worth recalling the first of Parkin's examples, cited above, in which X used Luganda to his Ugandan neighbour initially, but switched to English when the question of soliciting a job arose. Should one argue that the use of English here simply signals a change of topic within personal interaction, or might it be better to regard this as a 'metaphorical'[2] switch to a form of transactional interaction?

To investigate the phenomenon more closely a small experiment was carried out in Kenya during 1969. Since it was out of the question to plant tape-recorders, tap telephone conversations, etc., and since I wanted to avoid setting up artificial situations, it was decided to try time-sampling the phenomenon in the setting of a group of bars in a township about 100 miles

[1] 'On the ethnology of linguistic change', in *Sociolinguistics*, ed. W. Bright, Mouton, 1966, pp. 27–49, and also in 'Linguistic and social interaction in two communities', in the *Ethnography of Communication*, eds. J. J. Gumperz and D. H. Hymes, *American Anthropologist*, 66, 6, Pt. 2, 1964, 137–53.

[2] Suggested by J.-P. Blom and J. J. Gumperz in 'Some social determinants of verbal behaviour' (unpublished).

from Nairobi.[1] Two assistants were asked to select one of the bars, and, after a preliminary mingling with the drinkers, to select a conversation in which code-switching was taking place. They were then instructed to reproduce all they could of the conversation over a 1–3-minute stretch, and to repeat this at half-hourly intervals during the evening, the procedure being continued on every alternate day over a two-week period. Initially the assistants left the bar to write up their material, but finding that this attracted too much attention, they subsequently wrote down the conversations *in situ*, lending credence to the impression that they were writing letters to their girl friends whenever necessary. The results of the experiment have not yet been analysed, but it may prove to be a practicable and fruitful way of establishing when and to what extent some people switch, though naturally enough it provides no valid phonic data. One thing that is apparent is that switching often seems to be initiated by particular lexical items: one may say that they thus initiate a shift in topic or even in interaction type, but more commonly personal idiosyncrasy seems to be involved. This does seem to be a factor to be reckoned with, and in default of a better term I am temporarily labelling this 'idiosyncratic' switching.

At the outset of this introduction I referred to a long-standing belief that tribal units are characteristically unilingual. While it may be true that the most striking examples of individual multilingualism occur in areas of high linguistic heterogeneity, e.g. towns, large agricultural estates, factories, settlement schemes, etc., which may be of fairly recent origin, it is also fairly clear that long-standing patterns of trade, intermarriage, and interchange of cultural features and personnel have contributed to varying degrees of multilingualism within the tribal unit. This may be more marked in some areas than in others, restricted to certain groups or roles, more pronounced along the periphery than in the centre, but until now impressions have not yet yielded to systematic investigation. It is also important to remember that, from the earliest period of colonial administration, the division of countries into administrative units gave a

[1] The experiment could not have been carried out without the loan of the two assistants by Mr. H. C. A. Somerset of the Institute of Development Studies, University College, Nairobi, who also trained them. I would like to express my gratitude to him.

particular impetus to multilingualism in those areas where the administrative unit subsumed two or more tribal units. The contrast between Tanzania and Kenya in this respect has had, I believe, an important effect on the differential use of Swahili in the two countries.[1] Evidence for cultural interpenetration may be found at various levels: in ritual (see Southall, pp. 376 ff); in particular institutions, like that of the rain-maker among the Iraqw of northern Tanzania, or chiefship in both Bantu and non-Bantu societies of Eastern Africa; in specialist roles, e.g. iron-working; and possibly also in such institutions as that of age organization. Where the institution or feature has been fully assimilated into the host society there may be few linguistic traces of its origin except possibly in terminology.[2] Linguistic evidence for such transfer is notoriously difficult to assess, but one could plausibly argue that the relatively small proportion of the lexicon of particular Bantu languages, around 20 per cent, which can be related to cognates within the Bantu field, is at least suggestive of a substantial amount of accretion from outside sources, and constitutes a topic that would well repay detailed investigation.[3]

If tribal units are not unilingual, then just how multilingual do they become, and what form does this multilingualism take? Some preliminary investigations of this phenomenon were undertaken in rural Kenya during 1968/9. University students were used to carry out a 100 per cent sample of homesteads within a 1–5-mile radius of their own homes. Through questionnaire and interview people were asked to provide information on the extent of their multilingualism, their competence in each language, and the frequency with which they used it, together with information on their ability to write different languages, the frequency with which they listened to the Radio, and similar questions. Substantial samples have now been obtained from most Bantu-speaking areas of the country, plus

[1] See also my 'Factors Inhibiting or Engendering Language Policies in Eastern Africa' *in* J. Rubin and P. Jernudd, op. cit.

[2] There is one striking case of a language, Mbugu, in Tanzania, which operates a Bantu affixal system on non-Bantu roots. See my 'Linguistic hybrids', *African Studies*, 19/2, 1960, 95–7.

[3] Consider the evidence presented, for example, in Harold C. Fleming's 'Asa and Aramanik: Cushitic hunters in Masai-land', *Ethnology*, VIII, 1, 1969, 1–36, and in C. Ehret's 'Cattle-keeping and milking in eastern and southern African history: the linguistic evidence', *Journal of African History*, 8, 1967.

Luo and Kipsigis, and additional samples have been obtained for the Luo/Luhya, Luo/Gusii, Luo/Kipsigis, and Kipsigis/Masai border areas. The results of the survey will not be available for some time, but some very general remarks can be made. Firstly, as might be expected, the incidence of individual multilingualism is markedly higher in those areas characterized by a high degree of linguistic heterogeneity, and even in areas where individual multilingualism is low, e.g. Luo, there is a sharp rise along the borders, though Luo appear to be less inclined to learn Luhya than do Luhya to learn Luo. There is also a sharp increase in Luo use of Swahili along the border with Luhya, though it is still significantly lower than that for Luhya. In general, a high proportion of Kalenjin (Nandi/Kipsigis) appear to be competent in Swahili,[1] but whether this is due to a high degree of linguistic heterogeneity in the area or to some other factors, such as propensity for service with the Police or Army, cannot yet be determined. In some areas, e.g. Gusii/Luo, patterns of bilingualism appear to be most highly developed in the setting of buying/selling. These are merely isolated facts which invite further inquiry from a first glance at the material: whether such rural multilingualism is on the increase or on the decrease; what are its social implications; what is meant in precise linguistic terms by people's claim to specific degrees of competence; all these questions remain for further work. On the other hand, a good deal of basic factual material is now available, the study of which is likely to raise many new questions.

CONCLUSIONS

In the foregoing pages I have tried to focus attention on a few of the topics which provoked particularly stimulating discussion at Dar es Salaam. It will be obvious that for many topics the papers themselves constitute the best source for discussion and consideration of further work. I have said nothing on literacy, nor on the whole question of language modernization, nor on the contribution of social psychology to sociolinguistics,[2] but it

[1] This has been confirmed independently during a sociolinguistic survey of western Kenya carried out in 1968 by Dr. B. Heine of the University of Cologne, and noted in his 'On the Distribution of Swahili in Western Kenya' (MS).

[2] See also Fishman, op. cit. (1968).

will be seen that in this respect contributions to the present volume need no special commentary. At this point, however, I should like to conclude by considering briefly what is implied in the title of the Seminar 'The Social Implications of Multilingualism' and suggesting some possible lines for further research.

In societies which comprise ethnically and linguistically heterogeneous communities the choice of one language rather than another follows characteristic patterns at all levels of society, being affected by such factors as education, domain, topic, and locale. The range of choice itself, however, is powerfully influenced by policies adopted officially, whether these are promulgated in terms of an overriding 'national language' policy, as in Tanzania or Ethiopia, or adopted piecemeal in different institutions as in Kenya or Uganda, but in all these countries the weight given to an African as opposed to a European language is likely to be subject to the competing demands of modernity and authenticity. The rationale behind such planning and the planning processes themselves have only recently formed the subject of specific research, but since policy decisions are usually made on political or economic rather than on linguistic grounds, prospective research workers will be quickly made aware of Governmental sensitivity in such matters. This sensitivity has many strands: there is an awareness of imperfections throughout the organization; there is an apprehension lest such imperfections be exposed; and there is a dislike of what is often seen as expatriate meddling. It is evident, none the less, that there are considerable differences even within Eastern Africa: Tanzania has set up a National Swahili Council, and there is an Institute for Swahili Research at the University College, Dar es Salaam. While these are largely policy-implementing bodies, it would be rash to assert that the former, at any rate, played no role in policy-making. By contrast, in Kenya decisions in language matters do not appear to be made in consultation with any advisory body, at either the policy-making or the implementation level. Processes of implementation are easier of access, however, and it is hoped that the Survey of Language Use and Language Teaching in Eastern Africa will contribute substantially to our knowledge. When it comes to evaluating policies we are once again faced with a paucity of data. The field has so far attracted little attention,[1] and the prospective research-worker must not only recognize great regional and institutional variation in the manner and scope of policy implementation, but must face the difficulties inherent in evaluating policies whose objectives have never been clearly formulated. Only within the educational system does anything like a controlled situation obtain, and work is already in progress (see Gorman, pp. 198 ff) from which more specifically evaluative studies can derive. If there is an overall need for case studies of language-planning processes there is also a need for studies of Governmental attitudes towards planning in general and to the inclusion of language in such activities in particular.

At the other end of the scale are the problems of language use within the rural or urban family, and at friendship or network level. In the sense that functional specificity of language variants to particular domains or settings is a fact of social life anywhere, then the multilingual societies of Africa differ in degree but not in kind from monolingual societies. On the other hand, there is one important respect in which East African communities differ, namely the differential access to both languages of modernity and of authenticity displayed by members of different generations. In very many cases schoolboys of today cannot communicate with their fathers, much less their mothers, in English; and while communication is generally easier in Swahili, again this is difficult with older women. In the linguistically homogeneous rural areas the language of the homestead is the local language, and it is members of the younger generation being educated in Swahili and English who feel out of place. This is made abundantly clear in the autobiographical essays submitted to the Kenya Language Survey. In the linguistically heterogeneous urban areas, where Swahili and English are used much more widely, the local language may well be intrusive, and members of the older generation made to feel isolated. Inter-generational problems of communication are liable to be most acute at important ceremonies, such as funerals, weddings, baptisms, etc., when the use of a particular language for one generation may symbolize for

[1] On this point see Joan Rubin, 'Evaluation and Language planning', to appear in Rubin and Jernudd, op. cit.

another the forces of discontinuity and separation. One consequence of such discontinuity between generations might be for kinship ties to become shallower, and indeed Southall, in the Introduction to the first International African Seminar, commented, 'The most general statement that can be made is that in the new situations the scope of kinship rights and duties has narrowed and become more uncertain and the body of kin included in them become reduced.'[1] To argue that multilingualism is the critical factor in such situations would not only be difficult but, I believe, erroneous. Available evidence suggests that most of Africa has been multilingual for a long time, even if the domains of such behaviour were characteristically restricted, e.g. to trade or hostility. The present pattern of multilingualism is itself a concomitant of changes in the scale[2] and forms of social relationships resulting from the substitution of an expatriate Colonial authority for indigenous authorities, and the absorption of numerous ethnically based units into a new and wider territorially based one. The subsequent increase in the degree and pace of heterogenization, especially in the towns, elicited a linguistic response in an expansion in the use of Swahili. More slowly, but perhaps more significantly, came the drive to control the metropolitan language symbolizing status and power. There has rubbed off on those who achieved their objective something of the estrangement and sense of social distance which marked the relationships between expatriates and local people generally. The manner and extent to which the use of Swahili and English has been superimposed on existing patterns of multilingualism should therefore be seen as a response to change—in turn and necessarily shaping further changes—but being essentially an attempt to accommodate to and incorporate changes over which no individual had had control. The effect of the superimposition on local languages has been undeniable, but, like the superimposition itself, extremely variable. In some areas it has taken the form of compensation in domains where either Swahili or English is characteristic, as in the use of Luo or Luhya alongside Latin or English in separatist church services in Nairobi; in other areas,

[1] *Social Change in Modern Africa*, ed. A. W. Southall, Oxford, 1961, p. 31.

[2] I am using the term in the sense used by Godfrey Wilson in his *Social Change*, Cambridge, 1945, Ch. II.

e.g. Tanzania, the use of local languages has been actively discouraged as leading to separatism and tribalism; in other areas again it has been possible to resist the use of Swahili. What are now required are detailed studies of selected communities to follow up the experiments carried out by the Survey of Language Use and Language Teaching. In particular, it is on the relationship and interplay between language use and social change that attention needs to be focused and through which I believe a genuine contribution to sociolinguistics may be made.

A. GENERAL AND THEORETICAL STUDIES

I. National Languages and Languages of Wider Communication in the Developing Nations[1]

JOSHUA A. FISHMAN

The past quarter century has brought into the constantly fluctuating family of nations several score new members, formerly colonies of the Western capitalist democracies, referred to variously as new or developing nations.[2] However,

[1] The body of this paper was prepared for delivery as the keynote address at the Regional Conference on Language and Linguistics, Dar es Salaam, Tanzania, 18 December 1968. The entire paper, including footnotes, was prepared as a contribution to the Seminar on the Social Implications of Multilingualism in Eastern Africa, University College, Dar es Salaam, Tanzania, 15–20 December 1968. Preparation of this paper was facilitated by the Institute of Advanced Projects, East–West Center, University of Hawaii, where the author spent the 1968–69 academic year as a Senior Specialist.

[2] There is some slight inaccuracy about each of these designations. The designation 'new' is in conflict with the fact that several of the nations that are of interest to us enjoyed political independence within frontiers not markedly dissimilar from those obtaining today long before the period of Western colonization. The designation 'developing' poses other difficulties, since it is not at all clear how the line should be drawn between rapidly developing, slowly developing, negligibly developing, and negatively developing nations. However, these designations are probably adequate to serve as primitives for discussions that have as their goal not the refinement of these terms *per se* but, rather, the discussion of differing language planning processes and their concomitant societal contexts in the nations of Africa and Asia that attained political independence, either again or for the first time, subsequent to the conclusion of the Second World War. Such discussion should help us compare the prevalence of certain societal and language planning processes in various kinds of new or developing nations, or to compare their prevalence in certain of these nations with their prevalence in certain other nations that obtained political independence during other periods in history and that have had somewhat different experiences in connection with political consolidation, socio-cultural integration, industrialization, urbanization, etc. As a result, even those studies that do not aim at refining the concept of national development *per se* contribute indirectly to such refinement as a by-product of the contrasts or similarities that they disclose, between nations characterized by different developmental trends or indices.

Social-science theory and data in connection with national development are

not only is their political independence recent but their search for sociocultural integration,[1] on the one hand, and for operational self-management (i.e. for effectiveness in the realms of public order and public service, as well as industrially, commercially, educationally, diplomatically, and militarily),[2] on

---

currently undergoing both rapid expansion and refinement. For a brief review of the factors most frequently studied in connection with national developmental sequences see Hopkins and Wallerstein, 1967. The foregoing also constitutes an excellent review of the study designs employed in the comparative study of nations. An example of recent theoretical advances in the study of developing nations, new and old, is Johan Galtung's 'Sociological Theory and Social Development' (Galtung, 1968, particularly Part II: Socio-Economic Development). A helpful introduction to current issues and reformulations in this field is S. N. Eisenstadt's review article 'Some New Looks at the Problem of Relations between Traditional Societies and Modernization' (Eisenstadt, 1968). Eisenstadt concludes that recent research 'points out the need to examine the characteristics of those processes which may help in the transition to modernity as against those which may hinder it, and those which lead to the development and continuity of modern frameworks as against those types which impede the viability of such frameworks once they are established'.

Because the concepts of national development and modernization essentially relate to multivariate continua, much of what is said in this paper should pertain to nations outside of Africa and Asia as well. Certainly most of the nations of Central and Eastern Europe experienced problems of development and modernizations during the first half of this century that were very similar in many ways to those currently being studied in the new nations. (Non-Western models of development have thus far been little discussed. The need for such models is pointed out by Inayatullah, 1967.) Indeed, we need go back only a bit further in Western European social and political development in order to find there, as well, changes, problems, and processes quite similar in many ways to those evident in many parts of Africa and Asia today. Thus, while no unilinear or irreversible theory of development is being posited, it is hoped that the present paper can provide some historical perspective as well as conceptual parsimony for those seeking preliminary order in the welter of detailed information produced by language policy, language planning, and other sociolinguistic research in Africa and Asia today.

As do all theoretical formulations, this paper is intended to summarize and systematize the data, literature, and experience that is currently known to the author and, then, to function as a point of departure for subsequent empirical and theoretical efforts, many of which will undoubtedly necessitate the revision, refinement, or abandonment of the parameters here suggested.

[1] This term will be discussed and illustrated extensively below. In general, it refers to the never fully completed process of shaping and reshaping broader cognitive–emotional identifications and broader behavioural expressions of communality than are expressed via the narrow kinship, neighbourhood, and ethnic traditions that individuals recognize as a result of their early socialization experiences among family and friends.

[2] I use the term political integration or consolidation to cover all of these operational processes that are to such a large extent governmentally influenced or controlled and technological rather than ethnic in nature. Of course, political

the other hand, are often of even more recent vintage and of greater uncertainty than is their political independence *per se*. These nations have been subjected to a huge amount of social science attention—and, in very recent years, also to sociolinguistic scrutiny—so that the contours of their similarities and

---

consolidation and sociocultural integration are closely interrelated phenomena, although they may be studied separately. Education and transportation are not merely government services or operations without ethnic content or substantive ethnic consequence. They can both facilitate wider socio-cultural ties and the dissemination of integrative socio-cultural ideologies, loyalties, and behavioural realizations. Similarly, the adoption of wider ethnic loyalties and perceived similarities can serve to facilitate industrial and commercial operations. For further discussion of the *interdependency* between political and socio-cultural integration, as well as for indications of various stages of reintegration or reconsolidation, see Fishman, 1968. The interaction between various integrative factors is well presented in Spengler, 1961.

The concept of 'integration at the national level' has recently come to be of increasing interest to empirical social scientists. See, e.g., DeLamater, 1967; DeLamater, Katz and Kelman, 1967; Deutsch *et al.*, 1964; Jahoda, 1963; Katz *et al.*, 1963; Kelman, 1967; Lawson, 1963; Morse and Pearlman, 1968.

I do not refer here to the substantial literature on nationalism *per se* nor to the rapidly growing body of theory and data on cross-polity comparisons. The former is largely historical in nature (except for the still provocative volume by Karl W. Deutsch, *Nationalism and Social Communication*, 1953), and the latter, of necessity, deals only with nationwide indices (see, e.g., Merritt and Rokkan, 1966). Nevertheless, both of these research traditions can yield valuable hypotheses for those interested (as I am in my empirical work) in social behavioural data pertaining to national integration.

The legitimacy of the nation as a context for the comparative study of social process data is particularly strong in connection with language policy considerations, in view of the fact that such policies are so typically nationwide. To the well-known ideographic protest that 'you cannot add these units together, they cannot be compared', Galtung (p. 18, op. cit., footnote 1, above) replies: 'People saying this should never . . . count the members of their own family, for in a strict sense no individuals are identical. However, counting has never presupposed identity, only some kind of similarity used to define a *set*. . . . For the definition of a set all one wants is . . . at least one element that serves as the criterion for membership in the set—and then all kinds of comparisons can be carried out. But some people seem to feel that one can only compare identical elements, as if identity were the only relation in the world. Moreover, if the elements were really identical, what would be the use of comparing them?'

In a similar vein Moore comments '. . . for every generalization about structural relationships in social systems there is an exception, known best to the objector, in a suitably obscure corner of the world. Yet it is the point of view adopted here that it is possible and appropriate to deal with the major functional areas observable in any continuing society (e.g. biological reproduction, socialization of the young, economic production, maintenance of order) and to analyse the general or typological relations that pertain among the specific structures that fulfil these universal functions. Generalization also, however, involves a difficulty of an intrinsic sort. Theory construction is a process of abstraction, the counterpart of

dissimilarities (with respect to the paths that they have adopted in coping with the problems of socio-cultural and political-operational integration) are now beginning to be recognized.

As in all new areas of scientific inquiry, the study of the new nations is faced by two overriding problems, first, that of finding the most fruitful *dimensions* for analysis, and second, that of finding the most revealing *units* of measurement or description in connection with the aforementioned dimensions. In the comments that follow I would like to review six factors or dimensions that I believe to be heuristically useful in differentiating between the language policies and accompanying developments that tend to obtain where three different directions or clusters of cumulative decisions have been reached. For the moment I would like to refer to these types of decisions and directions merely as being of Type A, Type B, and Type C so that I can devote greater attention to the differentiating circumstances under which they are reached and implemented (in the hope that these are revealing also in their application to many countries), rather than attend to particular countries and their somewhat unique and even contradictory local circumstances at particular times.

TYPE A DECISIONS

Type A decisions are those which come about as a result of consensus (at least in 'leading circles') that there is neither an over-arching sociocultural past (i.e. no pervasive feeling of unity of history, customs, values, or missions traceable into the reasonably distant past) nor a usable political past (i.e. no pervasive tradition of independence, self-government, hallowed boundaries) that can *currently* serve integrative functions at the

---

which is loss of information. No theory will yield a *specific* prediction, or yield a *specific* guide to policy (given an end to be achieved) except by reversing the process and adding information to the general proposition (Moore, 1961, p. 58).

My own research goal in a forthcoming cross-national study of language planning processes will be to determine how particular population segments (e.g. teachers, University students) behave with respect to announced language policies, i.e. what they do, what they know, and what they think in connection with the language planning policies and products that are ostensibly directed towards them. Possible *types* of countries, as a context for such behaviour, are an important element in the design of such research.

nationwide level. It is felt by *élites* in decision-making capacities that there is as yet no indigenous Great Tradition (no widely accepted and visibly implemented belief-and-behaviour system of *indigenously validated greatness*) that all or most of the inhabitants can immediately draw upon to make them one people and their country one nation.[1]

[1] I have purposely stressed the phenomenological aspect of socio-cultural integration and political consolidation (i.e. what people believe and say, particularly what *élites* believe and say to each other, to specific audiences, and to the population at large) rather than purportedly more objective indices of these two phenomena. Once again, these two dimensions (the external or 'objective' and the phenomenological or 'subjective') are often highly related and mutually determining. If I tend to separate them here it is because of two considerations. First of all, such a separation enables one to study the absence or presence of interdependency between objective factors and surrounding belief systems—in a variety of contexts—rather than assume that this is always and everywhere the same. In addition, the separation of the two and the stress on the phenomenological dimension is necessary in order to recognize that we are dealing with a dynamic system in which there are always elements of tension, pressure for change, and redefinition on behalf of alternative decisions.

The same objective circumstances are differently viewed and defined, because of differing goals and values. So is it also with socio-cultural integration. Whereas some *élites* interpret the *status quo* in one way (e.g. that there is no usable past to unite the whole country, and therefore that only a superordinate future goal can serve this unifying purpose), others will interpret it differently (e.g. that local or regional socio-cultural unity is sufficient reason to set aside wider national unity as unattainable or undesirable and to opt for local autonomy instead). In the text of the present paper I have avoided most references to such internal differences and tensions only for the sake of the simplicity inherent in 'ideal' models. Instead, I have dealt with three different coherent rationales concerning socio-cultural integration. By keeping in mind that ideal models are intended to clarify the diversity of intermediate and shifting resolutions that actually obtains (treating it as error variance above and beyond which certain main effects are recognizable), it will more readily be understood that rarely does any of these ideal rationales command undisputed allegiance in any country at any time. Thus, it is always important to examine *which élites* (and other population segments) hold *which* views and, in addition, to determine the circumstances under *which* their views (and behaviours) with respect to national integration and language policy tend to change.

For a detailed discussion of how *élites* decide such matters as 'What shall be our history?', 'Are we many or are we one?', etc., see Bell and Oxaal, 1964. Bell, Oxaal, and their associates in several studies that have appeared since 1964 (e.g. Moskos, 1967; Oxaal, 1968; Mau, 1968) have admirably demonstrated how the views of *élites* can be exhaustively studied and insightfully related to their background characteristics (age, education, income, ethnicity, religion, political affiliation, etc.). However, what remains to be done in sociolinguistic extensions of such studies of *élites* is not only to trace the interest basis of their own views but, in addition, to trace the interest basis of the spread of these views to non-*élite* populations previously unaware of them or uncommitted to them. This can be accomplished via recurring studies which combine brief surveys of large

Both of these recognized lacks—i.e. the lack of perceived socio-cultural integration at the nationwide level and the lack of felt political-operational integration at the nationwide level—lead to the early and relatively unconflicted arrival at Type A decisions, i.e. the selection of a Language of Wider Communication as the national or official language.[1] With remarkably few exceptions, those nations in which views such as those just mentioned are widespread in leading governmental and intellectual circles have selected the language of their pre-independence Western rulers for all nationwide purposes. Similarly, a Western-trained and modernly oriented *élite* has usually been continued and favoured in positions of authority in all basic governmental services as well as in industry, commerce,

---

populations with intensive studies of specially selected naturally occurring groups or interaction networks.

Those familiar with the above-mentioned publications will realize that my concept of Great Tradition is not identical with Redfield's, in that it is for me primarily a phenomenological reality rather than either an objectively great or traditional system. The myths that integrate societies and polities are real enough as long as people strive for or against them, value or deprecate them, counteract or reinforce them. As a result of the power of these traditions, exoglossic societies throughout history have come to believe that their languages were genuinely their own, truly a reflection of their particular genius, and authentically related to their peculiar experiences. Thus, Type A decisions are often merely a beginning point from which subsequently indigenized language and behaviour systems not only may but frequently do arise. Both France and Roumania are equally proud today to be the bearers and perfectors of Roman civilization, disregarding the fact that neither of them is ethnically of Romance origin. Such unifying themes, dreams, and bonds are continually planned, discovered, revealed, and refurbished, and their status as Great Traditions is measurable only by their effectiveness rather than by any objective criteria of verifiability.

[1] There is so much variation, from country to country, in the use of terms such as 'national' language and 'official' language that it is no longer possible to use them without some ambiguity as to just what they imply. A distinction is sometimes made between them, such that more languages are recognized for 'official' *use* (in courts, government agencies, schools, mass media, etc.) than are accorded the honorific *status* of being 'national'. Thus, while the designation 'national' tends to stand for past, present, or hoped for socio-cultural authenticity in the ethnic realm (nationality being a broader level of integration growing out of coalescences between earlier and more localized ethnicities), the designation 'official' tends to be associated primarily with current political–operational needs. If the languages designated by the two terms are not identical this is indicative of the need to recognize political–operational demands that are (temporarily?) more pressing than the demands of socio-cultural authenticity.

The term national language is used in this paper to designate that language (or those languages) whose use is viewed as furthering socio-cultural integration at the nationwide (hence 'national') level.

education, and culture. Both of these decisions—the selection of a (usually Western) Language of Wider Communication and the continuation of a Western trained *élite*—are similarly justified by the basic need to obtain and retain as much tangible aid, as much trained personnel, and as much influence abroad as possible in order to meet the immediate operational demands of nationhood. Under these circumstances I would say that in nations in which Type A decisions prevail language selection serves *nationism* (i.e. the very operational integrity of the nation).

Nationism—as distinguished from nationalism—is primarily concerned not with ethnic authenticity but with operational efficiency. When Type A decisions prevail considerations of operational efficiency have often led to the adoption of local and regional languages for immediate operational purposes only, i.e. the predominant *élites* of such nations have tended to view local and regional languages as serving merely transitional purposes *vis-à-vis* the viability of the nation as a whole. Only the Language of Wider Communication is seen as fulfilling nation-wide purposes on a permanent basis, or as being linked to the developing national goals, national symbols, national rituals, national holidays, and national identifications that such nations—just as do all nations—need and create.

In view of their wholehearted reliance on a (usually Western) Language of Wider Communication, nations in which Type A decisions are preferred need engage in only limited language planning activities.[1] As long as the 'metropolitan' country's norms are also considered to be acceptable locally no indigenous attempts at language elaboration (i.e. the addition of technical vocabulary) or codification (i.e. standardization of grammar, orthography, lexicon, or phonology) are needed. The 'metropolitan' country's lead in these matters can be fully accepted with only relatively minor local adjustments. However, two

[1] The approach to studying language planning referred to in this paper is that developed by Charles A. Ferguson, Joshua A. Fishman, Jyotirindra Das Gupta, Joan Rubin, and Bjorn Jernudd in their outline of a model cross-national study of language planning processes (unpublished MS., Stanford University, 1968). This approach identifies several stages of language planning (policy formulation, elaboration and codification, implementation, evaluation and feedback, including cost–benefit analysis) as well as a host of interlocking questions and methodologies to be followed in conjunction with studies of each stage.

other kinds of language planning *are* often engaged in by nations making Type A decisions. In order to promote the acquisition and mastery of the selected Language of Wider Communication, a modicum of study of local languages may be fostered in order

NATIONAL LANGUAGES AND LANGUAGES OF WIDER COMMUNICATION IN THE DEVELOPING NATIONS

Factors	*I. Type A Decisions*	*II. Type B Decisions*	*III. Type C Decisions*
1. *Perceived socio-cultural integration*	*a. No* integrating *Great Tradition* at the national level	*a. One Great Tradition* at the national level	*a.* *Several Great Traditions* seeking separate socio-political recognition
2. *Selection of National Language*	*b.* Governed by considerations of political integration: nationism	*b.* Governed by considerations of authenticity: nationalism	*b.* Governed by need to compromise between political integration and separate authenticities
3. *Adoption of LWC*	*c.* Yes, as permanent, national symbol	*c.* Often transitionally: for modern functions	*c.* Yes, as unifying compromise (working language: W)
4. *Language Planning Concerns*	*d.* Minor: exonormative standardization of LWC	*d.* Modernization of traditional lang.: H or L?	*d.* Modernization of several traditional languages
5 .*Bilingualism Goals*	*e.* Local, regional; transitional to LWC	*e.* National; transitional to indigenous monoling.	*e.* Regional bilingual. (H & L, W & N) & national bilingual. (W & N)
6. *Biculturism Goals*	*f.* Transitional to modernity	*f.* Traditional plus modern spheres	*f.* Traditional plus modern spheres
Types	*I. A-modal Nations*	*II. Uni-modal Nations*	*III. Multi-modal Nations*

to facilitate the preparation of more effective (contrastively based) teaching and learning materials. These materials are often inexpensively available, both for younger and older learners, the latter often being reached via radio or other media that do not depend on the printed page. Nations making Type A decisions also may engage in a modicum of 'terminal literacy' work in some of the local mother tongues among older adults that require literacy (e.g. to attain agricultural modernization) but that can no longer be expected to master the adopted Language of Wider Communication. For them too, then, some special learning materials and teaching methods are devised.

Since the adopted Language of Wider Communication is the mother tongue of very few indigenous inhabitants, the very process of teaching it to the point of functional mastery itself engenders a certain amount of bilingualism when and where Type A decisions are preferred. More widespread in nations opting for Type A decisions is the traditional bi-(actually multi-) lingualism found in small but interacting societies throughout the world. However, bilingualism is viewed as having no nationwide function by the *élites* tending towards Type A decisions. It is not a characteristic of their ideal 'citizen of the future'. Bilingualism, widespread though it is, is viewed as having only a transitional role and even *that* primarily for two populations: the very young and the very old. The former manifest what we might call 'reading readiness bilingualism'. They have not yet fully encountered the institutions of nationhood: the school, the Government, the military, the higher culture. After this encounter occurs it is expected that their bilingualism will decrease. The old, on the other hand, are viewed as having already passed beyond major interaction with the institutions of nationhood. In both instances what is expected is bilingualism *en route* to monolingualism. The young are expected to give up their local tongues in exchange for the nationwide (and increasingly *national*) language, which is also usually a worldwide Language of Wider Communication.[1] The

[1] The expectation that local mother tongues will be totally displaced is probably unrealistic, particularly for sedentary populations that do not migrate from the villages of their birth to the capital or to other more urban places. In their case A. Tabouret-Keller has demonstrated that a diglossia pattern arises (primarily mother tongue at home or with intimates and primarily a 'wider' language at work or with non-intimates) which is very similar to that which still exists even among sedentary populations in Western Europe with respect to use of local varieties and national standard languages. (For further details see Tabouret-Keller, 1968.) Nevertheless, just as Provençal or Alsatian have absolutely no national significance in France, notwithstanding the diglossia patterns into which they enter *vis-à-vis* standard French, no national significance is attributed to or desired for the multitude of local vernaculars by *élites* favouring decisions of Type A.

old are expected to lose whatever smattering of the Language of Wider Communication they may have acquired and to revert increasingly to their various local tongue. Ultimately (i.e. given sufficiently many successive younger generations that have given up their local languages) the former process is expected to win out over the latter.

Biculturism is also viewed as merely transitional by leading circles favouring Type A decisions. The path that most *élites* and intellectuals ideologize is one that leads from tradition (with its so-called tribalism, localism, or particularism) in one or another new direction. One such new direction is modernity with its identifications on a larger and purportedly more rationally influenced scale.[1] Some *élites* that move nations towards Type A decisions are among the most modern and pan-Western in the world in so far as tastes, sentiments, and behaviours are concerned. They have struggled to leave behind their ethnicities—which they consider as merely childish, sentimental, or archaic *vis-à-vis* their current national roles—and they tend

[1] The traditionalism–modernity terminological dichotomy is widely recognized as pertaining to a behavioural–attitudinal–valuational continuum. This continuum has long been of interest to both empirical and theoretical students of society. In recent years the number of instruments and studies in this connection has increased many-fold. For an excellent summary and evaluation of social-science data and theory in this connection see the special issue of the *Journal of Social Issues* devoted to 'Modernity and Tradition' (particularly Gusfield, 1968). For other relevant studies see Dawson, 1967; Inkeles, 1965; Jahoda, 1961–2; Kahl, 1968; Levine, 1965; Little, 1965; Mayer, 1963; Smith and Inkeles, 1966. This last-mentioned paper not only presents a cross-nationally validated instrument for the measurement of 'overall modernity' but also provides a valuable bibliography of other attempts to measure and describe individual and societal modernity. For a critique of generalized measures of modernization and a plea for locally validated measures of modernism see Stephenson, 1968.

While I do not use the terms 'development' or 'modernization' to imply inevitable imitation or duplication of Western precedents, I have also not attempted to avoid the designation 'Western' when referring to certain languages and countries, on the one hand, or to certain socio-cultural and politico–economic developments, on the other. Regardless of how ethnocentric the former references may be, since east and west, north and south are certainly no more than relative rather than absolute designations, their usage is firmly established and quite unambiguous. As for the latter reference (e.g. Western life styles, Western outlooks, etc.) I obviously do not intend them in any invidious manner but merely as indications that, wherever they are encountered, they stem from social, political, and economic processes that were initially set in motion and that have been most continuously developed in those nations classically referred to as Western. While 'modernization' is assumed to imply Westernization in the latter sense, the concept of 'development' makes no such assumption.

to seek a thoroughly new socio-cultural order of national life rather than merely the modernization of an old indigenous order. Their image of the national future tends to be mono-cultural rather than bicultural. Such *élites* most often seek a predominantly Western life-style (urban, avowedly rational, technological), usually expressed via a Western Language of Wider Communication, to provide the modern socio-cultural and the stable political–operational integration towards which (they hope) their countries are moving.

Such views have been reported for *élites* of several developing nations, but three examples must suffice at this time. In his paper on Cameroonese *élitist* families, Alexandre comments:

> The country is one of the more heterogeneous in West Africa with a variety of language groups belonging to several families. . . . There is no nationwide lingua franca. . . . The official languages are English (W. Cameroon) and French (E. Cameroon) on an equal footing at the federal level (but with *de facto* predominance of French). The school system continues, on the whole, the French colonial tradition with an European language used as a medium from the start. There are a few literacy classes in some of the vernaculars organized by the Christian missions without any official recognition. Since independence there have been heated discussions among the intelligentsia between cultural nationalists, who favour a wider use of the vernaculars, and unificationists, who fear that this would consolidate tribal consciousness and be detrimental to nation building. The federal government—and its French technical advisors—support the latter view (Alexandre's paper in this volume).

That such reliance on the language of former colonial rule may yet come to be looked down upon by other or future *élites* in these same locales, just as they are already derided today in a number of developing countries that have already attained greater indigenous integration, is evidenced by the following observation recently published in a Dar es Salaam daily.

> There are leaders and bureaucrats who still look upon the English way of life as a superior culture, and, therefore English as the language of 'culture'. They seize every opportunity to speak English and flaunt their knowledge of English before peasants and workers in the fields and offices. Some of them will even proudly

assert that they can only think in English! ! This is one manifestation of cultural bankruptcy . . . [Others] who know little English nevertheless speak English after the manner of expatriate Englishmen. They do so because they subconsciously wish they were Englishmen (*The Nationalist*, 20 December 1968).

Considerations such as these frequently lead to the displacement of *élites* and to attempts to rationalize other types of decisions with respect to language policy and language planning.

Actually, the significant fact about *élites* forced to make and to confirm Type A decisions is not that they invariably stress Westernization but that they are in search of new and *effective* ideological and behavioural systems that promise rapid integrative returns on a large scale. Acceptance of the West, rejection of the West, region-wide and continent-wide integrative philosophies, all of these tend to be present and to displace each other with ambivalent rapidity. The same leaders who castigate their own indigenous ethnicity and predict that

> In three or four years, no one will remember the tribal, ethnic and religious differences which have caused so much difficulty to the country and the people in the recent past (p. 58).

may well also criticize their own strongest links with Western culture:

> The education that was given to us was designated to assimilate us, to depersonalize us, to Westernize us—to present our civilization, our culture, our own sociological and philosophical conceptions, even our humanism as the expression of a savage and almost conscious primitivism—in order to create a number of complexes in us which would drive us to become more French than the French themselves. (Sékou Touré, 1959, p. 156.)

While the erratic pursuit of new integrative principles continues, the demands of *nationism per se* require continual reinforcement of a Type A decision.

TYPE B DECISIONS

The contrasts between Type A decisions and Type B decisions are many and noticeable. To begin with, the nations in which

Type B decisions predominate tend to be based upon long-established socio-cultural *unities*, and, not infrequently, upon rather well-established political boundaries as well. There is widespread consensus—not limited only to *élites* but most consciously and ideologically elaborated by them—that a single Great Tradition is available to provide the indigenized and symbolically elaborated laws, beliefs, customs, literature, heroes, mission, and identity appropriate for nationwide identification. Of course, not all inhabitants may care to be identified with the nation, but in so far as such identification *is* desired and *is* expressed, there is only one hallowed Great Tradition that is felt to be available and appropriate for such recognized nationwide purposes.

The clearly preponderant Great Tradition available to nations in which Type B decisions prevail points to the selection of a single indigenous (or indigenized) language to serve as national language.[1] The Great Tradition and an indigenous (or indigenized) language have been associated with each other for so long a time that they are by now considered inseparable from the point of view of socio-cultural integration at the national level. Both are considered to be interdependent and undeniable dimensions of national authenticity. Both undeniably contribute to and benefit from *nationalism*, i.e. the ideology of authenticity or identity based upon broader kinship, broader custom, and broader cause. Whereas most nations making Type A decisions must first preserve the polity as an operational entity and then seek to develop national identity and identification over time, the *élites* of new nations making Type B decisions tend to believe that they already possess a strong national identity but must seek to render it more functional for the purposes of national well-being in the modern world.[2]

[1] It is reasonable to ask whether the link between Great Traditions and their uniquely related languages is merely a by-product of literacy, i.e. of a written Great Tradition. Although this is probably usually the case (i.e. most Great Traditions are written and, as a result, they intensify both their unifying functions as well as their language links), it is not necessarily so. The Algonquin and Iroquois Great Traditions were unwritten, as was the pre-Islamic Arabic standard developed by court-poets at a purely oral level. Other oral Great Traditions have existed (and continue to exist today) in other unified traditional societies. It therefore seems preferable to speak of unifying Great Traditions than of their probable but not absolutely necessary by-products: written texts and standard language varieties.

[2] The inapplicability of the foregoing paragraph to certain new nations that have adopted or developed inter-regional lingua francas as their national languages

The Dar es Salaam newspaper cited earlier expresses these views forcefully and in the very combination proposed by our conceptual scheme:

A common indigenous language in the modern nation states is a powerful factor for unity. Cutting across tribal and ethnic lines, it

---

is intentional. Such nations are intermediate between Type A and Type B. Like nations in which Type A decisions have been reached, they lack any overwhelming indigenous centre of gravity that clearly points to a single locus of socio–cultural integration at the national level. However, neither can all of the locally available tongues and traditions be considered equally inapplicable for wider roles, particularly those of a political–operational nature (such as commerce and communications between the provinces and the capital). Thus, an indigenous language (usually one that has already served as a lingua franca and therefore lost some of its originally regional or local connotations) may be selected as national or official at the same time as a Western Language of Wider Communication is utilized for higher education and High Culture pursuits. Obviously, the indigenous language so selected in such countries initially serves as an internal language of wider political–operational integration rather than as a language of socio–cultural integration. Similarly, the Western Language of Wider Communication serves *élitist* and international communication purposes.

These intermediate cases may more rapidly develop into nations making Type B decisions, i.e. they may more quickly succeed in developing 'national' loyalties, customs, missions, and symbols (anthems, costumes, celebrations, etc.) in what was initially only an internal language for political–operational viability than may be the case with nations that arrived at more 'classical' Type A decisions involving a Western Language of Wider Communication alone for nationwide purposes. Type A decisions, if they succeed in providing political–operational stability, are, by definition, ultimately self-liquidating. Under such circumstances an indigenized Great Tradition ultimately is fashioned which provides socio–cultural integration as well and which leads to self-perceptions and decisions of Type B. This transition between A and B, it might be hypothesized, is accomplished more quickly if an indigenous (rather than Western) Language of Wider Communication is employed. There is even some reason to believe that language policy *per se* is more successfully implemented when the later is the case, e.g.

> The adoption of *bahasa Indonesia* as the first language of the new state met no resistance, largely because the language so established was not the language of the majority ethnic group—the Javanese. The imposition of an Indonesian language was not symbolic of the imposition of a majority—and this largely removed the whole question from the role of politics (Fischer, 1965, p. 116).

Certainly, sustained failure to attain economic growth in nations making Type A decisions may lead to attempts to reach Type C decisions, or failing that, to subdivide into a number of separate units, each of which may attempt A, B, or C decisions, depending on their own integrative perceptions and capacities. Similarly, prolonged functional failures following upon Type B decisions may make new *élites* more sympathetic to Type C decisions than were their predecessors. Thus, the conceptual approach advanced in this paper does not assign permanent slots to *élites* nor to the types of decisions reached by them. Developmental changes in society, polity, and economy lead to changed language decisions, and such changes can be anticipated. However, no attempt is made to argue for smooth,

promotes a feeling of single community. Additionally it makes possible the expression and development of social ideas, economic targets and cultural identity easily perceived by citizens. It is, in a word, a powerful factor for mobilization of people and resources for nationhood.

In Tanzania we have been blessed with such a language—Swahili. Whatever the existing variation of dialect and diction, and local mutilation of meanings of given words notwithstanding, Swahili is spoken and understood throughout the length and breadth of the land. Indeed there is a noticeable trend towards designating Africans as Swahilis—though the historical Swahilis are a distinct ethnic and sociological grouping.

Quite obviously this common language is a precious heritage and asset. It can serve a double purpose. Firstly it can reveal the wealth of political, economic and social ideas and values of our past. In so doing, it can reveal part of the historical foundation of Tanzania as a nation. Secondly, it can be the medium of formulating the political, economic and social principles, plans and goals of our nation in this day and age. In so doing it will serve as the other linchpin in the foundation of our identity.

Unfortunately, as Mr. Kawawa hinted when opening the linguistics conference at the University College two days ago, the colonial era made a great many Tanzanians forsake their language and look upon English as a venerable substitute. Now this mistake has got to be corrected. Swahili must be accorded its legitimate place as the language of Tanzanians in political and economic communication, in social life, in administration, in education. At the same time it must be developed so that it answers to the complex features of life in this age. It is to be hoped that educationists, administrators, social workers and the public at large will take up this challenge (*The Nationalist*, 20 December 1968).

---

fixed transitions from one phase to the next. For a discussion of irregularity in sequences and regressions of the type anticipated above see Smelser, 1959, pp. 30–2.

The history of modernization and industrialization during the past 300 years provides ample evidence of the unevenness of this trend *within* the political boundaries existing at various points in time. As successive regions of polities become urbanized, industrialized, and modernized, the likelihood that they will seek separate socio-cultural and political–operational integration is great, particularly if a past history of such separate integration exists or can reasonably be constructed. The past history of successive subdivisions of this kind and their subsequent rationalization is reviewed by Inglehart and Woodward (1967). The likelihood of future revisions of the current ethnically meaningless boundaries of many developing countries (should they undergo marked regionally discontinuous economic development) is discussed in Kapil, 1966.

Because of the well-established 'gravitational pull' of authenticity-loyalties, when and where Type B decisions are preferred, any worldwide Language of Wider Communication tends to be allocated only transitional goals in connection with operational efficiency considerations. There may well be an admitted immediate need for a Language of Wider Communication for modern higher education (particularly in the areas of technology and science), but ultimately this is rationalized on the grounds of pure expediency. Inevitably, there is a tendency to ideologize a future time when the nation will be strong enough and adequately self-sufficient (in terms of trained personnel and in terms of training and production facilities) so that any Language of Wider Communication that may currently be needed will no longer have a *national* role to fulfil and will become a mere foreign language.

However, in order to hasten that earnestly desired time the indigenous (or indigenized) [1] national language must usually first be modernized so that it, too, can cope with modern technological, scientific, governmental, and high cultural discourse. Such modernization of the national language is frequently complicated in two ways in nations in which Type B decisions are preferred. First of all, a choice must often be made between a highly stylized, classical variety of the language (called H in the socio-linguistic literature) and one or another vernacular variety which has usually heretofore been considered unworthy of serious attention for serious purposes (called L in the sociolinguistic literature). Secondly, the chosen variety (H or L) must be subjected to the trials and tribulations of modernization *per se*, which process can take any one of several directions.

H and L may have parted company centuries ago and have gone widely separate ways in the interim, to such an extent that they are no longer mutually comprehensible. In some cases H and L have always been quite separate languages. In either case

[1] 'Indigenous or indigenized' is a necessary circumlocution if one wishes to cover national languages that are still intellectually recognized as 'imports' from other locales but that have been so thoroughly influenced by local sociolinguistic forces as to be given an independent honorific name (Yiddish and not Judeo-German, Riksmaal and not Dano-Norwegian, Afrikaans and not Afrikaner Deutsch, Ukrainian and not Little Russian, etc.), and associated with indigenous historical experiences or integrative activity.

(whether separate languages or separate varieties), they have both been long accepted for separate *intra-group* purposes in those nations that reach Type B decisions, and a choice must now be made *between* them with respect to modernization for national purposes. Because H is the language or variety that alone has been deemed appropriate for serious purposes it is also normally the variety that is selected for modernization. This choice is a troublesome one, since the bulk of the population usually does not master H and since H has its traditional (i.e. its pre-modern) caretakers (scribes, teachers, grammarians, poets, etc.) that resist its modernization and that often attempt to constrain it along very classical or puristic lines that are maximally distant from either vernacular or international sources.

Language planning in the context of Type B decisions is largely concerned with tasks furthering: (1) immediate instruction in the Language of Wider Communication which is ('temporarily') needed in the spheres of science, technology, higher education, and modern high culture, and (2) the modernization of that variety of the national language which is ('ultimately') to displace the Language of Wider Communication from all public national functions. For the purpose of advancing both kinds of language planning, institutes, centres, academies, committees, and/or commissions tend to be established, governmentally and extra-governmentally, some of which may well engage in considerable contrastive, historical, and dialectological work in the pursuit of their goals.

Most *élitist* and other population segments preferring Type B decisions tend to arrive at a rather different view of bilingualism than do their counter-parts where Type A decisions are reached. *That* bilingualism which involves the indigenous national language and the (usually Western) Language of Wider Communication is seen as having *current* functional significance but only transitional ideal significance at the national level, with the latter (the LWC) rather than the former (the indigenous language) destined to 'go'. Stable and widespread societal bilingualism (referred to as diglossia in the sociolinguistic literature) is foreseen and ideologized only in terms of H and L. H has 'always' been viewed as appropriate to *traditional* high culture: traditional religion, law, and scholarship. It is increasingly viewed as appropriate for serious *modern* purposes as well, when realized in its more modernized guise. L has 'always' been viewed as appropriate for everyday pursuits, for intimacy, humour, and emphasis, even among the fortunate few who have mastered H, and it is anticipated that it will continue to have these functions in the future. In short, many planners and policy-makers (when and where Type B decisions are in the ascendency) look forward to a somewhat modernized emendation of the traditional intra-group bilingualism (diglossia) that has 'always' characterized their societies.

The above expectation is strengthened by the bicultural image of the ideal citizen of the future in nations reaching Type B decisions. On the one hand, it is widely hoped he will command the old indigenous wisdom which corresponds to the national Great Tradition. On the other hand, it is hoped he will master the new 'foreign' skills which are needed for modern nationhood. Both the new skills and the old wisdoms are valued in their appropriate domains. They may each be associated with quite separate customs, diets, and behaviours, but, if this is so, these merely reinforce the widespread and stable diglossia by means of which they are controlled and combined.[1] Examples of such views and designs are ample among *élites* in those developing nations in which Islam, Hinduism, and other ethnic religious systems permeate all aspects of life. An example from China of several decades ago sums up the usual position quite strikingly:

> The old and the new must both be taught; by the old is meant the four Books, the five Classics, history, government and geography of China; by the new, Western government, science and history. Both are imperative, but we repeat that the old is to form the basis and the new is for practical purposes. (Chang Chih-Tung, *Learn*, translated by S. I. Woodbridge, as quoted by Rowe, 1959, p. 121.)

[1] The partial retraditionalization of hitherto westernized *élites* in many nations where Type B decisions have recently been attained is a sign of their increasing self-redefinition. As long as they were oriented entirely towards the West, traditional foods, dress, and pursuits could either be ridiculed, ignored, or patronizingly recognized at parties or other atypical occasions. With the growth of national integrative processes (and pressures) more definite and recurring realizations of national identification are called for and become socially rather than idiosyncratically patterned.

Statements from *élites* of other regions are equally revealing, e.g.

> In his [Gokälp's] opinion the Turks should accept from Western civilization only . . . its material achievements and scientific methods and from Islam its religious beliefs without its political, legal and social traditions. All other elements of culture, and particularly all the emotional and moral values, except the religious ones, should be drawn from the Turkish heritage per se. (Heyd, 1950, pp. 150–151.)

Finally, a summary statement by a scholar who is well aware of 'older traditions' may be read as pertaining to language matters as well as to other aspects of national development.

> The nationalist movement, especially in those under-developed countries which have older traditions, must willy-nilly make a new synthesis. The real problem of these societies is that of finding the terms on which they can coexist honourably with the technology and civilization of the West. There is no question of rejecting the latter; at the same time, however, it is not possible for these societies to accept the West completely, to forget their own past. (Gadgil, 1955.)

TYPE C DECISIONS

If Type A decisions are characterized by the perceived absence of a clearly overriding indigenous Great Tradition that is considered currently adequate to serve the purposes of sociocultural integration at the *national* level, and if Type B decisions are characterized by the felt *presence* of a single predominant indigenous Great Tradition that serves these very purposes, then Type C decisions are characterized by a *conflicting or competing multiplicity* of such Great Traditions. Since each of these Great Traditions is numerically, economically, and ideologically, strong enough to support separate and large-scale sociocultural and political–operational integration, their co-occurrence within a single polity makes for rather constant internal tension and for nationalistic disunity, particularly in the absence of superordinate threat. Indeed, in nations characterized by Type C decisions the nation itself must stand for a supranationalistic goal or purpose, since nationalism *per se* is a rather well developed but traditionally regional (i.e. sub-national) phenomenon. This fact has long been recognized by *élites* in several nations, whether facing problems of religious, political, or economic integration. Thus:

> Tilak faced the problem of identifying, indeed of inventing, an Indian nation. For such an identification he needed a glorious past in which Indians could take pride. The problem here was not that India lacked a glorious past, but that she had too many of them, and each was involved with communal animosities in the present. (Minogue, 1967, p. 98.)

At the regional level language selection in nations making Type C decisions is no more problematic than it was in nations characterized by Type B decisions, since, once again, regional Great Traditions inevitably have their language counterparts. It is at the broader national level, however, that language selection problems occur in nations characterized by Type C decisions since any indigenous candidate for the role of national language would yield an unfair advantage to its native speakers, to its native region, and to its native Great Tradition in the management of supra-regional, i.e. national, affairs. In order to avoid giving any party an advantage—and in order to avoid constant rivalry for greater national prominence among the various contenders—a foreign Language of Wider Communication is frequently selected *de jure* or utilized *de facto* as (co-) official or as working language (W) at the national level (sometimes in conjunction with an indigenous national language which may actually be little employed by those who are ostensibly its guardians).

As in the great empires of antiquity, a Language of Wider Communication is needed in nations characterized by Type C decisions primarily for purposes of political–operational integration and primarily at the level of written and formal interaction.[1] Whether established officially or not and whether

[1] Karl Deutsch's preliminary draft on 'Conditions for the Spread of Interregional Languages: the Experience of Medieval Europe' (prepared for the SSRC Conference on Language Problems of Developing Nations, Airlie House, Virginia, November 1968) is an instructive introduction to the historical precursors of today's Languages of Wider Communication. Deutsch points out how in the great empires of bygone days Languages of Wider Communication facilitated the introduction of new knowledge and 'new skills with relatively minimal

established permanently or not, the Language of Wider Communication comes to be particularly related to nationwide activities, such as central (i.e. federal) governmental functioning, interregional communication, and, ultimately, to those personal interactions for which supra-regional stature is implied.

However, in opting for Type C decisions (in contrast to decisions of Type A or B) the regional level of socio-cultural and political–operational integration remains extremely lively and important. As a result, each regionally recognized official language requires modernization for its own regional governmental, educational, technological, and modern cultural realizations. This means that the alternatives that we noted in our discussion of language planning in nations characterized by Type B decisions (namely, that a choice must often first be made between H and L varieties and that possibly divergent points of view must then be overcome with respect to classicization or vernacularization as guiding principles in modernization) are again present to complicate life in nations characterized by Type C decisions, but this time they are also present in each of several regional entities, rather than at the national level alone. This is not to say that no language planning is conducted at the national level in nations characterized by Type C decisions for that is not necessarily the case.[2] The national authorities are

---

disturbance of the traditional society. . . . Innovations are imported but contained. They are not infectious. They overlay and mask local diversity but change it only very slowly, if at all. Within limited sectors of each society their diffusion rates are high, but the assimilation rates of the bulk of each society to these new practices, culture patterns or languages are very small. . . . Together, the gaps between rapid diffusion on the surface and among the upper strata of a traditional agricultural society, and the slow assimilation of its sedentary masses, produces the typical image of a social layer cake. . . . Such societies do not teach the masses of their people how to learn and innovate more quickly in the future.'

Deutsch adopts the widespread American view that traditional life and socio-cultural diversity within national boundaries are undesirable. As a result, he fails to recognize that the problem—linguistically and behaviourally—is less often one of tradition *or* modernity (indigenous language *or* Language of Wider Communication) than one of tradition *and* modernity (indigenous language and Language of Wider Communication in appropriate domains of social interaction.

[2] For a very able delineation of regional language planning, on the one hand, and national language planning, on the other hand, in a nation currently characterized by decisions of Type C, when there is only a modicum of co-ordination between them, see Das Gupta, 1967. For an indication of the multiple diglossias that can exist in such nations see Gater, 1968.

frequently left with the delicate responsibility of planning for the wider acquisition of both the sometimes co-official Language of Wider Communication and the indigenous national language, each of which is likely to have opponents in one region or another.

Nations characterized by Type C decisions also present greater complexity when we come to consider their bilingualism goals. From an intra-regional point of view traditional diglossia involving H and L languages or varieties is normally justified on a permanent basis. The model regional citizen of the future is viewed as bilingual at the very least. From a national perspective, too, bilingualism is frequently considered the natural and desired state of affairs involving the indigenous national as well as the Western (or 'working') Language of Wider Communication. Once again, then the model citizen is viewed as multilingual, with each language having its well-defined and rather exclusive functions.

Both the old wisdoms and the new skills are considered desirable on a long-term basis with respect to the images of the future that are encountered in nations characterized by Type C decisions. Here again different patterns of dress, of diet, of recreation, and of education may co-exist within one and the same speech community as its members (or as certain networks of its members) go back and forth between traditional and modern behaviours during their daily rounds. These separate life styles emphasize and protect the separate validity of each of the intra-regional and inter-regional languages which are so plentifully evident in nations where Type C decisions prevail.

CONCLUSIONS

The major consideration that seems to govern subsequent language policy and language planning decisions in the new nations seem to be the interpretation locally made (and unmade) with respect to the absence or presence of socio-culturally integrating Great Traditions (and their integrative counterparts in economic, ethnic and attitudinal–behavioural terms) that correspond, at least roughly and at any given time, to the new boundaries of political–operational integration. *Élites* making Type A decisions perceive their countrymen as *amodal* in this respect. Type B perceive their context as *unimodal* in this respect. *Élites* opting for Type C decisions view reality as *multimodal* in this respect.[1]

Where new nations are self-defined as *amodal* (or where the modes that exist are considered less important than certain supra-national goals), the leadership tends to quickly select a (usually Western) Language of Wider Communication as the nationwide language in order to maximize political–operational integration (nationism). At least initially this language reveals exonormative standardization (i.e. it follows the norms of the 'metropolitan' country). Bilingualism is viewed as having only local and transitional significance. The model citizen of the future is viewed as a monolingual speaker of the Language of Wider Communication (which has been adopted as the official or national language) and as living as much in accord with a newly integrative socio-cultural pattern or life style as possible.

[1] It has been the purpose of this paper not merely to rationalize six dimensions that might be useful in differentiating between the variety of *élitist* views and behaviours concerning the language problems facing developing nations but also to indicate that these dimensions themselves lend themselves to empirical study and revision. If language policy and language planning dimensions like those suggested (together with other cross-polity dimensions like those listed in such compendia as Rudolph J. Rummel's 'The Dimensionality of Nations Project', in Merritt and Rokkan, op. cit., fn. 1, p. 28) could be examined in an appreciable number of new nations hypothesized as belonging to various types, then an R Factor by Q Factor analysis could be attempted. An R analysis would tell us what we can now only vaguely guess, namely, which dimensions are really separate and which are primarily redundant. Such analysis would enable us to determine how many orthogonal (i.e. clearly independent) *dimensions there are in the measurement and description of language problems and language policies in developing nations.* Similarly, a Q analysis would tell us how many different *types of developing nations* there really are in conjunction with the language and other dimensions utilized. Such an analysis would tell us, e.g., whether or not the hypothesized 'intermediate cases' between Types A and B are indeed a separate cluster.

As in all R by Q analysis, few 1·00 loadings are expected. If Table 1 can, for a moment, be considered the output of such an analysis (whereas it is really only the hypothetical input) we would expect each Q cluster of nations to have some loading on each R dimension or measure. Nevertheless, we would also expect the Q clusters to differ markedly in their relative loading patterns, and these profiles, then, would tell us which clusters of nations were most similar and which were most dissimilar on which descriptive dimensions. A pilot analysis of this kind could be undertaken even now on the basis of a few expert judgements with respect to the six dimensions suggested in Table 1 and selected dimensions from Rummel's studies.

For an example of how cross-polity data lend themselves to sociolinguistic research see my 'Some Contrasts between Linguistically Homogeneous and Linguistically Heterogeneous Polities', *Sociological Inquiry*, 1966, 36, 2, 18–30. For several examples of how R by Q factor analyses contribute to the compositing of sociolinguistic data see Fishman, *et al.*, 1968.

Where new nations are perceived by their decision makers as unimodal their most influential interaction networks tend increasingly to stress that indigenous (or indigenized) language most intimately associated with an existing or developing dominant Great Tradition. Considerations of more inclusive socio-cultural authenticity (i.e. nationalism) tend increasingly to limit the role of the pre-independence Language of Wider Communication to transitional roles in the spheres of technology, government, higher education, and modern High Culture. As the major indigenous language is modernized (the H variety normally being chosen for such treatment) it is expected to displace the (Western) Language of Wider Communication from the spheres in which it has only of necessity been retained. Even then bilingualism is often viewed as being desirable on a rather permanent footing involving the H and L varieties of the indigenous national language, each predominant in different spheres of an avowedly bicultural national life style that incorporates everyday informal rounds (L), traditional formality (H, classical), and modern skills (H, modernized).

Finally, those new nations that are self-defined as *multi-modal* with respect to Great Tradition-based socio-cultural integration gravitate towards recognizing regional languages for regional authenticity and a Language of Wider Communication (which may or may not be 'paired' with an indigenous national language) as a working language for the purposes of national political–operational integration. The several recognized regional languages are each modernized (once again, the H varieties usually being selected for modernization). Bilingualism and biculturism are viewed as stable and desirable phenomena, both at the regional and at the national levels. Regional and socio-cultural integration proceeds primarily on the basis of the regional L and H varieties. National political–operational integration depends on relatively widespread mastery of one or another of the working language(s). Both the new skills and the old wisdoms are retained in the image of the model citizen of the future.

Languages of Wider Communication seem likely to retain long-term significance under all three types of decisions. Under amodal perceptions it is hoped that they will increasingly displace local and regional languages. Under multi-modal perceptions they are depended upon to function as unifying working languages for political–operational integration at the national level. Under uni-modal perceptions they continue to serve as vital languages in certain higher and more modern domains, although it may be hoped they they can ultimately and ideally be dislodged.[1]

[1] Having carried my conceptual presentation this far purely in theoretical terms, it seems fitting to offer a few examples of how I would currently characterize the language planning decisions of a few nations with which I am somewhat familiar:

Type A	⟶	*Type B*	*Type C*
Cameroons	Philippines	Israel	India
Ghana	Indonesia	Thailand	Pakistan
Gambia	Tanzania	Somalia	Ceylon
		Ethiopia	Malaysia

The difficulties of utilizing the classification proposed in this paper when proceeding non-quantitatively become apparent if we compare the position I have assigned to Tanzania with that assigned to Ethiopia. Few Tanzanian leaders today might agree that Tanzania still lacks sufficiently integrating bonds to be classified as making Type B decisions, particularly if Ethiopia, where native speakers of the national language are also still a minority, *can* be so classified. (For an example of a more intermediate view of Tanzanian integration dated as recently as two years ago, see Mosha, 1967.) Of course, in the final analysis, phenomenological classifications must reveal the views of the beholders, because it is these views that lead to subsequent actions. However, quantitative factor loadings derived from such views and behaviours are also obtainable, and these would enable us to indicate the infinite *degrees* of similarity and difference that are actually provided for by the current conceptual approach in a fashion that simply cannot be matched by purely nominal classifications based upon the judged 'resultant of forces'.

The problem of classifying Ireland presents us with another opportunity for gauging the utility of the conceptual scheme advanced, given the unusual case of a well-nigh vanished vernacular that is still governmentally termed to be the national language and 'the first official language' (and, therefore, which is accorded every ceremonial honour), while an erstwhile foreign colonialist Language of Wider Communication has, long since, become the actual mother tongue of the vast majority of the population and the functional language of national integration. Nevertheless, certain *élites* have set their sights on Type B decision-making which would have Irish slowly but surely destined to displace English (much like certain *élites* might plan to have Arabic displace French in Tunisia). Most, however, claim (at least in private) that Irish is an excessively deified corpse in honour of which the nation has adopted Type C policies even though its population has—in the past 200 years—re-established a new Type B integration and only one ethnic group and one integrating Great Tradition are involved. The official position still maintains that Ireland consists of one people with two languages, each of which should be available to all for all national purposes and one of which requires substantial strengthening so that this goal may be attained. This official position is difficult to classify within our conceptual framework, since it involves a functional duplication (which may, indeed, help explain the singular lack of success in 'restoring' Irish after fifty years of politically independent policy on behalf of that

Indigenous national languages are in need of modernization (elaboration, codification, and, not infrequently, simplification) in order to render their H varieties suitable for modern national purposes, at the same time that their more traditional H and L varieties are retained for more traditional H and L functions in nations making Types B and C decisions. We have now entered a new phase of geographically widespread planning of indigenous languages that must be assisted in discharging new and complicated national functions. The *processes* of language planning are currently little known, and it is high time that sociolinguists turned their disciplined attention from an enumeration of new words to discovering what these planning processes really are and which of them differentiate between cases of successful and unsuccessful planning. National languages and Languages of Wider Communication constantly come and go on the world scene. We neither can nor should foresee the time of being able to get along without *both*. Our need, therefore, both for practical and for academic purposes, is to know the processes and the circumstances through which human decisions influence their adoption, cultivation, displacement, and replacement.

REFERENCES

Bell, Wendell, and Oxaal, I.
(1964) *Decisions of Nationhood.* Denver Social Science Foundation (University of Denver).

Das Gupta, Jyotirindra
(1967) *Language and Politics in India.* Ph.D. Dissertation, University of California, Berkeley; also, Berkeley and Los Angeles, University of California Press, 1970.

Dawson, J. L. M.
(1967) 'Traditional versus Western Attitudes in West Africa: the Construction, Validation and Application of a Measuring Device', *British Journal of Social and Clinical Psychology*, 6, Part 2, 81–96.

---

cause). The brunt of the actions and decisions actually taken during this period seem to me to be indicative of Type B decisions on behalf of a once foreign language which has slowly been completely indigenized and associated with a new indigenous Great Tradition, while forcing the old vernacular into being little but a vestigial rural marker, on the one hand (when spoken conversationally), and a ceremonial marker, on the other hand (when printed or spoken on formal occasions).

DeLamater, John
(1967) 'Commitment to the Political System in a Multi-state Nation.' Unpublished MS., University of Michigan.
DeLamater, John, Katz, Daniel, and Kelman, Herbert C.
(1967) 'On the Nature of National Involvement: an Empirical Study.' Unpublished MS., University of Michigan; also *Journal of Conflict Resolution*, 1969, 13, 3.
Deutsch, Karl W.
(1953) *Nationalism and Social Communication.* Cambridge: M.I.T. Prep. (2nd ed. 1966.)
(1968) 'Conditions for the Spread of Interregional Languages: the Experience of Medieval Europe.' (Preliminary draft prepared for the SSRC Conference on Language Problems of Developing Nations, Airlie House, Virginia, November 1968.)
Deutsch, Karl W., Jacob, P. E., Teune, H., Toscano, J. V., and Wheaton, W. L. C.
(1964) *The Integration of Political Communities.* Philadelphia: Lippincott.
Eisenstadt, S. N.
(1968) 'Some New Looks at the Problem of Relations between Traditional Societies and Modernization', *Economic Development and Cultural Change*, 16, 436–50.
Fischer, Joseph
(1965) 'Indonesia', in James S. Coleman (ed.), *Education and Political Development.* Princeton University Press.
Fishman, Joshua A.
(1968) 'Nationality-nationalism and Nation-nationism', in Fishman, Joshua A., Ferguson, Charles A., and Das Gupta, Jyotirindra (eds.), *Language Problems of Developing Nations.* New York: John Wiley; pp. 39–51.
Fishman, Joshua A., Cooper, Robert L., and Ma, Roxana
(1968) *Bilingualism in the Barrio.* New York: Yeshiva University. (Final Report on Contract OEC–1–7–062817–0297); also Bloomington (Ind.) Language Sciences Series, Indiana University, in press.
Gadgil, D. R.
(1955) *Economic Policy and Development.* Poona: Sangam Press.
Galtung, Johan
(1968) 'Sociological Theory and Social Development', *Nkanga*, No. 2. Kampala, Uganda: Transition Books Limited.
Gater, James W.
(1968) 'Sinhalese Diglossia', *Anthropological Linguistics*, Vol. 10, No. 8, 1–15.

Gusfield, Joseph

(1968) 'Tradition and Modernity, Conflict and Congruence', *Journal of Social Issues*, XXIV, No. 4, 1–8. (Special issue ('Modernity and Tradition', ed. Joseph Gusfield.)

Heyd, Uriel

(1950) *Foundations of Turkish Nationalism: The Life and Teachings of Ziya Gokälp*. London: Luzac and Harvill.

Hopkins, Terence K., and Wallerstein, Immanuel

(1967) 'The Comparative Study of National Societies', *Social Science Information*, 6, No. 5, 25–8.

Inayatullah

(1967) 'Toward a non-Western Model of Development', in Daniel Lerner and Wilbur Schram (eds.), *Communication and Change in the Developing Countries*. Honolulu: East–West Center Press.

Inglehart, Ronald F. and Woodward, Margaret

(1967) 'Language Conflicts and Political Integration', *Comparative Studies in Society and History*, 10, 27–45.

Inkeles, Alex

(1965) 'The Modernization of Man', *Conspectus*, India International Center, New Delhi, Vol. 1, No. 4. (Reprinted in Myron Weiner (ed.), *Modernization: The Dynamics of Growth*. New York: Basic Books.)

Jahoda, Gustav

(1961–2) 'Aspects of Westernization: a Study of Adult-class Students in Ghana', *British Journal of Sociology*, 1961, 12, 375–86; 1962, 13, 43–56.

(1963) 'The Development of Children's Ideas about Country and Nationality': Part I. *British Journal of Educational Psychology*, 33, 47–60, and 'National symbols and themes': Part II. *BJEP*, 33, 143–53.

Kahl, Joseph A.

(1968) *The Measurement of Modernism*. Austin: University of Texas Press. (Institute of Latin American Studies, Latin American Monographs, No. 12.)

Kapil, Raul L.

(1966) 'On the Conflict Potential of Inherited Boundaries in Africa', *World Politics*, 18, 656–73.

Katz, Daniel, Kelman, Herbert C., and Flacks, R.

(1963) 'The National Role: Some Hypotheses about the Relation of Individuals to Nation in America Today', *Peace Research Society Papers* (I), 1, 113–27.

Kelman, Herbert C.
(1967) 'Patterns of Personal Involvement in the National System: a Social-psychological Analysis of Political Legitimacy'. (Invited address presented at the Eleventh Interamerican Congress of Psychology, Mexico City, December 1967.)

Lawson, E. D.
(1963) 'Development of Patriotism in Children—a Second Look', *Journal of Psychology*, 55, 279–86.

Levine, Donald N.
(1965) *Wax and Gold*. University of Chicago Press.

Little, Kenneth
(1965) *West African Urbanization: A Study of Voluntary Associations in Social Change*. New York: Cambridge University Press.

Mau, James
(1968) *Social Change and Images of the Future*. Cambridge, Mass.: Schenkman.

Mayer, Philip
(1963) *Townsmen or Tribesmen*. Cape Town: Oxford University Press.

Merritt, Richard L., and Rokkan, Stein
(1966) *Comparing Nations: The Use of Quantitative Data in Cross-National Research*. New Haven: Yale University Press.

Minogue, K. R.
(1967) *Nationalism*. New York: Basic Books.

Moore, Wilbert E.
(1961) 'The Social Framework of Economic Development', in Ralph Braibanti and Joseph J. Spengler (eds.), *Traditional Values and Socio-Economic Development*. Durham: Duke University Press.

Morse, Stanley J., and Pearlman, Stanton
(1968) 'Nationalism, Political Protest and the Concept of National Role.' Unpublished MS., University of Michigan.

Mosha, M.
(1967) 'The Role of Language in Nation Building', *EAIS & CA-EAA Conference on Mass Media and Linguistic Communication in East Africa*, 31 March–3 April 1967, mimeo.

Moskos, Charles C., Jr.
(1967) *The Sociology of Political Independence*. Cambridge, Mass.: Schenkman.

Oxaal, Ivar
(1968) *Black Intellectuals Come to Power: The Rise of Creole Nationalism in Trinidad and Tobago*. Cambridge, Mass.: Schenkman.

Rowe, David Nelson
(1959) *Modern China: A Brief History*. Princeton University Press.

Rummel, Rudolph J.
(1966) 'The Dimensionality of Nations Project', in Richard L. Merritt and Rokkan Stein (eds.), *Comparing Nations: The Use of Quantitative Data in Cross-National Research.* New Haven: Yale University Press.

Sékou Touré, A.
(1959) *La Lutte du Parti Démocratique de Guinée pour l'Emancipation Africaine.* Conakry: Imprimerie Nationale.

Smelser, N. J.
(1959) *Social Change in the Industrial Revolution.* London: Routledge and Kegan Paul.

Smith, David H., and Inkeles, Alex
(1966) 'The OM Scale: a Comparative Socio-psychological Measure of Individual Modernity', *Sociometry*, 29, 325–77.

Spengler, Joseph J.
(1961) 'Theory, Ideology, Non-economic Values and Politico-economic Development', in Ralph Braibanti and J. J. Spengler (eds.), *Traditional Values and Socio-Economic Development.* Durham: Duke University Press.

Stephenson, John B.
(1968) 'Is Everyone Going Modern? A Critique and Suggestion for Measuring Modernism', *American Journal of Sociology*, 74, 256–64.

Tabouret-Keller, A.
(1968) 'Sociological Factors of Language Maintenance and Language Shift': a Methodological Approach Based on European and African Examples', in Joshua A. Fishman, Charles A. Ferguson, and Jyotirindra Das Gupta (eds.), *Language Problems of Developing Nations.* New York: John Wiley; pp. 107–118.

II. Communication Roles of Languages in Multilingual Societies

EUGENE A. NIDA and WILLIAM L. WONDERLY

INTRODUCTION

The purpose of this paper is to provide a model for studying languages in reference to their communicative functions, especially in multilingual societies; and to point out some of the factors that should be taken into consideration by educators and policy-making bodies who are concerned with the development of national languages and with making optimal use of other languages in their areas. In this approach the paper differs from a number of other studies of the role of language which focus on the function of language within different contexts.[1]

MAJOR COMMUNICATION FUNCTIONS OF LANGUAGE

A study of language in terms of the needs for adequate communication within a particular society has led to the recognition of three major communication roles:

1. The In-Group Language

The in-group language is the one used in any society for the basic face-to-face relationships with other speakers with whom the individual in question fully identifies. In so-called primitive societies this would quite naturally be the indigenous or tribal language. In certain large language communities such

[1] See especially William A. Stewart, 'An Outline of Linguistic Typology for Describing Multilingualism', in Frank A. Rice (ed.), *Study of the Role of Second Languages in Asia, Africa, and Latin America*, pp. 15–25. Washington, D.C.: Center for Applied Linguistics, 1962. (This volume contains several important articles and bibliographies related to the subject of the present paper.) Another volume of importance, both for the articles it contains and for its bibliographies, is John J. Gumperz and Dell Hymes (eds.), *The Ethnography of Communication* (Part 2 of *American Anthropologist*, Vol. 66, No. 6, 1964).

a face-to-face language might be the regional dialect as, for example, the case of Swiss–German.

In a large linguistic community which is relatively heterogeneous, in the sense that it has many so-called 'vertical dialects' (socio-economic distinctions in speech), the in-group form of language may be one of these levels; or it may be characterized by the use of colloquial levels involving special slang expressions, or it may even be a highly specialized jargon which is particularly important for in-group identification. Such forms of speech have been important for groups such as beatniks, and the in-group speech of English-speaking teen-agers reveals certain of these characteristics. Relatively elaborate underworld jargons have been known and studied by various language specialists.[1]

2. *The Out-group Language*

Almost all people living in a face-to-face speech community have some need for contacting people of groups outside their own community. The only exception to this situation might be some of the isolated tribes in Amazonia, but even among groups such as the Guaica (or Shiriana) Indians in northern Brazil and southern Venezuela (where some of the dialects are mutually unintelligible), there is a highly developed form of language used on all occasions when different tribal groups meet together. Even under these so-called 'primitive' circumstances an out-group form of language has developed.

In many parts of the world a trade language serves the purpose of out-group communication. In the lower Congo and the Kwilu valley a trade language called Kituba serves for most intertribal contacts. The Kituba language is actually a koiné form of Kikongo which has spread throughout the area as a medium of out-group communication. In the process of spreading it has become greatly simplified in its linguistic structures. In eastern New Guinea the language of out-group communication is a local pidgin language called Neo-melanesian, a name designed to give the language some status.[2]

[1] For a discussion of some of the varieties which can be found within a large linguistic community, see Wonderly, 1968, chapters 2 and 3.

[2] For a study of the characteristics of pidgin and creole languages, see Hall, 1966. For a listing and discussion of African pidgins and trade languages, see Samarin, 1962.

3. The Language of Specialized Information

In many areas where there are both in-group and out-group languages there is also the need for a language of specialized information. This is often the language of higher education or of specialized formal training. For example, in the Cameroons many of the speakers of local languages, e.g. Bafia, Bassa, Meka, and Kaka, also know the trade language Yaoundé (closely related to Bulu, which was promoted as a trade language by Protestant missionaries). Yaoundé serves as an important out-group language, but any person wanting to acquire specialized information, that is, information which comes from the world culture and not from the culture of the immediate out-groups, must learn French. Similarly, in the Philippines speakers of such languages as Cebuano, Hiligaynon, Pampango, and Samareño must learn Pilipino if they are to enjoy movies, watch television, read certain newspapers, and carry on trade in areas outside of their immediate tribal areas. But these persons must also learn English if they want to go on to secondary school or the university and if they wish to take positions of leadership in politics, business, or social life.

Though the preceding description of in-group languages, out-group languages, and languages of specialized information emphasizes multilingual situations, it must be clearly recognized that these three basic functions of language exist in a number of different linguistic settings. While the most obvious is no doubt the 'three-language structure', it would be misleading if we were not to recognize, also, certain essential features of a two-language structure, as well as those of a one-language structure, though these latter two will not here receive detailed treatment.

THE THREE-LANGUAGE STRUCTURE

A typical three-language structure may be found in Kenya, where people who speak various in-group languages, e.g. Luragoli, Kipsigis, Luo, Kikamba, and Kikuyu, find it highly desirable to learn Swahili if they wish to have much outside contact. At the same time, if such persons want to obtain a higher education or to participate as leaders in national life, English is indispensable.

In a typical three-language structure a so-called 'world language', e.g. English, French, Spanish, or Portuguese, tends to be the language of specialized information. This is due to the fact that technical information from the world culture comes to people primarily by means of such a language. However, a three-language structure does not always involve a so-called world language as the language of specialized information, for the linguistic world of a particular speech community may be highly restricted. For example, in the Kwilu area of Congo a Kihungana speaker certainly must learn Kituba if he is to have contacts with other tribal groups. Kituba thus becomes his out-group language. However, the language of the Army and of many local Congolese government administrators is Lingala. Within his restricted context, therefore, Lingala may be said to constitute the language of specialized information for him.

A similar situation exists in the northern part of the Philippines. Some of the small tribal groups learn Ilocano as the out-group language, but if they are to have much contact with the national life, then it is essential for them also to learn Pilipino, which thus becomes for them the language of specialized information.

There are, of course, some speakers who might be said to have a 'four-language structure'. Their own tribal language constitutes the in-group language, and there may be two different out-group languages, representing different 'grades' of usefulness and serving to communicate with different out-groups. Finally, they may have a fourth language for specialized information. However, this kind of four-language structure is relatively rare and does not usually involve any large number of individuals. Furthermore, the possession of more than one out-group language usually represents not so much a different functional level as the presence of diverse out-groups with whom the person has occasion to interact. It is thus only the exceptional situation in which a person is so placed as to find it important to know four languages representing four distinct levels of communication. Therefore we have not set up a four-language structure as being one of the basic structures for communication.

Focusing upon a three-language structure for different levels of linguistic usage does not mean, of course, that people necessarily restrict themselves to learning three languages. Quite the contrary, in Africa, where there is a greater percentage of multilingualism than in any other large speech area of the world, many persons know four, five, or six languages. However, these do not represent distinct grades in out-group language contacts, but rather the learning of specific neighbouring languages under circumstances where their acquisition has proved obligatory, inevitable, or highly useful. It is therefore necessary to distinguish between the learning of a specific out-group language which serves as a basis of contact with one particular group and the learning of an out-group language which may serve as a means of communication with a number of different groups. It is within the context of this type of distinction that the recognition of a three-language structure seems to be fully justified.

THE TWO-LANGUAGE STRUCTURE

In many places in the world speakers participate in a two-language structure rather than in a three-language structure. The second language serves both as the language of out-group contacts and also as the source of specialized information, e.g. Latin America, Haiti, Holland, Switzerland.

THE ONE-LANGUAGE STRUCTURE

Native speakers of major languages, e.g. English, French, German, Russian, or Chinese, have typically a one-language structure. They may actually speak a local regional dialect, for example, southern United States or Liverpool English, as the language of in-group identification; but the standard form of the language is used for most out-group contacts and for specialized information.

LANGUAGES AND POLITICAL ACTION

The above description of three-language and two-language structures has not indicated anything of the tensions or problems involved in such multi-level systems; but obviously the importance of language for interpersonal relationships and its symbolic value as a means of group identification (it is the most important because for one thing it is the hardest to change or falsify) make languages politically and socially very strategic. Hence, languages naturally become a prime element in the struggle for national unity. From the very beginning of the independence movement in Indonesia the trade language Bahasa Indonesia was proclaimed as the language of national unity. This was a fortunate choice, for though at the time that it was adopted as a language of national unity it probably did not have more than 10 million speakers, it nevertheless was a very effective instrument for rallying the total constituency of Indonesia. Even today there are only about 30 million speakers of Bahasa Indonesia, of whom perhaps not more than 3–4 million speak it as their mother tongue. In view of the presence of Javanese, which is spoken by some 60 million people, it is in a sense surprising that Bahasa Indonesia was chosen as the language of unity. But if Javanese had been chosen the attainment of national unity would have been highly questionable.

Bahasa Indonesia did have certain very distinct advantages as a national language. In the first place, its speakers were widely scattered throughout the whole region of Indonesia. In the second place, its structure is relatively simple and is closely related to all of the languages within the Indonesian area except those very few which are spoken in the highlands of West Irian. The very fact that Bahasa Indonesia was politically neutral did a great deal to make it acceptable to various groups who would have been unwilling to accept any other language as a dominant form of speech.

Bahasa Indonesia itself is derived from the Malay language as spoken in the northern part of Sumatra and the Malay peninsula. As it has spread throughout Indonesia it has adopted certain typically simplified structures which mean that it may be classified as a type of koiné.

In the Philippines the linguistic situation was somewhat different. The obvious choice for a language of national unity, in terms of the number of speakers, would have been Cebuano, since it is spoken by more persons than any other. However, Tagalog, as the language of the region of Manila, had much greater prestige and had been acquired by a number of speakers of other languages as their 'second language'. The influence of Tagalog as the language of Manila was, however, increasingly decisive, for the population of Manila is somewhat over 3 million persons out of a total population on the islands of 30 million. In other words, at least one-tenth of the total population of the country lives in Manila, and a very high percentage of persons go to Manila from time to time.

If, however, Tagalog was to be accepted by people generally throughout the Philippines certain concessions were regarded as essential. As one concession the national language has been called Pilipino, not Tagalog. Also, the promoters of the use of Pilipino have rejected the pressures which have come from the strict Tagalog purists, who wanted to establish Tagalog in its classical form as being the norm of the national language. Some persons, of course, promoted the use of English as a national language, since it was spoken at least in some measure by as many persons as any other one language of the Philippines. Nevertheless, English had a very decided disadvantage as an out-group language and as the language of national unity, since its structure is so completely different from that of the Malayo-Polynesian languages of the Philippines. Actually, a person who speaks any one of the Philippine languages can usually learn Pilipino within three to four months of residence in a Tagalog-speaking area. Moreover, the learning of Pilipino in the school is much easier than would ever be the case with English. Even though English has been retained as the language of advanced primary and secondary education and of university instruction, there is mounting pressure for the use of Pilipino as the medium of instruction throughout the secondary schools, except for courses in science, where it is recognized that students obviously need to be prepared to receive specialized information in a language in which a greater abundance of such information is available. The Indian situation differs markedly from the foregoing, but is well documented.[1]

NATIONALISM AND REGIONALISM

The very pressures that create the needs for some national language as a unifying force almost inevitably also create a contrary reaction in favour of regional languages. Whether people actually feel threatened by the emphasis upon national

[1] For various other aspects of the linguistic situation in India, see Ferguson and Gumperz, 1960.

unity in language is hard to say, but certainly the emphasis upon a single language very frequently makes them more and more aware of their own regional language.

This local emphasis on regional languages depends partly upon the degree of cultural vitality of the particular regional group, and upon the group's sense of identification or non-identification with the national society. In Latin America most of the indigenous groups have, through more than three centuries of uninterrupted Spanish- and Portuguese-speaking colonization and government, developed a feeling of inferiority with respect to their own Indian languages; while maintaining the Indian languages for purposes of in-group communication and identification, they have shown little interest in extending their use to that of out-group communication or the communication of specialized information. But as these groups progressively identify with the national society, they show increasing interest in the use of the national language, Spanish or Portuguese. The resurgence of Guarani in Paraguay is only an apparent exception, as this language has now taken on national status alongside Spanish, and has become a symbol of national, not just regional, identity.

In the Cameroons the emphasis in education has certainly been on French, and though there is no tendency to repudiate French as the national language nor as the language of specialized information, there has certainly been an emphasis upon regional languages, particularly within the Christian community. Here there has been a rapidly increased interest in the translation of the Scriptures into various languages. On the whole, however, this emphasis is not at the expense of the national language but at the expense of some former out-group languages. For example, Protestants in the Camerouns are no longer content to have their Scriptures in Bulu, which had become a kind of 'Protestant Latin' to many of the people. They insist that they want the Scriptures in French and their own local language, but not in a kind of 'half-way language' such as Bulu has seemed to be.

A NATIONAL LANGUAGE

For a language to become a national language certain very important features are needed. In the first place, it should be politically neutral. If it is not characterized by political neutrality it is too often regarded merely as a tool by which a particular language group seeks to extend its domination. Quite naturally, this is a cause for alarm among other language communities. In this respect, the development of Bahasa Indonesia has been very instructive, for under the circumstances there has been very little opposition to Bahasa Indonesia and almost no reaction in favour of regional languages. In the Philippines making Tagalog appear politically neutral has been exceptionally wise; and in East Africa Swahili has at least seemed to afford a neutral linguistic medium, especially in a nation such as Kenya, where the political centre of the country is not associated with traditional Swahili dominance.

In Nigeria there is simply no politically neutral language. In fact, the division into three major regions reflects the three language poles: Hausa, Yoruba, and Ibo. The political survival of Nigeria as a country would be even more seriously threatened than it is if any one of these languages were promoted by the Government as being the one national language.

If a language is to be a national language it should also be linguistically related to the various local languages of the area. One feature which makes Tagalog and Bahasa Indonesia so acceptable in their respective areas is that they are so closely related to all of the other languages. For example, a generative grammar of Tagalog, Ilocano, and Cebuano can be almost completely identical up to the point where morphemes have to be identified. In other words, the grammatical structure is essentially the same. It is only that individual lexical items tend to be different. With languages so very closely related, people can learn the national language in a very short time. It is so much easier than having to master an entirely foreign structure. In contrast, the fact that Spanish and Portuguese, as Indo-European languages, are so radically different from the Indian languages of Latin America is no doubt one of the important factors which has hindered the indigenous groups from learning the national language in these countries. Moreover, when persons are required to learn a completely foreign grammatical structure they often tend to develop a relatively distorted form of that structure as, for example, in the rather widespread modifications of French structure as now spoken in Congo.

For a national language to succeed it should also be spoken as a mother tongue by a substantial community of speakers who can serve as fully satisfactory models. In Indonesia an average of one person in ten could speak the language Bahasa Indonesia—with, of course, certain minor local variations, but always with complete mutual comprehension. The persons who serve as models for such a language should also be well distributed geographically and not concentrated in one place. The problem of French in the Congo is that after independence the number of people who spoke French as their mother tongue became increasingly more restricted (even a high percentage of the Roman Catholic missionaries in Congo were Flemish-speaking). The increasing absence of valid models creates a serious problem, for with rapid expansion of the school system and fewer and fewer native speakers as models for the language, students often become separated by a four-to-five 'generational gap' between the native speaker of French and the local teacher of French. As a result, a native French speaker often has real difficulty in recognizing his own language as spoken by such people. Almost the same thing is true of English as it is often taught in local schools in the Philippines. Accordingly, many persons speak of this form of English as 'bamboo English'.

THE NATIONAL LANGUAGE AND THE LANGUAGE OF SPECIALIZED INFORMATION

Almost inevitably, leaders of any nation attempt to make the national language also the language of specialized information. This is precisely what has happened in the case of Indonesia. At an earlier stage Dutch was the language of the university system in the area, but shortly after independence all instruction was carried out in Bahasa Indonesia. The rejection of Dutch is understandable not only because of its association with colonialism and the fact that its structure differs from that of Malayo-Polynesian but also because it has certain limitations as far as being a 'world language' is concerned. Dutch thus seemed to be an inadequate instrument for keeping abreast of technological developments throughout the world. English was considered as a language of specialized information, but only for certain restricted types of material. As a result, Bahasa

Indonesia was not only established as a national language but every effort has been made to raise it to the status of a language of specialized information. For the most part, however, language planners in Indonesia have had no adequate appreciation of the technical and economic problems involved. No provision, for example, has been made for the translating and publishing of necessary textbooks. There has even been drastic restriction on the importation of books, and as a result the level of training in the universities has suffered.

The very problem of specialized information is becoming more and more acute, for nothing in the history of the world has quite equalled the information explosion during the last thirty years. It is estimated, for example, that of all the scientists who have ever engaged in research and publication, at least 90 per cent are now alive and producing. Moreover, progress in the present-day world depends far more upon technological information than upon any other one factor. Therefore, if so-called developing nations do not wish to condemn themselves to perpetual dependency and to an ever-increasing lag they must make provision for either: (1) a sufficient number of persons fully educated in a language of specialized information and continually provided with books in such languages, or (2) adequate programmes of translation and publication of such materials in the national language, or (3) even better, a combination of these two approaches. Perhaps the basic difficulty is that governmental bureaux move with tragic slowness in such matters, and by the time books are approved, translated, and published they are very likely out of date. So rapid is the advance of knowledge in our day.

MEANS FOR PROMOTING A NATIONAL LANGUAGE

The most obvious means for the promotion of a national language would certainly appear to be the school system, and this is no doubt largely true. However, it is absolutely essential that in any such school programme a sufficient number of years of instruction be included so that a person actually develops adequate control of the language. Furthermore, he needs to have continued contacts with a national language or he soon loses facility. Where there are only three or four years of primary education in a national language, the tendency is to lapse into illiteracy or semi-literacy, and the continued influence of instruction in the national language becomes minimal. Such persons may know the alphabet and be able to write their name and read signs, but they are not really participants in the national-language community. The failure of continued contacts through papers, magazines, and inexpensive books also means that much of the value of primary education may be lost, for there is no continuing reading habit. In this respect, goals defined or carried out by government bureaux are often entirely too shortsighted.

Without at least certain supplementary means of promoting the national language, even a school system is likely to be largely ineffective. In reality, the informal means by which people learn languages are often far more satisfactory than the formal ones. In the Philippines and Indonesia, for example, movies constitute one of the very important techniques by which the national language is promoted in the provinces. In the Philippines comic books are particularly important. There are at least 120 different publications put out every two weeks, ranging in size of edition from 4,000 to 34,000 each. The contents include everything from Donald Duck stories to horror comics, but the important factor is that all of these are in Pilipino and they reach a very wide audience. In fact, these books are no doubt more important in spreading the use of Pilipino than any and all of the textbooks printed by the Government.

An important means of promoting the national language, but one which has not yet been sufficiently exploited, is that of serious literature on a level of language within reach of the poorly educated reader. Most serious reading matter tends to be on a level suitable only for the person who is well educated in the national language, leaving a gap between the primer stage and the stage of the experienced reader. Many persons who learn to read, therefore, lapse into semi-literacy or, at best, continue to nourish their intellect on comics and similar publications. However, techniques are available by which writers can be taught to prepare serious materials on a 'common' level which will be accessible to the poorly educated reader while still acceptable to the better educated—i.e. in a form of the language common to both groups.[1] Bible translations in such common or popular language are being made available in Spanish, French, English, and a number of other languages, and the same techniques used in preparing these could also be used for preparing all kinds of material of cultural and educational value.

Increasingly in the Philippines television is an important instrument for the spread of Pilipino. Local radio is often in regional languages, but it is economically impossible to provide television in the various local languages, and therefore the use of Pilipino serves an important function with an ever-increasing audience. The situation is no doubt similar in the case of other national languages; however, the persons who do not speak the national language frequently tend to be economically underprivileged, and thus their limited access to television places certain limitations upon the use of this medium for spreading the language.

GAPS IN VOCABULARY OF OUT-GROUP LANGUAGES AND OF LANGUAGES OF SPECIALIZED INFORMATION

It is a common assumption that a person educated in an out-group language or in a language of specialized information will have a vocabulary fully sufficient to cover the totality of his experience, for example, greetings, business, politics, family life, religion, and technology. This, however, is by no means always the case. A person may have received a relatively adequate technological education in such a language but still have little or no experience with that language in certain areas of his life, such as interpersonal relations and religion. It is, of course, possible for such individuals to have a 'consumer vocabulary' in such areas but to be pitifully inadequate as far as their 'producer vocabulary' is concerned.[2]

In the Philippines the national language Pilipino serves quite well as an out-group language for speakers of many other languages except in the areas of family and religion, where almost inevitably people revert to the local language if this is at all possible.

[1] Some of the techniques for preparing this type of literature, and of the problems relating to its preparation, are discussed in Wonderly, op. cit.

[2] Ibid., pp. 35 ff., for concepts of 'producer' and 'consumer' language.

There are some situations, however, in which religion seems to be primarily a subject for discussion in an out-group language, or in a language of specialized information. This type of behaviour may reflect some degree of insecurity as far as the local language is concerned. People may feel that a language other than the in-group language is necessary as a symbol of prestige due to the deity, and not infrequently the use of such a language expresses a people's desire to identify with a group of which they are not an immediate part. In Roman Catholicism the traditional tendency to use Latin reflects something of this same type of prestige status for a language of specialized information.

In circumstances where people do discuss religion (at least on certain levels) in a language other than that of the in-group there are usually two quite distinct levels of religion. The religion of the home is actually discussed primarily in the local in-group language. This is essentially the 'lower storey' of religion—what might be called the lower stratum of religious expression which lies beneath the veneer of a theologized form of expression. In contrast with this, the religion of the temple or the church may be expressed primarily in the out-group language or in a language of specialized information. Where there are two quite distinct languages involved in religious expression one will usually find quite distinct forms of religion, and in many instances people do not bring these two 'levels of religion' together, e.g. the existence among Latin-American Indians of folk-Catholicism or Christo-Paganism alongside of more orthodox forms of Catholicism, and of African religious elements in the Voodoo and similar religions of the Caribbean.[1]

THE MULTIPLE ROLES OF LANGUAGES

For the sake of simplicity of presentation the previous discussion has focused primarily upon the diverse roles of different languages in the distinct patterns of communication. Actually, however, the situation is far more complex than what might appear on the surface, for one and the same language may occur at different levels, even within a so-called three-language structure. For example, in Congo (Kinshasa) French may serve

[1] Cf. Nida, 1961; Metraux, 1959. See Luzbetak, 1963, pp. 239–64, for discussion and bibliography.

as an out-group language for certain types of general business contacts while at the same time serving as a language of specialized information. A language such as Lingala, which is an in-group language for many people, also serves as an out-group language for many others, especially on the lower levels of out-group contact in a capital such as Kinshasa.

LANGUAGE AND LEVELS OF STYLE

The distinction between in-group language, out-group language, and language of specialized information is closely parallel to certain distinctions in the level of style within an individual language. For example, an English-speaking person in the United States will generally use an informal or casual level of style in in-group contacts. For out-group contacts his level of style will probably be formal, sometimes called 'regular', while as a language of specialized information the level of style is rather largely technical.[1] A native speaker of English can regularly shift between these levels, and in fact is hardly aware of the existence of such differences. Nevertheless, a person who does not speak English as his own mother tongue and has learned only one of the levels becomes immediately conspicuous when he tries to communicate in an area for which his linguistic experience has not prepared him. For example, many students from India studying in the United States have mastered a form of English which is distinctly 'bookish'. Though such students are quite competent in the area of technical or formal speech, their attempts at casual or informal use of English quickly betray their background.

In some multilingual situations the functions of informal or casual style as over against a more formal or technical style are distributed among two or more languages. For example, bilingual speakers of Haitian Creole use the Creole in social situations that call for informal or casual speech, but standard French for more formal speech; so that standard French in Haiti tends to lack, for want of occasion for their use, the informal and casual expressions that are available in Parisian French, and the Creole of the same speakers tends to lack the potential for more formal use.[2]

[1] Joos, 1962; see also Wonderly, op. cit., pp. 13–17.
[2] Stewart, n.d.

LIMITATIONS OF THE IN-GROUP LANGUAGE FOR USE IN OTHER FUNCTIONS

Linguists have generally assumed that any language is adequate for communicating any and all ideas that the members of its speech community have occasion to deal with—granting, of course, that new terms may need to be borrowed or new expressions coined with the intrusion of new ideas. However, where the different communication functions are distributed among two or more languages, each of the languages is thereby, in actual practice, subject to certain limitations. The vocabulary gaps in out-group languages and languages of specialized information, as mentioned in a preceding section, are an example of this; as are also the limitations in style level in a case like that of Haitian bilingualism.

This is not a case of inherent inadequacy in either of the languages involved, but rather of a 'social handicap'—that is, of limitations placed on one or both of the languages by the society itself. An in-group language therefore tends to be limited in its function to the communication of the kinds of information normally transmitted in interpersonal relationships within the local society, largely on an informal or casual level. In many two-language or three-language situations the in-group language is unwritten, and is usually not standardized. 'Outside' information, whether communicated in spoken or written form, tends to be limited to the out-group language or the language of specialized information, at least until such a time as it has been taken into the society and assimilated as 'inside' information. Stewart mentions the possibilities of habilitating an in-group language such as Haitian Creole through standardization, to make it acceptable for other functions; but warns that a premature attempt to use it for other functions can lead to difficulties, 'since the use of a language outside of its prescribed function without an accompanying change in its status is likely to be considered locally as inappropriate or even ludicrous'.[1]

LANGUAGE AS A CLASS PRIVILEGE

In view of the increased importance of communication as a means of control of human beings, it is not at all strange that

[1] Stewart, 1962b, quoted from p. 49.

language should figure more and more prominently as a politically important instrument. The acquisition of a prestige language is thus regarded by many persons as one of the essential keys to success and social advancement. It is for this reason that many Indians in Latin America place such a high premium upon gaining a command of Spanish. Similarly, many Africans are keenly concerned about mastering English, French, or Portuguese, for such a language means not only acceptance by a ruling class but also the possibilities of participation in the national life of the society.

If, however, language acquisition can thus be viewed as an instrument of upward mobility the converse is also true. That is, the exclusive possession of certain language abilities can be regarded as a technique for perpetuating an oligarchic control. If a particular language is the exclusive language of education and if it is the essential medium for controlling technical information it may for this very reason serve also to 'keep people in their places' and thus guarantee a larger share of control for a privileged few. It is no wonder, therefore, that language policies are regarded by so many people as being the touchstone of class mobility and the guarantee of personal rights.

REFERENCES

Ferguson, Charles A., and Gumperz, John J. (eds.)
(1960) *Linguistic Diversity in South Asia.* Indiana Research Center in Anthropology, Folklore, and Linguistics, Pub. 13.

Gumperz, John J. and Hymes, Dell (eds.)
(1964) *The Ethnography of Communication.* (Part 2 of *American Anthropologist*, Vol. 66, No. 6.)

Hall, Robert A., Jr.
(1966) *Pidgin and Creole Languages.* Ithaca, N.Y.: Cornell University Press.

Joos, Martin
(1962) *The Five Clocks.* Indiana University Research Center in Anthropology, Folklore, and Linguistics. Pub. 22.

Luzbetak, L. J.
(1963) *The Church and Cultures.* Techny, Illinois.

Metraux, A.
(1959) *Voodoo in Haiti.* London.

Nida, E. A.
(1961) 'Christo-Paganism', *Practical Anthropology*, 8, 1–14.

Samarin, William J.
(1962) 'Lingua Francas, with Special Reference to Africa', in Frank A. Rice (ed.), *Study of the Role of Second Languages in Asia, Africa, and Latin America*. Washington D.C.: Centre for Applied Linguistics. 54–64.

Stewart, William A.
(1962a) 'An Outline of Linguistic Typology for Describing Multilingualism' in Frank A. Rice (ed.), op. cit., pp. 15–25.
(1962b) 'Creole Languages in the Caribbean' in Frank A. Rice (ed.), op. cit., 34–53.
(n.d.) 'The Functional Distribution of Creole and French in Haiti', in Georgetown University Monograph Series on Languages and Linguistics, No. 15.

Wonderly, William L.
(1968) *Bible Translations for Popular Use*. London: United Bible Societies.

III. Restricted Codes in Socio-linguistics and the Sociology of Education[1]

W. P. ROBINSON

INTRODUCTION

My label of 'social psychologist' requires that I have some knowledge about the perception of other people, and some recent studies of judgements about others have been set in the wider context of examining how far and in what ways people take the needs, wishes, and expectations of others into account. Since this seminar is organized for the immediate benefit of those engaged in surveys of languages and language usage in East Africa and the ultimate benefit of the African countries concerned, it seems most appropriate to attempt to re-organize our work in England with these considerations in mind. One result of this is that I have eschewed an exposition of Bernstein's theoretical framework and relevant evidence. Instead I have selected two main topics, one methodological, the other educational, which may bear directly upon the African surveys. The methodological section begins with a short history, but develops the theme of the usefulness of an approach to socio-linguistics which never forgets that language is used to serve many functions and always remembers that it is only one vehicle for communication among others. Even within the limited range of speech samples we have examined, we can show that the speech used varies across situations and persons, while the detection of these differences requires a prior consideration of functions and semantics, and an examination of grammar at

[1] The Sociological Research Unit at the Institute of Education, London, is directed by Professor B. Bernstein and supported by funds from the Department of Education and Science and the Ford Foundation, to whom grateful acknowledgement is made. The development of the research into children's answers is supported by the Joseph Rowntree Memorial Trust, to whom similar gratitude is expressed.

appropriate levels of analysis. The differences between persons show, not only that performance is a function of social variables, but also that the relationships are not necessarily monotonic and the influences not necessarily simple. Although we cannot yet provide a general description of these phenomena, our examples may be informative guidelines for others.

In the section about the sociology of education Bernstein's original linkage of a 'restricted' code to a particular social class is generalized and incorporated as one instance within a role theoretic framework which distinguishes between 'open' and 'closed' role systems. A further separation is made between 'object' and 'person' centred types of both 'elaborated' and 'restricted' codes. The relevance of these two theoretical refinements for the initiation and control of social change through the educational system is briefly examined.

THE 'RESTRICTED' CODE AND SOCIO-LINGUISTIC METHODOLOGY

For now we see through a glass darkly. My own vision in this fragile new world of socio-linguistics is too blurred as yet for me to discern even the proper universe of discourse for the discipline. The literature is at that early stage of development, when prescriptions and evaluations are commoner than descriptions and explanations, and priorities for action are asserted with more fervour than theoretical or empirical justification. Nevertheless, I have accepted one such set of priorities as the basis for a review of the research we have been doing on the language of primary-school children in an urban industrial society, to see how it may further our understanding. If I can show the significance of this perspective for work within a monolingual community, then its import may be that much greater in a multilingual society for reasons to be specified in the final paragraphs. The prescription comes from social anthropology and is summarized by Hymes (1967, p. 13):

> There must be a study of speaking that seeks to determine the native system and theory of speaking; whose aim is to describe the communicative competence that enables a member of the community to know when to speak and when to remain silent, which code to use, when, where and to whom etc. In considering what form socio-linguistic description might take, . . . , one needs to show

sociologists, linguists, ethnographers and others a way to *see* data as the interaction of language and social setting (Hymes, 1967, p. 13).

Such a demand implies that at a certain stage of inquiry a study of the manifest and latent functions of verbal acts will come to have a temporal priority over further detailed grammatical and lexical descriptions of language, dialect, or sociolect which ignore the context of the communication. For example, the form and content of verbal utterances may be relatively specific to particular 'registers', so that attempts to find more general similarities or differences will be confounded: real differences between persons and situations will remain hidden if heterogeneous groups of either are compounded.

If this is so we may wonder why these implications have not received greater attention from linguists, psycho-linguists, and socio-linguists. Some reasons can be cited, and these may serve as warning signs to potential field workers. Psychologists and sociologists have generally paid greater attention to phonetics, phonology, grammar, and lexis than to semantics and context. If we ask about the differences between these two sets of topics we may agree that the first have more readily available theoretical descriptions which offer ease of use without abuse, quantifiability, data with a respectably hard foundation, and a safety from criticism when one is outside one's own expertise. Such attractions contrast with the hazards of semantics and context. These might require preliminary reading of philosophy books, difficult to understand and uncomfortably close to the armchair speculation which is anathema to the current hard-data image of the behavioural sciences. The daunting prospects, in combination with the readily available escape routes provided by linguists, may have been responsible for the neglect of a perspective which can give direction and meaning to studies of language behaviour.

We began with Bernstein's theoretical framework (1961), which polarizes 'restricted' and 'elaborated' codes of language as 'ideal' types. We know that at each stage of primary and secondary education working-class children in Britain are more likely to move down any hierarchical divisions in the structure, that they perform less well within these divisions, and that they are less likely to be retained by that system.

The differential distribution of the two codes by social class was suggested as a possible major reason for these social differences in educational attainment. One alternative argument that these differences in performance are presently a reflection of differences in innate cognitive potential lacks force in several ways:

(i) The same pattern of differences survives any statistical partialling out of verbal intelligence test scores.

(ii) The test scores can themselves be influenced by changes in environment in predictable and controllable ways.

(iii) The discrepancies between verbal and non-verbal intelligence-test scores are greater in the working than the middle class, and the degree of correlation with social class is greater for verbal than non-verbal scores.

Since it is easy to demonstrate differences in the values, attitudes, and associated behaviour of middle- and working-class parents which would have these consequences, it is simpler to attribute much of the present variance to social rather than biological genes. It is argued that the command of an 'elaborated' code is a necessary, although not sufficient, condition of educational success. Possession of this code implies an orientation to language as a major vehicle for the intra- and interpersonal communication of many types of information about the physical and social world. Linguistically, the code has the possibility of exploiting the full grammatical and lexical potential of the language, while utterances in this code will have to bear a correspondence to the events being discussed. The middle class are socialized into the attitudes, knowledge, and skills which constitute this code. For the working class, especially the lower working class, language is not a medium of special significance. Speech has the primary function of defining the nature of such immediate role relationships as mother, mate, or boss. The 'restricted' code governing this speech has a specifiable linguistic structure commensurate with its social functions. It is unsuitable for the attainment of educational success for a number of reasons:

(i) It does not orient the speaker to language as the major vehicle for the communication of what schools are trying to teach.

(ii) Its grammar and lexis lack the hierarchical and flexible structure and range of units for the encoding and decoding of appropriate messages.

(iii) It lacks the requirement of a referential anchorage to non-linguistic events, since its own latent function is mainly to express effect or control behaviour directly.

These problems are exacerbated in the teaching situation. The superficial, but directly observable, similarities in the grammar and lexis of 'elaborated' and 'restricted' codes can lead to two types of misunderstanding:

(i) The teacher's speech in 'elaborated' code is decoded by the child as a message in 'restricted' code.

(ii) The child's 'restricted' code speech is decoded by the teacher as a debased level of operation in 'elaborated' code.

Such misunderstandings may well delay school progress, and the second condition may serve as the basis for the teacher's first judgement relevant to a selection procedure which will successively channel the child into the lower echelons of the system; the beginnings of a self-fulfilling prophecy.

It is important for an understanding of Bernstein's concepts not to invest the terms 'elaborated' and 'restricted' with all the meanings these words have in normal usage. They are the closest to the underlying ideas that we can find in the English language, but are far from ideal. 'Elaborated' is not to be interpreted as more complicated or more finely differentiated, and 'restricted' does not apply to all forms of constraint by user, usage, or situation. Utterances in 'elaborated' code may differ in their accuracy, level of analysis, or clarity, but are not rendered more or less 'elaborated' as a result of this. I think the most useful preliminary differentiating test is to ask whether an utterance functions to elicit or offer a proposition about the non-linguistic world, a statement which can in principle be accorded a *truth value*. If the primary focus is upon this referential usage, the utterance is probably in 'elaborated' code. Declarative statements and associated questions are the core of the 'elaborated' code. Such forms are also exploited in the 'restricted' code, but in this case the apparent and manifest purpose of the utterance will not be its true function. The 'restricted' code is concerned with control rather than information, prescription rather than description, commands and exclamations rather than statements and will contain questions which test affect and authority rather than fact. The emphasis is upon social identity and roles. The confusion between the two arises partly because utterances may serve both functions simultaneously, and partly because the 'restricted' code is perversely oblique with its usage of declarative sentences: it says 'Lovely day', it means 'Nice to see a friend', it says 'Have a fag', it means 'I'm willing to be friendly'.

Bernstein's is an imaginative and ingenious interpretation, but its plausibility has to pass into the empirical channel of the scientific process before the seal of 'not disproven' may be attached. Initial investigations by Bernstein, Lawton, and Robinson were directed to the question of the existence and nature of social class differences in verbal behaviour (see Robinson and Rackstraw, 1967 for a bibliography), and these gave general support to the requirements of Bernstein's theory for the adolescents studied. Small speech corpuses and small numbers of subjects probably attenuated the stability and generality of the differences found, but certain generalizations seem warranted:

(i) Working-class subjects use fewer complex clauses and verbal groups than their middle-class peers.

(ii) They use a narrower range of items in each of the four lexical form classes: nouns, adjectives, verbs, and adverbs, and their usage is more predictable.

(iii) They use more socio-centric sequences like 'you know!' and 'isn't it?', exemplifying a social bias in their verbal behaviour.

(iv) They show fewer grammatical changes when required to switch from descriptive and narrative speech to explanations, which is consistent with the idea that they may be confined to a single code.

These results obtained with both speech and writing across a variety of contexts with both boys and girls. In America, further and comparable results have been obtained with racial as well as social-class contrasts. Apart from the study of socio-centric sequences, it can be seen that the interest was in grammatical and lexical differences rather than the differential functions of language.

Subsequently, because there are important educational and social issues involved, research work has concentrated on schoolchildren, and much of it has been focused on to the behaviour of pre-school children and their families. The general intention has been to diagnose features preventing smooth integration into mainstream education and to use head-start or continuing special programmes to offset such disabilities (Corbin and Crosby, 1966; Deutsch, 1967; Gray and Klaus, 1965; Hess and Shipman, 1965).

Bernstein's Sociological Research Unit at the Institute of Education, London, has similar objectives. Among the research goals are a comprehensive linguistic description of social class and other differences in the speech of five-year-old Infant-school children, an examination of the relationships between language and school performance, and investigations of the social psychological antecedents of each, both at school and at home. At home the structure and content of the communication network of the family is a major area to be explored, but there is a further intention to link patterns of interaction back to the attitudes of parents. It should also be possible to give a sociological description and explanation for the differential location of these attitudes. Within the schools the relevance of teachers' attitudes and behaviour to the children's performance is under scrutiny, and a special 'Use of Language' programme has been introduced into some schools.

Some of these lines have been investigated further than others, but rather than provide a general tour of the results, I should prefer to use certain of them to trace the routes of inquiry followed, and point out possible ways of shortening the journey to make it less bumpy for others, bearing in mind Hymes' proposal.

The main sample of children's speech was collected from structured, but informal and friendly, interactions between a female research worker and the child. During this interview the child performed six tasks designed to sample a variety of contexts which we may label as aided and imaginative narration, picture description and interpretation, rule specification, explanation and conversation. (An exhaustive taxonomy of verbal activities at this degree of abstraction would be of great use.) This speech was tape-recorded, transcribed, and after a further fourteen hours linguists' sweat, was transformed into a sequence of symbols, based upon an extended version of Halliday's Scale and Category Grammar (Turner and Mohan, 1970). The main effort was centred upon the specification of social-class differences in grammar at or below the rank of sentence. Lexical counts were a second priority.

Accordingly, social-class contrasts were run on over 350 such grammatical items—and virtually no significant differences were obtained. It is true that many items had such a low incidence of occurrence that there was little variance to be accounted for. However, this is not the whole story, and for a brief moment we wondered whether social-class differences might not have appeared by this age. Two counter-arguments could be advanced: either that the particular grammatical analysis used was inadequate to reveal differences or that the research emphasis was unsound in some way. There is weight to both these arguments.

Hawkins' (1969) study of pronominal usage led him to label pronouns 'exophoric' when these units had no unambiguous reference objects backwards (anaphoric) or forwards (kataphoric), and he found that middle-class children used fewer 'exophoric' pronouns than their working-class peers. Neither grammatical criteria of location in structure nor frequency counts would show up such a distinction. A similar result obtained in Rackstraw and Robinson's (1967) analysis of children's explanations of how to play 'Hide and Seek', in which the working class were less adept at keeping their references to the separate roles linguistically distinct. This lack of sequential organization is one characteristic of the 'restricted' code mentioned earlier by Bernstein (1961), but to detect these important grammatical differences it was necessary to pitch the analysis at a supra-sentential level.

A weakness of the approach lay in the summation of scores across contexts. Further analyses conducted for single tasks yielded grammatical differences (Hawkins, op. cit.; Hakkulinen *et al.*, (in prep.); Rackstraw and Robinson, op. cit.), while Henderson (1970) has shown that the proportions of lexical form-classes used change from task to task, but more so for middle than working-class subjects, thereby demonstrating a connection between grammatical variation and the demands of the task, as well as suggesting that more 'registers' may be available to the middle class. These results enable us to make some statements about socially based differences in speech within limited contexts, but any attempted summation across contexts can obscure true variation. Each contrast sample needs to be made within a 'register', which must be so if the concept has any validity. It would be rash to infer that there are no universal generalizations to be made about social-class differences in the grammatical structure of the speech of five-year-olds, but it may be methodologically wiser to accumulate the differences within contexts and to see what higher-order generalizations can be made about these. It is certainly possible that such general statements will not be about the incidence of grammatical structures below the rank of sentence (and I suspect that an analysis which had counted transformations would have been no more successful). The Hawkin's and Rackstraw and Robinson's studies indicate that sequential organization, especially supra-sentential hierarchical structure, may be relevant, but what may be more important is the matching of form and content to the communicative requirements of the task in hand.

Lexical variation proved less difficult to account for. Type-token counts across four major lexical form classes for two of the six tasks (structured narrative and picture description and interpretation) were subjected to analyses of variance with independent variables of social class, sex, verbal-intelligence test scores, and an index of mother–child interaction. Within the parameters of the variables used, social class emerged as the major source of explained variance for types of nouns, adjectives, and verbs (Henderson, 1970). All was not quite so simple, and the complication can be used to show the dangers of summing scores across persons. Intelligence test scores, the index of mother–child interaction (Communication Index), and sex were each sources of variances in their own right, but there were significant interactions, for example, between verbal-intelligence test scores and social class for the incidence of noun token and types, while the nouns and adjectives types of boys were grossly depressed relative to girls in the high verbal-intelligence working-class group. Some relationships appeared to be curvilinear rather than monotonic. Finally, relationships among the dependent variables may differ across subgroups of subjects. The most extreme example so far is not with lexis but with intelligence, where an improved Control and Communication index correlates positively with the child's intelligence test scores in the working class, but negatively in the middle class.

Taken together, the grammatical and lexical analyses can be used as support for an argument that data collection and processing had best begin with homogeneous samples of persons operating in a situation requiring a single register. Although the data we have gives a comprehensive taxonomy of neither, they do illustrate the validity of Hymes' comments across a small range of person and context variables and show that analyses which are too crude or make false over-generalizations about the homogeneity of samples can obscure differences.

Whether language is viewed as the most appropriate or even a relevant medium of communication for given problems is taken up in our consideration of mother–child interaction, but in leading into this one further piece of evidence for the relevance of semantic criteria can be cited.

To describe and classify children's answers to 'wh' questions a taxonomic system was created which distinguished between the grammatical, lexical, and contextual aspects of answers in terms of appropriateness, completeness, and the amount of presupposition. It was also necessary to provide an initial categorization of 'mode' to allow for the permissible alternatives an answerer has, when he is posed certain 'wh' questions. For example, we distinguished nine modes for 'why' questions: denial of oddity, repetition of question as a statement, appeal to essence; direct appeals to emotion, appeals to authority, appeals to regularity, categorization, causal and consequence answers.

For all 'wh' questions we find differences between the social-class groups at age seven. There are grammatical and lexical differences in appropriateness and completeness, but some of the most pronounced are in mode and context, viz. the type and amount of information given. For 'when' and 'where' the middle class are more likely than the working class to use an objective temporal or spatial framework than a self-centred one. For 'why' answers the middle class use fewer simple appeals to regularity and more to categorization, cause, and consequence. When making appeals to authority, middle-class children are more likely to specify the authority for the judgement. In this study the significant sources of variation appear to be in the orientation of the children to 'wh' questions, and this is expressed more obviously in the content than the form of the answers.

When children's answers to 'why' questions are compared with the answers that mothers report they would give to them, there is considerable similarity in the use of modes and the amount of information offered. (We did not perform grammatical or lexical analyses for the answers to 'why' questions.) It does not do great injustice to the data to assert that the children's answers reflect their mothers' in these respects, and that in addition, the maternal answers imply a social difference in the use of language. Working-class mothers not only made more appeals to regularity and gave more repetitions of the question as statement, they were also less likely to answer the question at all, gave less information if they did, and expressed this in more 'noisy' speech. By their answers to 'why' questions they asserted their authority, whereas the middle class gave information.

These results go further than those indicating the dangers of faulty summation across independent and dependent variables by pointing to the value of a system of analysis based in the first instance on the semantic criteria of mode of answer.

The final lesson we might draw concerns the functions of verbal acts. The data provided by the mothers reveal contrasts both in how they report they behave and what beliefs and attitudes they have about the power or usefulness of verbal communication.

We have seen already that in the information-seeking situation, middle-class mothers respond to children's questions with information in acceptable modes, whereas the working class tend to assert their authority. This situation can be compared with a set of 'control' situations in which mothers answered how they would deal with certain discipline problems, e.g. the child's refusal to go to school. Both working- and middle-class mothers place most emphasis on verbal positional appeals to general status categories such as age or sex, e.g. 'Little boys go to school without a fuss.' However, given this degree of similarity, the working class show a greater preference for non-verbal control strategies and abrupt commands than the middle class, while the reverse is true for personal appeals based upon the behavioural and affective consequences of the misdemeanour for the child.

Although the information-seeking and control situations are encouraging the mothers to adopt contrasting tactics, mothers of each social-class group treat the situations as similar; the working-class mothers treat both as control problems, whereas the middle class use both as opportunities to teach the child. The working-class mothers use language to exert control, and it is but one means of achieving this, while the middle-class mothers use it as a medium of instruction. What is taught is also different. The working-class child has to work out what the rules of the socialization game are from successive non-verbal reinforcements or is told what behaviour is appropriate to certain simplified roles. The norms of these roles are given as universal generalizations, discreet and at the same level of abstraction—a set of rules of thumb, with little attempt at organization in terms of similarities and differences and no super-ordinate or sub-ordinate categories. The child must learn to ask which rule applies to particular situations. For the middle-class child what is taught has a different character. He is offered higher-order principles and an appreciation of similarities and differences. He has the chance of learning an internally consistent hypothetico-deductive system which can be generalized to new circumstances. He is directed towards controlled autonomy and is acquiring the requisite hierarchically organized and interconnected knowledge, beliefs, and skills to enable him to become an emancipated self-organizing system.

These ideas have been taken up through the questionnaires given to mothers at a second interview in which they were asked directly about the role speech played in her interactions with other people in general and her children in particular.

A series of twelve situations, such as 'finding out more about people', 'getting self across to others', 'comforting others in distress', and 'to increase the number of people I know', were classified into cognitive (epistemic), affective, and social categories. While there were no social-class differentials in the reported usefulness of language for the social category, working-class mothers stressed its significance in the affective area, whereas middle-class mothers emphasized its importance for epistemic problems. A second questionnaire asked about the difficulties a 'dumb' mother would encounter in child rearing. Again a differential obtained, with the working-class mothers feeling this would be more of a handicap in the teaching of non-verbal skills, but the middle class exhibited a relatively greater concern in interpersonal problems (Bernstein and Henderson, 1969). These results imply the priority of a functional analysis of language. What will different people see language as useful for? This question has precedence over problems of the quality of verbal activity. The data give added support to Bernstein's original contention that in the lower working class, language has primarily a social function. In retrospect I think we might have found the research problem easier if we had started the inquiries at this point of functions of language rather than with the grammatical analyses. This is not to deny the importance of grammatical or lexical studies, but to suggest a more profitable sequence of inquiry.

'RESTRICTED' CODES AND THE SOCIOLOGY OF EDUCATION

The methodological points have been mentioned both to illustrate the usefulness of a functional perspective in socio-linguistic studies and to stress the importance of conducting such investigations at an appropriate level of linguistic analysis within limited contexts for homogeneous groups of persons. Surveys of language use are not only concerned with such theoretical issues, however. They are often conceived with an intention to initiate social changes, probably to be mediated through the educational system. In so far as Bernstein's ideas correspond to the real social situation in Britain, the covert moral imperative has been to set up ways of achieving a switch from 'restricted' to 'elaborated' codes of language use, in order to give greater credibility to the principle of equal educational opportunity for all. Once in this realm of values, however, we have also to consider the consequences of a successful attainment of the delimited goals, in our case a switch to 'elaborated' code usage for individuals whose sociological expectation was a 'restricted' code. What losses can be foreseen, and how can these be minimized?

GENERALITY OF 'RESTRICTED' CODES

Before we try to do this we need to see whether Bernstein's linkage of social class and code is peculiar to mid-twentieth-century Britain or whether it might have more general application. It would seem plausible to argue by analogy that any society with similar or more extreme forms of social stratification will tend to generate 'restricted' codes in its low-status groups, and that any educational system controlled by the high-status groups will be designed to preserve the *status quo*. We have seen how the working class answers to 'why' questions and their disciplinary control strategies reduce the probability of a critical questioning of the established order and even encourage its preservation, and we have seen how the language barrier between working-class pupil and middle-class teacher can act as the basis for an early assignment to the lower streams of education and eventual recruitment to working-class adult roles.

As well as an argument based upon similarity across societies, we can also raise the theoretical level of analysis to 'open' and 'closed' role systems (Bernstein, 1968). In closed systems the roles prescribed are simplified and stereotyped with little personal discretion for variation in role perception or performance. Such systems will be associated with 'restricted' codes, whose structural, lexical, and semantic constraints will preclude possible re-organization of role components and the creation of new roles. High-status persons will also act within closed-code systems in certain limited contexts, but the critical question is whether the persons have only closed-role systems—and such is the alleged condition of the lower working class. In the same paper Bernstein also offers a list of conditions conducive to the development of closed role systems and 'restricted' codes.

If a social group, by virtue of its class relation, that is, as a result of its common occupational function and social status, has developed strong communal bonds; if the work relations of this group offer little variety; little exercise in decision-making; if assertion, if it is to be successful must be a collective rather than an individual act; if the work task requires physical manipulation and control rather than symbolic organization and control, if the diminished authority of the man at work is transformed into an authority of power at home; if the home is over-crowded and limits the variety of situations it can offer; if the children socialize each other in an environment offering little intellectual stimulation; if all these attributes are found in one setting, then it is plausible to assume that such a social setting will generate a particular form of communication . . . [viz. a restricted code] . . . "which will shape the intellectual, social and affective orientation of the children. . . ."

These determinants may not be an exhaustive list, and Bernstein does not go on to specify the precise character of the links between them and the 'restricted' code (viz. necessary or sufficient condition, reversible or irreversible, probabilistic or deterministic, sequential or co-extensive, additive, interactional, or multiplicative), but this reanalysis in role theoretic terms should provide readily operationalized and universal contrasts between open and closed systems, both within and across societies.

If these generalizations are valid Bernstein's theory escapes any charge of English parochialism, and should apply to societies regardless of the diversity of language obtaining, although in multilingual societies the additional contingency arises that a whole language may function as a restricted code. If this occurs that language may well lack the structural, lexical, or semantic features necessary for its utilization as a medium of instruction or as the language of textbooks.

Behavioural Consequences of Confinement to a 'Restricted' Code

To adopt such a view is to suggest that the immediate potential of a language as a medium of inter- and intra-personal communication and instruction will be in practice contingent upon the purposes for which that language is normally used. For example, I would hazard a guess that the competence models of language based upon transformational analyses of 'elaborated' code users are not valid predictors of the behavioural capacity of 'restricted' code users. We have little evidence as yet, but it would seem that the theoretical potential of the 'restricted' code which would be implied by a systematic linguistic analysis does not correspond to the person's behavioural capacity for generating a variety of utterances. This is a Whorfian view, and our studies must be distinguished from some aspects of those of Labov (1966) or Lambert (1967). Their work shows how a use of a particular phonology or language has social psychological functions: it gives an identity to the individual and serves for others to make inferences about the speaker. Non-linguistic markers could and do have comparable significance. There is no implication of more than a correlational link with psychological or sociological consequences. The Bernstein position adopts a stronger stance. Not only will the 'restricted' code have social psychological functions, it will also be psychologically relevant, constraining the processes and content of perception, thinking, remembering and learning. It will have the sociological function of maintaining a stable and passive sub-culture within a society. The 'restricted' code is an integral feature of feudalism, operating at the three levels of psychology, social psychology, and sociology.

Sociological and Psychological Significance of 'Restricted' Codes

To an extent this situation still obtains in Britain, and we can use role-theory language to provide a quick caricature. Adult society may be construed as a complex set of different roles into which young members are to be socialized. The society has means of differential recruitment to its adult role structure, and the educational system is one such process. Hence the educational order will select and channel individuals, directing and socializing them towards different roles. The system will be an approximate expression and means of realizing the values of the power structure of that society. Our present society has for many years used a high proportion of unskilled and semi-skilled labour, and the educational system acts selectively to recruit persons for such roles. That these people are confined to a 'restricted' code has a dual significance.

Firstly, from the point of view of society, especially its ruling groups, such people are both a quiescent source of unskilled and semi-skilled labour and also a reservoir of talent that can be tapped as changes occur in the qualifications and skills necessary for adequate occupational role performance. For example, an increasing demand for technologists can be met from this reservoir by a selective teaching of the relevant subject matter of the applied sciences. If Bernstein's (1970) separation of elaborated and restricted codes into two main categories (those concerned with 'object' relations in the material world and those concerned with 'person' relations in the social world) is valid only the former have to be learned for new occupational role performance, e.g. the codes of chemistry, electronics, or engineering. The social structure can remain intact if there is no positive transfer or leakage between object and person-centred codes. You will not provoke a revolution by carrying banners inscribed with chemical formulae, and you do not usually seek to alter the nature of your marital relationship with the language of calculus.

But from the point of view of the people confined to a 'restricted' code person relations, the code is functional rather than dysfunctional. The occupations pursued by the lower working class involve work which requires repetitive labour with induction into the roles probably based on modelling when any training is required. Language is unimportant for learning or performance. For those unskilled or semi-skilled jobs of a service nature (bus conductors, porters, etc.) only a minimal verbal repertoire is necessary. Such jobs are of only low prestige in a status-conscious society and offer little opportunity for intrinsic satisfaction. But confined to a 'restricted' code, such observations may not be made by the occupants of the roles, especially since they are supported by conservative social values transmitted through the appeals to regularity and tradition already cited. In these and other roles the 'restricted' code acts as a protection. Possibilities which could become aspirations unsupported by the means to achieve them are not conceived. Anomie is precluded. Children are not encouraged to ask a variety of questions quite outside the parents' competence to answer. Child rearing is simplified. The marital relationship is confined to a simplicity that the partners are able to enact. Sources of satisfaction are mainly in non-verbal activities. The price of this security is a lack of access to the accumulated experience of mankind, the functional gain an unawareness of what one is missing.

It is worth remembering these sources of satisfaction before we rush in with plans to equip persons with 'elaborated' codes. (Such plans will be caught up in the inertia of the educational system. To hope that the system could quickly be restructured to abolish the differential allocation of resources—and the consequential differential recruitment—or that teachers might all see the significance of an 'elaborated' code for enabling people to become self-organizing systems, is like believing that wars would cease if all the soldiers went home. Fortunately or unfortunately sociology exists!) This is not to say that such changes ought not to be made, but that the whole problem rather than part of it should be embraced, and these sources of satisfaction are part of what may be lost if the educational system succeeds in endeavours to equip persons with 'elaborated' codes. Those who acquire an object-centred elaborated code will have skills of considerable worth in industrializing and industrialized societies, and provided that job opportunities are available, the exercise of these skills and their other consequences may serve as sources of satisfaction. The extreme awkward case is probably that of the first-generation person-centred elaborated code user in an industrializing society. Jobs requiring such competence will not be common, and he will have forfeited the social satisfactions to be found in his original restricted code culture. Unfortunately it is also cheaper to educate people into this form of 'elaborated' code than into the object-centred one—a temptation to be resisted.

The conclusion seems to be that where there is a wish to industrialize quickly but with a minimum of social disruption, the main educational efforts need to be directed into science and technology rather than arts. This is a narrow view of 'education', but societies have only limited resources to deploy, and such decisions have to be based on politico-economic considerations as well as utopian hopes. A multilingual society may be at an advantage in such an endeavour, because it is possible to use the national or a metropolitan language for induction into the 'elaborated' codes of object-centred disciplines. This language can be clearly oriented to referential usage, while the vernacular can remain the medium of communication within the family. Such a division might minimize intergenerational separation and conflict, interpersonal and social confusion, but maximize industrial development. That there will be 'leakage' across codes and some positive transfer from object to person relations is probable, and this should facilitate the gradual re-organization of the social structure with the creation of a better quality of life for the members of that society. That this argument is naïve in its simplicity is obvious: it ignores the status differentials associated with the competence to use particular languages, and it ignores peer-group communication problems, as well as much else.

Its endorsement could enable an avoidance of the misunderstandings produced in a monolingual society where working-class children and adults may fail to see the possible relevance of language to education and of education to living, and where teachers may make inferences about brightness and aptitude on the basis of speech characteristics which they misjudge. Where different languages serve different functions the necessary perceptual discriminations may be easier to make. In monolingual England the educational experts are hardly aware of the nature of the problem of 'restricted' and 'elaborated' codes of language usage, and certainly this type of problem is not generally appreciated by teachers. In a multilingual community these differential functions may be easier to locate and make explicit.

REFERENCES

Bernstein, B. B.
(1961) 'Social Class and Linguistic Development: a Theory of Social Learning', in R. H. Halsey, J. Floud and C. A. Anderson (eds.), *Education, Economy and Society*. New York: Macmillan.

Bernstein, B. B.
(1970) 'A Socio-linguistic Approach to Socialization', in J. Gumperz and D. Hymes (eds.), *Direction in Socio-linguistics*. New York: Holt, Rinehart & Winston.

Bernstein, B. B. and Henderson, D.
(1969) 'Social Class Differences in the Relevance of Language to Socialization', *Sociology*, III, 1–20.

Corbin, R. and Crosby, M. (eds.)
(1966) *Language Programs for the Disadvantaged*. Champaign, Ill. National Council of Teachers of English.

Deutsch, M.
(1967) *The Disadvantaged Child*. New York: Basic Books.

Gray, S. W., and Klaus, R. A.
(1966) 'Deprivation, Development and Diffusion'. Peabody College, Nashville; Darcee Paper (1).

Hakkulinen, A., Lewis, B., and Taylor, S.
(In preparation) *Seven Year Old Children and the Contextual Use of Language*. London: Routledge.

Hawkins, P.
(1969) 'Social Class, the Nominal Group and Reference', *Language and Speech*, XII, 125–35.

Henderson, D.
(1970) 'Social Class Differences in Form-class Usage', in W. Brandis and D. Henderson, *Social Class, Language and Communication*. London: Routledge.

Hess, R. D., and Shipman, V.
(1965) 'Early Experience and the Socialization of Cognitive Modes in Children', *Child Development*, XXXVI, 860–86.

Hymes, D.
(1967) 'Models of the Interaction of Language and Social Setting', *J. Soc. Iss.*, 1967, *23*, 8–28.

Labov, W.
(1964) 'Phonological Correlates of Social Stratification', *American Anthropologist* (Special Publication), LXVI, 164–76.

Lambert, W. E.
(1967) 'A Social Psychology of Bilingualism', *J. Soc. Iss.*, II, 91–109.

Rackstraw, S. J., and Robinson, W. P.
(1967) 'Social and Psychological Factors Related to Variability of Answering Behaviour in Five Year Old Children', *Language and Speech*, X, 88–106.

Robinson, W. P., and Rackstraw, S. J.
(1967) 'Variations in Mothers' Answers to Children's Questions, as a Function of Social Class, Intelligence Test Scores and Sex', *Sociology*, I, 259–79.

Turner, G. J., and Mohan, B. A.
(1970, in press) *Linguistic Description and a Computer Program for Children's Speech*. London: Routledge.

IV. A Social Psychology of Bilingualism[1]

WALLACE E. LAMBERT

This paper examines bilingualism from a social–psychological perspective, one characterized not only by its interest in the reactions of the bilingual as an individual but also by the attention given to the social influences that affect the bilingual's behaviour and to the social repercussions that follow from his behaviour. From this perspective, a process such as language switching takes on a broader significance when its likely social and psychological consequences are contemplated, as, for example, when a language switch brings into play contrasting sets of stereotyped images of people who habitually use each of the languages involved in the switch. Similarly, the development of bilingual skill very likely involves something more than a special set of aptitudes because one would expect that various social attitudes and motives are intimately involved in learning a foreign language. Furthermore, the whole process of becoming bilingual can be expected to involve major conflicts of values and allegiances, and bilinguals could make various types of adjustments to the bicultural demands made on them. It is to these matters that I would like to direct attention. Although the research illustrations are drawn mainly from Canadian and American settings, the underlying processes, however, are likely to be universal ones.

What are some of the social psychological consequences of language switching? Certain bilinguals have an amazing capacity to pass smoothly and automatically from one linguistic community to another as they change languages of discourse or as they turn from one conversational group to another at multilingual gatherings.

[1] This paper is a revised and shortened version of an earlier paper with the same title (Lambert, 1967).

The social psychologist wants to know how this degree of bilingual skill is developed, what reactions the bilingual has as he switches languages, and what social effects the switching initiates, not only the suspicion or respect generated in listeners by an unexpected switch but also the intricate role adjustments that usually accompany such changes.

I will draw mainly on work conducted by a small group of us at McGill University in Montreal, a city where two major ethnic–linguistic groups are constantly struggling to maintain their separate identities and where skilled bilinguals are very common.

Over the past eight years we have developed a research technique that makes use of language and dialect variations to elicit the stereotyped impressions or biased views which members of one social group hold of representative members of a contrasting group. Briefly, the procedure involves the reactions of listeners (referred to as judges) to the taped recordings of a number of *perfectly bilingual* speakers reading a two-minute passage at one time in one of their languages (e.g. French) and, later, a translation equivalent of the same passage in their second language (e.g. English). Groups of judges are asked to listen to this series of recordings and evaluate the personality characteristics of each speaker as well as possible, using voice cues only. They are reminded of the common tendency to attempt to gauge the personalities of unfamiliar speakers heard over the phone or radio. Thus they are kept unaware that they will actually hear two readings by each of several bilinguals. In our experience no subjects have become aware of this fact. The judges are given practice trials, making them well acquainted with both versions of the message, copies of which are supplied in advance.

This procedure, referred to as the matched-guise technique, appears to reveal judges' more private reactions to the contrasting group than direct attitude questionnaires do (see Lambert, Anisfeld, and Yeni-Komshian, 1965), but much more research is needed to adequately assess its power in this regard.

Several of our studies have been conducted since 1958 in greater Montreal, where the conflict between English- and French-speaking Canadians is currently so sharp that some French Canadian (FC) political leaders in the Province of

Quebec talk seriously about separating the Province from the rest of Canada, comprising a majority of English Canadians (ECs). In 1958–9, we (Lambert, Hodgson, Gardner, and Fillenbaum, 1960) asked a sizeable group of EC university students to evaluate the personalities of a series of speakers, actually the matched guises of male bilinguals speaking in Canadian-style French and English. When their judgements were analysed it was found that their evaluations were strongly biased against the FC and in favour of the matched EC guises. They rated the speakers in their EC guises as being better looking, taller, more intelligent, more dependable, kinder, more ambitious, and as having more character. This evaluational bias was just as apparent among judges who were bilingual as among mono-linguals.

We presented the same set of taped voices to a group of FC students of equivalent age, social class, and educational level. Here we were in for a surprise, for they showed the same bias, evaluating the EC guises significantly more favourably than the FC guises of a whole series of traits, indicating, for example, that they viewed the EC guises as being more intelligent, dependable, likeable, and as having more character. Only on two traits did they rate the FC guises more favourably, namely kindness and religiousness, and, considering the whole pattern of ratings, it could be that they interpreted too much religion as a questionable quality. Not only did the FC judges generally downgrade representatives of their own ethnic–linguistic group, they also rated the FC guises much more negatively than the EC judges had. We consider this pattern of results as a reflection of a community-wide stereotype of FCs as being relatively second-rate people, a view apparently fully shared by certain subgroups of FCs. Similar tendencies to downgrade one's own group have been reported in research with minority groups conducted in other parts of North America.

Some of the questions left unanswered in the first study have been examined recently in a follow-up study conducted by Malcolm Preston and myself (Preston, 1963). Using the same basic techniques, the following questions were asked: (*a*) Will female and male judges react similarly to language and accent variations of speakers? (*b*) Will judges react similarly to male and female speakers who change their pronunciation style or the language they speak? Will there be systematic differences in reactions to FC and Continental French (CF) speakers?

EVALUATIVE REACTIONS OF ENGLISH CANADIAN LISTENERS

In this study it was found that the EC listeners viewed the female speakers more favourably in their French guises, while they viewed the male speakers more favourably in their English guises. In particular, the EC men saw the FC lady speakers as more intelligent, ambitious, self-confident, dependable, courageous, and sincere than their English counterparts. The EC ladies were not quite so gracious in their ratings, although they, too, rated the FC ladies as more intelligent, ambitious, self-confident (but shorter) than the EC women guises. Thus, ECs generally view FC females as more competent, and the EC men see them as possessing more integrity and competence.

FC men were not as favourably received as the women were by their EC judges; they are viewed as lacking integrity and as being less socially attractive by both EC female and, to a less marked extent, EC male judges. This tendency to downgrade the FC male, already noted in the basic study, may well be the expression of an unfavourable stereotyped and prejudiced attitude towards FCs, but apparently this prejudice is selectively directed towards FC males, possibly because they are better known than females as power figures who control local and regional governments and who thereby can be viewed as sources of threat or frustration (or as the guardians of FC women, keeping them all to themselves).

The reactions to Continental French (CF) speakers are generally more favourable although less marked. The EC judges appear to be less concerned about European French people in general than they are about the local French people; the European French are neither downgraded nor taken as potential social models to any great extent.

EVALUATIVE REACTIONS OF FRENCH CANADIAN LISTENERS

Summarizing briefly, the FC listeners showed more significant guise differences than did their EC counterparts. In general, the FC judges rated European French guises more favourably and Canadian French guises less favourably than they did their matched EC guises. One important exception was the FC women, who viewed FC men as more competent and as more socially attractive than EC men.

The general pattern of evaluations presented by the FC judges, however, indicates that they view their own linguistic cultural group as inferior to both the English Canadian and the European French groups, suggesting that FCs are prone to take either of these other groups as models for changes in their own manners of behaving (including speech) and possibly in basic values. This tendency is more marked among FC men, who definitely preferred male and female representatives of the EC and CF groups to those of their own group. The FC women, in contrast, appear to be guardians of FC culture, at least in the sense that they favoured male representatives of their own cultural group. We presume this reaction reflects something more than a preference for FC marriage partners. FC women may be particularly anxious to preserve FC values and to pass these on in their own families through language, religion, and tradition.

Nevertheless, FC women apparently face a conflict of their own, in that they favour characteristics of both FC and EC women. Thus, the FC female may be safeguarding the FC culture through a preference for FC values seen in FC men, at the same time as she is prone to change her own behaviour and values in the direction of one of two foreign cultural models, those that the men in her group apparently favour. It is of interest that EC women are confronted with a similar conflict, since they appear envious of FC women.

THE DEVELOPMENTAL STUDIES

Recently, we have been looking into the background of the inferiority reaction among FC youngsters, trying to determine at what age it starts and how it develops through the years. The results of a study by Elizabeth Anisfeld and me (1964) make it clear that, unlike college-age judges, FC children at the ten-year age level do not have a negative bias against their own group.

The question then arises as to where the bias starts after

age ten. A recent study (Lambert, Frankel, and Tucker, 1966) was addressed to solving this puzzle. It was found that definite preferences for EC guises appeared at about age twelve and were maintained through the late teen years. There was, however, a marked difference between private- and public-school judges: the upper-middle-class girl judges were especially biased after age twelve, whereas the pattern for the working-class judges was less pronounced and less durable, suggesting that for them the bias is short-lived and fades out by the late teens.

The major implication of these findings is that the tendency for certain subgroups of college-age FCs to downgrade representatives of their own ethnic–linguistic group, noted in our earlier studies, seems to have its origin at about age twelve, but the ultimate fate of this attitude depends to a great extent on social-class background. Those from upper-middle-class FC homes, and especially those who have become bilingual in English, are particularly likely to maintain this view, at least into the young adult years. This study, incidentally, used girl subjects only.

The pattern of results of these developmental studies can also be examined from a more psychodynamic perspective. The results are consistent with the notion that teen-age girls have a closer psychological relation with their fathers than with their mothers in the sense that the girls in the study rated FC female guises markedly less favourably than EC guises, but generally favoured or at least showed much less disfavour for the FC guises of male speakers. Social-class differences and bilingual skill apparently influence the degree of same-sex rejection and cross-sex identification.

Similarly, the reactions to 'same-age' speakers might reflect a tendency to accept or reject one's peer-group or one's self, at least for the monolinguals. The findings suggest that the public-school monolinguals are generally satisfied with their FC image, since they favour the FC guises of the same-age speakers at the sixteen-year level. In contrast, the private-school monolinguals may be expressing a marked rejection of themselves in the sense that they favour the EC guises. The bilinguals, of course, can consider themselves as being potential or actual members of both ethnic–linguistic groups represented by the guises. It is of interest, therefore, to note that both the public, and particularly the private-school bilinguals, apparently favour the EC versions of themselves.

This programme of research, still far from complete, does permit us to make two important generalizations. First, a technique has been developed that rather effectively calls out the stereotyped impressions that members of one ethnic–linguistic group hold of another contrasting group. The type and strength of impression depends on characteristics of the *speakers*—their sex, age, the dialect they use, and, very likely, the social-class background as this is revealed in speech style. The impression also seems to depend on characteristics of the audience of *judges*—their age, sex, socio-economic background, their bilinguality, and their own speech style. The type of reactions and adjustments listeners must make to those who reveal, through their speech style, their likely ethnic group allegiance is suggested by the traits that listeners use to indicate their impressions. Thus, EC male and female college students tend to look down on the FC male speaker, seeing him as less intelligent, less dependable, and less interesting than he would be seen if he had presented himself in an EC guise. Imagine the types of role adjustments that would follow if the same person were first seen in the FC guise and then suddenly switched to a perfect EC guise. Most EC listeners would have to reconsider their original classification of the person and then either view him as becoming too intimate in 'their' language or decide otherwise and be pleasantly amazed that one of their own could manage the other group's language so well. Furthermore, since these comparative impressions are widespread throughout certain strata of each ethnic–linguistic community, they will probably have an enormous impact on young people who are either forced to learn the other group's language or who choose to do so.

The research findings outlined here have a second important message about the reactions of the bilingual who is able to convincingly switch languages or dialects. The bilingual can study the reactions of his audiences as he adopts one guise in certain settings and another in different settings, and receive a good deal of social feedback, permitting him to realize that he can be perceived in quite different ways, depending on how he presents himself. It could well be that his own self-concept takes two distinctive forms in the light of such feedback. He may also observe, with amusement or alarm, the role adjustments that follow when he suddenly switches guises with the same group of interlocutors. However, research is needed to document and examine these likely consequences of language or dialect switching from the perspective of the bilingual making switches.

Although we have concentrated on a Canadian setting in these investigations, there is really nothing special about the Canadian scene with regard to the social effects of language or dialect switching. Equally instructive effects have been noted when the switch involves a change from standard American English to Jewish-accented English (Anisfeld, Bogo, and Lambert, 1962); when the switch involves changing from Hebrew to Arabic, for Israeli and Arab judges, or when the change is from Sephardic to Ashkenazic style Hebrew, for Jewish listeners in Israel (Lambert, Anisfeld, and Yeni-Komshian, 1965). We have adapted the procedure for work with American Negro speakers and listeners (Tucker and Lambert, 1967). The same type of social effects are inherent in this instance, too: Southern Negroes have more favourable impressions of people who use what the linguists call Standard Network Style English than they do of those who speak with their own style, but they are more impressed with their own style than they are with the speech of educated, Southern whites, or of Negroes who become too 'white' in their speech by exaggerating the non-Negro features and over-correcting their verbal output. More recently, Richard Tucker has applied the techniques in the Philippines, and discovered several unanticipated and socially significant reactions to various Philippine languages and speech styles (Tucker, 1969).

SOCIAL–PSYCHOLOGICAL ASPECTS OF SECOND-LANGUAGE LEARNING

How might these intergroup impressions and feelings affect young people living in the Montreal area who are required by educators to learn the other group's language? One would expect that both FC youngsters and their parents would be more willing, for purely social–psychological reasons, to learn

English than ECs to learn French. Although we haven't investigated the French Canadians' attitudes towards the learning of English, still it is very apparent that bilingualism in Canada and in Quebec has long been a one-way affair, with FCs much more likely to learn English than the converse. Typically, this trend to English is explained on economic grounds and on the attraction of the United States, but I would like to suggest another possible reason for equally serious consideration. FCs may be drawn away from Canadian-style French to English, or to bilingualism, or to European-style French, as a psychological reaction to the contrast in stereotyped images which English and French Canadians have of one another. On the other hand, we would expect EC students and their parents in Quebec to be drawn away from French for the same basic reasons. It is, of course, short-sighted to talk about groups in this way, because there are certain to be wide individual differences of reaction, as was the case in the impression studies, and as will be apparent in the research to be discussed, but one fact turned up in an unpublished study we conducted that looks like a group-wide difference. Several samples of Montreal EC, high-school students who had studied French for periods of up to seven years scored no better on standard tests of French achievement than did Connecticut high schoolers who had only two or three years of French training.

When viewed from a social-psychological perspective the process of learning a second language itself also takes on a special significance. From this viewpoint one would expect that if the student is to be successful in his attempts to learn another social group's language he must be both able and willing to adopt various aspects of behaviour, including verbal behaviour, which characterize members of the other linguistic–cultural group. The learner's ethnocentric tendencies and his attitudes towards the other group are believed to determine his success in learning the new language. His motivation to learn is thought to be determined by both his attitudes and by the type of orientation he has towards learning a second language. The orientation is instrumental in form if, for example, the purposes of language study reflect the more utilitarian value of linguistic achievement, such as getting ahead in one's occupation, and is *integrative* if, for example, the student is oriented to learn more about the other cultural community, as if he desired to become a potential member of the other group. It is also argued that some may be anxious to learn another language as a means of being accepted in another cultural group because of dissatisfactions experienced in their own culture, while other individuals may be as much interested in another culture as they are in their own. In either case the more proficient one becomes in a second language, the more he may find that his place in his original membership group is modified at the same time as the other linguistic–cultural group becomes something more than a reference group for him. It may, in fact, become a second membership group for him. Depending upon the compatibility of the two cultures, he may experience feelings of regret as he loses ties in one group, mixed with the fearful anticipation of entering a relatively new group. The concept of anomie, first proposed by Durkheim (1897) and more recently extended by Srole (1951) and Williams (1952), refers to such feelings of social uncertainty or dissatisfaction.

Robert Gardner and I (1959) worked with English-speaking Montreal high-school students studying French who were evaluated for their language-learning aptitude and verbal intelligence, as well as their attitudes and stereotypes towards members of the French community, and the intensity of their motivation to learn French. A factor analysis of scores on these various measures indicated that aptitude and intelligence formed a common factor which was independent of a second one comprising indices of motivation, type of orientation towards language and social attitudes towards FCs. Furthermore, a measure of achievement in French taken at the end of a year's study was reflected equally prominently in both factors. This statistical pattern meant that French achievement was dependent upon both aptitude and verbal intelligence as well as sympathetic orientation towards the other group. This orientation was much less common among these students than was the instrumental one, as would be expected from the results of the matched-guise experiments. However, when sympathetic orientation was present it apparently sustained a strong motivation to learn the other group's language, since students with an integrative orientation were more successful in learning French than were those with instrumental orientations.

A follow-up study (Gardner, 1960) confirmed and extended these findings. Using a larger sample of EC students and incorporating various measures of French achievement, the same two independent factors were revealed, and again both were related to French achievement. But whereas aptitude and achievement were especially important for those French skills stressed in school training, such as grammar, the development of skills that call for the active use of the language in communicational settings, such as pronunciation accuracy and auditory comprehension, was determined primarily by measures of an integrative motivation to learn French. The aptitude variables were insignificant in this case. Further evidence from the intercorrelations indicated that this integrative motive was the converse of an authoritarian ideological syndrome, opening the possibility that basic personality dispositions may be involved in language learning efficiency.

In this same study information had been gathered from the parents of the students about their own orientations towards the French community. These data suggested that integrative or instrumental orientations towards the other group are developed within the family, i.e. the minority of students with an integrative disposition to learn French had parents who also were integrative and sympathetic to the French community. However, students' orientations were not related to parents' skill in French nor to the number of French acquaintances the parents had, indicating that the integrative motive is not due to having more experience with French at home. Instead the integrative outlook appears to stem from a family-wide attitudinal disposition.

These findings are consistent and reliable enough to be of general interest. For example, methods of language training could be modified and strengthened by giving consideration to the social–psychological implications of language learning. Because of the possible practical as well as theoretical significance of this approach, it seemed appropriate to test its applicability in a cultural setting other than the bicultural Quebec scene. With measures of attitude and motivation modified for American students learning French, a large-scale study, very similar in nature to those conducted in Montreal, was carried out in various settings in the United States with very similar general outcomes (Lambert & Gardner, 1962).

One further investigation indicated that these suggested social–psychological principles are not restricted to English and French speakers in Canada. Moshe Anisfeld and I (1961) extended the same experimental procedure to samples of Jewish high-school students studying Hebrew at various parochial schools in different sectors of Montreal. They were questioned about their orientations towards learning Hebrew and their attitudes towards the Jewish culture and community, and tested for their verbal intelligence, language aptitude, and achievement in the Hebrew language at the end of the school year. The results support the generalization that both intellectual capacity and attitudinal orientation affect success in learning Hebrew.

BILINGUAL ADJUSTMENTS TO CONFLICTING DEMANDS

The final issue I want to discuss concerns the socio-cultural tugs and pulls that the bilingual or potential bilingual encounters and how he adjusts to these often conflicting demands made on him. We have seen how particular social atmospheres can affect the bilingual. For example, the French–English bilingual in the Montreal setting may be pulled towards greater use of English, and yet be urged by certain others in the FC community not to move too far in that direction, just as ECs may be discouraged from moving towards the French community. In a similar fashion, dialects would be expected to change because of the social consequences they engender, so that Jewish-accented speech should drop away, especially with those of the younger generation in American settings, as should Sephardic forms of Hebrew in Israel or certain forms of Negro speech in America. In other words, the bilingual encounters social pressure of various sorts: he can enjoy the fun of linguistic spying, but must pay the price of suspicion from those who don't want him to enter too intimately into their cultural domains and from others who don't want him to leave his 'own' domain. He also comes to realize that most people are suspicious of a person who is in any sense two-faced. If he is progressing towards bilingualism he encounters similar pressures that may affect his self-concept, his sense of belonging, and his relations to two cultural–linguistic groups, the one he is slowly leaving and the one he is entering. The conflict exists because so many of us think in terms of in-groups and out-groups, or of the need of showing an allegiance to one group or another, so that terms such as own language, other's language, leaving and entering one cultural group for another seem to be appropriate, even natural, descriptive choices.

Although this type of thought may characterize most people in our world, it is none the less a subtle form of group cleavage and ethnocentrism, and in time it may be challenged by bilinguals, who, I feel, are in an excellent position to develop a totally new outlook on the social world. My argument is that bilinguals, especially those with bicultural experiences, enjoy certain fundamental advantages[1] which, if capitalized on, can easily offset the annoying social tugs and pulls they are normally prone to. In a recent international study of the development of stereotyped thinking in children (Lambert and Klineberg, 1967), we found that rigid and stereotyped thinking about in-groups and out-groups, or about own groups in contrast to foreigners, starts during the pre-school period when children are trying to form a conception of themselves and their place in the world. Of relevance here is the notion that the child brought up bilingually and biculturally will be less likely to have good versus bad contrasts impressed on him when he starts wondering about himself, his own group, and others. Instead he will probably be taught something more truthful, although more complex: that differences among national or cultural groups of peoples are actually not clear-cut and that basic similarities among people are more fundamental than differences. The bilingual child, in other words, may well start life with the enormous advantage of having a more open, receptive mind about himself and other people, and he is likely to become especially sensitive to and wary of ethnocentricism. A current

[1] For present purposes discussion is limited to a more social advantage associated with bilingualism. In other writings there has been a stress on potential intellectual and cognitive advantages, see Peal and Lambert (1962) and Anisfeld (1964); see also Macnamara (1964) as well as Lambert and Anisfeld (1968). The bilingual's potential utility has also been discussed as a linguistic mediator between monolingual groups because of his comprehension of the subtle meaning differences characterizing each of the languages involved, see Lambert and Moore (1966).

study by Carol Aellen and myself (1968) examines this whole question in some detail.

This is not to say that bilinguals have an easy time of it. In fact, the final investigation I want to present demonstrates the social conflicts bilinguals typically face, but, and this is the major point, it also demonstrates one particular type of adjustment that is particularly encouraging.

In 1943 Irving Child (1943) investigated a matter that disturbed many second-generation Italians living in New England: what were they, Italian or American? Child uncovered three contrasting modes of adjusting to these pressures: some tried to belong to one of the two ethnic groups or the other, and some, because of strong pulls from both sides, were unable to belong to either.

Child's study illustrates nicely the difficulties faced by people with dual allegiances, but there is no evidence presented of second-generation Italians who actually feel themselves as belonging to both groups. When in 1962 Robert Gardner and I (1962) studied another ethnic minority group in New England, the French Americans, we observed the same types of reactions as Child had noted among Italian Americans, but in our study there was one subgroup of special interest. French American youngsters who have an open-minded, non-ethnocentric view of people in general, coupled with a strong aptitude for language learning, are the ones who profited fully from their language-learning opportunities and became skilled in both languages. These young people had apparently circumvented the conflicts and developed means of becoming members of both cultural groups. They had, in other terms, achieved a comfortable bicultural identity.

It is not clear why this type of adjustment did not appear in Child's study. There could, for example, be important differences in the social pressures encountered by second-generation Italians and French in New England. My guess, however, is that the difference in findings reflects a new social movement that has started in America in the interval between 1943 and 1962, a movement which the American linguist Charles Hockett humorously refers to as a 'reduction of the heat under the American melting pot'. I believe that bicultural bilinguals will be particularly helpful in perpetuating this movement. They and their children are also the ones most likely to work out a new, non-ethnocentric mode of social intercourse which could be of universal significance.

REFERENCES

Aellen, Carol, and Lambert, W. E.
(1968) 'Ethnic Identification and Personality Adjustments of Canadian Adolescents of Mixed English–French Parentage', *Canadian Journal of Behavioral Science.*

Anisfeld, Elizabeth
(1964) 'A Comparison of the Cognitive Functioning of Monolinguals and Bilinguals'. Unpublished Ph.D. thesis, Redpath Library, McGill University.

Anisfeld, Elizabeth, and Lambert, W. E.
(1964) 'Evaluational Reactions of Bilingual and Monolingual Children to Spoken Language', *Journal of Abnormal and Social Psychology*, LIXX, 89–97.

Anisfeld, M., Bogo, N., and Lambert, W. E.
(1962) 'Evaluational Reactions to Accented English Speech', *Journal of Abnormal and Social Psychology*, LXV, 223–31.

Anisfeld, M., and Lambert, W. E.
(1961) 'Social and Psychological Variables in Learning Hebrew', *Journal of Abnormal and Social Psychology*, LXIII, 524–29.

Child, I. L.
(1943) *Italian or American? The Second Generation in Conflict.* New Haven: Yale University Press.

Durkheim, E.
(1897) *Le suicide.* Paris: F. Alcan.

Gardner, R. C., and Lambert, W. E.
(1959) 'Motivational Variables in Second-language Acquisition', *Canadian Journal of Psychology*, XIII, 266–72.

Gardner, R. C.
(1960) 'Motivational Variables in Second-language Acquisition'. Unpublished Ph.D. thesis, McGill University.

Lambert, W. E.
(1967) 'A Social Psychology of Bilingualism', *The Journal of Social Issues*, XXIII, 91–109.

Lambert, W. E., Hodgson, R. C., Gardner, R. C., and Fillenbaum, S.
(1960) 'Evaluational Reactions to Spoken Languages', *Journal of Abnormal and Social Psychology*, LX, 44–51.

Lambert, W. E., Gardner, R. C., Olton, R., and Tunstall, K.
(1962) 'A Study of the Roles of Attitudes and Motivation in Second-language Learning'. McGill University, mimeo.

Lambert, W. E., Anisfeld, M., and Yeni-Komshian, Grace
(1965) 'Evaluational Reactions of Jewish and Arab Adolescents to Dialect and Language Variations', *Journal of Personality and Social Psychology*, II, 84–90.

Lambert, W. E., Frankel, Hannah, and Tucker, G. R.
(1966) 'Judging Personality through Speech: A French-Canadian Example', *The Journal of Communication*, XVI, 305–21.

Lambert, W. E., and Anisfeld, Elizabeth
(1968) 'A Reply to John Macnamara'. Mimeographed and submitted to *The Canadian Journal of Psychology*.

Lambert, W. E., and Moore, Nancy
(1966) 'Word-association Responses: Comparison of American and French Monolinguals with Canadian Monolinguals and Bilinguals', *Journal of Personality and Social Psychology*, III, 313–20.

Lambert, W. E., and Klineberg, O.
(1967) *Children's Views of Foreign Peoples: A Cross-national Study*. New York: Appleton.

Macnamara, J.
(1964) 'The Commission on Irish: Psychological Aspects', *Studies*, 164–73.

Peal, Elizabeth, and Lambert, W. E.
(1962) 'The Relation of Bilingualism to Intelligence', *Psychological Monographs*, LXXXVI, whole no. 546.

Preston, M. S.
(1963) 'Evaluational Reactions to English, Canadian French and European French Voices.' Unpublished M.A. thesis, McGill University, Redpath Library.

Srole, L.
(1951) 'Social Dysfunction, Personality and Social Distance Attitudes'. Paper read before American Sociological Society, 1951, National Meeting, Chicago, Ill., mimeo.

Tucker, G. R., and Lambert, W. E.
(1967) 'White and Negro Listeners' Reactions to various American–English Dialects.' McGill University, mimeo.

Tucker, G. R.
(1969, in press) 'Judging Personality from Language Usage. A Filipino Example', *Philippine Sociological Review*.

Williams, R. N.
(1952) *American Society*. New York: Knopf.

V. Cognitive Aspects of Bilingual Communication

JOHN J. GUMPERZ and
EDUARDO HERNANDEZ CH.

Socio-linguistic studies of bilingualism for the most part focus on the linguistic aspects of the problem. Having discovered that speakers alternate between what, from a linguistic point of view, constitute grammatically distinct systems, investigators then proceed to study where and under what conditions alternants are employed, either through surveys in which speakers are asked to report their own language usage (Fishman, 1965), or by counting the occurrence of relevant forms in samples of elicited speech. The assumption is that the presence or absence of particular linguistic alternates directly reflects significant information about such matters as group membership, values, relative prestige, power relationship, etc.

There is no doubt that such one-to-one relationships between language and social phenomena do exist in most societies. Where speakers control and regularly employ two or more speech varieties and continue to do so over long periods of time, it is most likely that each of the two varieties will be associated with certain activities or social characteristics or speakers. This is especially the case in formal or ceremonial situations, such as religious, or magical rites, court proceedings, stereotyped introductions, greetings, or leave-takings. Here language, as well as gestures and other aspects of demeanour, may be so rigidly specified as to form part of the defining characteristics of the setting—so much so that a change in language may change the setting. Similarly, ethnic minorities in complex societies often maintain a clear separation between the native language which is spoken at home and with in-group members and the outside language used in commercial transactions or at work with outsiders.

There are, however, many other cases where such correlations break down. Consider the following sentences from a recently recorded discussion between two educated Mexican Americans.

1. a. W. Well I'm glad that I met you. O.K.?
   b. M. *Andale, pues* (O.K., swell) And do come again. Mm.
2. M. *Con ellos dos* (with the two of them). With each other. *La señora trabaja en la canería orita*, you know? (The mother works in the cannery right now). She was . . . *con Francine jugaba* . . . (She used to play with Francine . . .) with my little girl.
3. M. There's no children in the neighbourhood. Well . . . *sí hay criaturas*) (There are children).
4. M. . . . those friends are friends from Mexico *que tienen chamaquitos* (who have little children).
5. M. . . . that has nothing to do *con que le hagan esta* . . . (with their doing this).
6. M. But the person . . . *de* . . . *de grande* (as an adult) is gotta have something in his mouth.
7. M. And my uncle Sam *es el mas agabachado* (is the most Americanized).

It would be futile to predict the occurrence of either English or Spanish in the above utterances by attempting to isolate social variables which correlate with linguistic form. Topic, speaker, setting are common in each case. Yet the code changes sometimes in the middle of a sentence.

Language mixing of this type is by no means a rarity. Linguists specializing in bilingualism cite it to provide examples of extreme instances of interference (Mackey, 1965), and middle-class native speakers in ethnically diverse communities are frequently reluctant to recognize its existence. Yet it forms the subject of many humorous treatises. In spite of the fact that such extreme code switching is held in disrepute, it is very persistent, occurring whenever minority language groups come in close contact with majority language groups under conditions of rapid social change. One might, by way of an explanation, simply state that both codes are equally admissible in some contexts and that code switching is merely a matter of the individual's momentary inclination. Yet the alternation does carry meaning. Let us compare the following passage from a recent analysis of Russian pronominal usage (Friedrich, 1966) with an excerpt from our conversation.

> An arrogant aristocratic lieutenant and a grizzled, older captain find themselves thrust together as the only officers on an isolated outpost in the Caucasus. Reciprocal formality at first seems appropriate to both. But while the latter is sitting on the young lieutenant's bed and discussing a confidential matter he switches to *ty* (tu). When the lieutenant appears to suggest insubordination, however, the captain reverts to *vy* (vous) as he issues a peremptory demand . . . (p. 240).

8. M. I don't think I ever had any conversations in my dreams. I just dream. Ha. I don't hear people talking; I jus' see pictures.
9. E. Oh. They're old-fashioned, then. They're not talkies, yet, huh?
10. M. They're old-fashioned. No. They're not talkies, yet. No. I'm trying to think. Yeah, there too have been talkies. Different. In Spanish and English both. An' I wouldn't be too surprised if I even had some in Chinese. (Laughter.) Yeah, Ed. *Deveras* (Really). (M. offers E. a cigarette which is refused.) *Tú no fumas, ¿ verdad? Yo tampoco. Dejé de fumar.*

The two societies, the social context, and the topics discussed differ, yet the shift from English to Spanish has connotations similar to the alternation between the formal (second person pronoun) *vy* (vous) and the informal *ty* (tu). Both signal a change in interpersonal relationship in the direction of greater informality or personal warmth. Although the linguistic signs differ, they reflect similar social strategies. What the linguist identifies as code switching may convey important social information. The present paper is an attempt to elucidate the relationship between linguistic form, interactional strategies, and social meaning on the basis of a detailed study of a natural conversation. The conversation was recorded in an institution specializing in English instruction for Mexican immigrants. The staff, ranging in age from recent high-school graduates to persons in their middle fifties, includes a large number of people of Mexican or Mexican–American descent, as well as some English-speaking Americans. Of the latter group several speak Spanish well. The recording was made by a linguist (E), a native American of Mexican ancestry who is employed as an adviser for the programme. His interlocutor (M) is a community counsellor employed in the programme. She is a woman without higher education who has been trained to assist the staff in dealing with the local community. She has had some experience in public affairs. In spite of the difference in education and salary, both participants regard each other as colleagues within the context of the programme. When speaking Spanish they address each other by the reciprocal *tú*. The programme director or a Spanish-speaking outside visitor would receive the respectful *usted*. Conversations within the office are normally carried on in English, although, as will be seen later, there are marked stylistic differences which distinguish interaction among Mexican Americans from interaction across ethnic boundaries.

For analysis the taped transcript was roughly divided into episodes, each centring around a single main topic. Episodes were then subdivided into 'turns of speaking' (i.e. one or more sentences reflecting a speaker's response to another's comment). The author and the interviewer co-operated in the analysis of social meaning. Two types of information were utilized. Turns containing a code switch were first examined as to their place within the structure of the total conversation in terms of such questions as: what were the relevant antecedents of the turn and what followed? What was the turn in response to, either in the same or preceding episodes? The purpose here was to get as detailed as possible an estimation of the speaker's intent. In the second stage the switched phrase would be substituted with a phrase from the other language in somewhat the same way that a linguistic interviewer uses the method of variation within a frame in order to estimate the structural significance of a particular item. By this method it was possible to get an idea of what the code switch contributed to the meaning of the whole passage.

LINGUISTIC ASPECTS OF CODE SWITCHING

Before discussing the social aspects of code switching some discussion of what it is that is being switched is necessary. Not all instances of Spanish words in the text are necessarily instances of code switching. Expressions like *ándale pues* (1) *dice* (he says) are normally part of the bilingual's style of English. Speakers use such expressions when speaking to others of the same ethnic background in somewhat the same way that Yiddish expressions like *nebbish*, *oi gewalt*, or interjections like *du hoerst* characterize the in-group English style of some American Jews. They serve as stylistic ethnic identity markers and are frequently used by speakers who no longer have effective control of both languages. The function of such forms as an ethnic identity marker becomes particularly clear in the following sequence between M and a woman visitor in her office.

Woman: Well, I'm glad that I met you. O.K.?
M: *Andale, pues*. (O.K. swell) And do come again. Mm?

The speakers, both Mexican Americans, are strangers who have met for the first time. The *ándale pues* is given in response to the woman's O.K. as if to say: 'Although we are strangers we have the same background and should get to know each other better.'

Apart from loan-word nouns such as *chicano*, *gabacho*, or *pocho*, the ethnic identity markers consist largely of exclamations and sentence connectors. For example,

11. M. I says Lupe *no hombre* (why no) don't believe that.
12. M. *Sí* (yes) but it doesn't.
13. M. That baby is . . . *pues* (then).

Mexican Spanish is similarly marked by English interjections. Note, for example, the 'you know' in the sentence:

14. M. *Pero como*, you know . . . *la Estela* . . .

The English form here seems a regular part of the Spanish text, and this is signalled phonetically by the fact that the pronunciation of the vowel *o* is relatively undiphthongized, and thus differs from other instances of *o* in English passages.

Similarly, words like 'ice-cream' have Spanish-like pronunciations when they occur within Spanish texts and English-like pronunciations in the English text.

The greater part of the instances of true code switching consist of entire sentences inserted into the other language text. There are, however, also some examples of change within single sentences, which require special comment. In the item below the syntactic connection is such that both parts can be interpreted as independent sentences.

15. M. We've got all these kids here right now, *los que están ya criados aquí* (those that have been raised here).

This is not the case with the noun qualifier phrase in item (4) and the verb complement in (5). Other examples of this latter type are:

16. M. But the person . . . *de* . . . *de grande* (as an adult) is gotta have something in its mouth.
17. M. *¿Será que quiero la tetera? para* pacify myself. (It must be that I want the baby bottle to . . .)
18. M. The type of work he did *cuando trabajaba* (when he worked) he . . . what . . . that I remember, *era regador* (he was an irrigator) at one time.
19. M. An' my uncle Sam *es el más agabachado* (is the most Americanized).

Noun qualifiers (4), verb complements (5), parts of a noun phrase (16), the predicate portion of an equational sentence (19), all can be switched. This does not mean, however, that there are no linguistic constraints on the co-occurrence of Spanish and English forms. The exact specification of these constraints will, however, require further detailed investigation. Clearly, aside from single loan words, entire sentences are most easily borrowed. Sentence modifiers or phrases are borrowed less frequently. And this borrowing does seem to be subject to some selection constraints (Blom and Gumperz, 1970). But some tentative statements can be made. Constructions like:

* *que* have *chamaquitos* (who have boys)

or,

* he *era regador* (He was an irrigator)

seem impossible.

THE SOCIAL MEANING OF CODE SWITCHING

When asked why they use Spanish in an English sentence, or vice-versa, speakers frequently come up with explanations like the following taken from our conversation:

If there's a word that I can't find, it keeps comin' out in Spanish. I know what word I want and finally when I . . . well I bring it out in Spanish, and I know the person understands me.

Difficulty in finding the right word clearly seems to account for examples like: *para* pacify myself (17). In other instances some items of experience, some referents or topics are more readily recalled in one language than in another, as in:

20. M. I got to thinking *vacilando el punto este* (mulling over this point).

21. M. They only use English when they have to . . . like for *cuando van de compras* (when they go shopping).

Linguistically motivated switches into English occur when the discussion calls for psychological terminology or expressions, e.g. 'pacify', 'relax', 'I am a biter'. Such expressions or modes of talking seem rarely used in typically Mexican American settings. On the other hand, ideas and experiences associated with the speaker's Spanish-speaking past, such as items (20) and (21), trigger off a switch into Spanish.

In many other instances, however, there seems to be no linguistic reason for the switch. *Sí hay criatures* (item 3) is directly translated without hesitation pause in the following sentence. Many other Spanish expressions have English equivalents elsewhere in the text. Furthermore, there are several pages of more general, abstract discussion which contain no Spanish at all.

One might hypothesize that codes are shifted in response to E's suggestion and that M answers him in whatever language he speaks. This is clearly not the case. Several questions asked in English elicit Spanish responses, and vice-versa.

In discussing the social aspects of switching it is important to note that while the overt topic discussed is the use of English and Spanish, much of the conversation is dominated by a concern with Mexican versus non-Mexican, i.e. common middle-class values or group membership. Spanish occurs most in episodes dealing with typically Mexican American experiences. In several places fears are expressed that Mexican American children are losing their language, and thus, by implication, denying their proper cultural heritage. To some extent the juxtaposition of English and Spanish symbolizes the duality of value systems evidenced in the discussion.

At the start of the conversation several exchanges dealing with the mechanics of tape-recorder operation are entirely in English. Code shifts begin with a sequence where M asks E why he is recording their talk and E responds:

22. E. I want to use it as a . . . as an example of how *chicanos* can shift back and forth from one language to another.

23. M. *Ooo. Como andábamos platicando* (Ohh. Like we were saying).

M's switch to Spanish here is a direct response to his (E's) use of the word *chicanos*. Her statement refers to previous conversations they have had on related subjects and suggests that she is willing to treat the present talk as a friendly chat among fellow *chicanos* rather than as a formal interview.

Codes alternate only as long as all participants are *chicanos* and while their conversation revolves around personal experiences. Towards the end of the recording session, when a new participant enters, talk goes on. The newcomer is an American of English-speaking background who, having lived in Latin America, speaks Spanish fluently. Yet in this context she was addressed only in English and did not use her Spanish. Furthermore, in the earlier part of the session, when E and M were alone, there was one long episode where M spoke only English even when responding to E's Spanish questions. This passage deals with M's visit to San Quentin prison, to see an inmate, and with prison conditions. The inmate was referred to only in English, and the conversation contained no overt reference to his ethnic background. Further inquiries made while analysis was in progress revealed that he was a non-*chicano*. It is evident from the first example that it is social identity and not language *per se* which is determinant in code selection. The second example indicates when conversations have no reference to speakers or their subjects' status as *chicanos* and when, as in the present case, a subject is treated in a generally detached manner without signs of personal involvement, code switching seems to be inappropriate.

On the whole, one has the impression that except for a few episodes dealing with recollections of family affairs, the entire conversation is basically in English. English serves to introduce most new information, while Spanish provides stylistic embroidering to amplify the speaker's intent. Spanish sentences frequently take the form of pre-coded, stereotyped, or idiomatic phrases.

While ethnic identity is important as the underlying theme, the actual contextual meanings of code alternation are more complex.

Turning to a more detailed analysis, many of the Spanish passages reflect direct quotes or reports of what M has said in Spanish or of what other Mexicans have told her, e.g.

24. Because I was speakin' to my baby . . . my ex-baby sitter. And we were talkin' about the kids you know, an' I was tellin' her . . . uh . . . '*Pero, como*, you know . . . uh . . . *la Estela y la Sandi . . . relistas en el telefón. Ya hablan mucho inglés*'. *Dice*, '*Pos . . . sí. Mira tú*', *dice*, '*Pos yo no sé de dode*' *dice*, '*Pos . . . el . . . las palabras del televisión. Y ya que me dice . . . ya me pide dinero pa'l "ayscrin" y . . .*' You know? . . . '*Y lue . . . y eso no es nada, espérate los chicharrones*, you know, when they start school' ('But, how, you know . . . uh . . . Estela and Sandi are very precocious on the telephone. They already speak a lot of English'. She says, 'Well, yes, just imagine' she says, 'well I don't know where they get it from', she says, 'well, the words on television. And she already tells me . . . she already asks me for money for ice cream and' . . . you know? 'And then . . . and that isn't anything, wait for the *chicharrones*, you know, when they start school')

Throughout the conversation Spanish is used in quoting statements by individuals whose *chicano* identity is emphasized. The following passage, in which Lola, who is of Mexican origin, is quoted in English, seemed to at first contradict this generalization.

25. An' Lola says, 'Dixie has some, Dixie'. So Dixie gave me a cigarette.

Lola, however, is in her late teens, and members of her age group, although they know Spanish, tend to prefer English, even in informal interaction. Later on, however, if they marry within the *chicano* community they are quite likely to revert to the predominant usage pattern. The use of English in her case reflects the fact that for the present, at least, Lola identifies with the majority group of English monolinguals with respect to language-usage nouns.

The pattern of quoting *chicanos* in Spanish and talking about them in English is reversed in the following passage, in which M. reports on the way she talks to her children.

26. Yea. Uh-huh. She'll get . . . 'Linda, you don' do that, *mija* . . . (daughter) *La vas* . . . (You are going to . . .) you're going to get her . . . give her . . . a bad habit.' *Le pone el dedo pa' que se lo muerda*, (she gives her her finger to bite), you know, '*Iiya*, she'll bite the heck out of you'. 'Ow!' *La otra grita*, (the other one yells). *So, una es sadist y la otra es masochist* (So, one is a sadist and the other is a masochist). (Laughter.)

Further inquiry again reveals that in M's family children are ordinarily addressed in English.

Aside from direct quotes, Spanish occurs in several modifying phrases or sentences such as: 'those from Mexico', *que tienen chamaquitos* (Item 4). The effect here is to emphasize the ethnic identity of the referent. The use of *sí hay criaturas* is particularly interesting in this respect. It is preceded by the following exchange:

27. M. There's no children. The Black Panthers next door. You know what I mean.
E. Do they have kids?
M. Just the two little girls.
E. No, no. I mean do some of the other people in the neighbourhood have kids?
M. They don't associate with no children . . . There's no children in the neighbourhood. Well . . . *sí hay criaturas* (yes there are children).

M. goes on to talk about the one other Mexican family in the building. The *sí hay criaturas* here serves to single out Mexican children from others and in a sense modifies the 'there's no children' several sentences above. The implication is that only the other *chicano* children are suitable playmates.

In a last group of examples the switch to Spanish signals the relative confidentiality or privateness of the message. The first example cited as item 2 above is a case in point:

28. With each other. *La señora trabaja en la canería orita,* you know. (The mother works in the cannery, you know.)

Here M's voice is lowered and the loudness decreases in somewhat the same way that confidentiality is signalled in English monolingual speech. Next consider the following:

29. E. An' how . . . an' how about now?
M. *Estos . . . me los hallé . . . estos Pall Mall's me los hallaron.* (These . . . I found . . . These Pall Mall's . . . they were found for me.) No, I mean . . .

M has been talking about the fact that she smokes very little, and E discovers some cigarettes on her desk. Her Spanish, punctuated by an unusually large number of hestitation pauses, lends to the statement an air of private confession. She is obviously slightly embarrassed. Note the almost regular alternation between Spanish and English in the next passage:

30. Mm-huh. Yeah. An' . . . an . . . an' they tell me 'How did you quit, Mary?' I di'n' quit. I . . . I just stopped. I mean it wasn' an effort I made *que voy a dejar de fumar porque me hace daño o* (that I'm going to stop smoking because it's harmful to me, or) this or tha', uh-uh. It just . . . that . . . eh . . . I used to pull butts out of the . . . the . . . the wastepaper basket. Yeah. (Laughter) I used to go look in the (. . . unclear . . .) *se me acababan los cigarros en la noche.* (my cigarettes would run out on me at night). I'd get desperate, *y ahi voy al basurero a buscar, a sacar,* you know? (Laughter) (and there I go to the wastebasket to look for some, to get some, you know?).

The juxtaposition of the two codes here is used to great stylistic effect in depicting the speaker's attitudes. The Spanish phrases, partly by being associated with content like 'it is harmful to me' or with references to events like 'cigarettes running out at night' and through intonational and other suprasegmental clues, convey a sense of personal feeling. The English phrases are more neutral by contrast. The resulting effect of alternate personal involvement and clinical detachment vividly reflects M's ambiguity about her smoking.

Our examples of bilingual communication indicate that language usage is closely tied to the position of *chicanos* as a minority group within the English-speaking majority. Selection of alternate forms is related to a variety of social factors such as ethnic identity, age, and sex (as in the case of Lola in item 25), degree of solidarity or confidentiality, etc.

In our conversational contexts at least the relationship of such factors to verbal messages is quite different from what the sociologist means by correlation among variables. We could not take a rating of, for example, ethnicity or degree of solidarity as measured by the usual survey techniques, or other scaling devices and expect this rating to predict the occurrence of Spanish and English in our texts. Such ratings determine the likelihood of a switch, but they do not tell us when a switch occurs in a particular case, nor do they predict the meaning of a switch. What seems to be involved rather is a symbolic process very much like that by which linguistic signs convey semantic information. Code selection, in other words, is meaningful in much the same way that lexical choice is meaningful. The regular use of particular speech varieties in speech events specific to certain classes of speakers and speaker-related activities sets up associations between these varieties and features of the social environment which are like the associations between words and objects. As long as the forms in question are used in their normal or regular setting, these associations convey no new information. But in contexts where—as in the examples cited here—there is an option, where one variety is merely normal and speakers can juxtapose another variety, selection becomes meaningful. The second, juxtaposed set of forms becomes socially marked in the sense that it introduces into the new context some of the semantic features of the speech events with which it is normally associated in the minds of the participants.

In the present conversation English is normal, except in a few passages with special content, and here the objective information is introduced in English, while the Spanish is marked and typically occurs in modifier phrases and sentences. Items such as 'there are no children' followed a few sentences later by *sí hay criaturas* or 'I got to thinking', or *vacilando el punto este*, where the Spanish elaborates on previous subject matter, exemplifies what we mean by marking through juxtaposition.

The decoding process by which speakers judge the significance of marked forms bears close similarity to normal semantic decoding. In other words, speakers select from alternate dictionary meanings or semantic features in accordance with the contextual constraints imposed by semantic and syntactic rules. In the present case Spanish derives its basic meaning from its association with communication among *chicanos*. But for *chicano* speakers in-group communication also carries secondary meanings of solidarity or confidentiality when compared to verbal interaction in a mixed group. The speakers judge what is meant in each case by evaluating the reasonableness of a particular interpretation in the light of the topic discussed and his own knowledge of social norms. Social structure, like syntax, aids in the interpretation of sentences. It is part of what a speaker has to know in order to judge the full import of what is said. Two speakers will make similar interpretations of a sentence only if they interpret it in terms of the same social assumptions.

CONCLUSION

The foregoing analysis has some important implications for the cross-cultural study of bilingualism. Since there is more to communication than grammar alone (I am using the term 'grammar' in the sense in which that term is usually defined by linguists), mere knowledge of the alternating varieties is not enough. The investigator must control the speaker's own system and must pay particular attention to the often quite arbitrary signs by which these values are signalled in speech.

To be sure, any analysis which, like ours, relies on a single case raises some question about the generality of the results. Are the processes discovered here peculiar to the present conversation and speakers, or do they account for the behaviour of larger groups? Goffman has shown that to assign others to social roles or categories is a common behavioural strategy. What seems to be peculiar about the present case is not what is done but how and by what linguistic means it is done.

As a behavioural strategy, code switching bears considerable similarity to the use of polite and familiar address pronouns in other societies. Our findings regarding the relation of ethnic identity and confidentiality parallel Brown's findings (1965) about the connection between high status and social distance. English forms ordinarily associated with non-members, i.e. non-*chicanos*, are like high-status pronouns, in that they convey formality or distance when used to refer to members, while customarily forms used among members, i.e. *chicanos*, are like familiar pronouns, in that they convey secondary meanings of solidarity and confidentiality.

How does the cognitive approach to bilingual usage relate to the more usual survey methods? Obviously, it does not eliminate the need for surveys. In the many little-known areas of the world language-usage surveys are essential tools for assembling basic data on usage norms and attitudes. But in the present rudimentary stage of our knowledge of language usage survey questions tend to reflect the analyst's, not the native's, theory of speaking. Analyses such as the present one which are not too difficult or time consuming may provide important background information to improve survey content.

Note:

Work on the present paper was supported in part through grants from the Institute of International Studies, University of California, Berkeley; and Office of Education, Bureau of Research, Department of Health, Education and Welfare, Washington D.C.

REFERENCES

Blom, Jan-Petter and John J. Gumperz
(1970) 'Social Meaning in Linguistic Structures: Code-switching in Northern Norway', in John L. Gumperz and Dell Hymes (eds.), *Directions in Sociolinguistics*. New York: Holt, Rinehart and Winston.

Brown, Roger
(1965) *Social Psychology*. New York: Free Press.

Fishman, Joshua A.
(1965) 'Who Speaks what Language to Whom and When', *La Linguistique* 2: 67: 88.
Friedrich, Paul
(1966) 'Structural Implications of Russian Pronominal Usage', in William Bright (ed.), *Sociolinguistics*. The Hague: Mouton. 214–53.
Mackey, William F.
(1965) 'Bilingual Interference: its Analysis and Measurement', *Journal of Communication*, 15, 239–49.

VI. The Interrelationships and Utility of Alternative Bilingualism Measures[1]

JOSHUA A. FISHMAN and
ROBERT L. COOPER

The work upon which the present report is based was designed to integrate those aspects of bilingual behaviour which had previously been studied separately. The paper considers two questions. First, what relationships exist among descriptions of bilingualism which employ methods derived from different disciplines? More specifically, to what extent do linguistic, psychological, and sociological measurements co-vary when applied to the same bilingual speakers? Second, what is the relative utility of such measures in terms of their ability to predict, both individually and jointly, the same criterion behaviours?

METHOD

Respondents

A variety of linguistic, psychological, and sociological measurements of bilingual behaviour were designed for use in a study of Puerto Ricans in Greater New York. Selected for particularly intensive study were the people living within the 'downtown' area of Jersey City. In this target area lived 431 persons of Puerto Rican background, comprising ninety households in all. More than half (58 per cent) had been born in Puerto Rico, and of these, more than half (60 per cent) had been

[1] A revision of 'Alternative measures of bilingualism', *Journal of Verbal Learning and Verbal Behavior*, viii, 276–82 (1969).

The research reported in this paper was supported by a grant from the U.S. Office of Education, Contract No. OEC–1–7–062817–0297, 'The Measurement and Description of Language Dominance in Bilinguals'. Data processing in connection with this research was supported by a grant from the College Entrance Examination Board.

living on the mainland for ten years or less. They were a very young group, with 60 per cent below the age of 18 and 28 per cent below the age of 6. In general, the adults were poorly educated, and they held low-income jobs. Half the adults had received no more than an elementary education, and of those who were employed, most worked as operatives or labourers.

Census

The first contact with persons living in the neighbourhood was by means of a door-to-door language census (Fishman, 1968). Bilingual census-takers asked a representative from each household to respond to a series of questions about himself and about the other members of the household. There were a series of language questions, including items assessing *proficiency* in various English and Spanish language skills (e.g. 'Can you understand a conversation in English?'), *frequency* of English and Spanish usage in different contexts (e.g. 'What language do you most frequently use at work for conversation with fellow-workers?'), and the *first language* learned for various purposes (e.g. 'What was the first language in which you read books or newspapers?'). Preceding the language questions were several demographic queries, including items dealing with age, sex, birthplace, education, occupation, and number of years of residence in the United States and in Jersey City.

Psycholinguistic Interview

Of those who were 13 years or older, over one-fifth ($N=48$) agreed to participate in a tape-recorded interview which lasted from two to four hours. An attempt was made to secure both male and female respondents who would represent the range of ages (of those 13 or older) and the range of educational and occupational backgrounds to be found in the neighbourhood. The interviews, which were held in the respondent's home or in a field office in the neighbourhood, were conducted by bilinguals who were able to use whatever language or combination of languages that was preferred by a given respondent.

The interview was designed for two purposes. First, it was devised to yield information about the respondent's performance on various proficiency and self-report devices adapted from the psychological literature. Second, it was designed to elicit samples of the respondent's English and Spanish speech under conditions of varying casualness or informality. The different sections of the psycholinguistic interview are briefly described below.

Listening comprehension. Five tape-recorded, naturalistic conversations, between Spanish–English bilinguals living in New York, were obtained and employed as tests of listening comprehension and interpretation (Cooper, Fowles, and Givner, 1968). Each conversation, in which speakers switched back and forth between English and Spanish, was intended to represent a different type of social situation or context. After hearing a conversation twice, respondents were asked a series of questions in order that their comprehension and interpretation of the conversation might be assessed. Several types of question were asked, including items testing comprehension of the Spanish portions of the conversation, items testing comprehension of the English portions, questions requiring the respondent to make inferences about the social relationships between speakers, questions asking the respondent to recall which speakers used which language and when, and questions about the appropriateness of using English or Spanish during specific portions of the conversation.

Word naming. Respondents were asked to give, within one-minute time limits, as many different English (or Spanish) words that named objects or items appropriate to a given context or domain as they could (Cooper, 1968). For example, respondents were asked to give as many different English (Spanish) words as possible that named things that could be seen or found in a kitchen. Respondents named words for each of five domains—family, neighbourhood, religion, education, and work—responding to all domains in one language and then to all domains in the other.

Word association. Respondents were also asked to give continuous associations, within one-minute intervals, to each of the following stimulus words: *home*, *street*, *church*, *school*, *factory*, *casa*, *calle*, *iglesia*, *escuela*, and *factoría*. These stimuli were intended to represent the five contexts or domains of family, neighbourhood, religion, education, and work. Responses were restricted to the language of the stimulus word. The word association task always followed the word naming task, but there was always at least a 10-minute interval between them, during which time another technique was administered.

Word frequency estimation. Respondents were asked to rate, on an 8-point scale, the frequency with which they heard or used each of 150 words, of which half were in Spanish and half in English (Cooper and Greenfield, 1968b). The 75 words in each language were made up of 5 sets of 15 words, the words for each set having been selected to represent a domain or context. The domains family, neighbourhood, religion, education, and work were employed. For example, some of the English words which represented the domain of education were *teacher, blackboard, history,* and *science.* Respondents rated all the words in one language before rating the words in the other. The items representing each domain were evenly distributed throughout the list of words in each language.

Spanish usage rating scale. Respondents were asked to rate, on an 11-point scale, the degree to which they used Spanish (relative to English) with *other Puerto Rican bilinguals* at home, in their neighbourhood, at church, at school, and at work (Cooper and Greenfield, 1968a). For each context, degree of usage was rated with interlocutors who varied by age, sex, and relationship to the respondent. For example, respondents were asked how much of their conversation was typically in Spanish when talking to Puerto Rican neighbours of the same age and sex, in their neighbourhood.

Linguistic elicitation procedures. Based both on the notion of verbal repertoire, advanced and elaborated by Gumperz (1964, 1967), and on the construct of linguistic variable, as developed by Labov (1963, 1966), an attempt was made to vary systematically the interview contexts in which English and Spanish were elicited (Ma and Herasimchuk, 1968). By extending Labov's method to bilingual speech situations, as suggested by Gumperz, an attempt was made to obtain speech in two languages that varied along a continuum of carefulness or casualness. Thus, the phonological variation associated with changes in the interview context could be observed in English and in Spanish. The degree of systematic phonological variation observed in each language could serve as one index of the extent of the speaker's linguistic resources or verbal repertoire. Phonological variation was observed in terms of five elicitation procedures or contexts. Described below, they are presented in order of the formality or carefulness of the speech elicited, with the most formal context first and the most casual last.

1. Word list reading. Two brief lists of words, one in English and one in Spanish, were given to the respondent to read aloud. The lists contained examples of sounds which were hypothesized to vary as a function of the elicitation procedure.

2. Paragraph reading. Four brief paragraphs, two in each language, were also given to the respondent to read aloud. Like the word lists, the paragraphs were constructed so as to include specified phonological variables.

3. Word naming. Performance on the word naming task (described earlier) was studied as an example of speech that was midway in formality between more careful speech, represented by reading aloud, and more casual speech, represented by free conversation.

4. Interview style. The speech produced during the formal question and answer periods of the interview, particularly responses to questions about the listening comprehension passages, were analysed as examples of relatively careful discourse.

5. Casual speech. The interviewers attempted to elicit casual speech in English and in Spanish by encouraging respondents to digress from the interview material and by asking questions designed to promote personal anecdotes or excited replies. Casual speech was sometimes also obtained fortuitously, as when the respondent was called to the telephone or when he spoke to a child who had come into the room.

Instruments: Summary

The techniques which have been described may be classified in terms of two variables: the type of behaviour described and the source of the observation. With respect to the first, the methods can be characterized as describing either language proficiency or language use. Language proficiency refers to what the person *can* do. Language use refers to what he *typically* does. With respect to the second category, the techniques can be described as relying either on the respondent's own performance, as on the word-naming task, or on a retrospective report of his behaviour. (The retrospective reports were either by the respondent himself, as on the Spanish-usage rating scale, or by someone who knew the respondent well, as on the census.) The intersection of these two types of performance and sources of observation forms a four-celled matrix into which each of the techniques can be placed. The four-way classification is presented in Table 1.

Table 1

Classification of Techniques for Bilingual Measurement

Source of observation	*Behaviour described*	
	Proficiency (What a person *can* do)	*Usage* (What a person *typically* does)
performance	phonological analysis (reading contexts) word naming word association listening comprehension	phonological analysis (speech contexts)
retrospective report	census (proficiency items)	census (usage items) usage rating scale word frequency estimation

SCORING[1]

Two types of scoring were employed: *a priori* scoring and *empirical* scoring. The former was based on *a priori* classifications (e.g. the average frequency rating given the fifteen Spanish words which had been selected to represent the domain of religion). The latter was based on factor analyses of all the items entering into the *a priori* scores for a given technique. There were two types of empirical score. One type was computed on the basis of *all* the items that clustered together into a 'factor'. This type of scoring was performed for the census data and the word frequency estimation technique. The second type of empirical scoring, which was used for all the other techniques, was based not on all items but only upon those that were *representative* of each factor (generally, the items with the highest loadings on the factor).

Both types of score, *a priori* and empirical, were studied in relationship to four *criterion* scores. These were based on ratings

[1] The scoring is described in greater detail in Fishman, Cooper, Ma *et al.* (1968).

made by two linguists who had scored the phonological variables and who had become personally acquainted with most of the interviewed respondents. These criteria, which were selected as representative of important types of language behaviour, are summarized as follows.

Accentedness. Respondents were rated in terms of the degree to which the phonological and syntactic structures of one language appeared to influence speech produced in the other. A seven-point scale was used on which high scores indicated Spanish influence upon English speech, low scores indicated English influence upon Spanish speech, and scores in between indicated maximum language distance, or no influence by either language upon speech produced in the other.

Bilingual reading. Based on their performance on the reading tasks (word lists and paragraphs), respondents were rated, on a five-point scale, in terms of their ability to read in the two languages. High scores indicated that the respondent could read only in Spanish (or not at all), low scores indicated that he could read only in English, and intermediate scores indicated that he could read in both languages.

English repertoire range. Respondents were rated in terms of the number of English speech styles which they appeared to use and the fluency with which these were employed. A six-point scale was used, ranging from knowledge of only a few words and phrases, at one extreme, to the ability to employ both careful and casual speech styles, in a maximally fluent manner, at the other.

Spanish repertoire range. Respondents were also rated in terms of the number and fluency of Spanish speech styles which they were judged to use. A four-point scale was employed, which ranged from the use of only a single, casual style to the fluent use of several speech styles, including more careful, formal Spanish.

Data Analysis

Two principal analyses were performed, a factor analysis and regression analysis.

Factor analysis. With the exception of scores obtained from one technique, all *a priori* and empirical scores were intercorrelated

The exception was in the case of the phonological analysis. Inasmuch as over 500 phonological *a priori* scores were computed for each respondent, only selected phonological *a priori* scores were used for the intercorrelational matrix. These were chosen on the basis of low loadings on the factors which had been determined for the phonological variables. Thus, the empirical scores from the phonological analysis were items with high factor loadings, and the *a priori* scores were items with low factor loadings. In all, 124 scores, obtained from seven techniques, were intercorrelated. Half the scores were *a priori* and half were empirical. A varimax orthogonal solution was then sought for the 124 × 124 matrix of intercorrelations.

Regression analysis. Intercorrelations were also obtained between the four criterion variables and the 124 *a priori* and criterion scores. Multiple-regression analyses were then performed between selected predictor variables and each of the four criterion variables. The predictor variables for each criterion were selected on the basis of their correlations with the criterion and on the basis of their correlations with each other as observed in the 124 × 124 matrix. A seven-factor solution appeared to be the best one yielded by the analyses of this matrix. For each criterion, the item from each factor that had the highest correlation with the criterion was selected. In this way, seven predictor variables were selected for each criterion. The selection procedure yielded maximum independence of predictors (since each entered into a different factor) combined with maximum power of individual predictors (since each had the highest correlation on its factor with the criterion), thus permitting maximum cumulative prediction of the criterion.[1]

RESULTS

Factor Analysis

The seven factors which were obtained were described as follows: (1) *Spanish productivity*, based primarily on performance

[1] Inasmuch as there were missing data for some of the predictor variables, the regression analysis also employed correlations between the criterion and the presence or absence of data from the predictors. In other words, where there were missing data, a multiple correlation was obtained between the criterion, on the one hand, and the predictor score plus a score based on the presence or absence of the predictor, on the other.

on the Spanish word naming and word association tasks; (2) *English productivity*, based primarily on performance on the English word naming and word association tasks; (3) *listening comprehension*, viewed in terms of degree of Spanish 'dominance'; (4) *claimed Spanish*, Spanish proficiency and usage as reported by the respondent or by a member of his household; (5) *unaccented English speech*, based primarily on the frequency of certain English phonological variables; (6) *sociolinguistic sensitivity*, based primarily on performance on listening comprehension items requiring the respondent to identify the use of English and Spanish and to make inferences about the social meaning of language usage; and (7) *Spanish word frequency estimation.*[1]

These factors may be characterized in terms of the different types of technique or task summarized in the four-fold classification of Table 1. Scores derived from the techniques categorized within a single quadrant, the proficiency scores based on performance, clustered into five different factors, namely 1, 2, 3, 5, and 6. Scores based on the techniques classified within two quadrants, retrospective reports of proficiency and retrospective reports of usage, clustered into two factors on the basis of the directness of the techniques employed. The scores obtained from the relatively direct questions used in the census and the Spanish usage rating scale formed one of these factors, and the scores obtained from the relatively indirect word frequency estimation task formed the other. Usage scores based on performance, which comprised the remaining quadrant, entered several factors without characterizing any.

The factors may also be characterized in terms of the two types of score which were employed. Factor 1 (Spanish productivity) was made up primarily of empirically derived scores and factor 3 (listening comprehension) of *a priori* scores. The other factors were each composed about equally of the two types of score.

It is also possible to describe the factors in terms of the disciplines from which scores were derived. Whereas all of the sociologically derived scores were confined to a single factor (claimed Spanish), the linguistically and psychologically derived scores contributed to all factors. Thus, the sociological

[1] The factors are described in greater detail in Fishman, Cooper, Ma *et al.* (1968).

scores were more homogeneous than were the scores derived from the other two disciplines. On three factors (listening comprehension, unaccented English speech, and Spanish word frequency estimation) psychological and linguistic scores were found in about equal proportions, and on three factors (Spanish productivity, English productivity, and sociolinguistic sensitivity) the psychologically derived scores predominated.

In sum, the most homogeneous scores were those derived from retrospective reports and from sociologically derived techniques. The most heterogeneous were performance scores and scores derived from the psychological and linguistic disciplines.

Regression Analysis

Table 2 presents the intercorrelations among the criterion variables. Three of the criterion variables displayed substantial correlations with one another (r's between 0·61 and 0·74), all of which were significant beyond the 0·01 level. The Spanish

Table 2

Intercorrelations among Criterion Variables

Variable	*Correlation*				$\bar{X}$	*S.D.*
	1	*2*	*3*	*4*		
1. Accentedness		0·74**	0·27	−0·69**	2·00	1·74
2. Bilingual reading			0·19	−0·61**	2·44	1·43
3. Spanish repertoire range				0·04	2·04	0·76
4. English repertoire range					2·84	1·61

** $p < 0·01$

repertoire range scale was not significantly related to the other criteria, however. As can be seen from the standard deviations of these variables (Table 2), the respondents were much more alike in terms of their Spanish repertoire ratings ($p<0·01$) than they were in terms of their scores on the other criterion variables. The non-significant correlations obtained with the Spanish repertoire scale can be attributed to the greater homogeneity of the Spanish repertoire ratings, a homogeneity which is consistent with the fact that for most of the respondents Spanish was the first language learned and was primarily a home and neighbourhood language. Thus, there was more opportunity for them to vary with respect to their English skills (due to differential exposure to English at school, at work).

Of the *a priori* and empirical scores that best predicted each of the four criterion variables, the census scores were by far the most successful. When the seven scores displaying the highest correlations with each of the four criteria were examined it was found that seventeen of the twenty-eight had been obtained from the census. Scores from other techniques, when added to those from the census, however, could sometimes substantially improve the prediction of the criteria. The improved predictions obtained by pooling scores from different factors can be

Table 3

The Cumulative Prediction of Accentedness

Cumulative predictors	r	R	R^2	*Cum R*	*Cum* R^2	F_{R^2}	ΔR^2	$F_{\Delta R^2}$
1. Language used more often at home (census)	0·847	0·847	0·718	0·847	0·718	102·57*	—	—
2. Word naming, education	0·509							
Presence *v.* absence of variable 2	−0·377	0·636	0·405	0·858	0·736	13·53*	0·018	1·29
3. Listening comprehension, third conversation	0·447							
Presence *v.* absence of variable 3	−0·119	0·462	0·214	0·861	0·742	5·35*	0·006	0·43
4. Listening comprehension, fifth conversation	0·398	0·398	0·158	0·861	0·742	7·52*	0·000	0·00
5. Word frequency estimation, education	0·379							
Presence *v.* absence of variable 5	−0·230	0·444	0·197	0·863	0·745	4·95†	0·003	0·21
6. Language used with bilingual men in neighbourhood (usage rating scale)	0·286							
Presence *v.* absence of variable 6	−0·149	0·319	0·102	0·864	0·747	2·32	0·002	0·13
7. Frequency of Spanish (ṽ̄ for v́N), word naming	0·206							
Presence *v.* absence of variable 7	−0·252	0·323	0·104	0·868	0·753	2·36	0·006	0·37

Note: Unless specifically noted, predictors are scales on which high scores represent Spanish dominance and low scores English dominance.

* $p < 0·01$
† $p < 0·05$

seen in Tables 3–6. These tables present the cumulative predictions obtained by successive additions of predictors which represent different factors (and thus tend to have relatively low correlations with one another).

Each table shows several types of figure, one of which indicates the correlation between the criterion variable and a single predictor (or, where data are missing for a predictor, between the criterion variable, on the one hand, and the predictor variable plus a 'dummy' variable which represents the presence or absence of the predictor, on the other). This correlation is in the column headed *R*. For example, the predictor variable Spanish literacy has a correlation of 0·586 with the criterion variable Spanish repertoire range (Table 6). The next predictor variable plus the presence or absence of that variable have a correlation of 0·343 with the criterion.

Table 4

The Cumulative Prediction of Bilingual Reading

Cumulative predictors	r	R	R^2	*Cum R*	*Cum* R^2	F_{R^2}	ΔR^2	$F_{\Delta R^2}$
1. Language used more often at home (census)	0·681	0·681	0·464	0·681	0·464	35·69*	—	—
2. Language used with older bilingual women in neighbourhood (usage rating scale)	0·423	0·423	0·179	0·735	0·541	8·95*	0·077	7·00†
3. Listening comprehension, fifth conversation,	0·502							
Presence *v.* absence of variable 3	−0·099	0·512	0·262	0·769	0·591	7·28*	0·050	2·27
4. Word frequency estimation, education	0·436							
Presence *v.* absence of variable 4	−0·322	0·542	0·294	0·784	0·615	8·17*	0·024	1·09
5. Frequency of Spanish (ṽ for ṽN), word naming	−0·383	0·383	0·147	0·793	0·629	7·00*	0·014	1·27
6. Language used with younger bilingual men in neighbourhood (usage rating scale)	0·306							
Presence *v.* absence of variable 6	−0·248	0·390	0·152	0·798	0·637	3·61†	0·008	0·36
7. Listening comprehension, third conversation	0·266							
Presence *v.* absence of variable 7	−0·217	0·343	0·118	0·803	0·645	2·68	0·008	0·36

Note: Unless specifically noted, predictor variables are scales on which high scores indicate Spanish dominance and low scores English dominance.

* $p < 0·01$ † $p < 0·05$

The method used requires the predictors to be added in a specified order. Predictors are usually added in order of their correlation with the criterion, with those having the largest

Table 5

The Cumulative Prediction of English Repertoire Range

Cumulative predictors	r	R	R^2	*Cum R*	*Cum* R^2	F_{R^2}	ΔR^2	$F_{\Delta R^2}$
1. Language used more often at home (census)	−0·603	0·603	0·364	0·603	0·364	24·27*	—	—
2. English word naming, religion	0·458							
Presence *v.* absence of variable 2	0·463	0·646	0·417	0·717	0·515	13·93*	0·151	6·25*
3. Listening comprehension, third conversation	−0·443							
Presence *v.* absence of variable 3	0·316	0·543	0·295	0·749	0·561	8·17*	0·046	1·92
4. Listening comprehension, fifth conversation	−0·542							
Presence *v.* absence of variable 4	0·184	0·573	0·328	0·784	0·615	9·65*	0·054	2·45
5. Word frequency estimation, education	−0·398							
Presence *v.* absence of variable 5	0·285	0·490	0·240	0·785	0·617	6·32*	0·002	0·08
6. 'Human response' ratio, Spanish word association, neighbourhood	0·290							
Presence *v.* absence of variable 6	0·492	0·565	0·319	0·793	0·629	9·35*	0·012	0·50
7. Frequency of English Vb [N]#, word naming	0·228							
Presence *v.* absence of variable 7	0·381	0·432	0·187	0·808	0·653	4·65†	0·024	1·33

Note: Unless specifically noted, predictors are scales on which high scores represent Spanish dominance and low scores English dominance.

* $p < 0·01$ † $p < 0·05$

relationship placed first and those having the smallest relationship placed last. The significance of the correlations between an individual predictor (including its presence or absence) and the criterion can be seen in the column headed $F_{R}{}^{2}$. Note that in the case of Spanish repertoire range only the first predictor is significantly related to it. However, the addition of other predictors cumulatively improves the prediction of that criterion. The significance of each successive addition can be seen in

Table 6

The Cumulative Prediction of Spanish Repertoire Range

Cumulative predictors	*r*	*R*	R^2	*Cum R*	*Cum* R^2	$F_R{}^2$	ΔR^2	$F\Delta R^2$
1. Spanish literacy (census)	0·586	0·586	0·343	0·586	0·343	21·44*	—	—
2. Sensitivity to language usage (fourth conversation)	−0·339							
Presence *v.* absence of variable 2	0·120	0·343	0·118	0·674	0·454	2·68	0·111	3·96†
3. Spanish word association, religion	−0·353							
Presence *v.* absence of variable 3	0·046	0·357	0·127	0·729	0·531	2·86	0·077	3·00
4. Frequency of Spanish ♯[*x*], casual speech	−0·281							
Presence *v.* absence of variable 4	0·116	0·302	0·091	0·807	0·652	1·96	0·121	6·10*
5. Frequency of English [*ai*], interview style	0·304							
Presence *v.* absence of variable 5	0·189	0·341	0·116	0·855	0·732	2·64	0·080	5·00†
6. Frequency of English [o^ə] CV, interview style	−0·205	0·205	0·042	0·857	0·735	1·83	0·003	0·37
7. Word frequency estimation (work factor score)	0·243							
Presence *v.* absence of variable 7	0·235	0·338	0·114	0·862	0·743	2·59	0·008	0·44

Note: Unless specifically noted, predictors are scales on which high scores represent Spanish dominance and low scores English dominance.

* $p < 0·01$ † $p < 0·05$

the column headed $F_{\Delta R}{}^{2}$. Thus, for Spanish repertoire range the addition of the second variable (although itself not highly related to the criterion) gives significantly better prediction than obtained by the first predictor alone. Similarly, the addition of the fourth and fifth variables significantly improves the prediction over that obtained by three and four variables, respectively.

For three of the criteria, substantial improvement in prediction was obtained by the use of additional variables. The most striking improvement was seen in the case of Spanish repertoire range, where the correlation between criterion and predictors went from 0·586, for a single predictor, to 0·862 for seven. For the criterion of accentedness (Table 3), however, the first variable had such a high correlation with the criterion ($r = 0·847$) that additional variables were unable to significantly improve prediction. For all criteria, the proportion of variance explained by multiple prediction was quite high, ranging from 64 per cent (Cum $R = 0{\cdot}803$) for bilingual reading to 75 per cent (Cum $R = 0{\cdot}868$) for accentedness.

DISCUSSION

The techniques described in the present report comprise a 'maxi-kit' from which the student of bilingualism can select the 'mini-kit' he needs for work in the field. Which ones should he select? The answer depends partly, of course, on what it is he wants to know, and partly on the socio-political climate in which he is operating. If he is interested in fairly unidimensional questions, and if language issues are not particularly sensitive, he can ask directly by means of a census-type approach. If, however, he is dubious about the validity of answers to such questions he should select a somewhat more indirect measure of proficiency and usage, such as the word frequency estimation technique. If the investigator is concerned with more complex criteria he may need to use a combination of techniques.

The selection of any particular 'mini-kit' for a particular population would ideally be made on an empirical basis. For example, let us suppose that our entire battery of techniques had been administered in Jersey City for the purpose of subsequently selecting the most effective instruments for a language survey to be performed upon a quite similar but much larger population. Let us suppose, further, that the larger survey would be conducted in order to describe Puerto Rican bilinguals with respect to the same criteria employed in Jersey City: accentedness, bilingual reading, English repertoire range, and Spanish repertoire range. If we wished to combine maximum prediction of all four criteria with a minimum of interviewing time we would select the following items or tasks[1]: (1) the three census items asking which language is spoken, written, and read at home; (2) the eight census items asking for ratings of Spanish proficiency and usage in terms of reading and writing skills; (3) one item asking how much Spanish is used

[1] The items chosen for the 'mini-kit' were in general those with the highest zero order correlations with the criterion. However, in two instances predictors with slightly lower correlations were chosen on the basis of their greater administrative convenience where no significant $F_{\Delta R^2}$ was involved between the most convenient and the most powerful predictors.

with older, bilingual Puerto Rican women in the respondent's neighbourhood; (4) a task requiring the respondent to name, within a one-minute period, as many different English words as possible that identify objects seen or found in a church; (5) a task requiring the respondent to listen to a brief, taped bilingual conversation and to comment on the appropriateness of the languages chosen for the particular purposes of that conversation; and (6) a rating (by the census taker on the spot, or later by a phonetic transcriber if the interview is tape-recorded) of the frequency with which the English variant [aɨ] is used during the interview.[1]

This six-item 'mini-kit' could be routinely administered in less than 30 minutes. It would yield the following cumulative multiple correlations (Cum R) with the four criterion measures: accentedness, 0·898; bilingual reading, 0·760; English repertoire range, 0·783; and Spanish repertoire range, 0·769. The first two criteria would be predicted as well (or in the case of accentedness, even better) by the mini-kit as by the full seven-factor battery. The last two criteria would be predicted quite well by the 'mini-kit', but the full seven-factor battery provides appreciably higher cumulative predictions for them (0·808 for ERR; 0·862 for SRR).

The apparent adequacy of a small 'mini-kit' of language measures should permit the future investigator of bilingual populations to spend proportionally more of his research time and funds on studying other-than-language behaviours. It should also permit him to study in more detail the behaviours underlying some of the less powerful but psychologically interesting predictors. For each of the criteria, but particularly for accentedness, the *first* predictor entering into the multiple-regression analysis was high enough to 'swamp' the other predictors, i.e. the best single predictor greatly out-weighed the others in the effective prediction of the criteria, even though adding the other variables substantially improved the prediction of three of the criteria. It would be an interesting subject for further research to control statistically or experimentally the 'swamping' variables in order to examine the relative potency of

[1] The variant [*aɨ*] is one of the possible realizations of the vowel that appears in *my*, *I*, *mine*, etc., words which in the normal course of a census interview ought to occur frequently if the interviewer is able to elicit English speech.

the lesser predictors.[1] Such an attempt ought to improve our ability to describe and to explain the determinants underlying individual differences among bilingual speakers. Why, for example, do scores obtained from *religious* word naming or word association enter into prediction of English repertoire range and Spanish repertoire range? And why does an *inverse* relationship appear to exist between Spanish religious productivity and Spanish repertoire range, whereas a *positive* relationship appears to exist between English religious productivity and English repertoire range? By magnifying the effects of the lesser variables, through controlling the effects of the 'swamping' variables, answers to such questions might be found.

In the present study techniques derived from separate disciplines contributed uniquely to the multiple prediction of complex criteria. Disciplinary uniqueness can also be concluded, of course, from the factor analysis, some of whose dimensions can be described primarily in terms of scores derived from a single discipline. The factor analysis, however, also revealed disciplinary redundancy, as can be seen from the clustering together, on several factors, of scores derived from separate disciplines. Such redundancy suggests that the bilingualism which has been studied separately by linguists, psychologists, and sociologists has been to a large extent the same phenomenon. However, the contributions made possible by disciplinary uniqueness also suggest that the phenomenon of bilingualism can best be described by an interdisciplinary approach. Although the disciplines overlap, none singly can describe it adequately.

SUMMARY

A variety of techniques for the measurement and description of bilingualism, derived separately from the disciplines of linguistics, psychology, and sociology, were administered to the same respondents, forty-eight Spanish–English bilinguals who lived in a Puerto Rican neighbourhood near New York, in order to assess the relationships among these measures and their relative utility as predictors of four proficiency criterion variables. A factor analysis, performed on the intercorrelations among 124 scores, indicated areas of interdisciplinary overlap as well as uniqueness. The best predictors of the criteria were

[1] We are indebted to Wallace E. Lambert for this observation.

obtained from retrospective reports of proficiency and usage. However, scores from other techniques provided significant increments in the cumulative prediction of the four proficiency criteria, a very high proportion of whose variance was explainable through multiple-regression analysis.

REFERENCES

Cooper, Robert L.
(1968) 'Two Contextualized Measures of Degree of Bilingualism', in *Bilingualism in the Barrio* (q.v. below), pp. 505–24. Also, *Modern Language Journal*, LIII, 172–8(1969).

Cooper, Robert L., Fowles, Barbara, and Givner, Abraham
(1968) 'Listening Comprehension in a Bilingual Community', in *Bilingualism in the Barrio* (q.v. below), pp. 577–97. Also *Modern Language Journal*, LIII, 235–41 (1969).

Cooper, Robert L., and Greenfield, Lawrence
(1968a) 'Language Use in a Bilingual Community', in *Bilingualism in the Barrio* (q.v. below), pp. 485–504. Also *Modern Language Journal*, LIII, 166–72 (1969).

Cooper, Robert L., and Greenfield, Lawrence
(1968b) 'Word Frequency Estimation as a Measure of Degree of Bilingualism', in *Bilingualism in the Barrio* (q.v. below), pp. 475–84.

Fishman, Joshua A.
(1968) 'A Sociolinguistic Census of a Bilingual Neighborhood', in *Bilingualism in the Barrio* (q.v. below), pp. 260–99. Also *American Journal of Sociology*, LXXV, 323–39 (1969).

Gumperz, John J.
(1964) 'Linguistic and Social Interaction in Two Communities', *American Anthropologist*, LXVI, 2, 137–54.
(1967) 'On the Linguistic Markers of Bilingual Communication', *Journal of Social Issues*, XXIII, 48–57.

Labov, William
(1963) 'The Social Motivation of a Sound Change', *Word*, XIX, 273–309.
(1966) *The Social Stratification of English in New York City*. Washington, D.C.: Center for Applied Linguistics.

Ma, Roxana and Herasimchuk, Eleanor
(1968) 'Linguistic Dimensions of a Bilingual Neighborhood', in *Bilingualism in the Barrio* (q.v. below), pp. 636–835.

Fishman, Joshua A., Cooper, Robert L., Ma, Roxana, *et al.* (1968) *Bilingualism in the Barrio*. Final Report, Contract No. OEC–1–7–062817–0297, U.S. Department of Health, Education, and Welfare. New York: Yeshiva University. Also, revised ed. 1 vol. Indiana University Language Sciences Series. Bloomington: Indiana University Press. In press.

B. EMPIRICAL STUDIES WITHIN AFRICA

VII. Linguistic Complexity in Uganda[1]

CLIVE CRIPER and PETER LADEFOGED

It is often assumed that there are obvious and inherent disadvantages suffered by states which are linguistically heterogeneous. Linguistic heterogeneity thus becomes a 'problem' to which an answer must be found, whereas linguistically homogeneous states do not share this problem. How far is this in practice true? The title of this seminar 'Social Implications of Multilingualism in East Africa' would seem to be asking precisely this question. The intention of this paper is to examine how we may describe the extent and degree of multilingualism in a nation and the problems arising from it, taking Uganda as an example. The point made is that it is necessary to examine different levels of political and administrative organization in order to define the type and degree of multilingualism that is operating at each level. No overall statements concerning the social implications of multilingualism in a nation are possible without considering the level at which they apply. What is a problem at county or district level may cease to be one at national level, and vice versa.

BACKGROUND TO UGANDA

The past history of the establishment of Uganda as an independent nation plays an important part in understanding the present situation of language use and policy. The first European influence in Uganda came with the advent of the missionaries in 1877. In 1894 the British Government took over rule of the area from the chartered East African Company and proclaimed a

[1] This paper was prepared during field work carried out for the Survey of Language Use and Language Teaching in East Africa. It was supported by the Ford Foundation. Dr. Ruth Glick was the third member of the team working in Uganda, and therefore also helped in the collection of material used in this paper.

British Protectorate. An agreement was signed with the kingdom of Buganda six years later, in which special status was accorded to Baganda practices and political institutions, thus setting them apart from the three kingdoms in the West and all the other administrative areas in the East and North of the Protectorate. Initially all contact of the Europeans was with the Baganda, and to a lesser (and more hostile) extent with the other Kingdoms. The economic and educational advantages of this contact were largely the monopoly of the Baganda. In the early part of the century they were used as colonial agents to establish a similar hierarchy of chiefs and bureaucracy to their own in the Nilotic and Sudanic areas to the north and in the non-centralized Bantu areas of the East. They established a hierarchy of administrative units paralleling their own system, which continues today.

The power and influence of the Baganda under the patronage of the British ensured the high status of their language and its position as a language of administration. Though the influence of Luganda in the Nilotic and Sudanic areas of the North has not lasted after the replacement of the Baganda agents by locally appointed chiefs, in certain districts of the East, e.g. Busoga, Bugisu, it has remained the official language taught in schools and used for public notices and meetings. Nevertheless, even among speakers of the closely related Bantu languages of Lusoga and Lugisu it has remained an alien language whose use and practice has depended upon the continuing high status, power, and achievement of the Baganda themselves.

When independence was achieved in 1962 the Kingdom of Buganda was granted federal status, with exclusive powers over its public services as well as powers over hereditary and ceremonial offices and other customary matters. Only the latter powers were given to the other Kingdoms of Toro, Ankole, and Bunyoro, and to Busoga. The remainder of the country was divided into a number of District Administrations. In 1966 the Kabaka of Buganda was deposed and the federal and quasi-federal status of the Kingdoms abolished. Though many Baganda remain in high positions in the civil service and elsewhere, this action has hastened the decline in their political power and prestige. Much of the latent hostility felt towards them on account of their previous position as agents of the colonial power and as a group having greater access to educational and economic opportunities is now expressed more openly.

One feature of this is the rejection of Luganda as either a national language or even as a lingua franca or official language to be used throughout the Bantu-speaking areas. Northern areas have always feared the privileged position of the Baganda and refused to countenance the use of Luganda, even though it is the sole indigenous language with a wide enough base in terms of first- and second-language speakers and of a published literature to become the national language. The possibility of this occurring has been finally removed by the political necessity of the Government having to break the power of the Baganda as an entity both separate and independent from the remainder of the country.

English was inevitably introduced as the major language of administration and law from an early stage, though Swahili held a rival official position for a brief period. There has never been any substantial number of non-Africans living and working in Uganda. In 1966 there were estimated to be only 110,000 non-Africans, of whom approximately 8 per cent were European and 80 per cent Asian. In 1948 only about a third of these numbers were present. Consequently a situation has never existed in which there has been a foreign (non-African) settler population. Europeans have primarily been employed in missionary work, in administration, and in the provision of services, while the Asian population has been restricted to commercial activity within the towns and trading centres. This perhaps explains to some extent the position of the two foreign languages which play such an important role in the country as a whole.

The various regions of Uganda differ from one another geographically, climatically, demographically, and economically. This widespread variation is paralleled by the ethnic and linguistic composition of the country's population. Broadly speaking, the Bantu-speaking groups occupy the southern half of the country, the majority of which were traditionally organized through the institution of a centralized state, e.g. such as in the Kingdoms of Buganda and Bunyoro. By contrast, the Nilotic groups were not so organized. Their movement southwards and westwards was carried out by smaller groups and chiefdoms. Successive waves of invaders have left a confused pattern of settlement, with no clear-cut boundaries between one ethnic group and another, though in general it is possible to associate the North-East with Eastern Nilotic groups (Karamojong, Ateso, etc.); the North with the Western Nilotic

Table 1

The Official Status of the Major Languages Spoken in Uganda

Language	*% population native speakers*	*hours/week Radio*	*% non-English Radio time*	*Literacy campaign*	*Newspapers: % of total circulation*	*Officially used in primary schools*	*Agriculture information services*	*Law Courts*
Western Nilotic								
Lango	5·6 }	12¾ }	11	X }	2·1 }	X }	X	
Acholi	4·4 }			X }				
Alur	1·9	3¼	3	X	0·2			
Dhopadhola	1·6	½	0·5	X				
Kumam	1·0	½	0·5	X				
Group totals	14·5	17	15	5	2·3	1	1	
Eastern Nilotic								
Ateso	8·1	12¾	11	X	0·9 }	X	X	
Akaramojong	2·0	3¼	3	X				
Kakwa	0·6	¾	0·5	X				
Sebei	0·6	3	3	X				
Group totals	11·3	19¾	17·5	4	0·9	1	1	
Central Sudanic								
Lugbara	3·7	5¼	4	X	0·2	X		
Madi	1·2	3½	3	X	0·1			
Group totals	4·9	8¾	7	2	0·3	1	0	
Bantu								
(E)								
Luganda	16·3	34	29	X	40	X	X	
Lusoga	7·8	6¼	5	X				
Lumasaba (Lugisu)	5·1	4½	4	X				
Lugwere	1·7	—	0					
Lunyole	1·4	—	0					
Lusamia/Lugwe	1·3	3½	3	X				
Group totals	33·6	48¼	40	4	40	1	1	
(W)								
Runyankole	8·1 }	9¾ }	8 }	X	0·8 }	X		
Rukiga	7·1 }							
Runyaruanda	5·9	—	0	X				
Rutoro	3·3 }	9¼ }	8 }	X }	0·8 }	X }	X	
Runyoro	2·9 }							
Rurundi	2·0							
Rukonjo	1·7	—	0	X				
Rwamba	0·5	—	0	X				
Group totals	30·5	19	16	5	1·6	2	1	
Non-Ugandan								
Swahili	—	—	0		2·4	(X)		
English	0·2	50¾	—		50·5	X	X	X
Gujerati	1·0	—	0		2·0			
Hindustani (Hindi/Urdu)	0·1	5	4					

groups (Lango, Acholi, Alur, etc.); and the extreme North-west with the Central Sudanic groups of Lugbara and Madi. None of these conglomerations of ethnic groups form exclusive territorial groups. Thus in the North-west, Kakwa, an Eastern Nilotic language, is spoken in what is predominantly a Central Sudanic area. Similarly in the East, groups of Western Nilotic Dhopadhola speakers and Eastern Nilotic Ateso speakers are interspersed within the Bantu-speaking group.

A picture of the distribution of the various languages shows the lack of any single dominant language. Luganda, the most important of the Bantu languages, is spoken as a first language by only 16 per cent of the total population. Yet it is by far the largest language, no other single language being spoken by more than 8 per cent of the population. There are only seven other languages spoken by more than 5 per cent of the population. The Bantu languages are quite closely related, and taken together, the Eastern Bantu languages are spoken by a third of the country's population, while the Western Bantu languages are spoken by almost an equal proportion (see Table 1). Thus nearly two-thirds of the population speak one of the closely related Bantu languages. Of the remaining third, 15 per cent speak one of the Western Nilotic languages (Ateso, Karamojong, etc.). The Central Sudanic languages, Lugbara and Madi, are spoken by a combined total of only 5 per cent.

In looking at the country as a whole the important features to notice are that the largest language is spoken (as a first language) by only 16 per cent of the population, that no other language is spoken by more than half this number, that there are a large number of languages spoken by small but approximately equal numbers of people, and that there are at least three (if not four) language subgroups.

CLASSIFICATION OF LINGUISTIC COMPLEXITY

These figures, on their own, hide rather than illuminate the degree of multilingual complexity to be found in Uganda, I shall go on to consider the type and extent of multilingualism found at national, district, county, and sub-county levels, and the problems associated with it at each level. But before we can do this we need a way of classifying the degree of linguistic complexity at each of these levels.

One way of classifying administrative units is by examining whether there is a language which can be considered dominant, using the arbitrary criterion that the number of its speakers must be at least double that of any other language spoken in the unit. When there is no such language the unit can be classified as *mixed.* If there is a major language of this kind a further sub-division can be made into *simple* units, in which there are no substantial monority languages, and *predominant* units, in which there is a major language, but in which there are also one or more other languages, spoken by substantial minorities (here taken arbitrarily to be more that 10 per cent of the population of the unit). In this terminology Uganda as a whole is a mixed unit, Britain is an example of a simple unit, and Canada of a predominant unit. The reason for making these divisions is to show up the very different political and administrative problems that arise. Mixed units clearly have their own problems, and predominant units differ from simple units in that it is only if there is a substantial linguistic minority that any political pressures may be exerted to have a language other than that of the majority given official recognition in some way.

NATIONAL LEVEL

The figures that have been cited above reveal the linguistic complexity of Uganda as a whole. In terms of numbers, Luganda, alone of the indigenous languages, has any possible claim to primacy. But, as we have seen, politically it is not in favour. English remains the national language of Uganda, the language of all administration from the District level up; officially the language of all processes of law from the lowest court up; the language of all education from the senior levels of primary school through secondary school to University, of most technical or vocational training, e.g. nursing, secretarial, agricultural; the language of parliament; the language of public address by ministers and officials; and the language of most offices and businesses. It is, in fact, the lingua franca of the educated *élite*. There is not any apparent substantial opposition to the continued use of English as a national language, partly no doubt due to the entrenched interests of those who have already mastered the language and whose positions have largely derived from such mastery, but partly due also to the previously noted fact that there is no indigenous language except Luganda, which is widespread enough and developed to a stage whereby a concentrated effort could turn it into a national language.

The only language besides Luganda and English which can be considered important when looking at the nation as a whole is Swahili. Unlike Tanzania and Kenya, Swahili in Uganda has no official status at all, and is, if anything, slightly discouraged at a national level. For example, there is no broadcasting in Swahili, even though broadcasting is carried out in a total of eighteen languages. In 1927 Swahili was proposed as the official language of all three East African territories. Its introduction in Uganda in schools and elsewhere met widespread opposition. This opposition was particularly successful in Buganda, and the use of Swahili in schools in that region was soon abandoned. Elsewhere, in the North, it continued to be used for several years longer. The opposition to Swahili came from those who feared the domination of Kenya with its different economic and settler interests. The Baganda also saw Swahili as a threat to the spread and dominance of their own language. The lack of a European settler community requiring unskilled farm and plantation labour helped in the successful campaign against Swahili.

Knowledge of Swahili today varies from district to district and also from old to young. The Asian population in the towns and trading centres helped its spread among the uneducated and also in certain areas of employment dominated by them, e.g. the railways, in which Swahili is still widely used. In the Army, the Police, and the Prison Service Swahili was the main language and acted as a lingua franca among the many different language speakers found in the forces. Though Swahili is still taught to those joining those services, its role is threatened by English, as the qualifications for entry are raised, with the result that all new entrants are able to speak English.

The variety of Swahili spoken varies from one part of the country to another. In many parts it differs substantially from standard Swahili, and speakers of it are often unable to understand the Swahili broadcasts from Kenya and Tanzania. While in the context of Uganda alone Swahili cannot be considered, *at present*, as a viable alternative to English as a national

L

language, considering East Africa as a whole, the importance of Swahili as an inter-territorial language, as an East African Community language, cannot be over-estimated. Shifting the focus from a national level to this regional level shows a different degree of multilingualism which has to be taken into account in political decisions regarding language policies.

In considering national language policies, differences in religion must be taken into account. Approximately 60 per cent of adults in Uganda are either Roman Catholics or Protestants, with the former being slightly more numerous. But neither Catholic nor Protestant hierarchies have adopted a nation-wide language to be used in services or church affairs. Such matters are decided at the lower level of the diocese. Islam presents slightly more of a problem, even though the total number of African followers is only about 6 per cent of the population (concentrated mostly in Buganda, the Eastern Region, and in West Nile district in the extreme North-west). Their heavy commitment to the use and knowledge of Arabic at the expense of English means that with the rising educational qualifications required for most jobs Muslims are being left at the bottom of the occupational-status ladder. Their opposition is to secular education, and it is this which is symbolized by the use of English. Though at a local level there may be few problems of integration or few problems arising from non-integration, at a national level a future problem is being laid by a section of the community consciously rejecting both the means of economic advance and also the means of integrating with the remainder of the nation. This is, of course, not a problem unique to Uganda.

So far we have been considering national language policies. But policies also have to be developed concerning the role of the vernacular languages. The problems that arise in formulating and carrying out a vernacular language policy depend upon the degree of complexity, in linguistic terms, of the administrative units with which the Government Ministries most directly deal. These units are the Districts. They vary in size from 49,000 in Sebei to 661,000 in Busoga, with the mean size just under 400,000. They were established in colonial times, and, like the other administrative units, were made to coincide, as far as possible, with ethnic or tribal boundaries.

In the terminology we are using for describing linguistic complexity three of the eighteen districts can be classified as mixed, in that there is no single major language. Of the remaining fifteen districts, seven can be classified as simple, in that they have no substantial minority language spoken, and eight as predominant, in that they have a substantial minority language present in addition to the major language. These facts are summarized in Table 2.

Table 2

Linguistic Complexity within Uganda as a Whole

	Simple	*Predominant with*		*Mixed*	*Total*
		1 minority	*2 or more minorities*		
No. of Districts	7	—	8	3	18

It is with this situation in mind that the government ministries have to adopt some attitude towards the vernacular languages. A summary of the policies of various departments is given in Table 1. The Ministry of Education lays down an official policy with regard to the vernacular language to be used in the early stages of primary education prior to the introduction of English. There are six such designated languages, the number being limited in order to reduce overall expense and minimize restrictions on the posting of teachers between different areas. The price of this economy is that, for example, a Kakwa child may be taught in the very different language of Lugbara or a Sebei child in Luganda.

Adult literacy campaigns are organized by a different department and are carried out in a number of languages not used in primary education. Differences between the two approaches are obvious. In the first case children have little or no choice, it is their parents who largely decide and, both for them and their children, the prize to be won is command of English, not of the vernacular. In literacy campaigns adults have to be persuaded to undertake any extra work, and the attractions of minimizing this by keeping to their own completely familiar language are obvious. With the exception of Luganda, vernacular-language newspapers play a very small role in the dissemination of news. English-language papers have the greatest circulation and, by definition, they are read only by the most educated.

Broadcasting is carried out in eighteen languages. Here the conflict lies between achieving the maximum coverage of languages, and hence the greatest flow of information to those unable to understand English, and the necessity to economize and not spread the limited amount of broadcasting time too thinly.

DISTRICT ADMINISTRATION

With the exception of broadcasting, all the policies of the government ministries have to be put into effect either by the local district administrations or by the district representatives of the ministries. The district forms a crucial link between the Government and the general population.

With the recent constitutional changes all districts (the ex-Kingdoms included) have been placed on an equal basis and are considered not as semi-autonomous administrations but as agents of the Government. The District Commissioner is the Government's principal agent in the district. He has the ultimate responsibility for maintaining law and order; he is responsible for ensuring that the District Administration does not act outside government policies as prescribed by law, and that its finances are properly run; he acts as a co-ordinator of all the government departments represented in the district, together with the D.A. in planning development.

Unlike the District Commissioner, the Secretary-General of the district is primarily a politician and, in theory, holds a similar position *vis-à-vis* the District Administration as a minister to his ministry. The task of detailed administration is carried out by the Administrative Secretary and his staff acting under the general directions of the Secretary General and the District Council. This latter body is composed of a number of elected (or, at present, appointed) members from each county within the district, who together act as an advisory body, without individually having any executive powers. Executive powers run from the Administrative Secretary down through his headquarters staff to appointed county chiefs, thence to sub-county and parish chiefs. All the chiefs are local, salaried, government employees, whose job it is to carry out orders issued by the District Administration and to ensure the proper administration of their area.

It is at the district level that many of the language problems are seen most acutely. All senior officers of the government departments represented in the district will be English speaking, and all administration within their departments will be carried out in English. These officers may be posted anywhere in the country, so many will not know the local language. (A major complaint that is often heard from such officials is that when they move their families around with them on successive postings their children are forced to attend schools where the teaching is being carried out in different vernaculars so that their progress is impeded.) All district administration working within the Headquarters will also be English speaking, so that there is no difficulty of communication at this level.

At lower levels of government departments problems of appointments begin to apply. This is particularly true in the case of the service ministries. The main task of the Forestry section of the Ministry of Agriculture and Co-operatives in West Nile district is the planting and care of the forest plantations. This is largely a technical matter, and the amount of contact or communications between forestry employees and the general public is minimal. In the Co-operative Development section, by contrast, the task of educating local farmers in the reasons for and ways of organizing co-operatives is paramount. The gap between the educated English-speaking official and the non-educated local-language-speaking farmers is at its greatest. Though senior district co-operative officials can use interpreters when visiting areas within their district, such a procedure would be impossible for junior staff, who are expected to be in constant touch with the people in their charge. This leads to the necessity of appointing junior staff to their own language areas, or accepting a very low rate of information transfer. A 'simple' district suffers much less, since local employees will all speak the same language and can be cross-posted within the district. It is also feasible to produce educational materials, such as posters and handouts, in a single language.

Similar problems of appointments occur within the District Administration over the appointment of county chiefs. Their function is both to act as the executive agent for the District Administration and also to be the focal point of information flowing downwards from the Government and upwards from the sub-chiefs and the people in their areas. One or other of these functions may be impaired according to the policy carried out in each district. On the one hand, if county chiefs are appointed in counties in which they cannot speak the predominant language their major communicative function is automatically impaired. If, on the other hand, chiefs are posted only within their own language area the freedom of the District Administration to move the right man to the right place is severely curtailed. Districts have followed different policies. Some have balanced numbers of chiefs appointed from the different ethnic groups within the district, but, ignoring the language problem, have posted them to any county within the district. Others have restricted the appointment of particular chiefs to areas in which they can speak the local language (though it may not necessarily be their first language). Similar examples could be multiplied, since this is a recurrent problem for almost all government departments. The extent of the problem in Uganda can be seen by looking at Table 3, showing the degree of multilingualism when looked at from the district level.

Table 3

Linguistic Complexity within Districts

	Simple	*Predominant with*		*Mixed*	*Total*
		1 minority	*2 or more minorities*		
No. of counties	69 (64%)	25 (24%)	6 (6%)	5 (5%)	105 (100%)
No. of counties with majority lg different from majority lg of district	10 (14%)	3 (10%)		2 (40%)	15 (14%)

Using the same criteria as with districts, 64 per cent of the counties in Uganda are classed as 'simple', that is they have a single dominant language with no substantial minority language; 30 per cent have a 'predominant' language but with one or more minority languages, and only 5 per cent are classed as 'mixed'. A statement of this kind hides part of the administrative complexity, for the problem to the administrator lies as much in counties which have a dominant language which is *different* from the dominant language of the district as a whole. While only five of the counties are 'mixed', fifteen (or 14 per cent of the total) have a language different from the majority language of the district as a whole. In an otherwise linguistically homogeneous district the presence of even a single 'different' county is likely to lead to political troubles if no account is taken of the linguistic and cultural differences.

A comparison can be made between the situation in Teso District, where there are 80 per cent Iteso and 12 per cent Kumam, and that in West Mengo, where there are only 60 per cent of the dominant Baganda compared with the Banyaruanda minority of 12 per cent. In Teso district the Kumam are concentrated within one county, in which they form the majority, whereas in West Mengo the Banyaruanda are spread throughout the district, and hence their language forms no rival to Luganda. In Teso, on the other hand, even though the number of Ateso speakers is proportionately greater, the demand for recognition of Kumam in education and administration is considerable, with resultant political strain.

COUNTY

Each county has an appointed chief as the principal representative of the District Administration. He has under him a number of headquarters staff, e.g. clerks, askaris, and is responsible for tax collection, for passing on information and orders received from the District Administration, and for transmitting back intelligence on the situation within his area. In addition to him and his staff, the District Administration employs numbers of people in local prisons, road maintenance, in dispensaries, etc.

There is no fixed qualification for appointment to chief, and hence educational background and knowledge of English vary widely from district to district and county to county. Many, if not the majority, of chiefs do not have a command of English. Correspondence between District Headquarters and County Headquarters is in English. The clerks at the county level are all, by definition, English speaking and may be required to translate correspondence into the vernacular. There is a move to raise the formal qualifications necessary for the post of chief so that over a period of years it is likely that all county and sub-county chiefs will have sufficient knowledge of English to deal not only with correspondence and notices in English but also with all the visiting government officials, whose only lingua franca is English.

Some correspondence to sub-county chiefs initiated from the District headquarters may be written in one of the 'official' district languages if it is imperative to avoid misunderstandings. Also some public notices of forthcoming visits or of job vacancies may be sent out to the county chiefs written in both English and the 'official' district language or languages. For example, in West Nile only Lugbara and Alur are recognized as 'official' languages in the district, and the other two substantial minority languages, Kakwa and Madi, are not used. In Bukedi, another 'mixed' district, Luganda is recognized as the official district language, even though it contains counties where Nilotic languages predominate.

At the county level the problems seem to arise more out of the fact that it is at this level that competence in the administrative language of the *élite* fades out, rather than out of the degree of linguistic complexity encompassed within the county. Sixty per cent of the total number of sub-counties are 'simple' (see Table 4 below). Of the remainder, one-third have a dominant language and only 7 per cent are 'mixed'. These proportions are very similar to those of the counties, but where they differ is in the number of sub-counties which have a majority language different from the majority language of the county. In only 4 per cent of the total is this found. In other words, there is even less problem of administrative complexity within the counties than within the district.

Table 4
Linguistic Complexity within Counties

	Simple	*Predominant with* *1 minority*	*Predominant with* *2 or more minorities*	*Mixed*	*Total*
No. of sub-counties	355 (61%)	146 (25%)	46 (8%)	39 (7%)	586 (100%)
No. of sub-counties with majority lg different from majority lg of county	3 (1%)	9 (3%)		12 (32%)	24 (4%)

SUB-COUNTY AND PARISH

Administration reaches down as far as sub-county and parish in the appointment of chiefs and officials. At these lowest levels the proportion of English speakers drops and traditional relationships between nearby or neighbouring ethnic groups play a greater role in determining the pattern of multilingualism; thus the Lendu minority are mostly bilingual in Lendu and Alur, the dominant language of the county, whereas comparatively few Alur understand the Lendu speakers in their midst. It is at this level that the degree of individual rural bilingualism is determined.

TOWNS

Towns have not been considered in this survey. In part, this reflects the overall predominance of the rural over the urban, with the consequence that the problems associated with urbanization have barely been felt. It is also partly due to the fact that with the exception of Kampala and Jinja the towns are primarily administrative and trading centres serving the districts in which they are situated. They tend to reflect the linguistic problems of the districts themselves. There is no space to discuss here the composition of such towns, their residential pattern, and the degree of multilingualism found in them.

CONCLUSION

In order to describe the degree of multilingualism in Uganda, it has been necessary to examine a number of levels of political and administrative organization. At each level it is possible to describe the degree of linguistic complexity and the resultant diglossia and individual bilingualism that is found. Conversely, in formulating language policies it is necessary to consider the method by which they will be carried out, which is itself constrained by the administrative organization of the country. While the Ugandan Government can consider the relative merits of English, Swahili, and Luganda as a national language throughout the country as a whole, it must take into account the linguistic complexity of the districts in formulating a vernacular language policy which is consistent throughout the various ministries. Only in this way can problems of economy and ease of communication be balanced against political pressures exerted by minority groups within the framework of district administration.

VIII. Tanzania's National Language Policy and the Rise of Swahili Political Culture

M. H. ABDULAZIZ

The political decision to adopt Swahili as the national and official language of Tanzania has created linguistic and socio-linguistic trends with few parallels in the rest of Africa. Notwithstanding the radical nature of this decision, the choice will be found to be a logical one when viewed in the context of Tanzania's political and social history and her modern political thought. Various historical, political, religious, and socio-cultural factors precipitated a linguistic situation which favoured the emergence of Swahili as an acceptable national language. This paper attempts to make a synoptic review of these factors and a broad examination of the linguistic implications arising from the choice of this language.

Tanzania is a large territory comprising 362,688 sq. miles. Except for urban centres and half a dozen or so regional areas of high densities of population, most of the country is sparsely populated, with large tracts of land almost bare of habitation. This geographical fact has always facilitated population movements, with consequent shifts in the linguistic situation. Even within this century, population splits and new groupings have occurred caused by such phenomena as population increases, famine, growth of urban centres and rural settlements, a state of affairs that has favoured the growth of a lingua franca, in this case Swahili.

Bantu languages of East Africa, of which Swahili is one, are very closely related with comparable structural organization at all the linguistic levels (a notable exception is absence of lexically significant tones in Swahili and a few other languages of this area). In addition, they have a large core of common basic vocabulary. This, together with comparable cultural systems, have given rise to a high degree of isomorphous semantic structuring which makes it easy for a speaker of one Bantu language to learn another language of this family, and even develop native speakers' competence in it. Acceptance of Swahili to a large extent is due to the fact that it can be learnt easily and even used creatively by speakers of other mother-tongues.

In Tanzania today there are over a hundred mother-tongue groups.[1] The biggest mother-tongue group are the Bantu-speaking Wasukuma, who number over one million. The number of speakers of other groups vary considerably, the smallest being those with less than one thousand native speakers.

The language situation is a very complex one. Very little research has been done as to what objectively constitute languages and what are dialects.[2] Language continuum is most evident in this Bantu area. Present institutionalized names of languages would seem not to be based on any scientific criteria. Some of them are comparatively recent names, and by no means the original names of the languages as known by the speakers. Kinyamwezi and Kisukuma, two of the biggest mother-tongue groups, provide a good illustration of the difficulties involved in deciding what constitute languages and language communities.[3] These two languages are closely related, and mutual intelligibility between them is very high. However, within each group are dialects which are much less mutually intelligible among themselves than they are with the neighbouring dialects of the other group. For example, the Kikadama dialect of Kisukuma is much more closely related to the Kinyamwezi dialects around Nzega than it is to such Kisukuma dialects as Kinyantuzu, spoken around Musoma.

[1] Mother-tongue group here is defined as a group of people who presently consider themselves, and are considered by others, as speakers of the same mother-tongue or first language. A mother-tongue group is normally associated with a particular geographical area and is thought to comprise members of the same ethno-cultural origin. More than 90 per cent of Tanzanians speak a Bantu language as their mother tongue.

[2] It is hoped that the results of the forthcoming survey of Language Use and Language Teaching in Tanzania will throw some light on this situation.

[3] Kinyamwezi is the name given to the group of dialects spoken in Unyamwezi proper, which includes the districts of Tabora, Nzega, and Kahama. Kisukuma comprises a dialect cluster found in Kwimba, Maswa, Mwanza Shinyanga, and Geita.

The Wasukuma themselves did not have one single tribal name for the clans inhabiting the districts of Shinyanga, Maswa, Kwimba, Mwanza, and Geita before the arrival of the European colonialists and missionaries. Consequently there was no single name for the cluster of dialects that include Kigwe, Kinyantuzu, Kiya, and Kinangweli, which today comprise Kisukuma. Furthermore, among the large groups of clans who today are divided into the Wasukuma and the Wanyamwezi, group names were often directional.

The Wanyamwezi called their neighbours to the north the Basukuma (northerners), from which the language name Kisukuma is derived. Within the Wasukuma, groups in the two districts of Mwanza and Geita are generally known as Banangweli (people from the West); those south of the present-day Sukumaland in the district of Kahama are known as Badakama (southerners). Incidentally the northern Wasukuma would regard the Badakama as more of Wanyamwezi than Wasukuma because of the way they speak, while the southern Wanyamwezi would consider the Badakama as Wasukuma for the same reason.

The foregoing is meant to emphasize the fact that demarcation between languages is often not clear. Also in several instances there is no clear-cut congruence between language and tribe, a point which may have some relevance to questions of language loyalties and resistance to linguistic shifts.

The growth of Swahili as a Tanzanian language is closely linked with the historical development of this country as a nation state. During European penetration of the interior of Tanganyika such auxiliaries as soldiers, teachers, policemen, guides, interpreters, junior administrative officers (*Liwalis* and *Akidas*) were Swahili, or Swahili-speaking Tanganyikans from other mother-tongue groups. This had the effect of further spreading the language and giving it a new prestige status as the language of administration, education, and modernity. For example, as early as the end of the nineteenth century, Pare[1] people were sending their sons to stations on the plains situated on the caravan routes to learn Swahili.[2] In some areas

[1] An area comprising the Pare Mountains, situated in the highlands of north-eastern Tanzania.

[2] 'Makenga, an influential man in the chiefdom of Usangi (Northern Pare), during early German rule sent his son Mashauri Makenga to the Sambaa settle-

there were cases of chiefs being deposed by the Germans because they did not speak Swahili. This policy of using Swahili in the lower levels of administration and in the field of education was continued during British rule.

European missionaries, too, played an important part in the spread of Swahili. The Universities Missionary to Central Africa (U.M.C.A.), for example, started using Swahili as far back as the 1890s. The reason for using this language was partly historical, their first mission centres being established in the coastal areas of Tanga and Zanzibar.[1] Most of their Letargic Books and religious hymns were written in Swahili. They even started Swahili religious newspapers and prepared a Swahili–English Dictionary. In fact what is considered as the first ever newspaper in Tanzania was in Swahili published in 1895 at Magila by the U.M.C.A.[2] It was called *Habari ya Mwezi* and contained articles of both religious and secular content. In 1908 the newspaper had its first African editor in Samwil Sehoza. The Lutheran Church, too, put an emphasis on Swahili and used it as the language of instruction in their schools. Another important religious body whose official policy was to use Swahili both in their schools and as the language of religious instruction was the German Benedictine Church. This Church was influential over the whole of southern Tanganyika. The White Fathers on their part encouraged the use of Swahili in their churches, especially those around Mbeya and near Lake Tanganyika. However, in the Lake provinces around Bukoba, Mwanza, and Musoma their policy was to use the vernacular languages. Today it would seem to be the

---

ment of Lembeni so that he could learn Swahili. The boy lived there for five years and learnt to speak and write Swahili fluently. This enabled him to be appointed first as interpreter for the German officials and later as *akida* (administrative officer) at the Moshi Boma to assist with the administration of North Pare area.' Reported by Dr. I. N. Kimambo of the History Department, University College, Dar es Salaam, who got the information from Mashauri Makenga himself on 27 September 1965. Mashauri Makenga is believed to be still living, in his late eighties.

[1] In 1894 a student, Yohana Abdalla, from the U.M.C.A. St. Andrews College, Kiungani Zanzibar, wrote to Isobel Hall saying: 'We are so many boys in this house, and of different tribes, Yaos, Makuas, Bondeis, and Nyasas; but we all speak Swahili language.' Yohana Abdalla to Isobel Hall, 2 January 1894, U.M.C.A. A/5.

[2] Another newspaper published by the U.M.C.A. in Swahili was *Pwani Na Bara*.

policy of most churches in Tanzania to use Swahili wherever they can.

One of the arguments put forward for the adoption of Swahili as the Church language was that it would provide an inter-tribal integrative factor that would help to build the new community of Christians, just as it had done for Islam. There was also the argument that Swahili already possessed a comprehensive Islamic theological vocabulary that could be well adapted and used to expound the Christian faith. There was also the practical consideration that if Swahili were used throughout the country it would greatly facilitate the transfer of teachers and missionaries to different mother-tongue areas; also that it would reduce the heavy load and the cost of translating the Bible into all the vernacular languages. Furthermore, Swahili was already being used by the Government as a language of Administration. Those who argued for the use of the vernaculars maintained that the Christian message would be properly understood only if it were taught in the mother-tongue. Of course, conversion to Islam often meant total assimilation to Swahili language and culture. Thus outside agents that tended to disintegrate tribal organization frequently paved the way for the diffusion of Swahili.

Swahili has played a very significant role in the development of political values and attitudes in Tanzania. Its integrative qualities have influenced the style of Tanzania politics, especially its non-tribal and egalitarian characteristics. All movements of national focus have used Swahili as an instrument for achieving inter-tribal unity and integration. The Maji Maji War of 1905–7 against German colonial rule drew its support from different mother-tongue speakers who already possessed a rallying force in Swahili. Other movements of national appeal which took advantage of the existence of a common Tanzanian language were the Tanganyika Territory Civil Servants Association (T.T.C.S.A.), founded in Tanga in 1922; the African Welfare and Commercial Association (A.W.C.A.), which was founded in Dar es Salaam in 1934 and aimed at looking after the interests of African traders; the Tanganyika African Association (T.A.A.), and T.A.N.U. The T.T.C.S.A. had a Swahili newspaper called *Kwetu*, which circulated between 1937 and 1952. The T.A.A., a territory-wide political movement which many people would consider as the fore-runner of T.A.N.U. did most of their organization in Swahili and had their constitution in this language. An illustration of the part Swahili played in T.A.A. political organization is provided by an incident that happened in 1947 during their annual meeting, which that year was being held in Zanzibar. Delegates from all parts of Tanganyika had attended the meeting. The Chairman made his introductory address in English, whereupon a number of delegates protested and demanded that the speech be translated into Swahili. It was no other than Shaaban Robert[1] who was asked to translate the address. From that incident it was agreed that all future T.A.A. meetings should be conducted wholly in Swahili.

It has been the policy of T.A.N.U.,[2] the present ruling party, right from the start to encourage the use and spread of Swahili. It is said that only on a few occasions during the whole of the T.A.N.U. independence campaign did Nyerere, the then party President, use interpreters in vernacular languages. The Policy of the Party and the Government has consistently been one of making Swahili an essential component of Tanzanian identity and culture. Swahili was declared the national language soon after self-government in 1961. From then onwards the Tanzanian Government has taken practical steps towards developing Swahili into a workable modern language for the nation.

A landmark in the history of the development of Swahili as the official language of Tanzania was the Republic Day speech of 10 December 1962 which President Nyerere delivered in Swahili. In it he declared that he had formed the new Ministry of Youth and Culture so that greater attention could be paid to the development of national culture. The following is an extract from that speech:[3]

'The major change I have made is to get up an entirely new Ministry: the Ministry of National Culture and Youth. I have done this because I believe that its culture is the essence and spirit of any nation. A country which lacks its own culture is no more than a

[1] The well-known Tanzanian writer and poet. He died in 1962.
[2] TANU was founded on 7 July 1954.
[3] Nyerere, 1966, p. 186, columns 37 and 38.

collection of people without the spirit which makes them a nation. Of all the crimes of colonialism there is none worse than the attempt to make us believe we had no indigenous culture of our own; or that what we did have was worthless—something of which we should be ashamed, instead of a source of pride'.

The fact that the President had delivered his Parliamentary speech in Swahili made a very big impact on the House. Commenting on the President's use of Swahili Sheikh Amri Abedi, himself on this occasion speaking in Swahili, told the house:[1]

an unprecedented thing that happened on that day was that His Excellency delivered his speech in Swahili. That moment was truly the beginning of a new era in the history of the development of this country in the fields of language, national development and the running of the affairs of the government . . . . Today we have been given the freedom to talk in our own language. We shall now enter the field of discussion with confidence, with no doubt as to the real meaning of what we are saying, nor, whether we are being correctly understood by others. . . .

In 1964 the post of Promoter for Swahili was created within the Ministry of Community Development and National Culture. Already a number of bodies and individuals dealing with Swahili were functioning. Notable among these were the University College Institute of Swahili Research, the Swahili Poets Association (parent organization to the present nation-wide *Usanifu wa Kiswahili na Ushairi Tanzania—Ukuta*), and *Jumuiya ya Kustawisha Kiswahili*. The Ministry of Education had its own group called the Swahili Committee which interested itself in Swahili teaching materials and organizing syllabuses. The function of the Promoter was not only to co-ordinate the work of the various Swahili groups in the country, but more importantly to disseminate the fruits of research and other language activities among the masses of the people in Tanzania. Cultural matters were to be made the interest and concern of the whole nation, and not only small groups of people or individuals.

[1] Sheikh Amri Abedi was a Swahili scholar and poet. He was then Minister of Community Development and Culture. He died in 1964. See Tanganyika Parliamentary Debates (*Hansard*), sitting from 10 December 1962 to 16 February 1963, Government Printer, Dar es Salaam, 1963, columns 37 and 38.

The people were to be fully involved because culture meant the culture of the people, the overwhelming majority of whom were peasants and workers.

The Promoter for Swahili was also charged with the task of setting up Swahili groups in the rural and urban areas, and among the workers in such places as factories. In June 1966 an *ad hoc* Committee was set up to review and widen the activities of the Swahili Youth Festival, hitherto limited to school participants. The Committee succeeded in encouraging workers in factories to write their own plays in Swahili and enter the competition. The workers succeeded in producing some of the best plays of the competition. Interest in cultural matters among the broad masses of people in Tanzania is growing. There are now regular literary and other cultural competitions which peasants and workers take great interest in.

The fundamental nature of this egalitarian-centred interpretation of culture cannot be overemphasized. In Black Africa many people would equate culture with the intellectual and material development of the small urban *élite*, whose way of life may have little in common, if anything, with the rest of the population. African literature, a term widely used to refer to literature written by Africans in such languages as English, French, and Portuguese, is still literature by the European educated *élite* aimed at readers who can read and understand material in these languages. Today in Tanzania there is great interest in writing prose, plays, and poetry in Swahili. Much of such writing is done by people who have received little or no formal education in European languages.

An immediate problem created by the Government's policy of encouraging the use of Swahili in the conduct of official business was the problem of finding Swahili words for concepts and terms that have been hitherto expressed in English. From the date of Independence up to 1965[1] a lot of new words and terms were introduced into Swahili; many of these were random fomulations, so heavy was the pressure on the departments to Swahilize the communication medium. So a main concern of the

[1] In December 1965 a conference in Nairobi organized by the East African Institute of Culture and Social Affairs passed a resolution urging East African Governments to adopt specific language policies. See East African Heritage Monograph No. 4.

Swahili promotion section was to lay down the procedure to be followed in adopting new words. The first step was to look deep into Swahili itself to see if there were old or obsolete terms that could be reviewed or given a new shade of meaning. Failing this, recourse was to be had to other Bantu languages. As a result of this policy a number of words from other Bantu languages are being added to Swahili. Notable of these words are *bunge* (parliament)—from Kisambaa and related languages meaning—a meeting-place; *ikulu* (Presidential Palace or State House)—a Bantu word used widely for a Chief's residence; *ngonjera* (poetry-reading drama)—another widely used Bantu word meaning social performances with instructive function.

The third source to be used was Arabic, the traditional borrowing ground for Swahili. Words borrowed from Arabic were to be fully Swahilized in their phonological form. The next source was to be English; again the words were to be fully Swahilized. In the event of failure to get an English term which could be suitably Swahilized, then a completely new term was to be created. An example of such a new coinage, which does not seem to have caught on, was *jokofu* for 'refrigerator', a word that is made up of the two morphemes *joko* (stove) and *fu* (dead-cold).

Early in 1967 Second-Vice President Kawawa declared that Swahili was to be used at all times and in all government and other national businesses wherever it was possible and convenient to do so, that is wherever this would not adversely affect efficiency in Tanzania. English would continue to be used as a secondary official language to supplement Swahili, especially in functions where the latter language still needed developing. To put into effect the above resolution an inter-Ministerial Swahili Committee was formed (under the Chairmanship of the Principal Secretary, Ministry of Community Development and National Culture), to accelerate the formation of technical terms to be used and also to prepare the *Government Directory* in Swahili. The first part of the *Directory* came out in May 1967.

An important step that the Government has taken in its efforts to promote the development and usage of Swahili in the country is the setting up of the National Swahili Council. The Council was established by an Act of Parliament in

August 1967. The Act spells out the functions of the Council as:

(*a*) to promote the development and usage of the Swahili language throughout the United Republic;

(*b*) to co-operate with other bodies in the United Republic which are concerned to promote the Swahili language and to endeavour to co-ordinate their activities;

(*c*) to encourage the use of the Swahili language in the conduct of official business and public life generally;

(*d*) to encourage the achievement of high standards in the use of the Swahili language and to discourage its misuse;

(*e*) to co-operate with the authorities concerned in establishing standard Swahili translations of technical terms;

(*f*) to publish a Swahili newspaper or magazine concerned with the Swahili language and literature;

(*g*) to provide services to the Government, public authorities and individual authors writing in Swahili with respect to the Swahili language.

The present policies of socialism, egalitarianism, and self-reliance enunciated by the Arusha Declaration[1] and the other policy-making statements are creating conditions that will further entrench the use of Swahili in the different spheres of national life. The Declaration states that T.A.N.U. must be 'a Party of Peasants and Workers and that it is necessary for the government to be elected and led by Peasants and Workers.' Already the ruling Party draws most of its support and leadership from the broad masses of the people. Knowledge of a European language is not a necessary qualification for leadership. On the other hand, good knowledge of Swahili is essential for those who want to participate fully in the national life of the country.

But perhaps of all the linguistic conditions that tend to favour the growth of Swahili as a modern language, none is so far-reaching as the decision to make it the language of instruction throughout primary education. This decision has had the immediate effect of making new demands on the language. New Primary School books covering such subjects as science, mathematics, and geography are now produced in Swahili.

[1] The Arusha Declaration was made on 5 February 1967.

Scientific and technical terms are being added to the language all the time. The majority are Swahili terms, either existing words used with greater precision to express scientific concepts or translations from English. Some of the new technical terms are loans from English or Arabic. Together with the development of this school technical vocabulary is the growth of new structures to handle scientific statements. Swahili, like most other African languages, is not well developed in the scientific register, and any trends that would help development along these lines would be most welcome.

Apart from the purely educational consideration of the efficiency of teaching children in a medium they have good control of, the new policies on the purpose of Primary education would demand the use of the national language as the medium of learning.

A quotation from the Government's blue-print on education entitled *Education for Self-reliance* will give some idea of the place of Swahili in the educational system of Tanzania:

> But even if this suggestion were based on provable fact, it could not be allowed to over-ride the need for change in the direction of educational integration with our national life. For the majority of our people the thing which matters is that they should be able to read and write fluently in Swahili, that they should have an ability to do arithmetic, and that they should know something of the history, values, and working of their country and their government, and that they should acquire the skills necessary to earn their living. (It is important to stress that in Tanzania most people will earn their living by working on their own or on a communal *shamba*, and only a few will do so by working for wages which they have to spend on buying things the farmer produces for himself.) Things like health, science, geography, and the beginning of English are also important, especially so that the people who wish may be able to learn more by themselves in later life. But most important of all is that our primary school graduates should be able to fit into, and to serve, the communities from which they come.

Education (in its formal and broad sense) and culture are considered most vital to the building of a new Tanzania. Education must 'nationalize' the children and give them a sense of common cultural identity compatible with the national ethos. It was not surprising therefore when it was announced last September that the Department of National Culture hitherto functioning in the Ministry of Regional Administration and Rural Development was now to be put under one Ministry with Education. Commenting on this move, the T.A.N.U. National Executive Secretary said:

> The Party feels that the young generation must be tempered with genuine national values, and side by side with academic studies the youths should absorb their national culture which is the totality of these values.[1]

Today about 90 per cent of the people in Tanzania have had contact with Swahili and speak it with varying degree of intensity and control. Degree and type of bilingualism (here defined as a linguistic situation involving the mother-tongue and Swahili) varies with different mother-tongue areas and individuals, making broad categorization difficult.[2] But certain general patterns are observable. In the urban areas, in the national institutions, such as schools, national service camps, army and police barracks, and along transport routes Swahili is the primary language. In the rural areas the extent of bilingualism varies from place to place. At the one extreme there are areas in which Swahili and the mother-tongue are both primary languages in the sense that they are spoken interchangeably. In such situations the functions of the two languages overlap considerably. The two languages are freely mixed, tolerance to language shift being very high. Examples of such areas are the rural suburbs of towns like Moshi, Tabora, Songea.

At the other extreme there are rural places where the vernacular is the predominant (and in a few cases exclusive)

[1] Party newspaper, *The Nationalist*, 12 September 1968. Addressing the Advisory Council on Education, Dar es Salaam, the new Minister of Education and National Culture reiterated the above theme:

> 'The function of my Ministry is to create the organizational framework in which a socialist education can thrive, to stimulate and publicise ideas for new projects and to provide teachers and teaching materials that they have been trained to use more successfully. . . . We need financial aid, but can accept only that which does not force us to compromise our political principles. We need technical manpower assistance but must reject programmes that will promote the cultural values of other societies.' *The Nationalist*, Tuesday, 22 October 1968.

[2] The actual linguistic situation is very much more complex. Many individuals are multilingual in Tanzania languages, and some may also have English in their language repertoire.

language of day-to-day communication. Notable of these are the rural areas of the West Lake Region and Sukumaland. Between these two extremes the general pattern in the rural areas is that the mother-tongue functions as the primary and Swahili as the secondary language.

Family and individual bilingualism correlates with the educational background and degree of urbanness of the people concerned. The greater the amount of schooling an individual has had in Tanzania the greater would his proficiency in Swahili be likely to be.

Children in the large urban areas, if bilingual at all (that is if not monolingual in Swahili), would still have Swahili as their primary language. In the rural areas the degree of bilingualism of children below school age would correspond to the linguistic situation at home and the neighbourhood environment. The situation changes when children start to go to school. Swahili is the medium of instruction and, generally, the primary playground language. Most children would have had contact with Swahili before they went to school. But extreme cases do exist where children have absolutely no knowledge of the language on the first day of their arrival at school, especially in the West Lake Region. However, such children learn Swahili very quickly, and by the end of the second term of their first year at school they would have learned enough of the language to follow instructions without difficulty.

Children from deep rural areas often do not realize before going to school that they are speaking or mixing up two different languages. This is due to absence of such sociocultural correlates as would mark one form of speech with a particular racial or mother-tongue group. Moreover, tolerance to language shift and mixing is often high and involves the whole community. At school there is the least tolerance to language shift, and children are at once made aware of the fact that there are two separate languages involved.

Swahili plays such a predominant role in the children's school life that before they leave primary school they have achieved perfect control of the language. Mother-tongue interference often persists, and is most noticeable in the variant qualities of phonemes and in intonation. Otherwise the new generation of schoolchildren would seem to have native competence in their control of Swahili. This tendency is giving rise to new dialects of Swahili that correspond roughly to the mother-tongue divisions. One of the main tasks of the National Swahili Council and other language-planning agencies would be codification of Swahili so that a standard form continues to be recognized and accepted. At the moment there is a more or less uniform system called standard Swahili which is manifested in school books, newspapers, radio broadcasting, official notices, and the Parliamentary *Hansard*.

An extra-linguistic factor which has given Swahili its great assimilating power in East Africa is its Bantu-based culture. Original Swahili culture in the coastal and island settlements grow as a result of continued contact between Bantu and Arab–Islamic Cultures. The Arab–Islamic component did not superimpose itself but rather acted as a strong cultural stimulus. Bantu culture responded well to this external stimulus and adapted itself over centuries to emerge as an urban form of local African culture. Early historians writing about the East African coast often underplayed, and in some cases even denied, the African initiative in the formation of this literate urban culture. Yet it was precisely this indigenous base which gave Swahili culture its assimilating qualities whenever it came into contact with other local cultures in East Africa. Being a product of the environment, it could easily be adapted in other areas, and was therefore almost imperceptibly assimilated.

Swahili culture has greatly influenced regional cultures in Tanzania. In turn, regional cultures have in many ways enriched Swahili culture. The result of this bidirectional influence is the gradual emergence in Tanzania of a national culture which is a true synthesis of the various cultures of the country. Strikingly similar patterns of behaviour are emerging throughout the country, and especially among schoolchildren. Swahili language is an important component of this national culture as well as its bearer. The language is therefore not just a vehicular lingua franca. It is an important factor for establishing cultural, social, and political values among its interlocutors. Today in Tanzania, and indeed the rest of East Africa, there is no serious alternative to Swahili as a basis of intertribal integration. No other tribal language in East Africa is likely to be accepted with less resistance over the whole area. Besides,

Swahili is the most developed of the local East African languages as a modern vehicle of expression, and the one receiving the greatest amount of international attention. English, potentially an alternative national language in Tanzania and the rest of East Africa, is still spoken by a very small percentage of the population. And even this small percentage have learnt it outside its cultural context to use it as an effective basis for expressing social and cultural values. In the colonial days English was learnt in the most formal circumstances: in schools, offices, shops, and inter-racial communication. There was rigid racial compartmentalization, and informal social intercourse between Africans and speakers of English was very rare. Perhaps as a consequence English has not so far provided a basis for integration in Tanzania or the rest of East Africa, neither among African speakers of different tribes nor between the different races. In fact, Western culture has tended to be isolative where it succeeded in implanting itself directly on African culture. Those who aspired to wholly imbue Western culture during the colonial days did so in order to attain a semblance of identity with the rulers. It often meant psychological and physical rejection of indigenous cultural values, and adoption of what was termed 'black European' mentality.

However, English as a language has still a very important function in the national life of Tanzania. The importance of English as a language of science, technology, higher learning in general, international trade, and communication is well recognized. In the educational system of Tanzania it still plays a vital role. It is a subject in Primary schools, and the medium of learning in Secondary schools and higher institutions of learning, including the University. It is also the main language of Banking and Commerce. It is used generally as the secondary or supplementary official language, especially in areas in which Swahili may not yet be in a developed enough position to function as efficiently. Division of roles between the two official languages is by no means clear-cut at the moment, and there is a great deal of overlapping of functions. But it would seem that in many areas English will progressively yield its function to Swahili, until such times as the two languages reach a more stable relationship.

CONCLUSION

In this paper an attempt was made to outline the background to the present language policies in Tanzania. (The word policies here is not meant to imply a formalized explicit theory governing a course of conduct on matters of language. Rather it refers to explicit statements and trends of events that have a direct bearing on the language situation.)

The paper discussed the main historical, socio-cultural, political, and linguistic factors that have favoured the diffusion of Swahili and its wide acceptance as the national language. Apart from its linguistic advantages over the other local languages, Swahili has the virtue of not being associated with any single politically powerful group. In spite of the natural inclination of the mother-tongue groups to use the vernacular when they are talking among themselves, there is a remarkable absence of clash of linguistic loyalties. There has not been any organized resistance to the adoption of Swahili. On the contrary, the existence of this comparatively well-developed inter-mother-tongue national language is generally considered a blessing in a contemporary Africa where tribal and national aspirations often clash. Swahili political culture in Tanzania has brought about a situation where mother-tongue sentiments have a harmonious inclusive relationship with the aspirations to build a new Tanzanian nation with an identifiable culture and ethos.

The very wide use of Swahili in the national life of Tanzania today has created natural linguistic conditions for the language to develop as a modern system of communication. Modern cultural, economic, and political terminologies and concepts are being added all the time and find a smooth entrance into usage. Swahili is also making it possible for the peasants and workers who might not have had formal education to take a full and active part in the political leadership of their country. The freedom and opportunity that a common native language such as Swahili gives are great, especially in the context of Black African countries, in which the more common situation is to have only a European language as official.

Swahili is coping well with the expanding demands of the nation. There has not been observable inefficiency caused by the wide use of Swahili as the primary language of official business, the forces, and Parliamentary debates. In fact, the standard of debating in Parliament has improved considerably, as people now speak with much greater spontaneity and confidence. In at least one part of Tanzania, that is Zanzibar, Swahili is the only official language.

The future of Swahili seems to be bright. The Government is determined to improve it at all levels. The Ministry of Education treats as very urgent the problems of improving Swahili teaching methods, and the production of Swahili teaching materials. In the Ministry's Institute of Education a group of trained staff are working on the production of Swahili science and mathematical texts, and on devising new methods of teaching in Swahili. At the University College Dar es Salaam the Department of Language and Linguistics already offers a B.A. Optional Course in Swahili Literature for students of Language and Linguistics, Literature, and Theatre Arts. This course is taught in Swahili. The plan to start a new B.A. course in Swahili and Linguistics as from the next academic year has already been approved. This course will include the study of Swahili structure, usage, literature (Old and Modern), the history of the development of the language and problems of codification and elaboration, and Swahili dialects. The Institute of Swahili Research which is to be incorporated into the Faculty of Arts will, it is hoped interest itself, *inter alia*, with the production of Swahili dictionaries for schools and the general public, a children's encyclopaedia, school materials, and the general promotion of Swahili research.

REFERENCES

Abrahams, R. G.
(1967) *The Peoples of Greater Unyamwezi, Tanzania.* London: International African Institute.

Bienen, H.
(1967) *Tanzania: Party Transformation and Economic Development.* Princeton, N.J.; Princeton University Press.

Bryan, M. A.
(1959) *The Bantu Languages of Africa.* London: Oxford University Press for International African Institute.

Gulliver, P. H.
(1959) 'Tribal Map of Tanganyika' *Tanganyika Notes and Records*, pp. 52–55.

Guthrie, M.
(1948) *The Classification of the Bantu Languages*. London: Oxford University Press for International African Institute.

Hyder, M.
(1966) 'Swahili in a Technical Age', *East Africa's Cultural Heritage*. Contemporary African Monographs Series No. 4. Nairobi: East African Institute of Social and Cultural Affairs.

Iliffe, J.
(1967) 'The Role of the African Association in the Formation and Realization of Territorial Consciousness in Tanzania', Paper for the University of East Africa Social Science Research Conference, Dar es Salaam, December 1967.

Lensdale, J. N.
(1968) 'Some Origins of Nationalism in East Africa', *Journal of African History*, IX, 1, pp. 119–46.

Mazrui, A.
(1967) 'Language and Politics in East Africa', *Africa Report*, XII, No. 6.

Mushi, S. S.
(1966) 'The Role of the Ministry of Culture in National Development', *East Africa's Cultural Heritage*, Contemporary African Monographs Series No. 4. Nairobi: East African Institute of Social and Cultural Affairs.

Nyerere, J. K.
(1967) *Education and Self-Reliance*. Dar es Salaam: Government Printer.
(1968) *Freedom for Development*. Dar es Salaam: Government Printer.
(1966) *Freedom and Unity*, London: Oxford University Press.
(1967) *Socialism and Rural Development*. Dar es Salaam: Government Printer.

Parliamentary Debates (1968) *Tanganyika (Tanzania) Parliamentary Debates (Hansard), 1959–1968*. Dar es Salaam: Government Printer.

Prins, A. H. J.
(1961) *The Swahili-speaking peoples of Zanzibar and East Africa Coast*. London: International African Institute.

Ranger, T. O.
(1968) 'The Movement of Ideas, 1850 to 1939.' Paper delivered at the Conference on the History of Tanzania, Dar es Salaam, 1968.

Resnick, I. N. (ed.)
(1968) *Tanzania: Revolution by Education*. Longmans of Tanzania Ltd.

Tanu,
(1967) *The Arusha Declaration*. Dar es Salaam: Publicity Section, Tanu.

Trimingham, J. S.
(1964) *Islam in East Africa*. Oxford: Clarendon Press.

Whiteley, W. H.
(1964) 'Problems of a Lingua Franca: Swahili and the Trade Unions', *Journal of African Languages*, III, 3.

IX. Islam and the English Language in East and West Africa

ALI A. MAZRUI

Muslims in Africa south of the Sahara have been both among those who have been relatively suspicious of the English language as a factor in cultural transformation and among those who have shown an aptitude for speaking it well. Their suspicion of English has been partly connected with the role of missionary schools in Africa. And yet English itself was later to find that its strongest indigenous rivals for supremacy in Africa were the leading Islamic languages of Africa.

This paper proposes to concern itself precisely with this interplay between language and religion in Africa's political experience.

RELIGION, LANGUAGE AND EDUCATION

Christian missionaries were, of course, a critical factor in the spread of education in Africa, especially in the early days of colonial rule. The only real alternative to the Christian mission as a major agency for building schools would have been the Government, but at the beginning of this century, state responsibility for education was not fully acknowledged, even in Britain itself, let alone in her colonies. In the field of welfare services the general ethos of *laissez faire* still exerted considerable influence. There was a strong belief in restricting the participation of the State in education and comparable areas of social endeavour. In the colonies the educational initiative was thus firmly left to private agencies, pre-eminently the Christian missionaries.

From quite early therefore the idea of Western education in Africa came to be almost equated with Christian education. But education in British colonies was also increasingly equated among simple folk with ability to speak English. There is no doubt that there was a strong connection between the prestige of the English language and the prestige of education at large. Command of the English language was often used as a criterion of one's level of education;

And still they gazed and still the wonder grew
That one small head could carry all the English he knew.[1]

A simplistic syllogism emerged out of this dual connection. The partial equation of education with Christianity, coupled with the partial equation of education with the English language, produced a partial equation of Christianity with the English language. In other words, given that education was Christian, and the English language was the very basis of education, was it not to be inferred that the English language was itself Christian too?

Of course, this was not a rigorous exercise in logical reasoning, but simply an exercise in psychological association. There was a time when an African who spoke English well was initially assumed, almost automatically, to be a Christian. In the trial of Jomo Kenyatta on charges connected with the founding of Mau Mau, you could almost see Judge Tucker's mind associating English with Christianity in the following brief exchange between him and a witness. The witness had expressed a preference to give his evidence in English.

Magistrate: 'Very well, you can give your evidence in English. You seem to speak it very well. Are you a Christian?
Witness Kegeena: 'Yes'.[2]

The equation of the English language with missionary education was a major factor in conditioning Islamic attitudes towards it. Muslims became suspicious of the English language on the basis of a presumed guilt by association. This was aggravated by the sense of cultural defensiveness which developed among Muslim communities in Africa as in other parts of the world. As I have had occasion to argue elsewhere, Islam has a deep-seated sense of insecurity in relation to Christianity. As modernization gathered momentum in the

[1] This point, including the paraphrasing of Goldsmith, is also discussed in Mazrui, 1966.

[2] Slater, 1965, p. 40.

nineteenth and twentieth centuries, it was clear that Christian countries were leading the rest of the globe towards new technological and intellectual achievements. Within the Christian countries industrialization and modernization were sometimes recognized as dangers to Christianity itself. They were in themselves secularizing agencies, and were therefore corrosive factors on religion and tradition. But observers in Muslim countries in the Middle East and elsewhere were not always aware of the fears entertained by Christianity itself about the new forces let loose by the Industrial Revolution. All that Muslim observers could see was that white countries still professing Christianity were in the vanguard of modernity. And European faith in progress and the rightness of their political and economic systems created in Islamic countries a great sense of unease.[1]

In Africa south of the Sahara, perhaps even more clearly than in any of the Arab countries, these new forces of modernity came riding on Christian horses. The civilizing crusade which came with Christian missions, and the evangelizing commitment of the early mission schools, helped to emphasize the intimate association between the forces of modernity and the forces of Christianity in a newly colonized Africa. The sense of insecurity among Muslims helped to aggravate their suspicion of these new forces, and encompassed also a suspicion of their linguistic medium in British Africa, the English language itself.

RELIGION, LANGUAGE AND COLONIAL POLICY

Although the mission schools were agencies for the spread of the English language, that linguistic dissemination was not always warmly welcomed by colonial authorities. Colonial administrators were, on the one hand, interested in the possibility of producing literate Africans to help in some of the more menial clerical positions in government and the private sector; and on the other hand, colonial authorities were all too aware of the potential for agitation inherent in Western types of education in the colonies. In Ghana the word 'scholar' came into being in the middle of the nineteenth century to designate the products of the new schools in the country. Before long there developed

[1] See my paper, Mazrui, 1967a.

a so-called 'colonial office attitude' to educated Africans—perhaps typified by an assessment registered in Colonial Office records in 1875 that 'educated natives' or 'scholars' 'have always been a thorn in the side of the government of the G. Coast. They have been at the bottom of most of the troubles on the Coast for some years past.'[1]

Knowledge of the English language was critical in all this. In the words of Lugard, perhaps the greatest of the British administrators in Africa, 'the premature teaching of English . . . inevitably leads to utter disrespect for British and native ideals alike, and to a de-nationalised and disorganised population'.[2]

And even the missionaries themselves were sometimes accused of attempting to suppress the spread of the English language. Thus arose the Christian missionaries' brave attempts to develop orthographies and systems of writing for local languages. F. B. Welbourn has gone so far as to assert that: 'It was, indeed, in the field of language and literary education that the missionaries were to make their most important contribution outside the strictly religious field. The local languages had to be learned and reduced to writing'.[3]

But way back in the 1920s the missionaries were being criticized even by British Government officials for their tendency to 'discourage the teaching of English by the teaching of the native languages and dialects and to seek to perpetuate them as written languages'.[4]

And yet, in spite of some distrust of the English language by colonial administrators, and in spite of the effect of missionary promotion of African vernacular languages, the English language assumed a vital role in education above the primary level in both East and West African British colonies. And the missionaries disseminated the metropolitan language almost in spite of themselves. They were instrumental in spreading the language because of their commitment to augmenting

[1] Minute of 6 February 1875, by A. W. L. Hemming (later head of the African Department of the Colonial Office); C.O./96/115. See Kimble, 1963, p. 91.

[2] F. D. Lugard, *Annual Reports*, Northern Nigeria 1900–1911, p. 646. Cited by Coleman, 1958, p. 137.

[3] See Welbourn, 1965, p. 82.

[4] *Annual Report*, Department of Education, Southern Provinces, 1926 (Lagos, 1927), p. 7. Cited by Coleman, ibid. (footnote), p. 443. On the role of missionaries in the development of the vernacular, see also Westermann, 1949, pp. 117–28.

educational opportunities for Africans, and because of their near monopoly of school education in British colonies for quite a while.

But if Lugard did not succeed in denying Africa the English language, he certainly did succeed in slowing down its spread in the Muslim areas he controlled. The whole doctrine of Indirect Rule which Lugard propagated found its finest fulfilment in the Muslim areas of Northern Nigeria. Institutionally, Indirect Rule was a commitment to try to utilize native institutions in the task of governing the colonies. But Indirect Rule has had also its broader cultural implications. In this latter context it constituted a reluctance to tamper too radically with the belief systems as well as the political institutions of subject peoples.

Among such peoples Indirect Rule worked best in those societies which had developed institutions of the kind which were either relatively familiar to the conquering power (as, for example, Islamic institutions observed elsewhere in the Muslim world before, and then found in Africa as well) or relatively centralized in their authority structures (as, for example, the institutions of Buganda in the eyes of Stanley and other European explorers at a critical stage of imperial evaluation).

The finest realization of Lugardism was, in fact, among the Emirates of Northern Nigeria. And this realization included the exclusion of Christian missions from the North. In Southern Nigeria there was a growing desire for education among the masses, arising out of a belief that 'Western education, and especially a knowledge of the English language, would equip them with the techniques and skills essential for the improvement of personal status in the emergent economic and social structure'.[1]

But in the North applied Lugardism excluded the missionary agent of change and, with him, the English language as a medium of intellectual transformation, occupational and social mobility, and the crystallization of national consciousness. There were long-term consequences of this. 'In the first place, the absence of an English-speaking educated class in Northern Nigeria in the early period necessitated the importation

[1] Coleman, op. cit., pp. 124–5.

of thousands of Southerners into the North as clerks and artisans'.[1]

Uganda was also a major achievement of applied Lugardism, and here too the Muslims were strikingly deficient in their possession of Western academic and linguistic skills. In 1893 the Muslims had been defeated in Buganda and from then on remained a small, even if politically significant, minority. Inevitably, they were not among the great beneficiaries of missionary education. Uganda Muslims have developed as simple traders, as butchers, taxi drivers, and petty shopkeepers.

In political affiliation the Buganda Muslims were often supporters of Protestants in their fights with Catholics. But even this had connections with the nature of missionary education. It has been suggested that the Protestants have perhaps been 'more ready to admit (the Muslims) into denominational schools without proselytism' than the Catholics have been.[2]

But whatever the relative affinity between the Muslims and the two Christian denominations, the reduced access to mission schools relegated the Muslims to a modest status. The contrast in Buganda was perhaps particularly striking—certainly more conspicuous than in other parts of the country where Muslims and Christians live together. The commitment to the creation of an educated African *élite* was stronger among missionaries operating in this region than elsewhere. Mackay defined the general direction. 'Instead of vainly struggling to perpetuate the method of feebly manned stations, each holding a precarious existence, and never able at best to exert more than a local influence, let us select a few particularly healthy sites, on which we shall raise an institution for imparting a thorough education even to only a few.'[3]

As David Apter has pointed out, this was precisely the model for the later pattern for education which resulted in Mengo High School (later King's College, Budo) and St Mary's College, Kisubi.[4]

[1] Coleman, op. cit., p. 140. The growth of a Southern population in the North holding skilled or affluent positions later became one of the precipitate factors behind the massacre of the Ibos in Northern Nigeria and some of the other events which led to the civil war.

[2] Welbourn, op. cit., p. 61. Consult also Low, 1957.

[3] See Harrison, 1890, p. 470.

[4] Apter, 1961, p. 74. Consult also Taylor, 1958, and Low and Pratt, 1960.

Evidently Indirect Rule in Buganda was not protecting the Baganda from the influences of missionary education, in the way that the Northern Nigerians had been protected under similar doctrines. Indirect rule in Uganda managed to foster a pride in indigenous culture among the Baganda along with an interest in metropolitan ways at the same time. There was respect for Kiganda culture as a moral force combined with a keenness on the acquisition of Western education and certain British modes of behaviour. Even the devotion to Luganda as a distinguished medium of local culture was combined with a quest for competence in the English language and an attachment to it as a symbol of intellectual modernity.

But the Muslims were left behind in this stream of social change. Early in the 1950s the late Kabaka Mutesa II of Buganda paid a visit to the Mombasa Institute of Muslim education. He arrived there after sunset with his entourage, but without notice to the institution. No special arrangements had been made to receive him and his group. I received a phone call from his host in town indicating that the group was coming to the Institute. The Institute, built in Arabian style in the immediate suburbs of Mombasa, constituted at the time one of the showplaces of the town. My own position in it then was that of boarding supervisor, a position somewhat comparable to that of a warden in a hall of residence. I was therefore available at night when the Kabaka and his group came to visit the Institute. I showed them round some of the major sections of the educational institution, and then entertained them to some refreshment in my modest flat.

I later discovered that one of the things which had impressed the Kabaka's group was the phenomenon of a young Muslim speaking English so 'fluently'. Apparently the Kabaka on his return to Buganda recounted the episode. More than ten years after the event I was myself a resident in Uganda and was introduced to one of the Muslim members of the Buganda royal house. When it was explained to the Prince who I was, complete with my family background, his eyes brightened up. He remembered so late in the day the comments made by the Kabaka and his group on their return to Buganda about a young Muslim in Mombasa who spoke English fairly fluently.[1]

ENGLISH, ISLAM AND AFRICAN LANGUAGES

Looking at Africa as a whole, the strongest rivals to metropolitan languages are, in fact, Muslim languages. The term 'Muslim' or 'Islamic language' is here used either in the sense that those who speak it as a first language are overwhelmingly Muslim or in the sense that the language itself reflects a very strong Islamic influence at both the explicit and the suggestive levels, or in both those senses simultaneously.

The three strongest rivals to metropolitan languages in Africa are Arabic itself, dominant especially in the North, the Hausa language leading in the West, and the Swahili language leading in the East. The Arabic language is, of course, the most explicitly Islamic of them all, partly because it is the language in which Islam was revealed by the Prophet Mohammed, and also because of the continued influence of the Koran in its original Arabic on the cultural and religious life of Muslims almost everywhere. In Africa the language's area of concentration is North Africa, but Arabic also plays significant national roles not only in the Sudan but also in countries like Chad and Somalia.

Then there is the Hausa language in West Africa. More than 40 per cent of the population of Northern Nigeria speak Hausa as their mother tongue. But in addition, Hausa-speaking groups are scattered all over West Africa, and the Hausa language and culture have exerted significant attraction on neighbouring communities and influenced the direction of culture change within those communities.

Then there is the Swahili language in East Africa. Only a small minority of those who speak the language speak it as a first language. The language's greatest success is perhaps in its effectiveness as a lingua franca over an area which includes not only Tanzania, Kenya, and Uganda but also the Congo and Malawi and Burundi. It has been estimated that the language

[1] For some background of the Islamic factor in East African education consult also *Kenya Education Report* (The Ominde Commission), Part I (Government of Kenya Publication, 12 December 1964), pp. 33–9; Gee, 1958; Trimingham, 1964, esp. pp. 171–4; Prins, 1961, esp. pp. 107–9; Lewis, 1966, esp. Chapters IX, XIV, and XV.

is the seventh most important international language in the world.[1]

These are the three most important non-metropolitan languages in Africa as a whole. Some might argue that Wolof is the fourth most significant trans-national indigenous African language in the continent. This is more debatable. And yet if it is accepted as a proposition Wolof, too, qualifies as a Muslim language in the senses mentioned above.

The relevance of these languages for African cultural nationalism is quite striking. The richness of the languages is sometimes attributed to their original indigenous subtleties but also at times attributed to their association with Islamic dynasties and Islamic cultural movements in the past.

Edward Blyden, perhaps the father of modern cultural nationalism in Africa south of the Sahara, discussed the role of the Arabic language in intellectualizing indigenous African languages where Islam held sway.

> Different estimates are made of the beneficial effects wrought by Islam upon the moral and industrial conditions of Western Africa . . .; but all careful and candid observers agree that the influence of Islam in Central and West Africa has been, upon the whole, of a most salutary character. . . . Large towns and cities have grown up under Mohammedan energy and industry. . . . Already some of the vernaculars have been enriched by expressions from the Arabic for the embodiment of the higher processes of thought.[2]

Later on those African languages which were deeply Islamized did in turn become carriers of Islamic influence on others, partly because of the prestige they had accumulated. Coleman and others have talked about the powerful 'cultural attraction' that the Hausa had exercised on the smaller tribes of the middle belt and indeed on some southern nationalists in old Nigeria. The prestige of Hausa for such nationalism stems partly from its relatively rich historical tradition, partly because of the pomp and splendour of the ruling class in the community which spoke the language, and partly because of distinctive architectural accomplishments associated with Hausa civilization.

[1] A useful study of the 'heart' of the Swahili-speaking population is Prins, op. cit.
[2] See Blyden, [1887] 1967, pp. 174, 186–7.

... the culture provides an alternative to the white European culture which the Hausa have been taught to emulate. . . . Culturally conscious Nigerians, both Hausa and non-Hausa from the South, seek to identify themselves with this tradition. In their view it provides positive proof that the white man is mistaken when he states that Nigerians have no culture, no history, and no experience in large scale political organisation. This tendency toward identification is manifest even among the educated Nigerians from the South who do not take on the external of Hausa culture.[1]

In East Africa Swahili is by no means uniformly prestigious. In fact in Uganda the language seems to carry proletarian associations, partly because many of those who speak it are immigrant labourers from neighbouring areas who have had to resort to Swahili as a lingua franca in their dealings with members of other tribes.

But in Kenya, and even more in Tanzania, Swahili is associated with a highly developed cultural tradition, and the language enjoys enough prestige to be a serious candidate as an educational medium in schools.

In fact, on this issue of national languages, it has indeed been precisely such Islamic or neo-Islamic languages which have even remotely approached the status of the metropolitan language in countries previously colonized. The case of Somalia is, of course, distinctive, as it is almost the only nation state of some size in Africa south of the Sahara in the classical European sense of cultural homogeneity. The country has a language of poetic power which is still in search of an adequate alphabet. But in Somalia the rivalry is perhaps ultimately between two Islamic languages, Arabic and Somali itself. English and Italian are at a second level of competition.

In Nigeria debate has intermittently erupted as to whether Hausa should become the national language. When in the old Federal Parliament it was proposed that Hausa should be so adopted, strong voices were heard against the proposal. Chief Anthony Enahoro, for example, said in Parliament: 'As one who comes from a minority tribe, I deplore the continuing evidence in this country that people wish to impose their customs, their languages, and even more, their way of life upon the smaller tribes'.[2]

[1] Coleman, op. cit., p. 22. Consult also Mackintosh, 1966, and Sklar, 1963.

[2] Cited by Schwarz, 1965, p. 41.

And a Nigerian Minister visiting India in 1953, in relating his country's problems with a comparable multilingual situation in India, reaffirmed that: 'We are not keen on developing our own languages with a view to replacing English. We regard the English language as a unifying force.'[1]

Yet the advocates for Hausa have by no means been silenced. Of particular interest has perhaps been the campaign of Mr. Tai Solarin, a weekly contributor for quite a while to the *Daily Times*, Nigeria's leading newspaper. Mr. Solarin established himself as a campaigner for the adoption of Hausa as the national language of Nigeria, both in his articles in the newspaper and in supplementary pamphleteering.

> When the state of Israel was established the Israelis chose Hebrew which was LEAST spoken by any group of Israelis . . . because it is native; it is indigenous. . . . We now come to Nigeria . . . I have noticed that the defenders of 'English shall be our lingua franca' are invariably those of us who appear better dressed in the 'English' suit than the English themselves. . . . Whatever Nigerian language we choose is, psychologically, a more acceptable language than any foreign language.[2]

In the wake of the Nigerian civil war, and the suspicion in some quarters of the potential Hausa domination of the country as a whole, it would now be rash to re-activate the campaign for Hausa.[3]

That other neo-Islamic language, Swahili, has fared better in the struggle to win recognition as a national language. In Tanzania, especially, there has been a big push forward to give Swahili a widening role in the national life of the country. Most political activity in the country is now conducted in Swahili. There is an increasing emphasis on its use as a medium within the educational system. A brave attempt has also been made to Swahilize the vocabulary of legal discourse and judicial transactions in the country. And organizations like the Poets Association have received encouragement and support from the

[1] Reported in *Uganda Argus* (Kampala), 13 November 1953.

[2] See *Daily Times*, 20 October 1966. See also Solarin, 'A Native Tongue as Lingua Franca', *Daily Times*, 5 February 1965. I am also indebted to Oluwadare Aguda, n. d., pp. 14–20.

[3] For general discussions on the Nigerian civil war refer, *inter alia*, to *Africa Report*, February 1968; *Current History*, February 1968; and *Transition* No. 36, 1968.

Government in their bid to 'enrich the nation's language and cultural heritage'.[1]

In Kenya Swahili's triumph is much less clear, though the language seems to have made significant gains in the last two decades. It is more widely understood and its role as a national language is now debated with greater feeling. The ruling party reaffirmed in April 1970 its commitment to build Swahili up into a national language. It seems likely that Swahili will ultimately conquer Kenya as effectively as it has conquered Tanzania.[2]

The chances are that the Swahili which would conquer Kenya would be somewhat less Islamic in its cumulative associations than the kind of Swahili heard in many parts of Tanzania. But the Islamic influences on the language are for the time being very much in evidence wherever Swahili is spoken correctly. Here again, then, it remains true that a major rival to a metropolitan language is an African language with Islamic associations.

LANGUAGE, THE KORAN AND THE BIBLE

At the back of the Islamic influence on such African languages as Hausa, Wolof and Swahili is the influence of the Koran. And this influence has been important in conditioning Muslim attitudes to European languages in Africa. Edward Blyden, who had himself knowledge of Arabic, and taught it, had occasion to quote a European Koranic scholar who wrote in 1869:

> The Koran suffers more than any other book we think of by a translation, however masterly. The grandeur of the Koran consists, its contents apart, in its diction. We cannot explain the peculiarly dignified, impressive, sonorous mixture of semitic sound and parlance; *sesquipedalia verba*, with their crowd of prefixes and affixes, each of them affirming its own position, while consciously bearing upon and influencing the central root, which they envelop like a

[1] Vice-President Rashidi Kawawa committed the Government more formally to support the Poets Association in a speech he gave in January 1965. These cultural and linguistic groups are by no means consistently active, but the policy atmosphere in Tanzania is still very favourable to endeavours in this direction. See also *The Nationalist*'s enthusiastic response to Kawawa's speech on the future of Swahili in Tanzania, 'Our National Language', editorial, *The Nationalist*, 20 January 1965. See also renewed discussion on widening the role of Swahili in Tanzanian newspapers in January 1967.

[2] Mazrui, 1967b.

garment of many folds, or as chosen coaches move around the anointed person of the king.[1]

Blyden goes on to observe that the African Muslim is no exception among the adherents of Islam in his appreciation of the sacred book. 'It is studied with as much enthusiasm at Boporo, Misadu, Medina and Kankan, as at Cairo, Alexandria, or Baghdad.[2]

It has also been suggested that the Baganda were first attracted to the Arabs by the magic of reading and writing. Joswa Kate Mugema, a leading Muganda Christian, baptized in 1885, is reported to have started the art of 'reading' with the Arabs. 'He was still signing his name in Arabic characters as late as 1904. But reading meant, largely, reading the Qur'an'.[3]

Because of the special status of the Koran in Muslim theology, there is a linguistic dimension is Islam which has no real equivalent in Christianity. The Koran is regarded not merely as divinely inspired but as literally the utterances of God. Every word, every syllable is supposed to be directly emanating from God. The Prophet Mohammed, when revealing the Koranic verses, was serving as no more than a channel of communication. In fact, in such moments of Koranic utterances by the Prophet, God was almost a divine ventriloquist, giving the Prophet a voice which was, in fact, God's own.

The language in which the Koran was originally revealed assumes therefore a special meaning within this belief system. The Authorized Version of the Bible in the English language may be as holy to the Protestant as any other version, but the Koran in translation loses much of its original spiritual stature. Since every Arabic syllable in it is directly from God, a substitution of syllables in the English language or in Gujerati dilutes the ultimate authenticity.

Related to this literal Godliness of the Koran is the doctrine of its inimitability. This is the assertion that the diction and structure of the Koran can neither be equalled nor imitated by a mortal author. And yet, curiously enough, the very prestige that the Koran has enjoyed as a work of literature has played a

[1] The quotation is from Emanuel Deutsch, *Quarterly Review* (London), October 1869. Consult also Guillaume, 1962, especially Chapter 3.

[2] Blyden, op. cit., p. 178. See also Kritzeck, 1964, especially pp. 33–74.

[3] Welbourn, op. cit., p. 60. See also Welbourn, 1965b.

great role in stabilizing the evolution of the Arabic language. It seems almost certain that the Arabic language in its written form would have changed more radically over the centuries had it not been for a constant attempt by Arab writers precisely to imitate the language of the Koran. This recurrent attempt to imitate the inimitable has been one of the major stabilizing influences on written Arabic over the centuries.

In Arabic south of the Sahara the classical neo-Koranic form of Arabic is important not only in written literature but also in Arabic speech where it occurs. What Edward Blyden said in the nineteenth century about the classical nature of African Arabic is true today as well.

> Those who speak Arabic speak the Koranic or book Arabic, preserving the final vowels of the classical language—a practice which, in the hurry and exigencies of business life, has been long discontinued in countries where the language is vernacular; so that in Egypt and Syria the current speech is very defective, and clipped and corrupted.[1]

The importance which the Koran has enjoyed in Muslim thought has at times retarded the evolution of secular schools. This was certainly true in those British colonies with sizeable Muslim populations. Koranic schools, in many ways deficient as instruments of education, were often a serious rival to modern schools in Muslim areas. And the very importance of the Arabic language as something to be coveted by those who do not speak it as a first language complicated the scheme of linguistic priorities in Muslim areas in Africa. In a Hausa-speaking region, for example, should the educational system promote Arabic first as the next target for acquisition, or should it promote the English language? The answer, at least in the earlier stages of colonial penetration, was by no means easy.

In addition, there was a tendency to assume that just because the believers could look to an ultimate authentic language of their faith, so, too, could the unbelievers be associated with a language of their own. Among simple people in British Africa the English language was at times regarded as a language of unbelief, a language of the *kafir*. Indeed, the Jesus of Christianity

[1] Blyden, op. cit., p. 185. One of the biggest contributions to the study of Islam in sub-Saharan Africa has been made by J. Spencer Trimingham. Of special relevance to this paper are Trimingham 1959, 1962, and 1964.

—unlike the Isa of orthodox Islam—was often conceptualized as a European. Where churches would be segregated, and angels described as white, it was not difficult to make Jesus wear the nationality of Europe. But a nationality, it was assumed, carried a language of its own. And in British Africa the European was decidedly English-speaking. It was an easy step to move from a white Jesus to an English-speaking Jesus. And the Bible in English coming into Africa was too readily made analogous to the Koran in Arabic entering the continent. The special status of Arabic in Islam led to assumptions about a special status of English in Christianity.[1]

Gradually many of the Islamic inhibitions in regard to the English language have been weakened, at least in some areas. Lamu, which used to be profoundly distrustful of the English language and the culture it represented, has now found a new enthusiasm for Government Secular Schools. Zanzibar capitulated much earlier, taking a dramatic lead in East Africa in *per capita* graduates. Islamic distrust of the English language and the civilization it represented in Mombasa and its vicinity began to crack after the Second World War, but it still remains true that Muslims in Kenya are among the least educated of the communities. Sir Philip Mitchell, when he was Governor of the country, was so aware of the educational retardation sustained by Muslims in Kenya that he made a special effort to obtain the necessary funds for the establishment of the Mombasa Institute of Muslim Education referred to earlier. The Institute, designed to be mainly technical, was intended to rescue Arab and African Muslims from general educational lethargy and occupational narrow-mindedness. In their defensiveness against Christianity these Muslims were letting modernity pass them by.

But where Muslims have finally capitulated to the pull of the English language as a medium of intellectual modernity they have been among the better speakers of the language. As it happens, this is basically a linguistic accident. In East Africa among the best speakers of the English language in diction and pronunciation are Zanzibaris, Coastal Tanzanians, and

[1] In his trial on Mau Mau charges, Jomo Kenyatta was accused, among other things, of having gone so far in associating Christianity with colonialism as to actually assert that Jesus Christ was an English gentleman. See Slater, 1965, p. 153. Kenyatta denied this charge.

native-speakers of Swahili along the Coast of Kenya. It seems quite clear that the command of the English diction which these people manage to achieve is directly due to the structure and sound range of the Swahili language with which they started. In other words, there was something in the kind of Swahili spoken in these areas which gave the native speaker a degree of adaptability in the acquisition of the sounds of the English language.

A similar phenomenon has been observed among Hausa speakers in Northern Nigeria. When they do get around to accepting the English language, and when they do succeed in learning well, the sound range of their native Hausa facilitates their assimilation into the sound habits of the English language. It was not for nothing that Alhaji Sir Abubakar Tafawa Balewa, the late Prime Minister of the Nigerian Federation before the first coup, acquired the admiring name of 'The Golden Voice of the North' among fellow-Nigerians.

CONCLUSION

We have attempted to demonstrate in this paper two major themes. One is that Islamic attitudes towards the English language in Africa have been conditioned by the missionary genesis of secular education in British colonies, as well as by the place of Arabic in Islamic systems of thought. The missionary factor behind the spread of education and of the English language retarded Muslim involvement in this wave of modernity. The place of Arabic and the Koran within the complex of Islamic attitudes complicated the problem of priorities and choices in African Muslim communities and diverted energies towards Koranic schools at some expense to other forms of education. Among the more simple of the adherents of Islam there was also an easy assumption that just because Islam had a pre-eminent and divinely hallowed language of its own, Arabic, so Christianity, too, must have one of its own, readily assumed to be the pre-eminent European language of the conquering power. It took a while, therefore, before Muslim attitudes to the English language were freed from a neo-religious suspicion.

The second theme of this paper has concerned the simple proposition that the strongest rivals to metropolitan languages in Africa have, in fact, been languages of Muslim communities or of Islamic cultural derivation. Arabic, Hausa and Swahili especially have come nearest to challenging the supremacy of metropolitan languages in the evolution of modern Africa. They have also succeeded more than any other in symbolizing a trans-national cultural pride and sense of dynastic historical grandeur.

In historiography, texts in the Arabic language have been part of the evidence that modern Africa has been producing to combat the assertion that Africa is a continent with no history. And the Sudanic civilizations, and their association with African Islam, have helped to give such languages as Hausa and Fulani a cultural prestige.

In East Africa Swahili's prestige is by no means uniformly acknowledged. There are, in fact, parts of the region where the language is more easily associated with humble proletarian origins than with glorious cultural ancestry. And yet there is no doubt that in Tanzania, Kenya and parts of the Congo Swahili enjoys sufficient status to pose a challenge to the imperial languages in at least some areas of national endeavour.

Behind these two themes of the paper—the nature and origins of Islamic attitudes to the English language, and the potential of new Islamic languages as rivals to imperial media—is the simple curiosity that among the best articulators of English sounds in African societies are precisely people who grew up speaking Swahili, Hausa, and perhaps Arabic.

This last paradox is essentially, as we indicated, no more than an accident in phonemes across distinct languages. But perhaps even such accidents have a wealth of symbolism in them. After all, Nkrumah defined his concept of consciencism as being a diffusion in the African consciousness of the three dominant traditions in Africa's intellectual evolution. These are, firstly, the indigenous elements themselves; secondly, the impact of Islam on Africa's history, language and cultural trends; and thirdly, the influence of imperial Europe in the phase of Africa's entry into the modern era.

The interplay between competing religions and competing languages is simply one aspect of this tripartite structure of Africa's cultural evolution.[1]

[1] Consult Nkrumah, 1964.

REFERENCES

Aguda, Oluwadare

(n.d.) *The Nigerian Approach to Politics*. African Studies Seminar paper N. 2, Sudan Research Unit, Faculty of Arts, University of Khartoum.

Apter, David E.

(1961) *The Political Kingdom in Uganda*. Princeton, N.J.: Princeton University Press.

Blyden, Edward W.

[1887] (1967) *Christianity, Islam and the Negro Race*. Edinburgh: The University Press (1967 reprint.)

Coleman, James S.

(1958) *Nigeria: Background to Nationalism*. University of California Press.

Gee, T. W.

(1958) 'A Century of Mohammedan Influence in Buganda, 1852–1951', *Uganda Journal*, 22.

Guillaume, Alfred

(1962) *Islam*. London: Penguin Books.

Harrison, J. W.

(1890) *Mackay of Uganda*. London: Hodder and Stoughton.

Kimble, David

(1963) *A Political History of Ghana: The Rise of Gold Coast Nationalism, 1850–1928*. Oxford: The Clarendon Press.

Kritzeck, James

(1964) *Anthology of Islamic Literature: From the Rise of Islam to Modern Times*. London: Penguin Books.

Lewis, I. M. (ed.)

(1966) *Islam in Tropical Africa*. London: Oxford University Press for the International African Institute.

Low, D. A.

(1957) *Religion and Society in Buganda 1875–1900*. (East African Research Series No. 8.) London: Routledge and Kegan Paul.

Low, D. A. and Pratt, R. Cranford

(1960) *Buganda and British Overrule, 1900–1955*. London: Oxford University Press.

Mackintosh, J. P.

(1966) *Nigerian Government and Politics*. London: George Allen and Unwin.

Mazrui, Ali A.

(1966) 'The English Language and African Political Consciousness', *The Journal of Modern African Studies*, Vol. 4, No. 3.

(1967a) 'Islam, Political Leadership and Economic Radicalism in Africa', in Ali A. Mazrui *On Heroes and Uhuru-Worship*. London: Longmans Green.

(1967b) 'The National Language Question in East Africa', *East Africa Journal*, June. (A version of this paper also appeared in *Africa Report*, June 1967.)

Nkrumah, Kwame

(1964) *Consciencism*. London: Heinemann.

Prins, A. H. J.

(1961) *The Swahili-speaking Peoples of Zanzibar and the East African Coast*. London: International African Institute. (Ethnographic Survey of Africa, East Central Africa, Part XII.)

Schwarz, F. A. O. Jr.,

(1965) *Nigeria: the Tribes, the Nation and the Race. M. I. T. Press.*

Sklar, Richard L.

(1963) *Nigerian Political Parties*. Princeton, N. J.: Princeton University Press.

Slater, Montagu

(1965) *The Trial of Jomo Kenyatta*. London: Mercury Books. (2nd edn. revised.)

Solarin, T.

(1965) 'A Native Tongue as Lingua Franca', *Daily Times*, 5 February.

Taylor, J. V.

(1958) *The Growth of the Church in Buganda. London: S. C. M. Press.*

Trimingham, J. Spencer

(1959) *Islam in West Africa*. London: Oxford University Press.

(1962) *A History of Islam in West Africa*. London: Oxford University Press (Glasgow University Press).

(1964) *Islam in East Africa*. Oxford: Clarendon Press.

Welbourn, F. B.

(1965a) *East African Christian*. London: Oxford University Press.

(1965b) *Religion and Politics in Uganda 1952–62*. Nairobi: East African Publishing House.

Westermann, Diedrich

(1949) *The African Today and Tomorrow*. London: Oxford University Press for the International African Institute. (3rd edn.)

X. Socio-linguistic Implications of a Choice of Media of Instruction

T. P. GORMAN

In this paper I wish to outline some preliminary results that I have obtained, and some tentative conclusions that I have drawn from an analysis of the results of the first stage of an inquiry into aspects of the language use and language attainment of children who entered secondary schools in Kenya in 1968.[1]

GENERAL AIMS

The first stage of the inquiry was designed to provide us with information about the functional importance and the functional range of different languages in the usage of children belonging to different language groups and attending school in urban and rural areas.[2] More particularly we were concerned with their exposure to and use of English, Swahili, and a Vernacular language or languages in specific situations of interaction and reception.[3]

[1] I would like to acknowledge with gratitude the assistance of Mrs. J. Wheeler, a psychologist with extensive experience in Africa, in the pre-testing and administering of the questionnaires and tests and in the statistical interpretation of certain of the results; and the cooperation of Mr. A. Bashir of the Kenya Institute of Administration in the construction of the cloze test in Swahili. This research project was supported by a grant from the Survey Council of the Survey of Language Use and Language Teaching in Eastern Africa.

[2]*a*. I am using the term 'functional importance' as in Weinreich, 1953.

b. The term 'functional range' is used in the sense of code specialization, 'the specialisation of particular languages or varieties to particular situations or functions' (Hymes, 1962).

[3] In describing language behaviour I have found it useful to distinguish between *situations of interaction*, which are characterized by reciprocal interaction, and *situations of reception*, in which the subject is the receptor in a non-reciprocal exchange (e.g. as in listening to the radio or to a sermon). In the latter, the degree of language choice involved, if it can be said to be involved at all, is characteristically more restricted than in the former.

I assumed also that the information gathered would provide an indication of any gross divergencies in the reported language behaviour of the children and their parents as may have resulted from the operation and implementation of successive educational language policies.

I am aware that the language behaviour of the members of the different speech communities has been, and is, influenced by diverse social forces and by numerous historical, political, educational, demographic, and linguistic factors; and that it would be fallacious to attribute to any one complex of influences, such as those associated with the formal educational process, any specific forms of language behaviour. However, in instances where parents and children are exposed in most respects to the same induced social forces but differ most evidently in their educational experience, and consequently in their exposure to formal language learning processes, the attempt to discern, if not to isolate, certain consequences of this difference is not, I think, without justification.

STRATIFIED SAMPLES

The populations to which the study was directed were the children in each of eight major language groups in the first year at Government-maintained and aided secondary schools. Data was also gathered about children speaking other languages, but this will not be reported in this paper.[1]

[1] The eight language groups were: Kipsigis, Luo, Kamba, Kikuyu, Kimeru, Luyia, Gusii, and Mijikenda. Over 80 per cent of the population of Kenya belongs to these eight groups (Kenya Population Census, 1962). The first two languages belong to the Nilotic Branch of the Chari–Nile family, the others to the Bantu branch of the Niger–Congo family.

The sample was taken from all maintained and aided schools in Central Province, Nyanza Province, Coast Province (including Mombasa), Kipsigis District, Meru District, Machakos District, Kitui District, and Nairobi.

In these areas all Form I streams were numbered, and from the list four streams were drawn randomly. The sampling fractions for the rural sample are shown below:

	Schools	Forms
Kikuyu	4/48	4/80
Luo	4/24	4/39
Gusii	3/9	4/13
Luyia	4/32	4/54
Kipsigis	4/7	4/9
Kamba	4/13	4/25
Meru	4/19	4/13
Mijikenda	3/11	4/15

Continued at foot of next page

A lack of adequate information about the individuals comprising these populations imposed limitations on our sample design. It will be recognized that in developing countries it is seldom possible to obtain with reasonable celerity the personal data necessary for the structuring of a random sampling frame. Nor was the information available to enable a purposive sample of a number of schools to be selected.

Consequently, a form of cluster sampling was adopted in the rural districts, in which the eight languages were known to preponderate; the school 'stream' rather than the individual child constituted the sampling unit. Streams were selected in each of the relevant districts or provinces.

In addition, two large urban samples were chosen in Nairobi and Mombasa on the assumption that each of the larger language groups would be sufficiently represented in the urban schools to allow us to draw meaningful conclusions about differences in the behaviour of children in urban and rural schools. In Nairobi we randomly selected 24 out of 80 streams available, and in Mombasa 13 out of 25. This selection had a different purpose from that attaching to the sampling procedure in the rural areas. Both the total set of clusters in each of the urban areas and any individual cluster were expected to be far more linguistically heterogeneous than any cluster total or any individual cluster in any rural area.[2]

In the whole rural sample:

By school type:	30 maintained schools (32 Form I classes)
By size of school:	15 forms in single-stream schools
	8 forms in two-stream schools
	8 forms in three-stream schools
	1 form in a four-stream school
By sex:	20 boys schools
	5 girls schools
	5 mixed schools
By residence:	16 boarding schools
	12 day schools
	2 day/boarding schools

These proportions are well distributed in the sub-samples, with the exception of the sex factor.

Five schools in the rural sample were excluded in the initial processing of the data as the questionnaires and tests were not returned in time. This meant that the Luo and Luyia speaking children in the sample are under-represented.

[2] Over three-quarters of the urban population of Kenya is located in these two towns. A large number of the children attending schools in these areas, however

Given the nature of this dual-purpose sampling technique, it is clear that one would not be justified in applying to the data statistical calculations relating to population values. The study has, however, provided indications of fairly consistent trends and patterns of language behaviour among secondary-school entrants which can now be investigated in greater detail.

INSTRUMENTS

To each child a questionnaire was administered together with a cloze test in English and Swahili.[1] The questionnaire was designed to elicit information relating to the following factors:

A. Languages known and used in different modes by the child and by members of his family of orientation. (Total verbal repertoires.) The child was asked to indicate which languages various members of his family could speak, write, read or understand and to rate their 'proficiency' in each mode of use along a four-point scale.[2]

B. Reciprocal language use in the domain of the family (Restricted dyadic repertoires). The child was asked to say which languages were spoken to him by, and which languages he spoke to, various members of his family, and to rate the frequency with which this was done along a three-point scale.

C. Active and passive non-reciprocal language use of the subject only in the locales of home and school. (Restricted individual repertoires.)[3]

---

have had their primary education in rural areas. It was considered important to secure a sample sufficiently large to contain a considerable number of children educated in the towns. In this paper the results derived from the answers of children in the Nairobi schools only, have been reported in the urban sample.

[1] We used passages in English and Swahili from which every fifth word had been deleted. The number of 'cloze units' attained constituted the score on each test (cf. Taylor 1953).

[2] It is perhaps unnecessary to mention that I am using the term 'verbal repertoire' in the sense it is used by J. Gumperz (cf. Gumperz, 1966), although in dealing with what I have termed 'total verbal repertoire' I am concerned only with distinct codes within the repertoire.

[3] The terms 'reciprocal' and 'non-reciprocal' behaviour are used in the senses defined by W. Mackey (Mackey, 1965). In describing the language use of the children in the sample, I have found it useful to distinguish *active* non-reciprocal language use such as is involved in the process of counting, and *passive* non-reciprocal behaviour such as occurs in situations of reception.

D. Reciprocal language use by the subject in certain situations of interaction outside the locales of home and school.

E. Attitudes adopted by the child and his parents to the use of particular languages.

F. Other information considered to be relevant to the language use of children, such as details of their primary school background and of the languages of instruction used in the primary schools attended; details of their age, sex, and the length of their residence in an urban or rural setting; and such questions as I considered might by appropriately included in a questionnaire of this nature about the educational background and socio-economic status of their parents. The teachers of English and Swahili in each school were asked to rate the children in what they considered to be the rank order of their level of attainment in the two languages. These ratings and the cloze tests were included to help us evaluate the accuracy of the child's self-ratings in the two languages. I also anticipated that the test results would serve to indicate any gross differences in the levels of attainment in Swahili and English of schoolchildren in the rural and urban samples; between children belonging to different language groups; and between children who had been initially educated through the media of Swahili or English or of their mother tongue.

I am aware of the difficulties involved in any attempt to draw valid conclusions about the language behaviour of a population of this size, using instruments of this kind; instruments that in two cases primarily provide information not about language behaviour as such but about ways of reporting such behaviour.

Self-report measures have a number of inherent limitations, but the use of survey or correlational methodology involving such measures can yield valid results in certain circumstances. In interpreting these results it is, of course, essential to recognize the distinction between what have been termed 'verbal' and 'action' attitudes; between what the respondents say and what they do. As Hovland has pointed out, the primary utility of such methods is to suggest hypotheses which can then subsequently be examined or tested under experimental conditions when possible (Hovland, 1959).

THE DEVELOPMENT OF EDUCATIONAL LANGUAGE POLICY

Before detailing in part certain results relating to reported generational differences in language behaviour within a number of groups, I think it would be relevant to indicate briefly some of the more significant changes that have taken place as regards the use of particular languages in the educational system as media of instruction during the period in which the children and the fathers of the children surveyed, attended (or did not attend) school.[1]

During the time that the parents of most of the children involved in the survey would have attended school the characteristic pattern of language use in schools in the rural areas was that after the initial stages, when such material as was available in the primary language of the majority of the children in the area would normally be used, Swahili was used as the medium of instruction. Those who went on to the intermediate schools were also usually taught in Swahili, but by the time of the publication of the *Ten Year Plan for the Development of African Education* in 1947 it was acknowledged by the authorities that Swahili was rapidly being replaced by English as the medium of instruction in these schools (Kenya Government Printer, 1948).

In towns and areas in which groups speaking different languages had settled Swahili was the medium of instruction in the lower primary schools. Secondary non-technical education was in all cases conducted in English. The proportion of the population who attended secondary schools before 1958, however, was inconsiderable.

The implementation of certain provisions of the *Report on African Education in Kenya* in 1950 (Kenya Government Printer, 1950) initiated a decade of considerable change in educational practice. However, the direction of change was not exclusively or even primarily in accordance with the recommendations of

[1] Almost all the fathers of the children in the survey who attended primary and intermediate schools did so between 1920 and 1948, the greater number attending between 1930 and 1940. The proportion of those who attended primary or intermediate schools named within each group, and ranged from nearly 60 per cent among the Luo group to approximately 20 per cent among the Mijikenda.

the Commission, which were in certain respects impracticable.[1] The most significant consequence of the Report in many rural areas seems to have been that the exclusion of Swahili as a medium of instruction was accelerated, as was the introduction of English as a medium. The trend towards the introduction of English as a medium of instruction at an increasingly early stage had, however, continued, and the majority of children who took part in the survey reported that they were taught predominantly through this medium from the beginning of the third year, and in some cases earlier, though there were considerable differences in this regard in the various districts and between schools in urban and rural areas.

To summarize: Swahili, and in some instances the mother tongue, were the languages of instruction to which the majority of the fathers of the children in the sample who attended primary school were exposed. The languages of instruction the majority of the children in the rural sample were exposed to were their Mother Tongues and English, with the exception of the children belonging to the Mijikenda group.

The percentages of the children in each group attending rural schools who claimed to have been educated through the media of English, Swahili, or their Mother Tongue is shown in Table 1.[2]

In urban areas, as I have implied, the situation was rather different. The recommendation made by the Beecher Commission that Swahili should remain the initial language of instruction in primary schools in towns and settled areas was still officially in operation in 1960, when most of the children involved in the survey began their schooling, but it is clear that it was not strictly implemented in many schools. In 1960 the English-medium experiment had been officially introduced into only one African school in Nairobi on an experimental basis

[1] The report recommended that in rural areas provision should be made for textbooks in Dabida, Kamba, Kikuyu, Masai, Kimeru, Nandi, Luyia, and Dholuo for the first four years of education, and advised that textbooks should be translated for the initial stages of education in Giriama, Pokomo, Galla, Sagalla, Taveta, Suk, Kisii, Tende, Tesiot, Boran, Turkana, and Somali. It also stated that after the initial stages, in areas where the second group of languages were spoken, 'Swahili should be used for literature while the vernacular continued as the medium of oral instruction'.

[2] The children were asked to indicate which language was used to teach most subjects in the first and third year.

before being introduced more widely.[1] However, 41 per cent of the children in the Nairobi sample reported that in the schools they attended English was used to teach most subjects in Standard 1. The percentage was higher in Mombasa, where the Aga Khan Education Board had introduced initial English medium instruction in schools under its jurisdiction as early as 1953. However, in 1960 Swahili was still widely used as a medium of instruction in schools in the towns, and in many cases it was also taught in the periods allocated for training in the Vernacular.

Table 1

Reported Languages of Instruction in Standards 1 and 3: Rural Sample

	Mother Tongue		*English*		*Swahili*	
Language Group	% Std. 1	% Std. 3	% Std. 1	% Std. 3	% Std. 1	% Std. 3
1 Gusii (n. 99)	95	26	1	67	4	7
2 Kipsigis (n. 130)	85	36	7	59	8	5
3 Kamba (n. 139)	93	46	3	51	4	3
4 Kikuyu (n. 126)	83	40	3	46	14	14
5 Luo (n. 80)	85	30	12	67	3	3
6 Luyia (n. 63)	85	44	6	49	9	7
7 Meru (n. 144)	98	56	2	44	—	—
8 Mijikenda (incl. Digo and Pokomo) (n. 78)	—	—	—	34	100	66

Assuming that Swahili was primarily acquired and transmitted through the formal educational system, one would expect that in the rural areas the proportion of fathers who were reported to have a knowledge of the language would be significantly greater than the proportion of children making the same claim and also that the proportion of fathers reported to have a knowledge of Swahili would vary in the different groups, and such variation would reflect the degree to which parents in the groups attended primary school.

Table 2 indicates the percentage of children and their fathers in the rural sample who were reported to have a knowledge of the language in the different groups.

The figures appear to bear out the general assumption that a knowledge of Swahili is characteristically acquired outside the formal educational system. However, to state that a person has a knowledge of a language is to make a claim of little utility, particularly when the language is used widely in attenuated

[1] This and related developments have been described in greater detail in a recent article on the subject (Gorman, 1968).

Table 2

Percentage of Subjects and Fathers in the Rural Sample Reported to Know Swahili

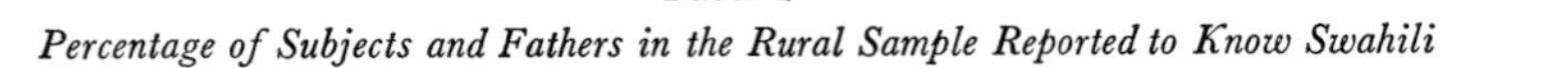

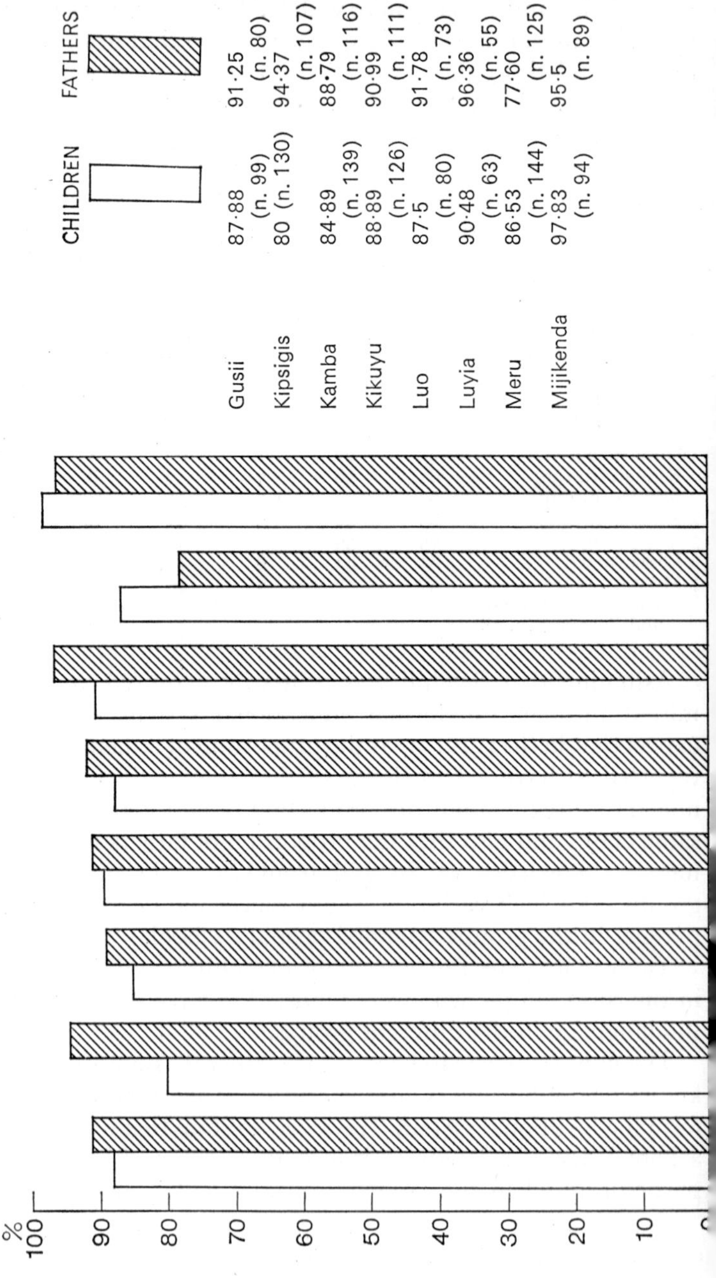

CHILDREN
FATHERS
Gusii 87·88 (n. 99) 91·25 (n. 80)
Kipsigis 80 (n. 130) 94·37 (n. 107)
Kamba 84·89 (n. 139) 88·79 (n. 116)
Kikuyu 88·89 (n. 126) 90·99 (n. 111)
Luo 87·5 (n. 80) 91·78 (n. 73)
Luyia 90·48 (n. 63) 96·36 (n. 55)
Meru 86·53 (n. 144) 77·60 (n. 125)
Mijikenda 97·83 (n. 94) 95·5 (n. 89)
%
100
90
80
70
60
50
40
30
20
10

forms, as is Swahili in many areas of East Africa. It is because of this that the children were asked to rate their proficiency in the language and that of their fathers on a four-point scale. Naturally these ratings have a comparative value only, but significant differences emerge when the degrees of proficiency attributed by the children by themselves and their parents are correlated. The relevant percentage of each group who were reported to speak Swahili in the two highest proficiency categories (Good or Very Good) is shown in Table 3.

Several deductions can be drawn from this data. It is evidently necessary for the children to know and to use Swahili, even if in an attenuated form, and this they do irrespective of their educational experience. Its relative disuse as a medium of instruction in rural areas since 1950 does not appear to have decreased its functional importance to young people living outside the towns. However, while the extensive use of Swahili as a medium of instruction before 1950 may have a bearing on the fact that the two generational groups are reported to use the language with different degrees of 'proficiency', the fathers' reported ability to speak the language proficiently does not appear to be significantly related to their educational experience, and this would lead one to look for factors outside the educational process to account for the distribution of proficiency ratings.

Similarly, in the urban samples the children in each group claimed to speak Swahili with very few exceptions, and as groups rated their father's proficiency above their own. There were no significant differences between the proficiency ratings given to the fathers of children in urban as opposed to rural areas. Significant differences were found in both urban and rural samples between the reported knowledge of the language on the part of parents of different sexes, but it is not relevant to detail these here.

When a similar comparison was made between the knowledge of English attributed to their parents by the children significant differences were found between ratings for male and female parents, and between those attributed to the children and their parents.

An indication of certain of these differences is given in Table 4, which shows the fathers' reported knowledge of

Table 3

Reported Proficiency Ratings in Swahili (Two Highest Categories) of Father and Children in the Rural Sample

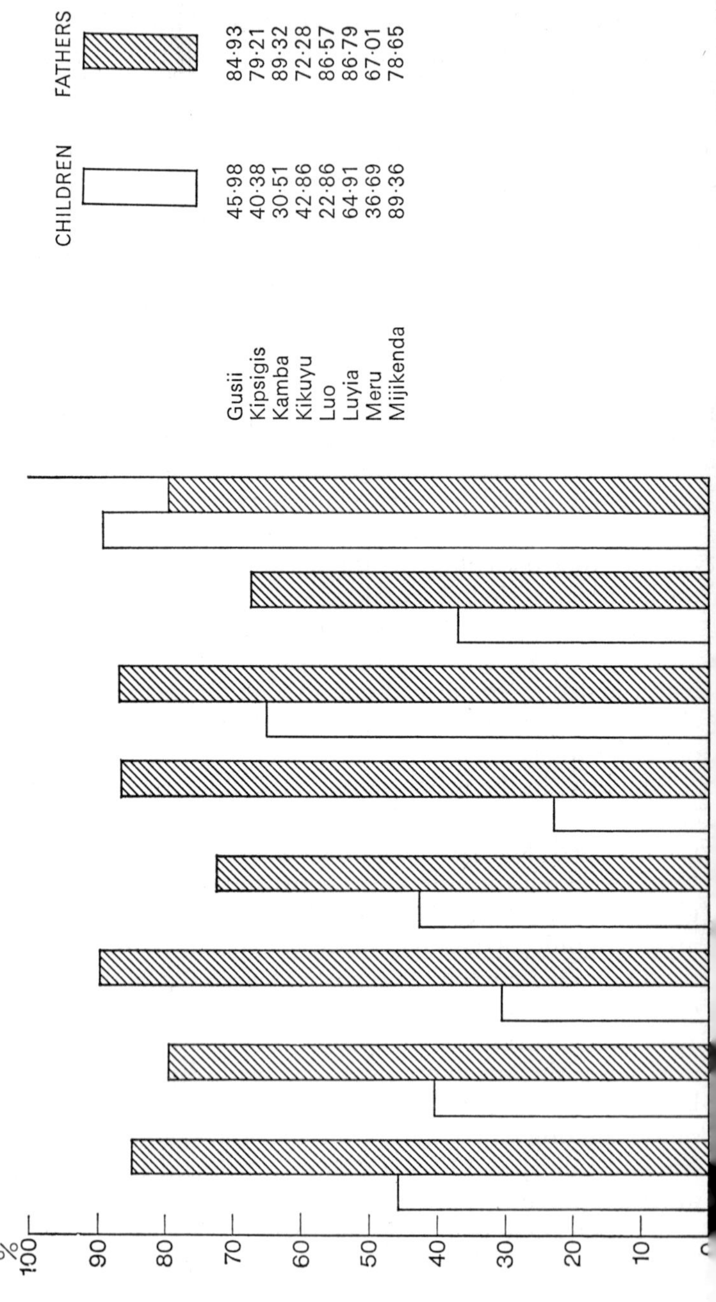

	CHILDREN	FATHERS
Gusii	45·98	84·93
Kipsigis	40·38	79·21
Kamba	30·51	89·32
Kikuyu	42·86	72·28
Luo	22·86	86·57
Luyia	64·91	86·79
Meru	36·69	67·01
Mijikenda	89·36	78·65

Reported Knowledge of English and Swahili by Fathers of Children in both Urban and Rural Samples

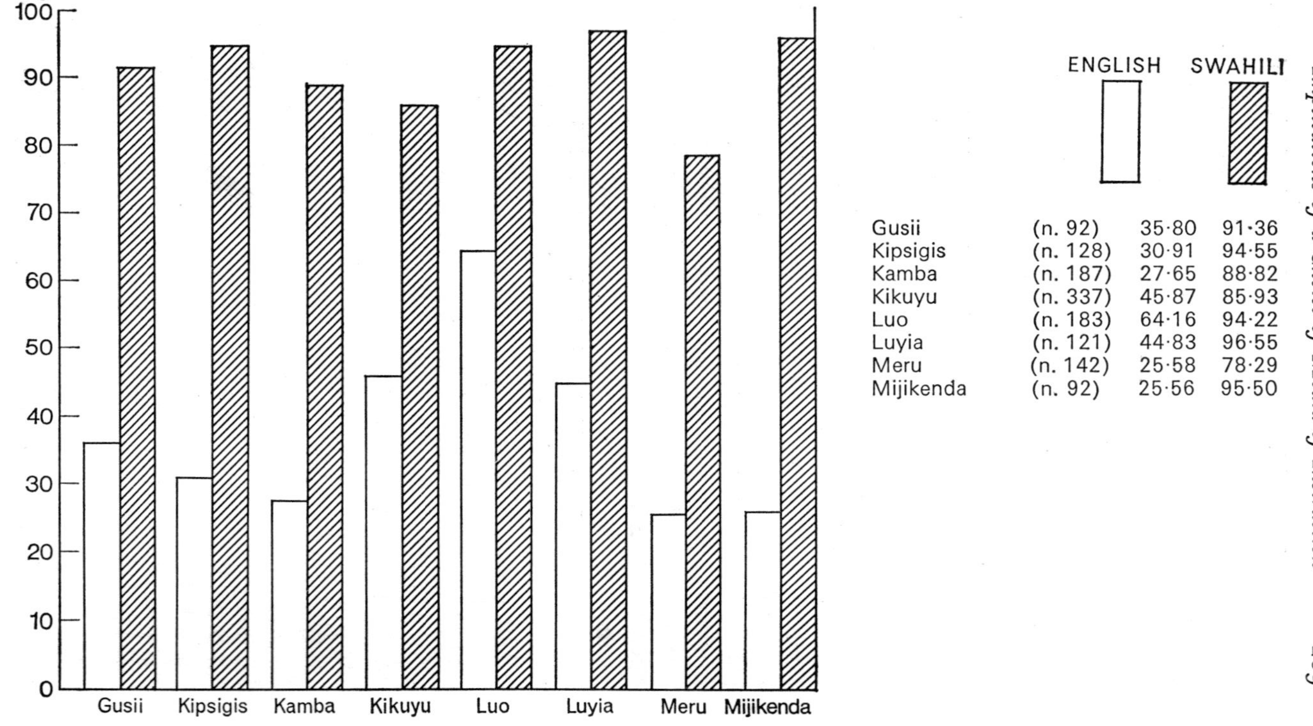

English and Swahili. In the Table the results derived from both urban and rural samples are combined.

When the relevant results have been correlated I think they will indicate that there is a positive relationship between educational background and reported knowledge of English among male parents, at least as far as members of those groups that do not constitute a significant part of the urban labour force are concerned. One can expect this, as it is apparent that the language is characteristically acquired through formal education.

The first section of the questionnaire provided further data about characteristic total verbal repertoires of the members of the different language groups and information about the functional importance of different vernacular languages within the groups, for instance, the percentage of children speaking Kimeru in the rural sample who claimed to speak Kikuyu was 42 per cent. The percentage of Kikuyu-speaking children who claimed to know Kimeru was 0 per cent. At this stage, however, I only wish to consider certain aspects of the children's reported use of Swahili, English, and their mother tongue in specific locales.

LANGUAGE USE IN THE HOME

The second part of the questionnaire asked for information about restricted dyadic repertoires used within the families of the children at home, and I would like to comment on certain aspects of the information obtained. I was primarily concerned with dyadic relationships in which the child was a participant. I assumed that in most families parental patterns of language use would tend to be normative, and that while overt parental pressure on the children to use or avoid the use of particular languages while at home appears to be exceptional in the groups concerned, one would expect that the inexplicit pressures on the children to conform to parental usage, or to limit their use of languages in the home to those understood by parents or grandparents, would be considerable.

In one of the questions about intra-familial language use the topic and locale were specified and held constant, as it were. The children were asked: 'What language or languages do you speak to the following members of your family at home when talking about school?' In another question the topic was not specified, and they were asked to write down the languages that different members of their family spoke to them at home.[1] As I have said, they were asked in each case to indicate the relative frequency on a three-point scale of the use of different languages. While the characteristic restricted verbal repertoires naturally varied within the different language groups, it is possible, without undue over-simplification, to make certain generalizations about patterns of intra-familial language use.

As would be expected the total verbal repertoires of both parents and children appear to be infrequently utilized in conversations in the home. The mother tongue of the children tended to be employed exclusively only in conversations between children and grandparents. To a lesser extent also, conversations between mothers and children tended to be monolingual. With these exceptions dyadic language behaviour tended to be multilingual.

Table 5 gives an indication of the extent of monolingual interaction between the children and certain members of their families. The figures indicate the extent to which children claimed that the mother tongue only was used in conversations with various members of their families.

The results seem to indicate that in each generational group the linguistic diversity of the interaction extends; that monolingual interaction is most prevalent between the children and their grandparents, mothers and the younger members of their families, in that order. Monolingual interaction between the children and older siblings is relatively rare. There are differences in the behaviour of a number of the groups which are significant, but the relative uniformity of the general configurations of language use within each group and in both rural and urban samples is perhaps the most striking aspect of the language behaviour reported.

Further information about language behaviour in the families of the children was obtained from their answers to questions

[1] They were asked to give details of languages used by and to their father, mother, and the male and female parents of these, and by and to their older brothers and sisters and younger brothers and sisters. 'Brothers and sisters' were defined as being 'sons and daughters of your father'. They were also asked to indicate which members of their family lived with them or within an hour's walk of their home. Table 5 is based on the answers given to the question in which the topic was unspecified.

Table 5

Reported Monolingual Interaction between Subjects and Members of their Families (Percentages)

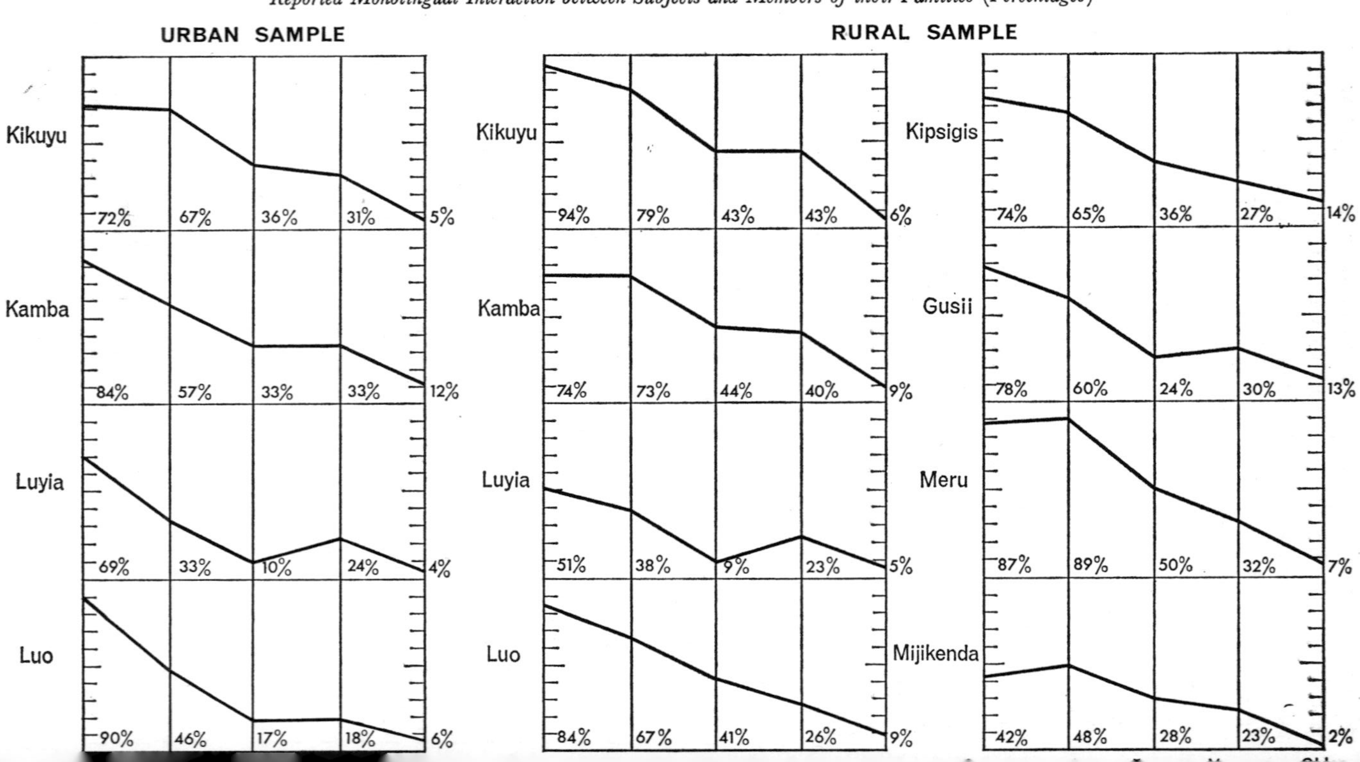

concerning their use of English and Swahili in conversations with the same members of their families. Table 6 shows the percentage of children in each sample who claimed to use either English or Swahili 'often' in conversations with members of their family. 'Often' was defined in the instructions to the

Table 6

Reported Habitual Use of English and Swahili

Rural sample	Grandfather Sw. %	Grandfather E. %	Mother Sw. %	Mother E. %	Father Sw. %	Father E. %	Younger brother Sw. %	Younger brother E. %	Older brother Sw. %	Older brother E. %
Gusii	8	3	2	0	8	4	5	9	14	37
Kipsigis	10	2	5	1	15	9	13	25	20	44
Kamba	5	0	5	0	7	5	5	17	15	33
Kikuyu	0	0	1	0	1	3	6	12	13	34
Luo	9	0	1	3	4	18	8	19	16	48
Luyia	14	4	9	1	31	18	16	18	24	43
Meru	3	0	2	1	3	3	7	17	17	36
Mijikenda	12	0	29	3	23	4	14	23	48	46

Urban sample	Grandfather Sw. %	Grandfather E. %	Mother Sw. %	Mother E. %	Father Sw. %	Father E. %	Younger brother Sw. %	Younger brother E. %	Older brother Sw. %	Older brother E. %
Kikuyu	5	0	5	7	6	9	15	18	30	30
Kamba	8	0	12	5	9	5	17	11	33	19
Luyia	8	8	12	3	13	16	21	14	25	48
Luo	3	4	7	6	11	23	33	25	26	53

question as meaning 'more than half the time'. Naturally this rating cannot be interpreted as having any literal validity in terms of the frequency with which the languages are used, but I think it can be understood as indicating that they are spoken habitually and that the information does not refer to the casual interpolation of elements of one or other of the languages in conversations between the persons concerned.

Again, certain common patterns of language use are evident. Swahili is characteristically used more frequently than English in conversations with fathers and less frequently in conversations with siblings, although there are exceptions to this trend in the urban sample. In most cases, and particularly in the urban sample, there is an increase in the extent to which both English and Swahili are used habitually by members of the younger generation, as compared to their parents. If one interprets this development diachronically as it were, and as an integrated phenomenon, one could say that in successive generations the code matrix used in the domain of the family characteristically increases in complexity and there is an alteration in the relationship of one code to another, in terms of the frequency with which they are used. Other evidence obtained also indicates this process of linguistic diversification in the younger generation. For example, Table 7 shows the extent to which the children claimed that in conversations with the fathers and their older brothers they use at various times Swahili, English and their mother tongue. The table shows the combined results of the urban and rural samples. The relevant percentages are indicated.

It is apparent that in the experience of the average school-going child in Kenya, the transition from monolingual behaviour which is associated in some measure with a monocultural environment to more diverse forms of language behaviour associated with more complex forms of social interaction is accomplished during his primary school experience; at which period the child is exposed to forms of activity that require in many cases the knowledge and use of English, Swahili, and his mother tongue. The basic pattern of institutional bilingualism in social interaction in Kenya is essentially a triadic one in which the three codes or sets of codes are in certain respects assigned complementary functional ranges; and the diversification of the children's language behaviour reflects this fact, though it has not always been reflected in the organization of the school curriculum.

A further indication of the direction of change and the nature of the diversification is given in the answers that the children gave to a question in which they were asked to indicate the language they *preferred* to use when talking to older and younger brothers and sisters *about school at home*. It is perhaps necessary to emphasize again that the reports simply provide an indication of an attitude or mental set that the children have regarding the languages that they consider would appropriately be used in a particular set of circumstances to the two groups of siblings.

Table 8 shows the statistical tables used to yield a chi-square test of significance of difference for subjects in the three largest language groups. The tables are constructed to indicate the answers of girls and boys in the three groups for reasons that will be indicated.

Reported Trilingualism in The Urban and Rural Samples

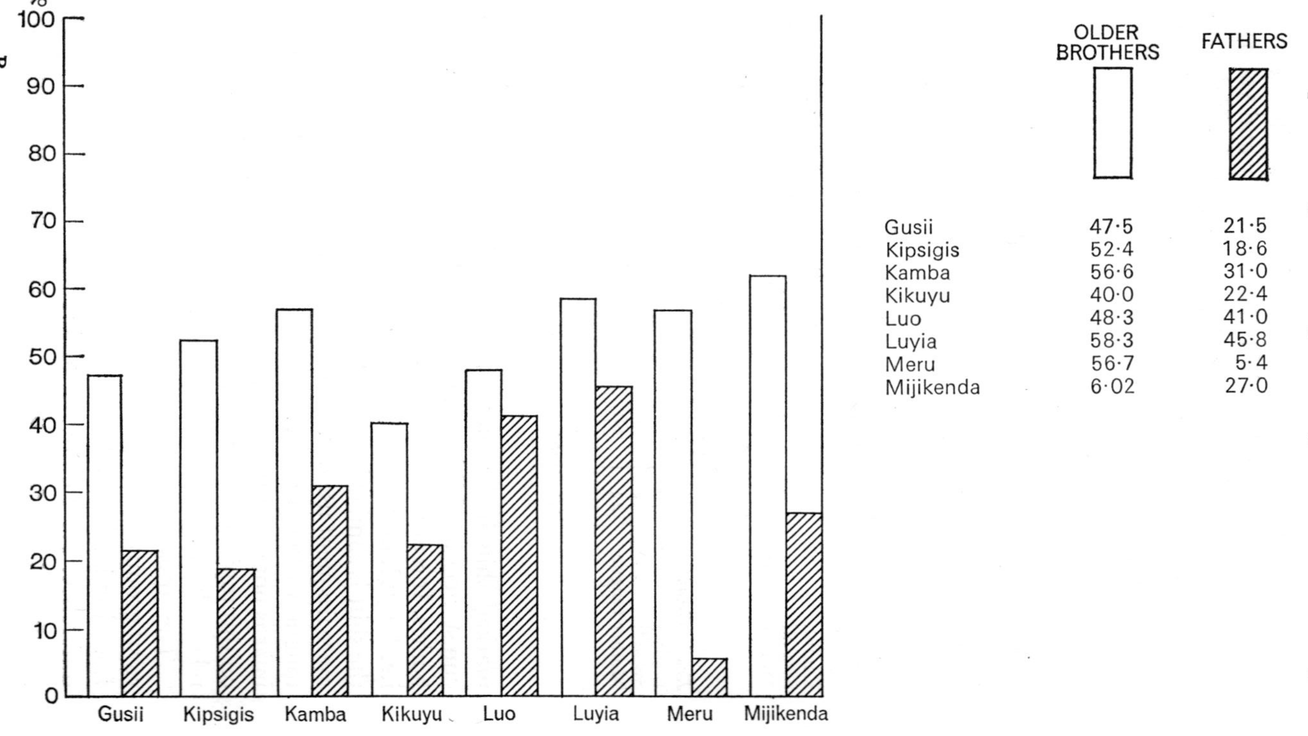

In each case there is a highly significant difference in the behaviour of the subjects in talking to older and younger siblings about this particular matter in this locale. If the reports, which are in several respects markedly consistent, give an accurate indication of patterns of behaviour it is clear that a very

Table 8

	Girls			*Boys*		
	Older siblings	*Younger siblings*	χ^2	*Older siblings*	*Younger siblings*	χ^2
Kikuyu Group						
English	87	17	61·2081	142	73	26·3421
Swahili	5	22	7·9011	27	35	0·6214
Mother tongue	18	93	38·2680	49	123	27·6830
	110	132	107·3772	218	231	54·6465
	($P < 0·001$)			($P < 0·001$)		
Luo Group						
English	37	17	9·0067	80	34	23·0698
Swahili	4	8	1·0500	13	26	3·1833
Mother tongue	10	30	8·5592	36	82	13·8222
	51	55	18·6159	129	142	40·0753
	($P < 0·001$)			($P < 0·001$)		
Kamba Group						
English	76	20	31·0071	60	23	19·5857
Swahili	2	10	5·5787	11	6	1·8962
Mother tongue	23	68	23·6355	26	76	20·7419
	101	98	60·2213	97	105	42·2238
	($P < 0·001$)			($P < 0·001$)		

marked shift in language behaviour takes place in these circumstances as children grow older and before they leave their homes. It is also clear that the shift primarily involves two codes, i.e. English and the children's mother tongue. The direction of the shift is similar in each case, in that the trend is towards the more frequent use of English to older siblings and of the mother tongue to the younger. The use of Swahili, which one might infer is not generally thought to be appropriate in conversations on this topic in this locale, is more restricted and in contrast is relatively stable.

The answers to the question of children in the urban and rural groups of the four major language communities (Kikuyu, Luo, Luyia, and Kamba) were also tested for significance of difference. No significant differences were found in any one group that related to urban and rural divisions. However, an overall comparison of the four urban and rural groups showed a significant difference in reported behaviour ($\chi^2 = 9{\cdot}46$ $P < 0{\cdot}01 > 0{\cdot}001$), which appeared to derive from the greater preference for Swahili in the urban groups (11·41 per cent, as opposed to 5·23 per cent in the rural sub-sample said that they preferred to use Swahili in conversations with older siblings).

Other socio-linguistic inferences can be drawn from the table, such as the fact that the boys in the Kikuyu-speaking group are decidedly more disposed to use English in this situation than the girls, as with one degree of freedom the relevant contributory χ^2 is significant beyond the 0·001 level and remains above 0·01, even if the confidence limits are lowered;[1] but this inference, though interesting, is not immediately relevant, except in so far as it indicates that other social forces apart from those associated with the educational system strongly influence the patterns of language use that are characteristic of the children surveyed.

I think that it would be wrong to assume that the configurations of language use in the home that were reported among siblings indicate that the use of English is, in certain respects, 'displacing' the use of the mother tongue of the children; this is, that it is being used in situations of interaction in which the mother tongue would formerly have been used. I think that subsequent research may indicate that the use of English in the home and outside it by the children in question is in part concomitant upon their assumption as educated people, of *additional* 'roles', as it were, with which the use of English is associated. It is usually accepted that 'different forms of social relations can generate quite different speech systems' (Bernstein, 1965). I think it would not be difficult to demonstrate that the partial corollary of this is also valid, namely, that the 'possession of different speech systems' has the effect of increasing the number of occasional roles that a child (in this instance) can assume and the number of role relations into which he can enter, and consequently the number of contexts in which a language or languages can be used.

The inquiry also provided information about aspects of the children's language use in school and locales outside the home and school when talking to their peers. No significant differences

[1] If χ^2 is multiplied by 4, $P < 0{\cdot}001$.

were found in their answers to the questions on these aspects of their behaviour that related to urban and rural divisions, though there were differences between the behaviour of pupils in the two samples in specific language groups. Again, the relative uniformity of the children's reported behaviour in both samples is itself a matter of some interest.

For example, in answer to the question in which they were asked to indicate what language or languages they preferred to use when talking, firstly, to older brothers and sisters, and secondly, to their closest school friends 'about school, outside their homes, e.g. in a bus or shop', a large majority of the pupils in all the groups in the urban and rural samples in answer to both parts of the question said that they preferred to use English. One is perhaps justified in drawing the conclusion that to the children in these circumstances, the language serves to some extent as an index of group identity whose display is not required within the 'closed networks' of home and school, where their status as educated people is recognized.

It is perhaps worth noting at this point that the two areas of reciprocal interaction in which the language choices of the children appear to be the least restricted are in their conversations with brothers and sisters at home and in conversations with their peers at school. In both cases the participants could be said to be 'equal' and 'solidary', to use the terms defined by Brown and Gilman to characterize the social relationships that they considered to be most evidently relevant to language behaviour (Brown and Gilman, 1960). The relative lack of restriction in language choice at school, however, applies only outside the classroom. Language use in the classroom is, to use Herman's phrase, 'task oriented', and the use of English is prescribed for most purposes (Herman, 1961); even when it is not prescribed, as, for instance, in certain kinds of active non-reciprocal activity associated with the school environment, such as the process of counting, it was reported to by used by all but a very small proportion of the children in the sample.

The reported language use of the children in the contexts I have just described tends therefore to be similar, irrespective of the group to which they belonged or of the language in which they received their initial school instruction. This seems to indicate that, in the contexts so far considered, their early educational experience is not a highly significant factor determining patterns of language use at this stage in their development, except in the sense that the use of English can be acquired only through the educational process.

However, before it will be possible to arrive at meaningful conclusions regarding the possible effects of the use of different media of instruction in primary schools on the subsequent language behaviour of the children, it will be necessary to obtain more detailed 'profiles' of language use for a smaller group of children in more varied situations of interaction and reception, and to devise effective methods of isolating and measuring certain of the language skills involved in the production and reception of English and Swahili and in a number of vernacular languages. The second stage of the project, which is now in progress, is primarily directed towards the achievement of these two aims.

REFERENCES

Bernstein, B.
(1965) 'A Sociolinguistic Approach to Social Learning', *Survey of the Social Sciences*, ed. J. Gould, p. 151.

Brown, R. and Gilman, A.
(1960) 'The Pronouns of Power and Solidarity', *Style in Language*, ed. T. Sebeok, pp. 253–76.

Gorman, T.
(1968) 'Bilingualism in the Educational System of Kenya', *Comparative Education*, IV, 3, pp. 213–21.

Gumperz, J.
(1966) 'On the Ethnology of Linguistic Change', *Sociolinguistics*, ed. W. Bright, pp. 27–49.

Herman, S.
(1961) 'Explorations in the Social Psychology of Language Choice', *Human Relations*, 14, pp. 149–64.

Hovland, C. I.
(1959) 'Reconciling Conflicting Results Derived from Experimental and Survey Studies of Attitude Change', *The American Psychologist*, Vol. 14, p. 299.

Hymes, D.
(1962) 'The Ethnography of Speaking', *Anthropology and Human Behaviour*, ed. T. Gladwin and W. Sturtevant, pp. 13–53.

Kenya Government Printer.

(1964) *Kenya Population Census 1962*, vol. II, 1964

(1948) *The Ten Year Plan for the Development of African Education*, Nairobi, p. 4.

(1950) *Proposals for the Implementation of the Report on African Education in Kenya*. Sessional Paper No. 1 of 1950, Nairobi.

Mackey, W.

(1965) 'Bilingual Interference, its Analysis and Measurement', *Journal of Communication*, XV, No. 4, Dec., pp. 239–49.

Taylor, W.

(1953) 'Cloze Procedure', *Journalism Quarterly* Fall, p. 416.

Weinreich, V.

(1957) 'Functional Aspects of Indian Bilingualism', *Word*, 13.

XI. Socio-linguistic Problems and Potentialities of Education through a Foreign Language

JOAN MAW

My own first introduction to questions of perception of reality and reflections of social organization in language came through teaching in a secondary school (Junior and Senior) in Uganda in 1955–8. I went to teach Art and Music, but I also taught English. The language of instruction in the school was English, but the youngest pupils had very little. I think a few anecdotes from this period are worth telling.

It was in painting that linguistic conflicts became manifest in a non-linguistic medium. First, as might be expected, there were problems of organization. The first language (Luganda) of the majority of the pupils contains the following words most commonly used for colours:

-myufù	'red, brown'
-yengèvu	'yellow'
kìragala	'green'
-ddùgàvu	'dark'
-êru	'white'
`bbululû	'blue'

(The last term, obviously a loan, is the only one referring specifically to colour. The others have also other meanings such as 'yellow, ripe', 'green, appertaining to leaves', and so on[1]). In the school the children used powder-paints, and they had available black, white, crimson, vermilion, ochre, raw umber, chrome yellow, lemon yellow, cobalt, and indigo. Mrs. E.

[1] In fact, of course, other colour terms could be produced, but on the comparative principle, e.g. 'buffalo-dark' ('black'); 'as if unripe' ('light-coloured'—used of a person); etc.

Engholm, in her book *Education through English* (Cambridge, 1965), has related how a boy in her class painted a picture of a vermilion canna lily raw umber, suggesting that the boy asked himself what colour the flower was, decided on *-myufù*, and took at random a colour from his palette covered by this term, which happened to be umber. Such instances can be multiplied from my experience. For example, pupils were quite likely to paint tree-trunks or people vermilion or indigo. These were presumably covered by *-ddùgàvu*, 'dark'.

On the other hand, the opposite situation arose when I asked a class to paint a picture including cows. They drew happily, but then several said they could not paint because they hadn't got the right colours. I asked what they wanted, and they could only say 'brown', but looked lost when I suggested umber. When I showed them how to mix different shades they were pleased, and each cow was painted a different colour and pattern, impossible to describe in English, but obviously real and recognizable to the children. The same boys who painted crimson tree-trunks and blue faces would not think of painting two cows alike, and took great pains to get the exact shade they wanted. In a society where cows are wealth, not kept for meat or milk but as capital, used for bride-price but rarely killed or sold, there are many words for describing distinctive markings, obviously of real importance to the members of that society.

Blue (cobalt) was a special case. Although it had a name in Ganda, this was a loan-word, and the children seemed to use the colour as a general substitute, to fill up spaces (rather as English children sometimes use brown) and to replace any colour they had not got. It was most often used for green, when children had forgotten how to make it.[1] (I did not buy green, because the only one available was jade, not very useful; and also as an economy measure, and to try to force mixing.) Blue did not seem to exist in its own right. So one day, as a preliminary to their painting someone resting on a hot day, I asked a class what colour the sky was. After a long silence someone said red. A number of the class agreed, and I said well, it could be

[1] Indeed, one boy habitually painted trees with vermillion trunks and branches and cobalt leaves—very attractive, and a useful object lesson in judgements on the nature of the artist's vision. One is reminded of the controversies about Homer's 'wine-dark sea'.

red sometimes, at sunset, for example. But what else could it be? Someone else said white, and got more agreement. I said it could be white when it was very cloudy, but this day was supposed to be hot. What other colour could it be? No further suggestions came, so I took them outside to look. All chorused 'blue', in tones of relief and revelation. Why had they said red? Red seemed to be associated with heat (charcoal or wood fires glow red), and on a hot day the heat comes from above, therefore the sky is red. Why white? The word *-êru* is also used for 'empty, clear, colourless'. On a hot day there are no clouds, and (quite the opposite of my suggestion) therefore the sky is clear, i.e. 'white'.

These examples show clearly, if further proof were needed, that not only do speakers of different languages divide up the spectrum differently (no new observation) but that their linguistic distinctions may influence their behaviour (in painting); and that the distinctions made may depend on other factors—socio-economic in the case of the cows; other physical properties in the case of the sky. One might well suppose that in other areas of experience also different distinctions and relationships are perceived, and that these differences will cause difficulty not only in manipulating another language but also in dealing with the concepts and relationships implicit in that other language, as well as confusion when dealing with non-linguistic phenomena.

In *Language in Africa*—papers of the Leverhulme conference, edited by John Spencer (Cambridge, 1963), several contributors suggested that the teaching of a second language might well begin in Art and Craft lessons, since these are practical subjects where demonstration proceeds along with language. This would be true only where the teaching consisted of instruction rather than of education. It is still more disheartening to read in such papers as that of Peter Wingard opinions such as that the use of English is to be merely that of an educational medium; that the English currently used in E.A. schools should be collected and made the basis for future courses; and the hypothesis—which his own experiments up to the time of his writing did not support—that, 'linguistic simplification will yield very large benefits'.

It seems to me mistaken to suppose that any language can be

only a medium of instruction; this ignores all recent work on the relation between conceptualization and language. Whether we like it or not, a change of medium will have some effect on the thought processes and conceptualizing of the learner; simplified language and courses based on existing unsatisfactory material are going to produce a progressively more poverty-stricken set of concepts, both of ideas and relationships. This is not to say that teaching should be unstructured but it should be progressive and aim at the fullest possible use and comprehension of the language used, and also pay attention to the learner's need for psychological and social development.

To take only this matter of a colour system. The introduction in art classes of distinctions in new areas (e.g. shades of red) with distinct names of course induces easier recognition of such distinctions, but the matter goes deeper than that. It seemed that the conception of colour as an abstract quality was difficult to grasp, and indeed many children could not make use of the distinctions between 'colour' and 'paint', and would continually ask for 'some more red colour, please'. This is not surprising, since, as has been pointed out, the basic colour-words often have other connotations such as 'ripeness', which is intrinsic and closely associated with the actual colour. As Professor M. A. K. Halliday has pointed out (*The Linguistic Sciences and Language Teaching*, Longmans, 1964, p. 113), one cannot compare one language with another, but one can compare the systems of one language with those of another. To compare the colour terms of one language with those of another would tell a great deal about both, but it is also of interest to see how these terms are used grammatically. For example, in English the colour adjective normally precedes the noun, though we are familiar in poetry with 'mantle of blue', 'little bird of blue', etc. In Swahili there are three forms in regular use, viz:

gauni jeupe	'a white dress'
kilori cha buluu	'a blue rattle-trap lorry'
ndege wenye nyekundu	'a red bird'

The choice is not free, but I frankly do not know what governs it, though one might suspect it was something to do with how intrinsic the colour was considered to be. But one might well find that this was not based on actual criteria (e.g. dye *vs.* paint, or skin pigmentation *vs.* fur). It might not be too much to suppose that the study of the colour systems of two languages could, under a sensitive teacher, lead not only to the enrichment of the student's vocabulary and a development of his sensitivity to particular colour ranges but also to a consideration of some of the areas of particular interest in his own and the new society (I am sure that a concern with the weather, judged by the appearance of the sky, would be found to be very important in English!) Women's fashions might figure in both cultures; and one might go further to a consideration of attitudes to colour, for example, in their ceremonial use. The fact that this differs between cultures (take the connotations of white and red in European and Oriental cultures, for example) might help to dispel the conception of an intrinsic 'meaning' of colour, or an implied hierarchy of value. The study of metaphors and idioms, etc. (black as ink/coal/my hat/the ace of spades/Newgate knockers; white as snow/chalk/a sheet, whiter than white; and so on) can enrich vocabulary, but again can give further insight into this new culture and, by comparison, into one's own; which is far more important.

It may be that Basil Bernstein's concepts can be useful here. John Spencer (op. cit.) has suggested that in bilingualism 'each language (is) efficiently used in a complementary set of contexts', and we hope that the current Survey of Language Use will throw some light on this hypothesis. It has also been suggested that bilingualism might be regarded as an extreme form of the use of different styles—in Bernstein's terms, elaborated *vs.* restricted codes. This may be true. But so far the assumption implicit in educational policy has been that in Africa the indigenous languages are in the position of the restricted codes—it has even been suggested that some languages consist solely of restricted codes—and that the language of education would be in the position of the elaborated code. If this were so it would incidentally be a further reason for avoiding 'simplified' forms of the second language.

The multilingual situation is likely, however, in my opinion, to be more complex than the monolingual in terms of restricted *vs.* elaborated codes. If one took, for example, the linguistic background of an individual living on the coast of Tanzania one would be likely to find something like the following. The first language might be, say, Bondee, used within the family, and Swahili, used outside the immediate family, learned by children from their peers. A child going to a Koran school would learn a certain amount of Arabic by heart—not necessarily with much comprehension—and to write Swahili in Arabic script. This would be a fairly usual prelude to a Government primary school, where the Roman script would be learned and teaching would be through the medium of Swahili. English would be introduced as a subject, and would generally be the medium of instruction in the secondary school. Swahili for most people would be the language of normal business and social contact, with the use of various debased forms for use with Europeans and Asians. Some of these language usages would be in a restricted code, e.g. the Swahilis for use with Europeans and Asians, the English of the primary school lessons, and the Arabic of the Koran school. The traditions of learning by heart, begun in these schools, and in any case natural in a country where writing materials are expensive and vernacular reading matter scarce, is one which would seem to encourage the widespread use of restricted codes. On the other hand, there is also a tradition of oral entertainment, particularly of story-telling, and great respect is shown to a person whose Swahili is said to be 'tasty' or 'sweet'. There will be general agreement among people, educated or not, as to whose Swahili is good, and such a person seems to have not only a wide vocabulary, and an interest in discussing and expounding the meanings of words, but also a gift for coining vivid phrases and expressions, the self-confidence to push grammatical possibilities to their limits, and subtle use of the phonetic resources of the language. To hear the delighted exclamations of the audience at such a speaker, and to note how people repeat what seem to be felicitous expressions under their breaths, is surely to witness a performance in an elaborated code, recognized and admired by others. The same kind of pleasure shown under these circumstances is not the same as that shown when a speaker introduces well-known saws and proverbs into a speech, nor that when an audience makes a traditional response, as in the preliminaries to a story, for example.

It seems likely, then, that Swahili at least does offer a range of possibilities to its speakers. On the other hand, the type of English at present used in primary and secondary schools is generally that of a restricted code. Are we really performing an educational service in the deepest sense if we offer only this kind of selective, stultifying language which gives no scope for imagination and invention? Teaching which ignores the already full, rich life of the pupil is liable at best to be boring and ineffective, and at worst to produce literate zombies. And the biggest tragedy is that a bilingual or multilingual situation *could* give pupils an insight into new cultures, as well as, by comparison, into their own, and could rouse some speculations into the nature of culture and society itself. We could take any aspect of life: artistic, such as public recitation; art-cum-craft, such as pottery making; craft-cum-practical, such as house-building. These activities have a place in most societies, but a different place. And vocabulary, techniques, and uses cannot be discussed in any intelligent way without mutual enlightenment and the surprise that may lead to a re-assessment of preconceptions, which is education. I am reminded of a colleague explaining to a Galla that European houses had a sort of pipe in the wall, and if you turned a knob water came out. 'They must be very happy', the Galla commented. Not all, explained my colleague, in fact sometimes people are so unhappy that they even commit suicide. A pause, then, 'They must be mad', was the verdict.

Of course, the direction of imagination and invention in a second language will not be exactly the same as that of a native speaker, but at its highest it may, I suggest, produce something entirely new, neither wholly indigenous nor wholly foreign, but an amalgam. However, a child trained in English on exercises of the filling-in type (and I quote) such as:

> The opposite of polite is . . .

or answering questions such as:

> Do you do stupid things or do you do cruel things?

or

> Write down one English word which means *a male pig*.

is, I submit, highly unlikely to produce language such as the following extracts, taken from compositions by children of the same age, or slightly younger, than those at whom the exercises were aimed.

Subject: Picking Cotton

'I went and told my grandmother that our cotton was ready now and we were going to start picking it on the next day but I did not know if she wanted to go the next day. She answered me, "I will go but I am not going to work hard. I am not well".'

[On seeing the cotton field] 'Then I saw the bright colour and I said in my heart that it looks like angels.'

'As it was easy we picked it as a play, we danced, singing. Although we were dancing and singing we were working, but dancing only with our feet.'

'Some of the children were not old enough to carry the basket all over the place. My mother told them to tie a belt round their centre and put cotton underneath their dresses. It was very interesting to see someone with a big stomach full of cotton.'

'My mother and father picked as if they were not human beings, very very fast and left not even a spot of white colour in a ball. . . . As the cotton balls were fluffy I did not pick them fast for I kept putting a ball of it on my cheek and feeling it.'

'When we heard that we started picking very quickly and we did not mind whether the cotton was silky and fluffy or not because our aim was not picking good cotton but filling the basket.'

'My brothers started to cry and some started to say that they were very ill but my mother said to those that were ill. "Would you like some food?" and they said, "Yes Madam." So mother thought that they were hungry but they were not ill.'

'The cotton was put on a bicycle and was driven home. I thought that it was very happy to ride on a bicycle.'

'We were all very tired and only gazing.'

'When a child cried I went to see very quickly what had happened to him. But I did not go for that, but because I was tired.'

Here a number of points could be made. The general impression of a happy, communal occasion is original, as is the general insistence on utter weariness by the evening. Observation of character is very clear. Retelling of amusing incidents was probably stimulated by the discussion at the beginning of the lesson. Some new vocabulary was offered, and it is plain that the words *silky* and *fluffy* had an immediate appeal.

Subject: My First Visit to a doctor

1. In the waiting room there were many notices. One of them was 'Do not shout'. But there were other people who did not care about it, they were shouting and coughing as if they were in their own house.

2. Then he dressed my ankle. I was a bit proud because my leg looked pretty to me.

3. . . . as we were unable to read the hand-writing of the doctor my father asked me to go back and ask him what disease I had.

4. [In hospital] They went on day and night, all things that I did not want to have done to me were done.

5. Then he pulled the tooth out. But I asked him to give me my tooth so that I might know what was wrong with it.

6. . . . but I could not move my leg then. So my father lifted me up. I was very happy because I was lifted up and I wished to be ill so that I might be carried, which was not nice however to be ill.

7. The time came for me to go and see him in the surgery. I was very pleased because he asked me in my language which I know very well.

8. I was very frightened thinking that there was something very important to be done to me. The doctor might say, 'Oh, this is a very bad cough so he must be cut up.'

9. We were home with my mother saying that I had escaped being eaten by the doctor.

10. Then he gave me a piece of paper like a ticket and sent me to the upper house, I mean upstairs where the tooth was going to be pulled out.

11. Early in the morning I awoke and sat outside for the cold air to come to my foot.

12. . . . he put a stethoscope on my back and heard what was inside.

13. . . . he put his stethoscope in his ears and on my back and listened whether my blood worked very well.

14. I was breathing very heavily because I was very frightened when he put that stethoscope on me.

15. But what made me very very frightened was to see him putting his something which I afterwards understood to be a stethoscope in his ears and the other side on my chest. I almost ran out of the room. I started shivering with fear because I thought that he was putting my blood out of my body.

The quotations here give quite a different effect. Obviously the experience was a frightening and lonely one; even though in many cases the child was accompanied by an elder, he usually saw the doctor alone. The need for reassurance and love shows particularly in extracts 6 and 7. Even the geography was strange (extract 10); and of all the technical terms supplied, the stethoscope seemed to be the instrument that made the greatest impression—it was even more frightening than being given an injection. Incomprehension seemed general, which makes the faith more touching.

Further quotations will be found in the appendix. The point I want to make is that a second (or third, etc.) language is here being used to *make specific* as well as to describe experiences common in both a traditional and a changing society, and that in the process attitudes may also change and become something new—neither specifically English nor specifically Ganda. What the teacher is concerned with is that the attitudes should be both informed and sensitive.

It has been suggested that one of the functions of a tribal language is the preservation of the social *status quo*, stressing the concept of the group as opposed to the individual. I quote Barby, *Democracy and Dictatorship*, 1956.

> From the analysis of the primitive's behaviour one cannot easily conclude that he possesses the feeling of the specific character of his personality, or that the various situations in which he may find himself have their own specific character. His reactions are guided by specific formulas. . . . Any act of adjustment to the primitive's world requires the individual's identification with his group. This type of adjustment . . . leads . . . to Gleichschaltung and communion, to the annihilation of the individual character of things and persons. . . . (Its opposite) creates formal relations, it preserves and increases the individual character of things and persons that forms the framework of a democratic way of life.

One wonders how correct the first conclusion is. One piece of evidence which might seem to support it is a remark by a child in a composition on being ill. He reported that he had a bad headache, but that until his mother told him that the pain was in his head *he thought it was in the ceiling*. The child must have been quite old to have had this conversation and to remember it, and it might seem to suggest a retardation of the concept of the separateness of the individual from his environment. Nevertheless, such linguistic evidence should be very carefully assessed: the meaning might have been merely that the *sensation* was that of pressure from above.

But whatever the nature of any particular world-view, if it is accepted that there is a connection between language and thought, between a particular language or language-group and a particular mode of thought, then we must also face the fact that in moving from one language to another in an educational system we are not simply changing the medium through which facts about geography or arithmetic are conveyed; we are, however imperfectly, presenting a new Weltanschauung. This may or may not be desirable or necessary, but it is inevitable. In discussing a language policy, practical considerations, such as those outlined in the working-party reports of the Leverhulme conference, are obviously of importance, but the deeper psychological and sociological problems raised are the important ones for the educationist, and, in the long run, the results on the national life of a country may be very far-reaching.

APPENDIX

Picking Cotton

'My grandmother also came with us but unwillingly for she was very tired of moving about but on the other hand she did not want to stay at home.'

'Before we went he asked us to pick in twos and said that those who would bring the highest amount of cotton would receive a present. He said this because he knew if he did not give a reward no one would take any trouble except my mother and my aunt perhaps and I because I was old enough to do what was good.'

'All the garden was white as my white shirt.'

'It was wonderful to look at. There were small balls of cotton but all the trees were full of white.'

'My youngest brother John started to throw the balls of cotton at me so that I would join his game, but I didn't. He threw them to my sister, oh she was very pleased, the game went on very nicely and I liked it very much and I wished I could join it.'

'My young brothers broke sticks and beat each other like knights.'

'This time one basket was full and my brothers started to

play with cotton. They wanted to lie in the cotton because it was silky. So my father wanted to beat them, and they stopped that moment and they picked some to be thrown in the air. They said that the aeroplane flew in the air going to England.'

'I was getting tired too, and I said to my mother, "Let me give the child some milk and let me make him happy by giving him some cotton to play with". But my mother knew the point and said that she would make him happy herself.'

'Although I was tired it was not yet time to stop. So I did all kinds of things to show my parents that I was tired. But a great sorrow for me was that they laughed and went on with their work.'

'My father told me, "If you want to sleep, I shall come with my stick and hit you".'

'When the time came to go home we were very tired and we did not want to walk. My father asked me to carry the basket which was very big. I hardly knew what to do because I was forced to do it. I carried it and by the time that we reached our home I couldn't even speak but I sat down and went to sleep.'

'Finally our baskets were full and we were tired. We finished picking and my father took a big one and I took a big basket but my mother took a little one because she carried the little child as she was really tired. As I was going I fell down because the basket was so heavy.'

'My grandmother who was very tired and hungry was now sleeping and groaning as she did so. When it was too hot we went home and I was very tired so that I thought I had an ache in my foot but my mother told me I was only lazy and that was my reward.'

'I was very hungry and it was very hot so that I started remembering a pawpaw I saw on the tree that morning and a big ripe guava I saw the day before. Mother was also hungry but she did not look so.'

'My father said to us, "I am very pleased for your work which you have done", and he gave us every one sweets, except the three porters.'

My First Visit to the Doctor

'I went unwillingly. My father pushed me inside angrily because of my fear. The doctor called me to him also because I was crying because of the medicine smells, water boiling on a stove, and a kind of pin with a medicine glass on the table.'

'He was a very fat man with a very big voice.'

'She said, "Come here". I tried to refuse but my father told me not to be afraid. I went to her and she dressed my foot. She spoke kind words and when I went out I told my father that the nurse who had nursed me was a kind woman.'

'The doctor brought a stethoscope and put it on my chest. I cried very loudly thinking that he was injecting me which I feared very much.'

'As I lay he pricked me with his pin which went deep in my body. I cried very loudly that he laughed until he nearly fell.'

'One who sat next to me had a very bad foot that was stinking nastily so that I nearly got sick, but as this room had an antiseptic spread on the floor it was alright.'

'I was much afraid because I found there an English woman and I did not know what she was going to do to me.'

'I was frightened a bit to see the doctor with all sorts of things on his ears and on the table.'

'The nurse saw that I was frightened and told my father to hold me firmly.'

'When the doctor saw me nearly crying he comforted me.'

'My little brothers and sisters were surprised to see my leg dressed in such a way.'

'I thought in my heart and said bad words to the doctor because he did not care about hurting someone's illness.' (On having a broken toe set.)

XII. Contrasting Patterns of Literacy Acquisition in a Multilingual Nation

C. A. FERGUSON

National multilingualism, the use of different language codes by substantial segments of the population of a country, is a well-recognized phenomenon, and a number of lines of research on it are currently being pursued. A less well-recognized socio-linguistic phenomenon is the coexistence within a nation of different approaches to the acquisition of literacy, not in the limited sense of different methods of instruction within a single framework of national purpose but in the sense of fundamentally different patterns which represent different aims, utilize different methods, tend to apply to different segments of the population, and have different outcomes. Thus, in a given nation there may be a contrast between a 'traditional' literacy with its goals and procedures, on the one hand, and a 'modern' literacy with different goals and procedures, on the other. Or a nation with a predominant and universally acknowledged pattern of literacy may have a different pattern, followed by a religious minority or by the majority but as a supplementary literacy for particular religious purposes. This phenomenon of national diversity in styles of literacy is the subject matter of the present paper.

In some ways this phenomenon could be better treated as a small part of different total patterns of education in a nation, and treatments of it in this more general context can doubtless be found. The purpose of the present paper, however, is to focus more narrowly on the actual processes of the acquisition of the ability to read, since it is at this point that the insights and methods of linguistics can be of greatest value in the analysis and characterization of the different patterns. The findings on this limited phenomenon may then prove of relevance for larger-scale treatments of educational processes.

The phenomenon of varied patterns of literacy acquisition within a nation can be found in many African countries, and it deserves study from a number of points of view. Here a single country will be examined, Ethiopia, and a single technique of analysis will be used, contrastive presentation of basic facts assembled in terms of a check list of questions. The data have been obtained from interviews, published studies, and observation of behaviour in literacy learning situations.

Ethiopia has a number of patterns of literacy acquisition, each with distinctive aims, methods, and results, and each followed by substantial numbers of people. It also has intermediate, ill-defined patterns, and a number of minor patterns in terms of number of people involved. Three fairly well-defined major patterns will be examined here. Several preliminary observations must be made: first, the overwhelming majority of Ethiopians do not become literate at all; second, there seems to be at present no widespread well-defined pattern of learning to read Amharic in the schools, although Amharic is the national language, it is the medium of instruction in primary education, and almost every educated Ethiopian is literate in it. Third, the majority of Ethiopians do not have Amharic as their mother tongue, but speak one of the other two major languages (Galla or Tigrinya) or one of the seventy-odd minor languages of the country.

The three patterns of literacy acquisition to be studied are church school pattern, adult campaign pattern, and Quranic school pattern. Each is examined in terms of five questions: (1) What are the apparent *goals*? (2) What is the nature of the *writing system* to be mastered? (3) What *language* or languages are involved? (4) What *methods* of instruction are employed? (5) What is the *setting* in which instruction takes place?

I. CHURCH SCHOOL PATTERN

Goals

The traditional church-school literacy training provides a basic competence for participation in the services of the Ethiopian Orthodox Church, and completion of the training gives a particular status in the society or marks a particular stage in an individual's life (*Dawit däggämä*, 'he repeated David'). This training may serve as the first stage in the comprehensive traditional system of church education; more often at the present time it serves as preparation for entry into a government school or other educational institution. The traditional church education is described in Haile Gabriel (1966) and Imbakom (forthcoming): briefer accounts appear in O'Hanlon (1946), Pankhurst (1966), and Girma (1967). The most detailed description of the Ethiopian writing system is Cohen (1936); some additional information appears in Wright (1964).

This pattern of literacy acquisition is essentially acquisition of the ability to read aloud material written in Geez, the classical liturgical language of Ethiopia. The process involves memorization of the characters and their pronunciation, in the traditional order, reading of traditional selections from Scripture and liturgical texts, and memorization of certain texts. Ability to write the characters is secondary, and literacy in Amharic, the national language of Ethiopia, is a by-product of the process. Typically instruction is by a priest (the school is commonly called *yä-qés temhert bét*, 'priest's school'), at a site in the vicinity of a church, and the pupils are boys about 5–8 years of age.

Writing System

The Ethiopian writing system consists of a core of 33 characters, each of which occurs in a basic form and in six other forms with diacritical additions representing vowels, a total of 231 different characters. These do not constitute 231 unrelated items to be learned since: (*a*) the basic shapes show similarities; (*b*) one feature is in effect a diacritic for palatalization; and (*c*) each diacritical vowel addition shows some kind of basic invariance, ranging from the unvarying small loop to the right for *é* to the various largely unpredictable shapes for *e*. In addition to the 231 there are nearly 40 characters which contain a special feature usually representing post-consonantal *w*; of these, 20 are often listed as a kind of appendix to the alphabet proper and the others are not commonly listed. There is no capital/lower-case distinction, and the use of different type fonts or styles is not well developed. The writing goes from left to right.

Punctuation and numerals constitute additional components in the writing system. Core elements of punctuation are a word-divider and a full stop (consisting of two dots and four dots respectively); recent additions include equivalents for comma, colon, and question mark. The numeral system consists of 20 characters (1–10, 20–100, 1,000) used in a positional notation without a zero, always accompanied by horizontal strokes above and below each character.

Language

The subject-matter language of traditional church schools is Geez, and the medium of instruction is normally Amharic. The same writing system is used for Geez, Amharic, and Tigrinya, and in rare instances for other languages of Ethiopia. The traditional pronunciation of Geez uses only Amharic phonemes, and the sound-symbol correspondences are identical for Geez and Amharic. Tigrinya preserves several consonants lost in Amharic but originally present in Geez; apparently Tigrinya speakers who study in church schools usually learn the Amharic pronunciation of Geez rather than using a Tigrinya pronunciation of the extra consonants. For Geez, as for Amharic, a written text provides an unambiguous guide to the consonants and vowels of the corresponding oral rendition, with the exception of two features: (*a*) gemination of consonants, which is of considerable frequency and grammatical significance in both Geez and Amharic, and (*b*) absence of vowel in consonant clusters, which is represented by the same characters as consonant + /e/. For the speakers of Amharic these features are relatively unimportant, in spite of fairly frequent spelling ambiguities, because the context is usually sufficient to make the proper identification. For Amharic speakers reading Geez and for non-Amharic speakers reading Geez or Amharic these features are more troublesome and are the occasion for corrections by the teacher.

Since there were more consonant phonemes in Geez than there are in Amharic, and Amharic words related to Geez tend to be spelled similarly to their Geez counterparts, Amharic orthography is in a many-to-one relationship with Amharic pronunciation, i.e. the Amharic speaker who wants to spell a word he knows must select the appropriate *h*, *s*, *ṣ*, or vowel carrier (see Table). Contemporary Amharic spelling exhibits considerable variation on these points and several others, and various suggestions have been made for standardization of the spelling (see Cowley, 1967, for discussion and further references).

Geez spelling and pronunciation; Amharic spelling		Amharic pronunciation
አ ዐ	(ʾ ʿ)	*ϕ* (vowel carrier)
ሀ ሐ ኀ ኸ	(*h ḥ ḫ x*)	*h*
ሰ ሠ	(*s ś*)	*s*
ጸ ፀ	(*ṣ ẓ*)	*ṣ*

Method

The method of instruction varies from place to place, and modernizing elements are entering, but the traditional procedures are as follows:

(1) The pupils are shown the letters in the arbitrary traditional order: *hä hu hi ha hé he ho*; *lä lu li lé le lo*, etc., left to right on the chart, and memorize them in this sequence. The pupils 'read' the characters aloud one by one as the pointer indicates them, and they do this over and over again until the whole set of 231 or 251 is learned. At this stage the pupils may have, in effect, memorized the letters by their position, and a pupil may be bewildered by having a particular letter pointed out for naming outside the sequence.

(2) A second traditional order of the alphabet (the *abugida*) is then used for further drilling to make certain that the pupils know all the letters independently of their position in the sequence. This second order is closely related to the usual order of letters in Semitic (and Latin) alphabets. It is generally believed, however, that this order does not continue the probable order of South Arabic letters, which were the starting-point of the Ethiopian syllabary, but was introduced at a later date by someone familiar with another alphabet (see Getachew, 1966–7).

(3) Next the *fidälä hawareya*, 'apostles' alphabet', consisting of the first several verses of the 1st Epistle of John, is 'read' and memorized. This passage seems not to have been selected for its simplicity or ease of comprehension, nor for the distribution

of different characters within it. The purpose behind the selection was very probably that the passage would serve as a preparation for reading the Gospel and Epistles of John and the Book of Revelation, which are favourite parts of the Bible in the Ethiopian Church. The text is first read letter by letter (the *quṭer* style), then in a singsong manner by pairs of letters (the *ge'ez* style). Next the pupil reads out in a slow singsong way short phrases of two or three words (the *wärd näbab* style), paying special attention to gemination, word connections, and accent. Finally, he reads connectedly (the *qum näbab* style).

(4) The next stage consists of learning to read and/or memorize selections from Scripture and the prayers and songs of the Church. The actual selection of texts varies from school to school, depending on the decisions of the teacher and the availability of manuscripts at the particular church. Typically, certain commonly recited prayers and hymns such as the Praises of Mary and the Lord's Prayer are learned, but the training may also include selections from the Gospel of John or other texts.

(5) Additional selections of Scripture are then read and reread. The most important of them, which forms a part of all church school literacy training, is the book of Psalms (*Mäzmurä Dawit* 'Psalms of David'). When the pupil has gone through the entire 151 psalms to his teacher's satisfaction (usually three or four times through) the pupil is 'graduated' and his family traditionally has a feast of celebration at which the boy reads or recites some of the psalms or other material he has learned. Up to this point little or no attempt has been made to explain the meaning of the material or to teach the Geez language as such.

(6) Traditionally writing is not taught as such during this period, but some teachers now give instruction in writing. The traditional method, formerly used at a more advanced level of study, uses reed pens, ink made by the pupils from leaves and soot, and slabs of wood or bone on which to write. The traditional instruction in writing usually takes about three or four months. Some pupils may learn to write by observation or self-instruction. Many pupils, by the time they have finished their Dawit, have acquired enough competence in writing and reading the Ethiopian syllabary to write letters in Amharic for illiterates.

Setting

In general, every parish church and every monastery has a school associated with it. In addition, many wealthy people have a teacher in the household to conduct classes, and there are also teachers who offer instruction independently. The usual setting is outside, with the pupils sitting on rocks in a rough circle. Much of the teaching is done by the more advanced students, and students of all levels are mingled in the same 'classroom', each moving at more or less his own pace. Recitation is often simultaneous. The schools average about 30 pupils per teacher, but the number of pupils may be as high as a hundred. The teachers are priests, monks, or laymen (*däbtärä*) with Church education. Many of the teachers at this level do not have a clear understanding of the content of the Geez material they are teaching.

II. ADULT CAMPAIGN PATTERN

The adult campaign pattern of literacy acquisition consists of acquiring the ability to read (with understanding) and write Amharic material. The writing system has already been described in the preceding section, but the methods of teaching are quite different. Some indications of the methods can be found in *Alphabetization* (1966), Djaletta (1964), Getachew (1962–3), 'Notes on a New Method . . .' (n.d.), and in the introduction to various primers.

The principal agencies sponsoring adult literacy campaigns have been the Ministry of Education, UNESCO, various missions, churches, church-related organizations (e.g. Yemissrach Dimts, Sudan Interior Mission), and the National Literacy Campaign. Other agencies have also been involved, both governmental and non-governmental (e.g. Ministry of Community Development, National Lottery, Philips Co.). Although the various agencies may have somewhat different aims, and the various instructional materials differ in a number of ways, there is a fundamental similarity in aims and methods.

The pupils in adult literacy campaigns may be of almost any age, but are predominantly 15–45. They may be of any native language, but are predominantly non-Amharic speaking; of any religion but predominantly Christian or under Christian influence, often non-Orthodox. The teachers are sometimes volunteers, often high-school students, and the classes take place in buildings intended primarily for other purposes, most often schools or churches.

Method

The adult campaign pattern differs from the church-school pattern in having clearly delimited lessons presented in a primer or charts or both, each lesson treating a selected portion of the writing system. The selection of lesson material is based either on the shape of the letters, the frequency of occurrence of the letters, or both. Some primers start with the full set of basic characters and then gradually add the various vowel 'orders'. Others start with a small group of similarly shaped letters of high frequency and progress towards the less regular and less frequent. Some emphasize the use of real words from the first lesson, many have pictures, either to illustrate words to be learned or to be associated with the shape of the first letter of a key word. One system has even used colour coding of the various vowel orders. Whatever the details of the methods, all are based on the notion that the material to be learned should be presented systematically and in small units.

The adult campaign pattern also differs from the church-school pattern in providing teachers' manuals with discussions of method and justification for the particular approach followed. One set of materials even has a special book for inspectors who travel from class to class to make sure the work is going properly. Another difference between the more traditional church-school pattern and the adult campaigns lies in the nature of the 'follow-up' material, i.e. the reading matter provided for the pupils when they complete the first step of literacy acquisition. In the church-school pattern the material is chosen for its value in religious education, without regard for its usefulness in preserving or extending competence in reading and writing. In the adult campaign pattern, however, follow-up material is often prepared expressly for the newly literate and is intended to improve his reading skills. Some of this material has a religious flavour, and in the opinion of the producers it may be directly related to a Church message, but much of it is not obviously religious in content.

Setting

Adult literacy classes are generally conducted in classroom settings, often in school rooms after hours, but sometimes in other facilities which approximate classroom characteristics. The teachers are people with some degree of modern education in Amharic, often high-school students or high-school graduates. A large proportion of adult literacy teachers are unpaid volunteers, but the more successful programmes generally have paid part-time teachers, and there exists a small corps of experienced full-time teachers and inspectors in various literacy programmes. A number of these people have had specialized training in literacy work, ranging from a few days orientation to intensive workshops in foreign literacy centres.

III. QURANIC SCHOOL PATTERN

Goals

The Quranic school literacy training provides a basic competence for Muslim religious observances and may also serve as the first stage in the comprehensive system of Muslim education, which reaches its culmination in study at a Muslim centre outside the country. More often at the present time it serves as a preparation for entry to a government school or another educational institution. The system of Muslim education in Ethiopia is described briefly in Trimingham (1962). The Arabic writing system is described in Mitchell (1953), where particular attention is paid to the techniques of writing, and Blachère (1952, pp. 58–65), where its historical development is summarized.

This pattern of literacy acquisition is essentially acquisition of the ability to read aloud and write certain kinds of material in Arabic. The material consists chiefly of parts of the *Quran* and the prescribed forms of daily prayer.

Writing System

The Arabic writing system consists of a core of 28 characters, most of which show variations in shape, depending on whether they are connected to the left, the right, both, or neither. Six characters never connect to the left, and no characters connect at word boundaries, which are thus marked by space. The variation in shape per character ranges from essential invariance in the case of a letter like <*w*> to four quite different shapes for <*h*>. Several sets of characters have similar or identical forms, except for diacritical marks consisting of various numbers of dots over or under the letter. In addition to the core characters there are about a dozen special signs which are used as diacritics to indicate short vowels (otherwise not marked), gemination of consonants, presence of glottal stop, certain endings, and other features. These additional signs, referred to collectively as *taškīl*, are not usually present in written Arabic texts, although they are generally used in texts of the Quran. There is no capital/lower-case distinction, but there are several different styles of script. The writing goes from right to left.

Punctuation and numerals constitute additional components in the writing system. The most important item of punctuation is a sentence marker, but equivalents of the comma, question mark, and other European signs of punctuation are increasingly used. The numeral system is a decimal notation in a one-to-one correspondence with the so-called Arabic numerals used in Europe, but the shapes of the numerals are quite different.

Language

The subject-matter language of traditional Quranic schools is Arabic, and the medium of instruction is usually the mother tongue of the group (e.g. Galla, Somali) or Amharic. For a very small minority of the pupils Arabic is the mother tongue. For a substantial number of other pupils some form of spoken Arabic is familiar as a lingua franca. For some pupils, also, the Quranic school is an important part of the process of acquiring a spoken use of Arabic. It must be noted, however, that most of the pupils do not learn spoken Arabic and acquire only a very limited ability to use written Arabic. It must also be noted that the difference between the forms, syntax, and lexicon of written Arabic and of spoken Arabic is very great (Ferguson, 1959), considerably greater than between written and spoken Amharic and roughly comparable to the difference between Geez and Amharic.

The sound system of the Arabic language differs from the sound systems of the various mother tongues of Ethiopian

Muslims. No other language in Ethiopia has a set of 'emphatic' consonants like those of Arabic, although a number have glottalized consonants which sometimes serve as counterparts in phonological adaptations in loan words, etc. Some languages of Ethiopia have velar spirants and pharyngeal sounds like those of Arabic, others do not. No other languages of the country seem to have interdental spirants like those of Arabic.

For (Classical) Arabic a written text provides an unambiguous guide to the consonants, but without the *taškīl* the short vowels, gemination of consonants, and the distinction between long vowels and diphthongs are not shown. The Arabic writing system with full *taškīl* is fundamentally similar in nature to the Ethiopian syllabary, but there are important differences: connected versus separate letters, difference in direction of writing, usual omission of *taškīl* versus obligatory vowel diacritics.

Method

In the most traditional schools the pupil uses a wooden plate (*lawḥ*) on which he writes and erases. The Arabic letters are taught in the traditional ABC order, first by name then by sound with each vowel mark (e.g. *a*, *ba*, *ta* . . .; *'a*, *'i*, *'u* . . .) and with some of the other special signs. Many of these sequences are recited in special singsong manners. The pupils then progress to words. The first connected text is usually the *fātiḥa*, the opening sura of the Quran, which is used on many occasions. This is followed by other passages from the Quran, prayers, and other items of religious importance. In those schools which use textbooks the commonest beginning work is a primer printed in Singapore (*Qāᶜida Baghdādiyya*) which includes practice material in letters and words, the *fātiḥa* and other Quranic material, and instructions for ritual prayers and ablutions.

After the earliest stage most emphasis is given to the memorization of the Quran and other religious texts, particular attention being paid to correct recitation (*tajwīd*), including both pronunciation as such and musical tone, since all these texts are chanted in accordance with traditional practice. Relatively little attention is given either to the meaning of the material or to the structure of the Arabic language.

Setting

In general, every village mosque has some kind of Quranic school associated with it. In addition, some of the towns and cities have separate Islamic schools, varying in nature from very traditional to quite modern. The former are usually conducted by a local imam or a visiting shaykh who offers his services. The latter are run by a founder-director or by a board of interested citizens. The pupils in all these schools are nearly 100 per cent Muslim, although a few non-Muslims can be found. A high proportion of the teachers speak Arabic either as their mother tongue or as a second language; of these many seem to be Hararis, whose native language is Adare but who are multilingual from an early age, in three or more of the following: Adare, Arabic, Amharic, Galla, Somali, French, English, Italian.

IV. TRENDS

The characterizations of the three preceding sections attempted to give a picture of each pattern of literacy acquisition in its most typical form at the present time. Each pattern has also, of course, a history which deserves separate study, and each pattern shows tendencies of change which are important to understand either for assessment by planners and policy-makers or for the formulation of general hypotheses on the processes of national development. This section presents six apparent trends.

Expansion

Since two of the three patterns of literacy acquisition are traditional in nature and aimed at goals not clearly related to national development, it might be supposed that they are diminishing in numbers of people involved and in general importance. This does not seem to be the case. Although no figures can be presented, it seems clear that the number of pupils following the traditional patterns is increasing, and although the function of these patterns in the 60's may be shifting and certain features of methods and materials may be changing, their importance does not seem to be diminishing. The adult campaign pattern, as might have been expected, is also increasing, and new elements of both diversification and co-ordination of efforts are appearing. In short, for some years to come all these patterns will probably continue to expand, and no new pattern of school reading instruction is likely to emerge.

Modernization

All three patterns show strong trends of modernization in teaching methods and in the instructional materials utilized. In the church schools in Addis Ababa, for example, it is almost impossible to find copies of the traditional manuscripts in use. Printed single sheets are now usually available, containing the field in both traditional orders, the numbers, the beginning of the first Epistle of John in Geez, and in addition, the Roman alphabet and Arabic numerals, an advertisement for the printing press, and a picture of the Emperor. Also several printed editions of the Dawit are available, some including also devotional material (all in Geez), and there is even an authorized edition of the Psalms with parallel Geez and Amharic. All these materials are increasingly used in traditional church schools, especially in Addis Ababa, and although most of the schools in the provinces are much less modernized, the trend is unmistakable. The greatest modernization in methods is the tendency to teach writing at an early stage; schools can now be found in which the priest-teacher is trying to teach a skill which he himself has not mastered, since in his own training writing had not been emphasized.

The Quranic schools show similar kinds of modernization. In Addis Ababa the traditional wooden boards seem nowhere to be in use, and even the most traditional school visited by the author had wooden benches, a blackboard, and a few books, although the basic classroom technique was memorization from oral models. The most important change taking place is the use of modern printed textbooks in Islamic schools; in place of the Singapore primer, primary school textbooks from Egypt and Lebanon are increasingly used. These textbooks are intended in their country of origin for speakers of Arabic, while in Ethiopia the pupils may have little or no knowledge of Arabic when they come to school, but the use of pictures, graded lessons, exercises, etc., is clearly an example of modernization. One Islamic school in Addis Ababa has even printed its own first- and second-grade primers for Arabic instruction (*'Abīd*, 1950), and there is also a beginning book in Arabic with text in Amharic, printed in Asmara (Sayyid Ibrahim, 1959–60).

The adult campaign materials from the beginning had a 'modern' appearance, but even here examples of further modernization can be found, such as new and improved wall charts and follow-up readers with colour illustrations. The most striking example is the consideration being given by one mission group to make use of a cassette-type magnetic tape set with accompanying printed materials for pre-literacy and literacy work in non-Amharic-speaking areas.

Governmentalization

All three patterns of literacy acquisitions have been chiefly non-governmental in sponsorship, financing, and actual operation. Each pattern now shows signs of becoming more closely connected with the government. A considerable number of church-run schools now follow the government curriculum and receive from the Government the usual financial support in terms of teachers' salaries, etc. These schools are included in the Ministry of Education's statistics on schools, and although they may vary considerably in the nature of the instruction offered, they are basically equivalent to government schools rather than traditional Church schools. The pupils attending them may indeed have first acquired literacy at a priest's school. Although this governmentalization represents an addition to traditional schools or a replacement of church education beyond the beginning stage, it is bound to have ever stronger effects on the traditional systems themselves, and clearly is an example of close connection with government.

Quranic schools are similarly moving towards governmentalization, although at a much slower rate. Direct governmental sponsorship exists in at least one Islamic school: the primary school associated with the mosque in Addis Ababa, which follows the government curriculum (plus Arabic and religious studies), has government-supplied teachers, and is government financed. In a few other schools the Government supplies some teachers although no other financial aid. In many Islamic schools in the towns and cities, as opposed to the situation in rural areas, the most important trend to governmentalization is the increasing use of the government curriculum, so that sixth-grade students are prepared for the national sixth-year examination. Up to the present there are apparently no Islamic schools as such beyond the sixth grade, except for a single school in Asmara affiliated to an Egyptian university, and Muslim students must attend government or private secondary schools where no Arabic or Muslim religious studies are offered.

Tying to National Development

The two traditional patterns of literacy acquisition were not explicitly related to national development—indeed, the concept of national development is itself a recent notion in the Empire—and the adult campaign pattern in many instances was conceived of as contributing to Christianization or to spiritual growth within Church congregations. Increasingly, however, in both governmental and non-governmental circles, all three patterns are regarded as contributing to national socio-economic developments, and changes in operation and methods are initiated with this new goal explicitly used as justification. The Government in its development planning assigns a place to literacy instruction. (Cf. Second Five Year Development Plan, p. 268, 'Action against Illiteracy' and also p. 260, 'as far as reducing the rate of illiteracy and the extension of basic primary education are concerned, the contribution of the church schools cannot be ignored'.)

The most striking explicit tie between literacy training and national development, as might be expected, is being made in the adult campaign pattern. The connection was already recognized in earlier campaigns (cf. Djaletta, 1963), but recent trends emphasize it even more. The recently inaugurated UNESCO-sponsored Work-Oriented Adult Literacy Project ties the teaching of literacy directly to agricultural and industrial development projects.

Decline of Traditional Higher Education

The two traditional patterns of literacy acquisition have served as preparation for traditional systems of higher education, within the Orthodox Church schools of various kinds or

Islamic schools. In the past only a small percentage of those who had completed the literacy training went on to higher education, but at the present time even this number is rapidly declining. The Islamic schools above the beginning level of Quranic school are in the process of disappearing in Ethiopia, and the practice of going outside Ethiopia to an Islamic country (e.g. Sudan, Egypt, Aden) for higher education has decreased sharply. At the present time Quranic schools generally feed into government or other non-Islamic schools.

The traditional higher schools of the Ethiopian Orthodox Church are of various kinds, each devoted to a special kind of study, including: religious music; Geez language and literature, including the composition of poetry; the books of the Old and New Testaments, including commentaries; the writing of the Church fathers; works on monastic life; the mathematics and astronomy related to the calculation of the Ethiopian Church calendar; and the specialized arts and crafts within the Church. Students normally attend several different schools, following their own interests; it has been estimated (Imbakom, forthcoming) that it would take about thirty years to complete study in all the different kinds of schools. At the present time all these kinds of schools exist, and there are hundreds of students in them, but the attendance is declining, and one observer has predicted that within a generation these higher schools will have disappeared.

V. PEDAGOGICAL IMPLICATIONS

The specialist in language teaching or the teaching of reading will be disconcerted by at least two features of the three Ethiopian patterns of literacy acquisition described here. In the first place he will be surprised to find that the majority of Ethiopians first become literate, by these methods, in a language which they do not speak. The language of literacy may be a classical language of limited functions in the society (e.g. Geez or Arabic) or it may be the national language of Ethiopia (Amharic) for a non-Amharic speaker. The first reaction of the specialist would be that the normal pattern of literacy acquisition should be in the mother tongue of the learner, but where this is not possible special teaching methods and materials should be used. Generally in Ethiopian literacy acquisition there is no explicit recognition of the difference between mother-tongue literacy and literacy in another language, apart from Eritrea and some scattered mission programmes. Before passing judgement, however, the specialist might well investigate the importance of such factors as strength of motivation for literacy acquisition, religious values associated with literacy, and the special status of the national language. In the only experiment related to this question which has been reported for Ethiopia the non-Amharic speakers made somewhat better progress in literacy acquisition than the Amharic speakers using the same materials (adult campaign pattern). (Cf. Brooks, 1916.)

The second surprise for the specialist would be the very great emphasis placed on memorization, especially in the two traditional patterns. A reading teacher from the United States, for example, would be astonished to hear 3- and 4-year-old children reciting or singing from memory hundreds of lines of text in languages they do not speak or understand. The first reaction is likely to be one of disapproval, both because of the apparent irrelevance of the subject matter and because of the apparently excessive use of memorization as a teaching technique. Here again further investigation might be in order. The memorized material may have high relevance in terms of ability to participate in religious ceremonies or to exhibit one's skills to admiring adults, and even in terms of the child's own pleasure in rhythmical verbalization, comparable in some ways to nursery rhymes with nonsense material in them. Finally, the excellent pronunciation achieved by many of the children in this kind of memorization may even suggest its usefulness for second-language teaching at the early ages. For example, some children observed by the author used phonological features of Arabic in their recitation which they did not have in their mother tongue, including post-velar and interdental consonants and the distinction between long and short vowels. There is certainly opportunity here for careful pedagogical experimentation, and some of the results might even have theoretical significance in understanding the essentially mysterious processes of child language development and literacy acquisition.

REFERENCES

The works listed below were consulted in the preparation of this paper. They are arranged in alphabetical order by author, by first names for Ethiopian authors, and surnames for non-Ethiopian authors. All Ethiopian and Muslim calendar dates have been converted to the Gregorian calendar, e.g. 1968–69 is put for 1961 Eth. Cal. Where an Ethiopian author's preference for Amharic spelling in known, this is used; otherwise the transliteration system of the *Journal of Ethiopian Studies* is followed (cf. Wright, 1964). The same transliteration is used for Amharic titles.

Abīd, Muḥammad

(1950) *Mabādi' al-Qirā'a ar-Rashīda* (Principles of Correct Reading), Vols. 1 and 2. Cairo: Dar Al-Maaref.

(1966) *Alphabetisation and Adult Education by Radio.* (Foreword by Dr. R. A. J. van Lier.) Eindhoven, Netherlands: N. V. Philips.

Blachère, R.

(1952) *Histoire de la Littérature Arabe,* Vol. 1. Paris: Adrien-Maisonneuve.

Brooks, Kenneth G.

(1966) *The Campaign against Illiteracy in Ethiopia.* Report prepared for UNESCO. (Mimeo.) Addis Ababa.

Cohen, Marcel

(1936) 'Ecriture', in *Traité de Langue Amharique,* pp. 17–28. Paris: Institut d'Ethnologie.

Cowley, R.

(1967) 'The Standardization of Amharic Spelling', *J. Ethiopian Stud.,* pp. 1–8.

Djaletta Jaffero

(1962) *Inspectors' Training Manual,* Yemissrach Dimts Literacy Campaign. Mimeo. bd. in heavy paper. Addis Ababa. (2nd ed., 1964).

(1963–4) *Amareñña Manbäbiya* (Amharic Reader), 1st Book. Addis Ababa: Central Printing Press.

(1963) *Follow-up Work Training Manual.* Yemissrach Dimts Literacy Campaign. Mimeo., bd. in heavy paper. Addis Ababa.

(1964) *Teachers' Manual.* Yemissrach Dimts Literacy Campaign. Mimeo., bd. in heavy paper. Addis Ababa.

Ephraim Isaac

(1964?) *Ethiopia's Problem of Illiteracy.* Pamphlet. Cambridge, Mass. (?)

Ferguson, Charles A.

(1959) 'Diglossia', *Word,* XV, pp. 325–40.

Getachew Haile
(1966–67) 'The Problems of the Amharic Writing System'. A paper prepared in advance for the Interdisciplinary Seminar of the Faculty of Arts and Education. Mimeo. Addis Ababa: Haile Sellassie I University.
(1962–3) *Teachers' Manual.* Addis Ababa: National Literacy Campaign.

Girma Amare
(1967) 'Aims and Purposes of Church Education in Ethiopia', *Ethiop. J. Educ.*, I, l, pp. 1–11.
(1963) 'Memorization in Ethiopian Schools', *J. Ethiopian Stud.*, 1, pp. 27–31.

Hagner, Olle
(1952) *Kunama Aurabu Kolattama Kida Kitaba.* Eritrea: Evangelical Mission (printed by Svantessons Boktrykeri, Hässkholm, Sweden).

Haile Gabriel Dagne
(1966) 'Struktur des kirchlichen Schulwesens', in *Versuch einer Erziehungsreform in Äthiopien.* Unpubl. Ph.D. Thesis. Free University of Berlin.
(1968) 'The Entoto Speech on Church School Training', *Ethiop. J. Educ.*, II, 1, pp. 11–14.

(n.d.) *Hullu Yemmar*
(Each one Learn). Manual of the National Literacy Campaign Association. Addis Ababa: Commercial Press.

Imbakom Kalewold
(Forthcoming) *Traditional Ethiopian Church Schools.* (Tr. by Menghestu Lemma with preface by R. K. Pankhurst.) New York: Teacher's College Press.

Mitchell, T. F.
(1953) *Writing Arabic.* London: Oxford University Press.

Muḥammad 'Abdurraḥmān
(1964) *At-Tadrīj lil-Madāris al-Athyūbiyya* (Primer for Ethiopian Schools). Vol. 1. Addis Ababa: Jam'iyyat Nashr al-Thaqāfa.

Mulugéta Sämruna and Asräs Däjäné.
(1964–5) *Manbäbenna Mäṣaf bä-Radiyo* (Reading and Writing by Radio). Addis Ababa: Instructional Materials Production Center.
(n.d.) 'Notes on a New Method of Teaching Amharic Reading and Writing'. (Addis Ababa?).

O'Hanlon, Douglas
(1946) 'Ethiopian Church Schools', in *Features of the Ethiopian Church*, pp. 13–21. London: S.P.C.K.

Pankhurst, Richard K.
(1962) 'The Foundations of Education, Printing, Newspapers, Book Production, Libraries, and Literacy in Ethiopia', *Ethiopia Observer*, 6, pp. 251–3.
(1966) 'Ethiopia', in David G. Scanlon (ed.), *Church, State, and Education in Africa*, pp. 23–58. New York: Teacher's College Press.
Qā'ida Baghdādiyya.
(1932?) Singapore: Maktaba wa-Maṭba'a Sulaymān Mar'i.
Sayyid Ibrahim
(1959–60) *Yäarabeñña Qwanqwa Astämari* (Arabic Language Teacher). Asmara: Fioretti Press (?).
(1962) *Second Five Year Development Plan.* Addis Ababa: Imperial Ethiopian Government.
(1966–7) *Se'lawi Fidäl* (Picture Primer), 1st Book. Addis Ababa: Ethiopian Publishing S.C., Berhanena Selam.
Tafarra Wondimagnehou
(1955–6) *Andäññaw Yanbab Mäṣhafé* (My First Reading Book). Asmara: Ministry of Education and Fine Arts.
Trimingham, J. Spencer
(1962) *Islam in Ethiopia*, London: Frank Cass. (2nd printing, 1965).
(1962–3) *Yä-Amareñña Fidäl Mämariya* (Amharic Alphabet Manual). Addis Ababa: National Literacy Campaign Organization.
(1968) *Yä-Añua Mämariya* (Anyuak Primer). Also Anyuak title. Bilingual Anyuak-Amharic. No authors, date, or place of publication indicated. (Addis Ababa.)
(1967?) *Yä-Wangél Fidäl: bä-Qällal Mängäd Kä-Fidäl esk-Anbab* (Gospel Alphabet; from Alphabet to Reading by an Easy Way). Addis Ababa: SIM Press (?).
Wäldä Ab Wäldä Mariam
(n.d.) *Tegreñña Nejämmärti* (Tigrinya for Beginners). Asmara: Education Department, Brit. Mil. Aden.
Wright, Stephen
(1964) 'The transliteration of Amharic'. *J. Ethiopian Stud.*, II, 1, pp. 1–10.

XIII. A Few Observations on Language Use Among Cameroonese *Élite* Families

PIERRE ALEXANDRE

Lovers of privacy should never ask a social scientist to dinner. Anthropologists, psychologists, and linguists share a common occupational disease: they take mental notes and are deplorably prone to turn their hosts and fellow guests into case-story subjects. I have done it before, and am doing it again—with some limitations. What I mean is that I have limited the sample in this paper to rather close friends from Cameroon, leaving deliberately aside people from other countries. There are several reasons for this choice, the main one being that I think a homogeneous sample to be more significant, in so far as my sample from other countries is very dispersed in many respects (I had only three usable cases from Senegal, two from Togoland, and one each from Congo-Brazzaville, Niger, Dahomey, Gabon, Ivory Coast, Guinée, and Chad). Moreover the people concerned all know I have been observing their language policy and have discussed it with me.

In fact, my sample is, if anything, all too homogeneous. In each of the fourteen families one at least of the spouses is a Bantu-speaker from southern Cameroon. All are nominally or actually Christian. All men have had a post-secondary education—university or *grandes écoles*.

Professional repartition of husbands runs as follows:

5 university lecturers

4 engineers

4 civil servants of administrative rank

1 secondary school teacher

Out of sixteen wives eight are or have been engaged in paid occupations after marriage:

3 teachers
1 engineer
1 interpreter
1 social worker
2 secretaries

Seven of the wives have had post-secondary education, five post-primary, two primary only, one sub-primary (vernacular literacy course in Christian mission), one none at all.

Average number of children:

Per pair	3·6
Per family	4·1

All families have at some time lived in France; present residences are:

Yaounde area	7
Paris	3
United Kingdom	1
Other	3

One of the husbands has taken a second wife recently (I have not met her as yet), another intends to take one presently. Two have divorced their first wife and are therefore entered twice in the table.

The data in the table have been left sketchy on purpose, so as to prevent easy recognition of the families involved. It reads as follows:

Ethnic groups (columns 2 and 4) and languages are indicated either by an initial—F for French, E for English, K for Wes Kos Creole—or by the group number in Guthrie's classification. In case 7, '10[a]' and '10[b]' means that the spouses belong to different tribes within the same group.

Language use is indicated for the following speech situations:

H to W : husband talking with wife
H to C : ,, ,, ,, children
W to C : wife ,, ,, ,,
C: children to one another

/ means alternate use of two languages, with rather higher frequency for the first one. When frequency of use seems equivalent for both languages / is replaced by &. When there is a definite order of frequency languages are enumerated in decreasing order, separated by commas. 'Some' means occasional and non-fluent use.

Thus F/E should read 'use of either French or English, with somewhat higher frequency of French'.

F & E 'use of French and English with equal ease and frequency'.

F, E 'Use of French and English with distinctly higher frequency for French'.

Religious affiliation is indicated (P for Protestant, C for Catholic), as it has some influence on language use, due to different missionary policies. Parentheses indicate non-practising P's or C's.

Level of education is graded

0 : illiterate
1 : pre-primary (vernacular literacy class)
2 : primary
3 : post-primary
4 : post-secondary

'Observations' are mainly concerned with children of school age.

In cases 1A to 6 the spouses belong to the same tribe; in 7 they both belong to Guthrie's A10 group—and speak Duala, A24, the coastal lingua franca; in cases 2A to 9 the spouses belong to different language groups; in cases 1B to 14 the wife is French.

Children in 1A, 2A, 8, 11, and 12 have speech difficulties, poor school results, or character troubles. Children in 2B, 3, 6, 10, and 14 have better than average school results. Non-linguistic factors are involved, yet it is to be noticed that all children of the second group are bilingual, i.e. shift from one language to the other and back without any apparent difficulty and without any preferential use of either. Children of the first group, on the other hand, while they may have a fair working command of several languages, are not really bilingual, and, according to their African relatives, are not very good speakers of their 'main' language.

Identi-fication	*Husband* *Ethnic group*	*Religion*	*Wife* *Ethnic group*	*Rel.*	*Ed.*	*H to W*	*H to C*	*W to C*	*C*	*Observations*
1A	A70	P	A70	P	0	A70	F/A70	A70	A70 some F	C have character difficulties; school results bad
2B	A40	P	A40	P	3	A40/F	A40 & F	F/A40	F & A40 some A70	C bilingual with good command of A70; school results good
3	A20	P	A20	P	3	A20, F	A20/F	A20/F	F/A20	C bilingual; school results above average; resident in France
4	A70	C	A70	P	4	A70/F	F/A70	F/A70	A70 & F	C bilingual; good school results
5	A70	C	A70	C	2	A70, some F	A70/F	A70, some F	A70	C under school age; difficulties in speech
6	A40	C	A40	C	4	A40/F	F/A40	A40/F	A40 & F	C bilingual; school results above average
7	A10[a]	C	A10[b]	C	2	A20, E, some F	F/E/A20	A20/E(K) some F	A20/K, E, some F	C had bad school results in France and E. Cameroon, fair in the United Kingdom
2A	A40	P	A70	C	1	A70, F	F	A70	A70, F, later A40	C have serious speech troubles. Now live in A40 milieu, seem to forget A70, have difficulties in French
8	A40	P	A70	P	4	F, some A70	F	F	F, A70, some A40	C have speech troubles
9	H10	C	A40	C	4	F	F	F	F	Live in France. H hopes C will be trilingual in Africa. C under school age
1B	A70	P	F	(C)	3	F	F, some A70	F	F/A70	
10	A20	P	F	(C)	4	F/A20	A20/F	F/A20	A20 & F	C bilingual
11	A70	P	F	(C)	3	F	A70/F	F, some A70	A70/F	C have some speech troubles; school results under average
12	A70	P	F	P	3	F	A70/F	F, some A70	A70 & F	C show character troubles. School results fair
13	A70	C	F	C	4	F	F, some A70	F	F	Live in France. H intends C and W to learn A70 in Cameroon
14	A70	C	F	C	4	F, some A70	A70, some F	F/A70	F & A70	C bilingual; school results above average

At this point and before going into a sampling of some motivations of language choice in these families it may be useful to recall some general traits of the overall language situation in the Cameroon Federation.

This country is one of the more heterogeneous in West Africa, with a variety of language groups belonging to several families: Greenberg's Afro-Asiatic and Niger–Kordofan, with languages of the Chadic, Benue–Congo (Central Branch and Bantu), West Atlantic, Adamawa–Eastern and Chari–Nile groups. There is no nation-wide lingua franca. The main provincial vehicular or trade languages are dialects of A70 (Ewondo/Bulu), A20 (Duala), Fulfulde, Mbum, and Wes Kos Creole. The official languages are English (West Cameroon) and French (East Cameroon), on an equal footing at the federal level (but with a *de facto* predominance of French). The school system continues, on the whole, the French colonial tradition, with a European language used as a medium from the start. There are a few literacy classes in some of the vernaculars, organized by the Christian missions without any official recognition. Since independence there have been heated discussions among the intelligentsia between cultural nationalists, who favour a wider use of the vernaculars, and unificationists, who fear that this would consolidate tribal consciousness and be detrimental to nation building. The federal government—and its French technical advisers—support the latter view.

This general situation is, naturally enough, reflected at the family level and explains the prevalence of French even in linguistically homogeneous families. In non-homogeneous families French has to be used, since there is no African lingua franca available. This is especially true of families where the wife is French: only two French wives in my sample are fluent in their husband's mother tongue. In homogeneous families, on the other hand, a preferential use of the vernacular at home was to be expected. The interesting fact is that this use of the vernacular outweighs only slightly the use of French. Moreover, the choice of either or both languages is, in many cases, fully conscious and motivated: when living in an African milieu parents make efforts to use French, when living in France to use the vernacular. In the first case they intend to train their children for maximal efficiency at school, in the second case they try to preserve their sense of national (tribal) identity while living abroad.

Really bilingual children belong to families—in two cases non-homogeneous with French wife—where this policy of deliberate language choice is applied by parents with equal (e.g. 10) or nearly equal (1B) levels of education. Contrariwise children have serious speech troubles in the three families (1A, 5, 2A) where there is a serious educational gap between spouses; in cases 2A this gap is compounded by tribal heterogeneity; yet comparison of 1A and 5 with 11 and 12 suggests that educational differences within a homogeneous family may have results as detrimental as linguistic heterogeneity. In cases 7 and 9, the main or sole family language is, so to speak, 'neutral', i.e. is not spoken as a mother tongue by either parent. In both cases children do not show any speech trouble. In case 8, with a similar situation, children do have speech difficulties. The differential element seems to be residence in an area where the wife's language is widely and predominantly spoken, which probably introduces some kind of conflict in family relationship, even if parents strive to use the 'neutral' language at home.

To sum up, the situation in Cameroonian *élite* families is to some extent reminiscent of the situation which obtained a century ago in French families living in the provinces where French was not spoken as a mother tongue (Provence, Brittany, Flanders, Alsace, Gascogne, Basque country). At this time *élite* families were bilingual, with French in a position similar to the one it occupies now in Eastern Cameroon. *Élite* families had to use the vernaculars to communicate with the lower orders of society, often including their poorer relatives. Later on, with the coming of compulsory free education, French became the universal medium of linguistic communication in France, and *élite* families, especially urban ones, abandoned the vernaculars, which nowadays remain chiefly used in the countryside by lower-income families. It seems probable that, despite the extension of the French-medium school system, Cameroonian vernaculars will show a stronger resistance than Basque, Breton, and other vernaculars spoken in the French provinces. There is, however, some chance, in view of the lack of any nation-wide African lingua franca, that *élite* families, especially ethnically mixed ones and those living in towns where tribal affiliations are weakened, may in time become unilingual with French, or a dialect of French, as first or main language. In fact, some of my informants are making conscious efforts to address their children in the vernacular to prevent them from forgetting it, from de-Africanizing.

The importance of a nation-wide lingua franca is evidenced by a comparison with Sénégal, which has the same type of school system and a far longer history of culture contact with France. In Sénégal Wolof is spreading quicker than French and is used as a second language by non-Wolof *élite* and non-*élite* families alike, and this despite the fact that it lacks a standardized spelling and is practically never used in written form, except for a few religious tracts and hymnals. It is, in fact, well on its way to becoming the *de facto* national language of a country whose official language is French. Knowing Wolof may well be in many cases a better-paying proposition than knowing French, which is not the case for any Cameroonian vernacular (a pedlar plying his trade between Garoua and Douala, for instance, would have to know at least three vehicular languages). This holds true even for the *élite* professions: a lawyer, prefect, medical doctor, or teacher can use Wolof, with most members of the non-French-speaking public over almost all Sénégal. Their Cameroonian counterparts cannot use Fulfulde, Ewondo, or Duala outside limited areas of the country.

It would be interesting to make similar comparisons between former British colonies with and without a nation-wide lingua franca to see how it affects attitudes *vis-à-vis* English and the vernaculars.

ADDENDUM

Before this paper was read I showed the draft to Messrs. 2 and 14 (separately) and discussed it with them. We made a list of twenty more families—common friends of ours—in comparable circumstances and tried a cursory review of the language situation in these families. Our general impression was that French is, on the whole, the dominant language of this social stratum, even if some parents try to privilege the use of a vernacular. In fact, French tends to become a class marker—the discretive trait of a U:Ū opposition.

While both of these informants are trying to train their children in the correct use of their Bantu vernacular, they are far less optimistic than I was about the children's proficiency in it. One of them tells me that his children speak 'Bantu' pretty much as my own children did when I was a D.O., i.e. in conversations with domestic servants, makit mamies, and lower-class age-mates, using a pidginized dialect with a simplified class system and a high proportion of French and Wes Kos lexemes. The other is more satisfied with his children's performance in the vernacular, but insists that the high standard they achieve is due to his mother's influence: the old lady lives with the family, helps to care for the children, and teaches them folk-tales in the vernacular, as she cannot speak French. This influence of grandparents seems to be an important factor which I overlooked in the first draft of this paper. This is also true, to a lesser extent, of poorer relatives staying with the family as a kind of domestic help.

Both informants also mention that children seem to avoid using the vernacular in public when living in a French-speaking milieu, or even in a situation when French, rather than the vernacular, is used by their parents (e.g. when I am visiting them with my wife).

They finally tax me with a dose of somewhat naïve gullibility for believing some of our common friends when they tell me they are trying to preserve African cultural values among their children. It seems they do it in part to humour my own prejudices.

XIV. The Role of Broadcasting in the Adaptation of the Somali Language to Modern Needs

B. W. ANDRZEJEWSKI

Within the last twenty-five years considerable changes have taken place in the lexical resources of the Somali language. A large number of words and phrases have come into existence, and many old words have changed their meaning. The changes which have taken place are, in the vast majority of cases, concerned with the adaptation of the language to the needs of modern life: politics, administration, technology, and science.

In discussing these adaptive changes it will be worth our while to reconstruct the state of the Somali language before 1943, a date which is of particular importance in Somali cultural history, since it was then that the first regular broadcasts of world news in Somali began.[1] Although there are no adequate written records on which one can rely for information, the period of change and that which immediately preceded it can easily be reconstructed from the living memories of those speakers of the language who are now over forty-five or so, since the new lexical items still retain their freshness for those who witnessed their first arrival.

In the Somali language before 1943 no words or phrases were in general circulation which would describe, for instance, socialism, capitalism, diplomatic relations, independence, secession, *coup d'état*, president, economic development, progress, or trade union. Likewise, it was difficult to speak in Somali about

[1] For a detailed account of the development of broadcasting in Somalia see References (below) under *Somali Republic*. Prior to 1943 broadcasting in Somali on a limited scale was undertaken, mainly for military purposes, in 1940–41 by the Italians from Addis Ababa and by the British from Aden and later from Hargeisa between 1941 and 1943.

such things as hydro-electric dams, short waves, anaesthetics, or tear gas, unless one used lengthy circumlocutions. That this should be the case even towards the end of the first half of the twentieth century was because there was very little modern education in any of the territories where Somali was spoken, due to various factors which it is best to leave to historians to discuss. Any news from the great world outside was usually brought to the general public by word of mouth: by sailors, migrant workers, soldiers who had served abroad, or by itinerant men of religion who sought higher learning of the traditional type in the great centres of Islam. It would be wrong, however, to assume that the Somali language at that time suffered from any inadequacy other than the absence of modern terms. It is certain that as far as oral traditions can reach, the Somali language has always had a vast vocabulary relating to all aspects of the existing Somali culture, including numerous specialized terms connected with animal husbandry, agriculture, weather-forecasting,[1] various skills and crafts, traditional medicine and veterinary science, and social organization. It acquired a fairly large number of Arabic borrowings throughout centuries of contact with the Arabian peninsula, which may have started even before the advent of Islam; these words were, and still are, particularly common in spheres of life connected with urban civilization and religion.

Moreover, among Somalis the art of alliterative poetry,[2] with its vast vocabulary and vivid imagery, has always been a particularly well-favoured form of entertainment, and also a means of influencing public opinion. Since some of the poets travelled widely or had contact with travellers and foreigners, world events were often brought into their poems; in most cases, however, they were mentioned as part of the poetic imagery or as illustrations or cautionary examples, while the main theme was concerned entirely with local affairs. Thus, when the great

[1] For a good example of specialized terminology in Somali traditional science see Musa Galaal, 1968. The book also contains a bibliography of that author's other publications.

[2] For general information about this poetry see Andrzejewski and Lewis, 1964; for bibliographies of published material see Johnson, 1967 and 1969. Note that there are several unpublished collections of Somali poetry in existence and that Radio Mogadishu and Radio Hargeisa have a large collection of tape-recordings of Somali poetry.

Somali poet Omar Hussein Gorse,[1] in a poem composed some time before the Second World War, tries to reconcile a particular tribe to some territorial losses he brings in the consoling thought that such things have happened before, even to the most mighty men of this world: witness the defeat of the Germans by the British in Tanzania in the First World War, and the difficulties in which some notables in Zanzibar apparently found themselves.[2]

Carradii Taboora iyo dhulkii canabku laallaaday
Jermalkii cammiray waa horaa cawda Loo rogay e
Calanka ma nashiro Kayserkii cadhada waallaa ye
Sinjibaar cuqaashii faddhiday carare qaarkood e
Raggii Daar Cajaayibo lahaa ka ma casheeyaan e.[3]

From the land of Tabora, and the country of pendent grapes
The Germans who had developed them were sent packing.
The quick-tempered Emperor no longer hoists his flag there.
Of the chiefs who dwelt in Zanzibar, some made their escape;
The men who owned the House of Wonders no longer sup there.

Similarly, another poet, Mahammed Nuur Fadal,[4] while reproaching a friend for his disloyalty, illustrates his theme by the evils which he saw in the world of his time, when Ethiopia was invaded by the Italians and China by the Japanese.

Cigow, daacadchumo waa wacha Laysku dilayaa ye

. . . . .

Waa wacha dawaankii chidhay ee dumiyay Liiggii ye
Waa wacha dacwiga kiimankii ugu dibboodeen e
Waa wacha dalkii Chabashiyeed dab uga qiiqaa ye
Waa wacha dadkii Shiine dhalay Loo deldelayaa ye.

[1] His name in Somali is *Cumar Chuseen Gorse* and he is also known as Omar Ostreliya (*Cumar Ostreeliya*). He is one of the greatest living poets of Somalia and a well-known broadcaster on Somali traditional culture at Radio Hargeisa. See also Note 3.

[2] This passage has been taken from Musa Galaal's collection of Somali oral literature. As far as I know his is the largest and the best collection of Somali oral literature in existence.

[3] All Somali words and texts in this paper are given in the transcription, which is explained in Andrzejewski and Lewis, 1964.

[4] His name is pronounced in Somali *Machammed Nuur Fadal.* A poet of great distinction who travelled widely in East Africa and died in Nairobi about 1950. This extract is also taken from Musa Galaal's collection.

O Cige, it is because of disloyalty that men come to blows

. . . . .

It was because of it that the register was closed and
the League (of Nations) was destroyed
It was because of it that kings spent sleepless nights
in council
It is because of it that the land of the Ethiopians is
now in smoke and flames
It is because of it that those begotten by China are
massacred.

Yet such poetic commentaries were only marginal to the general interest of the public; the small world of their own immediate environment usually had a more powerful appeal. It was not until the Second World War that the Somali nation was brought within the orbit of world events, and in 1940 the Somaliland Protectorate was occupied by Italian troops, forcing the British administration to withdraw to Aden.

The Italian occupation lasted only till March 1941, when both the Somaliland Protectorate and the Italian colony of Somalia found themselves under British military administration. After some initial experimentation regular broadcasts in Somali were introduced in 1943 from Hargeisa, and were accepted by the public as a welcome innovation. News bulletins were translated from English, and the skill of interpreting at a high level had to be acquired as a matter of urgency and new demands on the lexical resources met. A public whose awareness of the aesthetic side of their language had been nurtured for centuries on fine poetry would not be satisfied with slipshod translation; they expected news bulletins and commentaries which were both clear in their sense and felicitous in style and use of words. The early broadcasters rose to the occasion and set a pattern of adaptation which has been followed by their colleagues and successors ever since, both in Somalia and abroad. Their difficulty lay almost entirely in the field of vocabulary, which was deficient in words connected with modern life. The gaps could have been filled by massive borrowing from English or Arabic, but this would have placed a heavy burden on the listener's memory and would interfere with a full understanding of what was said. Moreover, such a course of action would amount to a humiliating admission of the intellectual inadequacy of their mother tongue, a language of great poets, story-tellers, and preachers. The path which was followed was probably inspired by the tradition of coining new words which pervades all Somali poetry, and may be connected with the heavy demands of alliterative verse, where the same alliteration has to be carried through the whole poem. The Somali broadcasters invented new words and phrases for the purposes of translation, leaving, to a large extent, the old, well-established loan words in peace, at least for the time being.[1]

For a linguist, their actual methods of word-coining present a well-known pattern, much the same as is found in many neologisms introduced in German, Arabic, or Polish in the first half of the twentieth century. To illustrate this point a selection of newly coined words and phrases is listed below: they are capitalized so that they can be distinguished from the older, ordinary words given for comparison.

AFGEMBI, *coup d'état*
afgembi, turning (a vessel) upside down
ARGAGGICHISO, terrorists
argaggichi, to terrify[2]
BARWAAQASOORAN, Commonwealth
barwaaqo, prosperity, good season
la sooran, to share (profits and losses) with
BOQOLKII BA SHAN, five per cent
boqol, one hundred
-*kii* (definite article)
ba, each, every
shan, five[3]
CAGAFCAGAF, tractor
cagafcagaf, an onomatopoeic word suggesting a heavy and noisy movement

[1] Some people were so enthusiastic about Somalizing the vocabulary that they even tried to replace well-established loan-words. Thus the word *ruboc*, 'quarter', which is of Arabic origin and is frequently used in telling time, was substituted by *waach*, which denotes the same fraction but is basically a meat division term. This gave rise to many jokes, and the innovation did not gain the acceptance of the public in that context.

[2] All verbs given in this list are quoted in the lexical entry system adopted in the Notes to Musa Galaal, 1956. For a bibliography of works on Somali grammar see Johnson, 1967 and 1969.

[3] Naturally, any other number can be substituted for *shan*.

CHARUN, headquarters, centre, capital
Charun, name given to the headquarters of the Dervishes during the 1899–1920 insurrection
CHIDHIIDHKA SIYAASADDA, diplomatic relations
chidhiidh, bond, tie, connection, tying the leading rope of a camel to the tail of the preceding camel in a caravan
-*ka* (definite article)
siyaasad politics, policy, deceit (Arabic)[1]
-*da* (definite article)
CHOOGGA DALKA, the National Army
choog, strength, force
-*ga* (definite article)
dal, country
-*ka* (definite article)
CUNAQABATEE, to blockade, to apply economic sanctions
cunaqabatee, to seize by the throat, to throttle
DADWEYNE, general public
dad, people
weyn, to be large
-*e* (nominal suffix)
DAYACHGACMEED, artificial satellite, spacecraft
dayach, moon
gacan, hand
-*eed* (a genitival suffix suggesting here the meaning 'hand made')
DHAQAALE, economy, economics
dhaqaale, thrift, looking after livestock and property with care
DHEGAYSTAYAAL, listeners
dhegayso, to listen
-*st*- (positional variant of -*so* in *dhegayso*)
-*ayaal* (nominal suffix + plural termination)
DHUCHUSHA DHULKA LAGA QODO, coal
dhuchul, charcoal
-*sha* (definite article)
dhul, ground
La-, someone, people
-*ga*, from
qodo, 'which (people) dig' (dependent form of *qod* 'to dig')

[1] All the Arabic loan-words mentioned in this list were fully naturalized long before the advent of broadcasting.

DUR, to give an injection
dur, to prick with a strong direct thrust, to cast a spell (said of djinns)
DUUB, to tape-record
duub, to coil, to wind, to roll (thread, rope, cloth)
GAADIID, transport
gaadiid, burden beasts used for transport
GOBANNIMO, independence
gobannimo, being of noble birth or noble character
GOOSATO, secessionists
gooso, to cut off for oneself
-to (nominal suffix)
GUMEYSI, colonialism
gumeysi, treating a person as inferior or contemptible, cf.
gun, bottom, person of low birth or mean character
HANTIWADAAG, socialism
hanti, wealth, livestock
wadaag, to share
HEESTA CALANKA, the national anthem
hees, song
-ta (definite article)
calan flag (Ar.)
-ka (definite article)
HIRARKA GAAGGAABAN, short waves
hirar, distant objects sighted on the horizon, gusts of rain, waves
-ka (definite article)
gaaggaaban which are short (dependent, reduplicated form of the verb *gaaban* 'to be short')
HOYGA MADADDAALADA, the National Theatre[1]
hoy, home
-ga (definite article)
madaddaalo, entertainment
-da (definite article)

[1] In the sphere of spreading modern terminology, especially that which is concerned with nationalism and politics, the Somali theatre fulfils an important role. Plays in alliterative verse are shown in Mogadishu and other towns and enjoy great popularity. Some have been adapted for broadcasting.

Since this paper was submitted for publication HOYGA MADADDAALADA has been gradually replaced by GOLAHA MADADDAALADA (*gole*, 'meeting ground', 'large circle drawn on the sand in traditional games'; *-ha* definite article).

HUBKA IS WADA, guided missiles
hub, weapons
-ka (definite article)
is, self, oneself
wada, 'which drives' (dependent form of the verb *wad*, 'to drive')

II DHEH, advertisement
ii = i + u
i, me
u, for
dheh, say, announce (imperative form of the verb *yidhi*, 'to say')

ISKA WACH U QABSO, self-help scheme
is, self oneself
-ka (definite article)
wach, thing, things, something
u, for
qabso, seize, undertake (imperative form of the verb *qabso*, 'to seize, to undertake')

KELIGITALIYE, dictator
keli, being alone
-gi, his
taliye, person who gives advice or rules

KONTON MAYL OO KU WAREEGSAN, fifty square miles
konton, fifty
mayl, mile (English)
oo, and
ku, on, in
wareegsan, which extends around, which encompasses (dependent form of the hybrid verb *wareegsan*, 'to extend around, to encompass')

MIDABKALASOOC, racial discrimination
midab, colour
kala, apart
sooc, to separate, to select (often applied to domestic animals)

LA WAREEG, to take over, to nationalize
la, with
wareeg, to turn around, to move over

QAL, to operate on
qal, to butcher

QIIQA ILMADA KEENA, tear gas
qiiq, smoke
-a, (definite article)
ilmo tear
-da (definite article)
keena 'which brings' (dependent form of the verb *keen*, 'to bring')

QURUUMAHA MIDOOBAY, United Nations
quruumo, nations
-ha (definite article)
midoobay, which have become united (dependent form of the verb *midow*, 'to become united, to become one')

SUUCHI, to apply full anaesthetics
suuchi, to cause to lose consciousness, to cause to faint (rare)
suuch, to lose consciousness, to faint

URURKA SHAQAALAHA, trade union
urur, group, cluster, Pleiades
-ka (definite article)
shaqaale, workers (Ar.)
-ha (definite article)

WADAJIR, federation
wada, together
jir, to be in a place

WADDANNADA SOO KORAYA, developing countries
waddanno, countries (Ar.)
-da (definite article)
soo, towards (the centre of attention)
koraya, which are climbing, which are going up (dependent form of the verb *kor*, 'to climb, to go up')

WARGEYS, newspaper
war, news, information
gee, to convey, to take to
-s (nominal suffix)

WASAARADA WARFAAFINTA, Ministry of Information
wasaaro, ministry, the office held by a vizier (Ar.)
-da (definite article)
war, news, information
faafi, to cause to spread, to send (animals) out to graze
-n (nominal suffix)
-ta (definite article)

From 1943 onwards political changes brought educational progress to the Somali people, and in the 1950s secondary education at home and scholarships or secondments abroad began to produce a new educated *élite*, some of whom were absorbed by the expanding broadcasting system. At the same time programme organizers realized that oral literature and historical traditions could be used both as entertainment and as a form of education. Poets, poetry reciters, storytellers, and experts on traditional sciences and folklore have all found an appreciative, often enthusiastic audience. Many of them were monolingual, illiterate men of the traditional pastoral or agricultural environment; it is due to real patriotism and the good linguistic sense of the new broadcasters that instead of looking down on these bearers of the old Somali culture, they humbly accepted them as authorities on the language and respectfully listened to their judgements and suggestions in the field of modern terminology. Frequently a broadcaster educated abroad would carefully explain the meaning of a particular English or Italian word or phrase to an old bard and ask him for guidance in coining a Somali equivalent.

The pattern set by Radio Hargeisa and later by Radio Mogadishu was imitated by foreign stations: the Somali broadcasters in Cairo, London,[1] and Moscow all vie in their desire to please the public by maintaining high aesthetic standards and avoiding unnecessary loan-words, especially from European languages. The Somali audiences have always been very sensitive on this point. A broadcaster using many foreign words would immediately come under their criticism, voiced with great vigour, going even so far as demanding his dismissal.

Broadcasting has had another important effect: it has helped to strengthen the position of one dialect type as a standard acceptable everywhere. I use the term 'dialect type' in order to describe a concept which though vague and elusive (like 'educated American English' or 'neo-classical Arabic') is yet a recognizable social reality in the Somali context.

The dialect type in question, which has been described in Andrzejewski and Lewis, 1964, as Common Somali, covers a

[1] The Somali Service of the British Broadcasting Corporation has a particularly fine record in this respect.

group of dialects characterized by full mutual intelligibility. It is spoken throughout the Ogaden, the northern regions of the Somali Republic (i.e. the former British Protectorate), Mijurtinia, Mudug, and in parts of Hiran and Lower Juba; it is also spoken by all Somalis in French Somaliland and by the vast majority of Somalis in the North-Eastern Province of Kenya. Moreover, in most towns, even outside these areas, large sections of the population speak Common Somali, as do Somali communities settled in Aden, Tanzania, and Great Britain.

Common Somali contrasts with the Coastal and the Central dialect types spoken mainly in Benadir and Upper Juba respectively,[1] but a large number of speakers use an approximation to Common Somali (varying in degree) as a lingua franca outside their immediate home environment. Common Somali (or Standard Somali might perhaps be a better phrase) has been used in this capacity for a very long time, possibly several centuries, and its spread is no doubt due to trading activities, to the constant movement of religious students in their quest for learning, either individually or in itinerant colleges,[2] and to the frequent pilgrimages to the tombs of Somali saints from one end of the Somali-speaking territories to the other.

Broadcasting stations use Common Somali in all their news bulletins, commentaries, and announcements, and this includes not only Mogadishu, Hargeisa, Djibouti, Nairobi, and Addis Ababa but also Cairo, London, Moscow, and Rome. In fact, they all confirm by implication the status of this type of dialect as the accepted spoken language of the Somali nation.[3] Owing to unfortunate conflicts of opinion among the Somali public, the language has as yet no official orthography,[4] though several different systems are in private use. But in spite of the total absence of a daily press or of school books in Somali, it is

[1] Common and Coastal Somali are fully mutually intelligible after a few weeks of intensive contact between the speakers, while Common and Central Somali become so only after a few months of such contact. Note that Somali dialect divisions do not always coincide with tribal groupings, and it is very confusing to refer to Somali dialects by tribal names.

[2] For a brief account of these itinerant colleges see Andrzejewski and Musa Galaal, 1966.

[3] Common Somali is the generally recognized form of oral communication in the National Assembly, government offices, the police, the Army, and in business in Somalia.

[4] For an account of this complex problem see Andrzejewski, 1962, and Pirone, 1967.

possible to discuss, without resorting to a foreign language, things that matter in the modern world; if a decision is reached one day on an official orthography it would be possible to start printing intelligently written newspapers within weeks, since the necessary modern terminology would be known to the reader through the influence of broadcasting.

REFERENCES

Andrzejewski, B. W.
(1962) 'Speech and Writing Dichotomy as the Pattern of Multilingualism in the Somali Republic', *Report of the C.C.T.A./C.S.A. Symposium on multilingualism in Africa*, Brazzaville, pp. 177–81.

Andrzejewski, B. W. and Musa Galaal
(1966) 'The Art of the Verbal Message in Somali Society', *Neue afrikanistische Studien*, (ed. J. Lukas), V, Deutsches Institut fuer Afrika-Forschung, Hamburg, pp. 29–39.

Andrzejewski, B. W., and Lewis, I. M.
(1964) *Somali Poetry: an Introduction.* Clarendon Press. Oxford Library of African Literature.

Johnson, John William
(1967) *A Bibliography of Somali Language Materials.* Hargeisa: U.S.A. Peace Corps.
(1969) 'A Bibliography of Somali Language and Literature', *African Language Review*, VIII (in the press).

Musa Galaal
(1956) *Hikmad Soomaali.* (ed. B. W. Andrzejewski). Oxford University Press.
(1968) *The Terminology and Practice of Somali Weather Lore, Astronomy and Astrology*, Mogadishu (available from New Africa Booksellers, Mogadishu P.O. Box 897).

Pirone, Michele
(1967) 'La lingua somala e i suoi problemi'. *Africa* [Roma], XXII, 2, pp. 198–209.

Somali Republic, Ministry of Information
(1968) *The Development of Broadcasting in Somalia.* Mogadishu.

XV. The Elaboration of Basic Wolof

First results: The most frequent one hundred words: The problems raised by the lexicological analysis of a great African language

MAURICE CALVET

One of the most urgent tasks set by the development of African countries is the correct promotion of a linguistic policy necessarily based on multilingualism. If English, French, Spanish, and Portuguese were imposed as written, schooling, and official languages at the time of colonization, and later on kept as such for lack of choice when independence came, the part that the main African languages can and must play in the development of Africa must no longer be underestimated. The transformation of traditional African societies into modern nations requires recognition of the linguistic problem which can be solved only within a multilingualism that will ensure the promotion of national-popular African languages. There can be no nation without a relative linguistic unity; there can be no modernity and no development without massive resort to writing in the national language.[1]

A national consciousness through a common language, culture, and history, and a common socio-economic progress is possible in Africa and is already being realized in some states of North, Southern, and East Africa. The main drawback, however, is the arbitrary outline of frontiers drawn by colonizers and the ethnic division which results in linguistic balkanization. And yet this ethnic fragmentation and segregation should not be over-exaggerated. In many West African states, apparently condemned to linguistic balkanization, a national consciousness is now emerging; it is often strengthened by the development of

[1] In its final resolution, the 5th Intercommunal World Conference, which met in Royan from 15 to 18 April 1968, 'asks the next United Nations Conference at Teheran for the inscription among Man's fundamental rights the right to a bilingual education allowing any man to talk to his kind'.

a local lingua franca which is known by most people and makes possible, at a popular level, inter-ethnic, i.e. national, communication, as is necessitated by common everyday life and the sharing of the same destiny.

The position of Senegal in this respect is highly interesting. With its 3,110,000 native inhabitants[1] Senegal is peopled by five main ethnic groups:

1. The Wolof–Lébou group numbering	1,147,000
2. The Peul-Toucouleur group numbering	652,000
3. The Serer group numbering	595,000
4. The Diola–Bainouk group numbering	296,000
5. The Bambara–Malinké group numbering	198,000

To these numbers one must add:

(*a*) All the Casamance ethnic groups	100,000
The Sarakolé group	65,000
Other small Senegalese ethnic groups	30,000
Mauritanians	48,000
(*b*) The non-native population	
Europeans, almost all French	40,000
Natives of Lebanon–Syria	15,000
Miscellaneous (mainly Portuguese and half-breeds from Cape Verde Islands)	8,000

To this ethnic diversity is added a corresponding linguistic one. If, at first sight, Senegal seems to be an ethnic mosaic, like the other French-speaking African countries, one must note that, unlike many African states, such as Ivory Coast or the Cameroons, Senegal is not characterized by linguistic balkanization.

This is what the C.L.A.D. statistically proved in 1964–66 at the end of a socio-linguistic inquiry which was answered by nearly 36,000 pupils, that is to say, all the children entering primary schools in 1963.[2] At the end of this inquiry we pointed

[1] The figures we give are those drawn from the study by L. Verrière 'La population du Senegal', 1965 (a former director of Statistics in Senegal). These figures date back to 1961–4. They are below the present facts.

[2] See C.L.A.D.'s Study No. 11 by F. Wioland: 'Enquête sur les langues parlées au Senegal par les élèves de l'enseignement primaire—Etude statistique 1965', including a map; and the report on it by Calvet-Wioland 'L'expansion du Wolof au Senegal', IFAN *Bulletin*, XXIX (B), 3/4, 1967.

out that, if the Wolof ethnic group represents only 36 per cent of the Senegalese population, the Wolof language, on the other hand, is spreading, since it is commonly used by the overwhelming majority of young Senegalese people (about 80 per cent). At the same time this inquiry taught us that French was used in the family circle by a mere 0·22 per cent of the Senegalese population.

We drew a double conclusion: (*a*) the necessity of learning French as a foreign language in Senegalese schools, using the techniques belonging to the up-to-date teaching methods of modern languages; (*b*) the necessity of regarding Wolof as the lingua franca of the country and likely to become the first African national language in Senegal.

As a corollary to these basic linguistic data we understood that we had to create a new method of teaching French based on the thorough study of Wolof influences on French, and prepare a reliable and firm basis for a harmonious French–Wolof bilinguism in Senegal.[1]

Finally, to complete these first data, according to the same inquiry carried out by Louis Verrière a year or two before ours, 12 per cent of the Senegalese people, only 1 per cent were women, stated that they knew how to read or write French.[2]

Although from a scientific point of view one can say that Wolof is in the process of becoming the first national-popular language of Senegal, it is still very difficult to get it accepted in this country. Opposition is met with from all sides:

(*a*) From French people working in Senegal, especially teachers of the Technical Aid Programme, who still regard Europe as being the centre of all things, believe in a civilizing mission, and generally consider African languages to be vulgar, provincial dialects.

(*b*) From the representatives of other large ethnic groups, particularly the Peul–Toucouleur. The specificity of Peul culture, the range of its groups scattered over several states, yet united by a common language and culture, are factors which give the Foulahs of Senegal a great aversion to the

[1] See C.L.A.D.'s, study No. XXIV; 'L'enseignement du Français au service de la Nation Sénégalaise', by Pierre Fougeyrollas.

[2] L. Verrière op. cit., p. 80.

idea of seeing the Wolof language endowed with a privileged status.

(*c*) From many Senegalese people, themselves Wolofs, from two walks of life: at a popular level, illiterate parents who have made great sacrifices to send their children to school want them to be taught in French and not 'cheaply' in their mother tongue. Often such people do not understand how useful a primary school education in the mother tongue can be, since the key to social success is through mastery of the French language and obtaining corresponding diplomas; at a higher level (among certain civil servants, teachers, engineers, doctors, magistrates, officers formed and moulded by the French system of education) one notes a confusion, if not an aversion to the idea that Wolof, their mother tongue, might one day become a written language, the first schooling language and even the national language of Senegal. For to them it means questioning again accepted ideas, and especially the acquired knowledge that justifies their social privileges.

It would certainly be interesting to start an extensive inquiry in Senegal among the adult population in order to find out exactly what proportion of Senegalese people favour the introduction of five main Senegalese African Languages (Wolof, Peul, Serer, Malinké, Diola) in primary and secondary school education; and whether or not they are ready to recognize Wolof as the first national-popular language in Senegal. But at present political reasons would not permit such an inquiry to be carried out. It could, moreover, be organized only at the demand of the Senegalese Government. Let us note that a first preliminary problem, that of the transliteration of the main Senegalese languages has very recently been settled. In his decree No. 68,871 of 24 July 1968, published in the Senegalese *Official Gazette* No. 3984 of 31 August, the Head of State fixed the unified alphabets of these languages. These alphabets admit only two new letters[1] and differ from the propositions made by the commission of experts which met in Bamako from 28 February to 5 March 1966 at Unesco's request. At present the Senegalese people are slowly becoming conscious of the promotion of the country's main languages. A lecture given by Professor Pierre Fougeyrollas at C.L.A.D.'s request on 14 April

[1] η for velar nasals and ʁ for sonant uvular occlusives.

1967 at Dakar University and later heard over the radio by the whole country, provoked a real psychological shock to both French and Senegalese opinion.[1]

Despite the difficulty of the undertaking, the opposition, and the psychological aversions, from 1964 we at C.L.A.D. understood that we must prepare, on a scientific plane, for the passage to writing and the introduction into the teaching programmes of the country's lingua franca, Wolof. A considerable subsidy was granted to us in 1965 by the Ford Foundation, partly to carry through this plan.

WORKS ON WOLOF

Of all the languages in Senegal, the best known and described is Wolof. In their work *Wolof and Serer*, published by the Faculté des Lettres at Dakar University, Professors G. Manessy and S. Sauvageot inventoried 110 publications on Wolof or in Wolof, not all of the same quality, which were brought out between 1732 and 1962. One of the most important of these works is the Wolof–French dictionary by Monseigneur Kobes which first appeared in 1873 and was republished in 1923. Since 1962 an average of one study a year has been published on Wolof. Recent contributions to the study of Wolof by Professor Sauvageot and C.L.A.D.'s research workers have been substantial, but the need for a scientifically compiled modern Wolof dictionary appeared to us as urgent, since Monseigneur Kobes's dictionary is now out-of-date (and out of print).

BASIC WOLOF

We undertook this study with the collaboration of: Professor Muller, a lexicologist at Strasburg University; Professor Rivenc, Toulouse University, who directed the elaboration of Basic French and Basic Spanish; and Professor Quemada, the director of the Centre of Studies of French Vocabulary at Besançon.

THE ENQUIRY

Its aim: to collect a corpus of 500,000 words.[2] Three of C.L.A.D.'s Senegalese research workers of Wolof origin under-

[1] Cf. C.L.A.D.'s study No. XXIV: 'L'enseignement du Français au service de la nation Sénégalaise'.

[2] The corpus of words for Basic French was only 340,000 words.

	Cap Vert region of Dakar	*Diourbel*	*Thies*	*Sine Saloum*	*Casa-Mance*	*Fleuve*	*Senegal Oriental*	*The whole of Senegal*
Demographic distribution of Wolof	213,000	374,000	183,000	260,000	21,000	93,000	3,000	1,147,000
Percentage in relation to the total Wolof population	18·44%	32·57%	16%	22·71%	1·88%	8·15%	0·25%	100%
Words necessary for the corpus of 500,000 words, in terms of the demographic distribution	92,200	162,850	80,000	113,550	9,400	40,750	1,250	500,000
Number of speakers	185	326	160	227	19	82	3	1,002
Number of typed pages	295	530	255	365	20	125	5	1,595

took a systematic survey of the seven principal regions of Senegal, from October 1966 to October 1968, according to the above demographic distribution.[1]

The research workers, under the guidance of a Senegalese sociologist, had to respect every parameter: regional origin, social origin, level of education, profession, sex, age. The representative sample of the population interviewed in this way forms a group of a thousand or so Senegalese people.

In each of the regions prospected the research workers interviewed speakers, over the age of 18, and representing the various socio-cultural and socio-economic levels. Each speaker was identified and coded carefully with the aid of an interview form. The researchers were instructed to instigate familiar dialogues, each speaker having to deliver a sample of his everyday speech, in a maximum fifteen minutes interview recorded on a portable tape-recorder. The researchers[2] when necessary, initiated conversations, trying to make the people speak of their environment, their activities, their daily worries, and their family preoccupations. These 'directed' conversations unfortunately cannot be avoided, as it is very difficult in this kind of inquiry to record clearly spontaneous family discussions.

In their reports our research workers state the difficulties they met with on the spot: the mistrust of most of the speakers; inhibitions caused by the sight of the microphones (our research workers are taken for State agents or Radio Senegal reporters on an obscure mission);[3] difficulty of obtaining the identity of the speakers; obligation to brush aside grievances, political criticism, and vulgarity, and to limit chatter displaying pom-

[1] It must be noted that more than 50 per cent of the population are less than 20 years old. Only speakers more than 18 years old whose mother tongue is Wolof were interviewed.

[2] Socio-cultural level of the three research workers:

Dr. Ousmane Silla: 31 years old, a Wolof–Senegalese sociologist at Ifan in Dakar (he is in charge of the inquiry).

Oumar Ben Khatab Dia: 40 years old, a Wolof–Senegalese man of secondary-school education who is a primary-school headmaster.

Samba Sar: 30 years old, a Wolof–Senegalese man with G.C.E., a student reading English, completing his B.A. and teaching in a Dakar comprehensive school.

[3] We must point out that our linguistic inquiry, intended to help in the elaboration of basic Wolof, was initiated on the sole decision of C.L.A.D. We have never received instructions, or official orders, from the Senegalese Government. At the very most we have profited by personal and official encouragement from Mr. Mohktar M'Bow, the Minister of Education of Senegal from 1966 to 1968. This

pous wordiness (as was the case of the Griots in talk devoid of spontaneity). The research workers pay the speakers at the rate of 100 CFA francs for each twenty-minute session. An atmosphere favouring everyday and relaxed talking is generally created by offering tea. Our investigators would have liked a tape-recorder and microphone that one can hide, which would have made their task far easier.

The corpus of 500,000 words is at present entirely recorded on tapes and is being carefully examined. It represents two hundred recording hours with a thousand or so Wolof-speaking Senegalese people. It was collected within two years, from November 1966 to 1968. Recordings made in the phonetics laboratory from 1963 to 1967 have been included in this corpus.

THE ANALYSIS

The Transliteration

The recordings are all phonologically transliterated (I.A.I. system) by Madame Aram Diop,[1] who is helped in this work by Mr. Ben Khatab Dia. The texts of the first under-corpus of 100,000 words have also been phonemically transliterated by Madame Diop, in the interests of homogeneity. Madame Diop is practically the only Wolof specialist at present capable of giving a good phonemic notation of Wolof. On the ground of the first under-corpus of 61,500 words we have just built up the alphabetical dictionary of the 6,000 different words it contains according to the first list given by the Centre of Studies of French Vocabulary at Besançon. In this way it is now possible to entrust several transliterators with the transliterating of the next part of the corpus. They can constantly refer to this dictionary-for-home-use, so that its phonemical spelling is scrupulously respected.

Once they are transliterated, the texts are typed on two 'Imperial' typewriters with international phonetic type by two Wolof–Senegalese typists. Then the texts are pre-edited under Madame Diop's control according to a code worked out

---

absence of official support for our undertaking has obviously complicated the task of our research workers among both the people and the local administrators.

[1] Madame Aram Diop, B.A., a Wolof–Senegalese lady, is completing her doctorate in linguistics. She is a linguist at Ifan in Dakar.

with the Centre of Studies of French Vocabulary at Besançon. The texts are then sent to the Centre of Studies of French Vocabulary at Besançon, where they are set on perforated cards. A copy-list of the perforated cards is immediately sent from Besançon to C.L.A.D. This copy-list is then corrected, if necessary. The corrected list is sent back to Besançon, where the Centre of Studies of French Vocabulary then carries out the computer examination, analysis, and classification with Bull machines.

In the Septembers of 1967 and 1968 the members of C.L.A.D.'s team entrusted with the transliteration, pre-edition, coding, and typing attended courses at the Centre of Studies of French Vocabulary at Besançon, in order to perfect the method of work between the two Centres.

Placing on Perforated Cards

The Centre of Studies of French Vocabulary has already completed its work on the first under-corpus. The second under-corpus is now being worked on. All the words of the first under-corpus, with the exception of proper names, have been put on to perforated cards. Words borrowed from the French are the subject of a separate analysis which will allow a study on the quantity and quality of words borrowed by Wolof from the French. On the advice of Professor Muller and for reasons of economy, we have decided to sift out the hundred most frequent words on the basis of the first under-corpus in order to economize on the corresponding treatment of half the remaining corpus.

(a) *The Problem of Economy of the Hundred Most Frequent Words.* The corpus in view is of 500,000 words, a range superior to that used for Basic French and equal to that adopted for A. Juilland's (Stanford University) inquiry into the Romance languages (written) which includes French, yet inferior to the limits accepted for German and Spanish. This corpus will be divided into 10 groups of 50,000 units, determined by the recording dates. In all inquiries of this kind, and whatever the language studied, one sees that a small number of words (grammatical ones) covers a large proportion of the text; in general, the thirty to fifty most frequent words represent 50 per cent of occurrences. As a result of leaving these words out of the analysis, a considerable amount of time and money is saved. It was a matter of deciding on a method which, without lessening the scientific value of the results, would allow the 500,000 occurrences to be found in the quickest possible time and at the least cost.

(b) *Lexicological Analysis.* (This has been embarked on under the control of M. Ladroit at the Centre of Studies of French Vocabulary at Besançon.) Requested by the Centre of Applied Linguistics of Dakar at the beginning of 1967 to proceed to an analysis of Wolof interviews, the laboratory of lexicological analysis began in the September of the same year with the perforation of card-indexes.

1. Organization of the Corpus

Unlike the two basic languages (German and Spanish) already treated by the laboratory, the analysis of Basic Wolof is divided into two under-corpuses. The first, (initially comprising 50,000 words) was in fact of 100,000 words, which represent an exhaustive analysis of the corpus. The second, of 450,000 words, excluded the terms (grammatical and lexical) whose total of frequencies reached 50,000 and for which the distribution was regular in the first under-corpus.

2. Problems Relative to the Analysis

As far as the analysis in itself is concerned, one great difficulty was that Wolof is a vehicular language using phonetic symbols. Thus, in preference to transliterating the whole of the corpus into Latin letters, a long and expensive task, it was necessary to modify transliterating chains of type and the tabulators on which the work was done. Another difference between the work on German and Spanish is at the level of the creation of context cards. In fact, this was not justified for Wolof, since the homophones were codified on the interviews at the time of pre-editing according to the following systems:

Column 61: grammatical category. 0 nouns; 1 pronouns; 2 personal mood verbs; 3 impersonal mood verbs; 4 qualifying adjectives;[1] 5 co-ordinating adverbs and conjunctions; 6 articles;

[1] We used the code but with slight modifications, taking into account the structure of the language: the 'qualifying adjectives' were codified 2, for in the language they have the same behaviour as verbs.

7 adjectives other then qualifying ones; 8 prepositions; 9 subordinating conjunctions; rien interjections.

Column 62: used only in cases of perfect homophony (of the kind 'voler' in French). A code is there to indicate what the meaning is.

The word-cards were treated with sociological information about the speaker so that it might eventually be possible to proceed to studies of a sociological kind from the basis of the language. References to the text equally figure in order to allow a term to be replaced in its context, which, in the course of the work, makes it possible to clarify litigious cases.

3. Statistical Documents

The alphabetical filing of these word-cards will make it possible to establish:

(*a*) A statistical alphabetical list taking into account homophonous cases and giving for each term: the overall frequency; the frequency in each unit of 5,000 words of uninterrupted text; and a card-index of recapitulatory cards, i.e. bearing the whole of the information collected: frequencies, words, and, for homophones, grammatical category.

(*b*) The recapitulatory cards thus created will make it possible to establish a list of decreasing frequencies from a sorting out according to frequency.

(*c*) The first card-index will later allow a regrouping of weak forms of the same word to obtain the list of frequencies and of distribution of words.

4. Lists of Available Words

Any inquiry of this kind cannot bring to light certain words which, however, are 'available' to most speakers. Thus the word 'coude' never appeared in the recording for the inquiry on basic French. On the other hand, in one of these recordings made with a charwoman the 'suçeuse' often appears. This word, unknown to the average French speaker, refers to the metal nozzle to be fixed on to the hose of a vacuum-cleaner.

In order to evoke the 'available' word in the linguistic consciousness of most speakers, whatever language they speak, one must resort to 'lists of available words', as a complement to the inquiry.

We shall undertake this complementary inquiry in 1969. To help us we shall have the experience and advice of Professor Rivenc, of Toulouse University, who is completing the elaboration of Basic Spanish with his team. Professor Rivenc allowed us to draw upon the lists he made and dealt out in the higher forms of Spanish schools. To draw these lists up about fifteen topics have been selected: the body, clothes, the family, school, the town, the seasons, plants, etc. For each topic pupils must, within a given time (twenty minutes), write down all the words that enter their minds (a distribution in three categories will be set: substantives, adjectives, verbs).

In this kind of complementary inquiry we intend to proceed in an original way, that is without resorting to writing: pupils, aged 18 and over, will be asked to sit in the booths of a language laboratory, and a Wolof-speaking research worker will ask them, from the control desk, to enumerate, within the space of ten minutes, the words suggested to them by such and such a topic. Their answers will be recorded and then analysed.

We expect to publish the Basic Wolof first, at the end of 1969. It will number the 3,000 most frequent words. Then we shall draw up a comprehensive glossary of all the terms met (6,000 at present).

Lexical Problems to be Foreseen at a Later Date

These essentially concern borrowed words. If an African oral language is to attain the rank of a written language, of a national language, it is essential that it should be open to change in order to allow for the translation and expression of modern concepts. But African languages have a traditional, archaic 'view of the world'. Two courses are open to us: (*a*) Resort to borrowing from one or several of the great international languages (French or English) to name objects, techniques, modern concepts. This is the course chosen by the Israelis for Modern Hebrew. It is what the Wolof language is already doing in both a dynamic and an archaic way. (*b*) Resort to the substance of the language. This is the solution advocated by

M. Cheikh Anta Diop.[1] In Wolof an aeroplane is called a 'flying machine' (*fofal naw*), for example. This solution has also been adopted by the Finns for Modern Finnish.

In our view only a 'Superior Council of the Languages of Senegal', composed of competent persons and with a section for each language, will be able to opt for one or the other of these solutions. We ourselves consider that the norm, good use, is, above all, the use by the greatest number. In this respect our basic glossary, established on statistical bases, will provide a foundation for solid reflection.

CONCLUSION

Our purpose here has been to give a general view of the problems raised by the elaboration of the basic glossary of a vehicular African language which is still only oral. We have attempted to show how we have launched this venture in Dakar.

The results we present, particularly the first 100 words, are temporary and still imperfect. We do not maintain that our method and organization are exemplary in this field. We do, however, consider that our experience may be useful in order that other teams in Africa should correctly take up this more and more necessary type of research work.

We are anxious to point out that, in the history of human languages, Wolof is the first African language whose basic glossary is scientifically drawn from a large corpus collected from a representative sample of the population. To date only Indo-European languages, such as French, German, English, Spanish, or Roumanian, have been the subject of such a lexicological treatment. On the firm basis of a Basic Wolof dictionary it will soon be possible in Senegal to elaborate alphabetization methods, to build up popular education programmes, and to lay the foundations of a Senegalese literature which will be genuinely national, independent of orality, and independent too of European written languages.

[1] Cheikh Anta Diop 'Etudes de linguistique Ouolove', *Présence Africaine*, Dakar–Paris, 4, 1948, pp. 672–84.

REFERENCES

Calvet, M.
(1964) 'Interférence du phonétisme wolof dans le français parlé au Sénégal', *Bulletin IFAN*, XXVI (B), 3/4, 518–31.
Etude phonétique des voyelles du wolof', *Phonética*, No. 14, 138–68.

Calvet, M. and Wioland, F.
(1967) 'Expansion du Wolof au Sénégal', *Bulletin IFAN*, XXIX (B), 3/4.

Diop, Cheikh Anta.
(1948) 'Etudes de linguistique Ouolove', *Présence Africaine*, 4, 672–84.

Fougeyrollas, P.
(1967) 'L'enseignement du français au service de la Nation Sénégalaise', *Etude C.L.A.D.*, no 24.

Gougenheim, G. and Rivenc, P.
(1969) *L'élaboration du Français Fondamental.* Paris: Librairie Didier.

Grelier, (Mme) S.
(1967) 'Essai de comparaison morpho-syntaxique de l'anglais, du wolof et du français—Le Nominal', *Etude C.L.A.D.*, No. 19.
(1967–8) 'Recherche des principales interférences dans les systèmes verbaux de l'anglais, du wolof et du français', *Etude C.L.A.D.*, No. 31.

Kobes, A. and Abiven, O.
(1923) *Dictionnaire Wolof-Français* Dakar: Mission Catholique.

Le Boulch, P.
(1967) 'Un cas de trilinguisme—L'apprentissage de l'anglais par les élèves sénégalais—Interférence des phonétismes wolof et français', *Etude C.L.A.D.*, No. 22.

Sauvageot, S.
(1965) *Le parler du Dyolof.* Dakar: *I.F.A.N.*

Sauvageot, S. and Manessy, G.
(1963) *Wolof et Sérèr.* Dakar: Faculté des Lettres, No. 12.

Stewart, W.
(1966) *Introductory course in Dakar wolof.* Washington: Center for Applied Linguistics.

Verrière, L.
(1965) *La population du Sénégal.* Dakar: Faculté de Droit.

Wioland, F.
(1965) 'Enquête sur les langues parlées au Sénégal par les élèves de l'enseignement primaire', *Etude C.L.A.D.*, No. 11 (including one linguistic map).

XVI. Loan-words in Luganda: A Search for Guides in the Adaptation of African Languages to Modern Conditions

M. MOSHA

INTRODUCTION

Background

Africa is going through a crucial period of transition which is characterized, *inter alia*, by tremendous desires and struggles to transform traditional political, economic, and social structures and systems into modern ones in a bid to cope with the exacting demands of the twentieth century. Of the many problems that have to be surmounted by such an effort, those relating to language are in many ways fundamental, and as such must be solved effectively in order to give the processes of national development a chance to succeed by providing the developing nation with: (*a*) an adequate system of linguistic communication, national identification, and consciousness, and (*b*) a means to cultural unity (see Knappert, 1964; Mosha, 1967).

A vital aspect of the language issue is that of the choice and adaptation of a local or a foreign language to be used either as a national language or as an official medium of administration and instruction either at all levels or at certain stages of the educational system. If it is a question of adapting a local language one would like to know whether there are linguistic and sociological factors which could be used as a guide. In this paper, therefore, an effort is made to survey in general terms the treatment of loan-words in Luganda (see Kirwan, 1951; Ashton *et al.*, 1954; Chesswas, 1959; Tucker, 1962; Cole, 1967) with special reference to words acquired from Kiswahili (see Inter-Territorial Language Committee, 1939; Tucker, 1942; Ashton, 1962) and English. The main aim of the study is to throw some light on some of the linguistic and socio-linguistic factors which could act as a guide in the adaptation of African languages to modern conditions—the assumption being that what holds true for Luganda will be useful elsewhere, even if the detailed findings about the treatment of loans differ significantly.

Introductory Remarks about Luganda

Luganda is the native tongue of the Baganda (see Fallers, 1964; Roscoe, 1965), an Inter-Lacustrine Bantu group numbering about 1½ million people, who live in the Buganda Region of Uganda. Linguistically, Luganda is geographically in contact with Kihaya (or Ruhaya) in the south-west, Runyankore–Rutooro–Runyoro to the west and north-west, Lwo to the north-east, and Lusoga to the east. It is also in contact, in varying degrees and circumstances, with Kiswahili, English, several languages of the Indic branch of IE (e.g. Hindustani and Gujerati), Arabic, Latin, and so on.

In Uganda Luganda, though not officially recognized as Uganda's lingua franca, has a position which compares somewhat favourably with that of Kiswahili in up-country Kenya, in that it is spoken or understood by at least over 3 million people. Of Uganda's local languages, Luganda has the largest number of speakers outside its tribal boundaries, and at one time it used to be the medium of instruction as well as a curriculum subject in many primary and junior secondary schools outside Buganda, particularly in the Eastern Region. But with advancement in these areas local languages have been replacing Luganda in the classroom. Moreover, with the spread of educational facilities, along with the fact that English, which is the official language of the Republic, is receiving an ever-increasing emphasis in the schools, Luganda is bound to lose its claim as a lingua franca for Uganda.

In Buganda, however, Luganda continues to be the language of instruction in primary schools, except in the urban centres. It is also taught in some secondary schools as an examination subject for the Cambridge School Certificate. It has, by East African standards, considerable literature, and there are several Luganda newspapers. It has more air time on Radio Uganda than any other indigenous language, while on UTV Luganda and English are the official languages.

Cultures in Contact

The way of life in Buganda has been changing very rapidly in the last sixty years. The single main factor in this great change has been—and will, for some time, continue to be—the contact with and the impact of the West European way of life. This contact and its great impact on the social, economic, and political pattern of Kiganda culture have directly and indirectly produced both lasting and transitory effects. Loan-words from English, for instance, are bound to remain a lasting legacy from the encounter. It is very likely, however, that word borrowing from the languages in geographical contiguity with Luganda, e.g. Lusoga, Runyoro, etc., as well as from languages not geographically contiguous, e.g. Arabic from the north along the Nile Valley, had been going on before the advent of Europeans. Word borrowing as such should therefore not be thought of as dating from their arrival. Nevertheless, their coming did not only provide new languages from which words could be borrowed but also accelerated both the need to borrow and the actual borrowing.

As already stated, the present study will concentrate on those loan-words that have been acquired by Luganda from English and Kiswahili. Loans from other languages that got into Luganda directly, i.e. without going into, say, Kiswahili and thence into Luganda, will have to await future investigation. But it is important to point out that with the exception of loans from Latin (in the case of Catholics) and Portuguese it is extremely difficult to establish whether loans from, say, Arabic or Hindustani came into Luganda directly or indirectly through Kiswahili. However, it has been felt reasonable to assume—on historical, geographical, and cultural grounds—that the majority of loans from Arabic, Hindustani, etc., were first borrowed into Kiswahili and then into Luganda from Kiswahili. It has to be admitted, however, that on purely linguistic grounds it is difficult—if not impossible—to establish whether a given loan-word in Luganda, which is not Bantu in origin but which has a corresponding form in Kiswahili, was borrowed directly from the source language into Luganda or indirectly from the source language through Kiswahili. Both historically and geographically, foreign contact with Buganda from the East African Coast had to go through the coast, where Kiswahili was the lingua franca. Because of the great distances involved, the lack of fast means of transport, and the tendency for those who ventured far inland to stay at the coast for some time first, it is likely that loans went into Kiswahili long before such foreign contact got to Buganda. Furthermore, it was customary for traders, hunters, explorers, and so on moving inland to avail themselves of Kiswahili speakers as interpreters. It is thus likely that the Baganda borrowed new words from the Kiswahili interpreters long before they borrowed from the Arab or Indian traders.

It is almost impossible to establish whether a certain loan-word in Luganda was borrowed directly or indirectly from the source language, because both Kiswahili and Luganda are members of the same language group, i.e. Bantu. There are, for example, a large number of words of Bantu origin in Luganda that closely resemble in form and meaning words found in Kiswahili (examples 1–4 below).

The symbols used in the transcription of Luganda and Kiswahili data are those of the IPA (1961) except that *g* is used for a voiced velar stop; *c* is used for a voiceless palato-alveolar affricate; *j* for a voiced palato-alveolar affricate; and *y* for a palatal frictionless continuant. For Luganda a single consonant symbol, e.g. *d*, stands for a short consonant, while a doubled symbol, e.g. *dd*, refers to a long consonant. High tone is unmarked, while low and falling tones are represented respectively by the grave ˋ and circumflex ˆ accents. For typographical convenience, these are placed immediately before the sounds to which they refer. When a consonant has the same tone as that of the *following* vowel the consonant as such is not marked.

Luganda			*Kiswahili*	
1. *ˋokˋuyˆi:mba*	Class (Cl.) 15	'to sing'	*kuimba*	Cl. 15
2. *ˋokˋufˆa*	Cl. 15	'to die'	*kufa*	Cl. 15
3. *ˋokuzi:ka*	Cl. 15	'to bury'	*kuzika*	Cl. 15
4. *ˋe:nzige*	Cl. 9/10	'locust'	*nzige*	Cl. 9/10

The transcription of English examples follows that of Jones, 1960a and 1960b, except that *g* is used for a voiced velar stop.

Luganda could therefore borrow words, say, from Arabic directly and Lugandanize them into forms that resemble in many ways the Kiswahili forms for the same Arabic words. It is thus impossible on linguistic evidence alone to establish, for instance, whether Luganda *`ekitabo*, 'a book', came straight from Arabic or whether it was borrowed from Kiswahili *kitabu*, 'a book'. It is a pity that Luganda as a written language did not exist during the initial stages of borrowing. As a result, there are no written records to which the investigator can turn for clues.

GRAMMATICAL CATEGORIZATION OF LOAN-WORDS

Factors Influencing Borrowing and Degree of Lugandanization

Why should Luganda borrow words from other languages? Who are the agents of borrowing? To what extent are loan-words fully assimilated into the phonetic, phonological, morphological, and lexical systems of Luganda?

As with other languages (see Weinreich, 1953; Whiteley, 1963), Luganda word borrowing is motivated by several factors. In the case of Luganda, the most important factor has been the non-existence of indigenous vocabulary for new and alien material objects and abstract ideas that have been coming into Kiganda culture from other cultures. For example, Christianity brought in many physical objects and abstract ideas, e.g. the physical object 'font' and its abstract associates 'baptize' and 'baptism'. Both the object 'font' and the non-material aspect of 'baptism' were originally new and alien to the Baganda, and as a result their indigenous vocabulary had no words for either 'font' or 'baptize–baptism'. Consequently, Luganda borrowed and Lugandanized 'baptize' to derive words for both the object and the abstract 'baptize–baptism', namely *`e`bbatirizo*, *`okubatiza*, *`bb`ati:s`imu*, respectively. But religion was not the only force at work.

Side by side with religion came new forms of dress, food, administration, law and order, communication, farming, commerce, industry, education, recreation, and so on. All these brought new objects and ideas for which the Baganda had to find names. The following examples will illustrate this.

The lending languages are indicated thus: (Ara.) for *Ara*bic, (Eng.) for *Eng*lish, (Hin.) for *Hin*dustani, (Kis.) for *Kis*wahili,

(Lat.) for *Lat*in, (Por.) for *Por*tuguese. The symbol < means 'from'.

5. *\`e\`ssu:t\`i*	Cl. 9/10	(Eng.)	'Suit'
6. *\`om\`up^u:ŋga*	Cl. 3/4	(Kis.)	'rice (in any form)'
7. *\`kk\`ami:son^a*	Cl. 1/2	(Eng.)	'Commissioner, e.g. a D.C.'
8. *re:rw\`e*	Cl. 9/10	(Eng.)	'railway'
9a. *\`e\`ddeb\`e*	Cl. 5/6 or Cl. 9/10	(Kis. < Hin.)	'a 4-gallon container'
9b. *\`e:ndeb\`e*	Cl. 9/10	”	” ”
10. *\`e\`mme:z\`a*	Cl. 9/10	(Kis. < Por.)	'table'
11. *\`e\`kkireziy\`a*	Cl. 9/10	(Lat.)	'church (Catholic)'

The prestige of the source language has been another factor. Since ability to read and speak English was (and still is) an indication of educational advancement, and since education was (and still is to a lesser extent than before) the key to a greatly improved personal, social, economic, and political status, there has been a tendency for some Luganda speakers to use Lugandanized English words even where indigenous words occur. Examples:

Indigenous Words		*Loan-words*		*Lending Language*	
12. *\`om\`usaw\`o*	Cl. 1/2	*\`ddok\`ita*	Cl. 1/2	(Eng.)	'doctor'
13. *\`e\`ns^o:nda*	Cl. 9/10	*\`e\`kko:na*	Cl. 9/10	(Eng.)	'corner'
14. *\`amasaŋŋa:nzira*	Cl. 6	*\`e\`ss\`ite:s\`eni*	Cl. 9/10	(Eng.)	'station'

The prestige of English alone would not, however, have been very influential were it not for the fact that the culture of the English speech community and the members themselves have, on the whole, enjoyed great esteem—even in cases where reason calls for condemnation or rejection. The blind desire among many Africans to live, dress, eat, and look like their European colleagues, neighbours, bosses, etc., is evident everywhere in spite of the cries against colonialists, imperialists, and the like. There exists an irrational vogue that what is European must be superior to anything else!

Kiswahili and the other languages do not enjoy similar prestige because of a number of reasons which will not be discussed here. It may be observed, however, that in the case of Kiswahili neither the language itself nor its speakers, native or otherwise, have ever won the respect of the Baganda. Consequently, loans from these languages are fewer than those from English, and typically fall into the category of words that refer to items that Luganda *had* to borrow. Here the relationship between, on the one hand, the recipient language and its native speakers and, on the other, the source languages and their speakers has operated against an extensive borrowing of words from Kiswahili and the other languages.

For a number of Luganda speakers, borrowing has been motivated by the need to differentiate semantic fields that were not differentiated before or by the desire to be more precise by avoiding ambivalent words. For example, a number of Baganda use *ˋomˋusawˋo* to mean a native doctor who deals in herbs and white magic, while *ˋddokˋita* stands for one trained in modern, i.e. European, medicine. Monolingual Baganda, when pressed to distinguish the two kinds of doctors, resort to the phrases: *ˋomˋusawˋo ˋomˋugˆaında*, 'a Muganda doctor', and *ˋomˋusawˋo ˋomˋuzˆuıŋgu*, 'a European doctor'.

Desire by government and other institutions to avoid undesirable designations and connotations has also enhanced the acquisition of loan-words. For instance, since the Luganda rendering *ˋeınsˆi ˋeyeıkyeıtwaırˋa* for' Republic' equates Uganda with Smith's Rhodesia, it has been decided that on Radio Uganda and UTV only the Lugandanized form of 'Republic', namely *ripˋaburiıka*, should be used. These two mass media and newspapers have also led to word borrowing by regularly presenting Luganda listeners and readers with Lugandanized forms which are eagerly accepted.

Another factor which must be considered is the quest for recognition and acceptance, which drives the less educated Baganda deliberately to use loan-words for purposes of showing off. Moreover, younger people have an inclination towards borrowing as a piece of adventure, fun, glamour, and stylistic effect (see Mosha, 1966).

Extent of education and specialization also affects borrowing, in that a Muganda who is forced to use English regularly for the greater part of each day because of the nature of his work gradually tends to lose his fluency in Luganda as years go by. As a result, he uses loans more frequently than is necessary, and his ability to keep the two languages apart dwindles.

There are also cases where phenomena that were traditionally rare, and the denotators of which had, therefore, a low frequency of occurrence, have become frequent and loans are replacing the Luganda words. One example of this is *mˋaraıyˋa*

(Kis.), 'prostitute' which is now more common than Luganda *ˋomweːnzi*, 'prostitute'. Finally, Luganda has borrowed some words in order to resolve homonyms. Originally, Luganda *ˋomˋuweːrˋeza* covered both 'a paid servant/workman' and 'an unpaid assistant'. Today, however, some Baganda distinguish the two workers by using *ˋomˋupakˋasi* (Kis.) for the former and *ˋomˋuweːrˋeza* for the latter.

It will have become evident from the foregoing that in Luganda word borrowing is not confined to a particular person or group. Every Muganda who is able to come into contact with the new ideas and objects becomes an agent. However given loans may be peculiar to a given occupation. For instance, the loans of a houseboy will predominantly refer to new food items, kitchen utensils, etc., while those of a lawyer will reflect preoccupation with legal processes.

The influence of these factors and their consequences have not failed to attract the attention of some Baganda who, because of their interest in and natural loyalty towards their mother tongue, have tried to discourage extensive word borrowing (see Nsimbi, 1962). They argue that borrowing should occur only in those situations where Luganda cannot provide indigenous denotators for alien ideas and objects. They point out that in many instances Luganda has named foreign objects and ideas: (*a*) by extending the meanings of indigenous words to them, e.g. *ˋekikuːnta*, 'barkcloth for covering oneself at night', now means 'a blanket' as well; and (*b*) by using a descriptive approach, e.g. *ˋomureːŋgaːɲjubˋa*, literally 'that which aims at the sun' designates the sunflower plant. But their position is a difficult one, because most Baganda entertain neither puristic notions about their language nor concern that Luganda is declining because of loans.

The extent to which a loan-word is assimilated depends on a number of factors, which may be described as being social and/or economic in nature. For example, a loan-word which refers to an object or idea of great actual or potential pragmatic, social, or prestige value stands a better and greater chance of quick and complete Lugandanization than one which has no such value. Furthermore, if in addition to being of great value the item or idea is of easy accessibility to most people the chances of its denotator becoming Lugandanized are even greater. An item which cannot be easily acquired by the common man because of its cost (or some other reason) will not spread to the masses, and hence a loan referring to such an item will not be Lugandanized as quickly and fully as one that refers to an item which can be afforded by many people irrespective of their economic or religious standing.

Thus whereas ˋ*e*ˋ*ssaɪt*ˋ*i* (Eng.), 'shirt', is a fully Lugandanized word that is known by practically every Muganda—old and young, literate and illiterate, westernized and unwesternized—ˋ*ʃʃaɪmp*ˆ*eɪni* (Eng.), 'Champagne', is known to relatively very few people. The former is said to be fully Lugandized, because all the sounds in it are Luganda sounds. On the other hand, the latter is partially Lugandanized, because ʃʃ is a foreign sound, which may not Lugandanize like its counterpart in 'shirt' to *ss* so long as the drink and its denotator 'champagne' are restricted to the literate and westernized Baganda. Similarly, religious items of a given religion give rise to loan-words that tend to be known only to the followers of that particular religion. However, even in such cases some loans spread across religious boundaries for several reasons. For example, ˋ*ppenite-ɪns*ˋ*iya* (Lat.), 'penance', is most likely to be known only to Catholics, whereas ˋ*pp*ˆ *aɪpa* (Lat.), 'Pope', is a loan-word known to many non-Catholics. Undoubtedly, Protestants and Moslems have loan-words that may not be known to those who do not belong to these religions.

Moreover, education and age influence both the desire to borrow words as well as the extent to which such words are Lugandanized. However, age alone has little influence, since the question of whether one is literate or illiterate is important.

For example, a young Muganda who is illiterate and who has lived largely with his old parents will speak Luganda with few loan-words just as his parents do. The young and educated Muganda, on the other hand, will use a great number of loan-words. The former will mainly use loans that are inevitable, i.e. loans that refer to items for which there are no indigenous words. The latter, however, will, in addition to using inevitable loans, use loans for which indigenous words exist. Furthermore, the former's speech will contain loan-words that are fully Lugandanized, while the latter's will consist of a number of loans that are partially Lugandanized. For example, the latter is likely to use ˋ*ddoˋkta* (Eng.), 'doctor', while the former will use ˋ*ddokˋita* (Eng.), 'doctor'. It may be mentioned here that this explains to some extent why a number of loan-words have more than one pronunciation. In short, the greater the popularity of a foreign object or idea, the quicker and fuller the process of Lugandanizing its denotator.

Grammatical Word-classes Involved

Most loans in Luganda are nominals, namely nouns and a few adjectives. In addition, there are several nomino-verbals and verbals. Examples:

(*a*) NOUNS:			
15. ˋ*eˋbbasiko:tˋi*	Cl. 9/10	(Eng.)	'waistcoat'
16. ˋ*eˋssˋa:ffˆa:ri*	Cl. 9/10	(Kis. < Ara.)	'journey, tour'
(*b*) ADJECTIVES:			
17. ˋ*ssimˆa:ta*		(Eng.)	'smart'
18. ˋ*i:nterˋidʒe:nti*		(Eng.)	'intelligent'
(*c*) NOMINO-VERBALS:			
19. ˋ*okˋufe:rˋi:ŋga*	Cl. 15	(Eng.)	'to fail'
20. ˋ*okˋusakˋisi:di:ŋga*	Cl. 15	(Eng.)	'to succeed'
(*d*) VERBALS:			
21. ˋ*ono:fe:rˋi:ŋga*			'You (*sg*) will fail'
22. ˋ*ana:sakˋisi:di:ŋga*			'He/she will succeed'

Morphological Lugandanization

Morphologically, Lugandanization produces several interesting features, although, on the whole, it follows Luganda morphological structure. In the case of nouns and adjectives, one important point to observe is whether or not initial vowels (IVs) and class prefixes (CP) occur. Many loans in these two categories exhibit a tendency towards the non-occurrence of IVs even where Luganda usage requires them. With regard to CPs, again many loans have no overt CPs. But this is partly because many loans fall into classes 5/6 and 9/10. Class 5 has a large number of indigenous words with a zero CP and usually long consonants in stem-initial position. Classes 9/10 have less indigenous words without an overt CP, but most of the loans which go into these classes have no overt CP.

There is also a tendency for borrowed nouns to belong to both classes 5/6 and 9/10. For instance, one speaker may use the loan ˋ*eˋddu:kˆa* (Kis. < Ara.), 'shop', with the concord system of class 5, while another uses the same word with the concordial agreement for class 9. Sometimes the speaker may vary the concordial elements—saying at one time: *\`è\`dduık^a r\`ino*, Cl. 5, 'this shop', and at another time: *\`è\`dduık^a \`eno*, Cl. 9, 'this shop'.

Loans were encountered for the remaining classes except for classes 15, 16, 17, and 18. In the case of loans in Luganda classes 1 and 3 from Kiswahili classes 1 and 3 (with or without a syllable bilabial nasal CP), the phonological shape of the CPs is CV-. See, for instance, examples 26 and 27 on p. 299 and example 34 on p. 301.

Adjectives from English exhibit neither IVs nor CPs. Those from Kiswahili, on the other hand, pattern like the nouns. With regard to loans from English, morphological Lugandanization of nomino-verbals and verbals is characterized by the use of the empty morph *-iıŋg-* (as in examples 19–22 above). In Lugandanized forms it occurs immediately after the radical. All extension and tense affixes occur after and not before it. The loans *\`okubatiza*, 'to baptize', and *\`okukanika*, 'to carry out mechanical work or repairs', were the only ones recorded that did not have *-iıŋg-*. It is conceivable that Luganda treats the *-iz-* and *-ik-* of respectively *bæpˈtaiz* and *miˈkænik* as if they were Luganda extension elements *-iz-* and *-ik-*, and thereby supposing that Lugandanization has already occurred and therefore the addition of *-iıŋg-* is out of the question. Note that in *\`okukanika* Lugandanization has dropped the first syllable in the source language. There are a number of such cases, and sometimes such syllables are equated with a CP. The only feature of importance in the case of the Lugandanization of Kiswahili nomino-verbals is the occurrence of the IV *o-* (cf. Luganda and Kiswahili, Examples 1–3 on p. 291).

Finally, it is important to note here that Lugandanization of loans is producing a number of root structures that are longer than the typical Luganda -CVC- structure.

PHONOLOGICAL LUGANDANIZATION

The paper will now outline how loans are Lugandanized into the phonetic and phonological systems of Luganda. The pronunciation of individual members of each source language as well as the pronunciation of non-native speakers of the source language have had significant effect on the actual sounds of the loans. Both Kiswahili and English have not been presented to the Baganda with a uniform pronunciation. It is also reasonable to assume that the Kiswahili speakers from whom Baganda acquired loans were mostly not native speakers of Kiswahili, but people who spoke it with many instances of transfer and interference from their own mother tongue. This explains why several loans from Kiswahili show sound differences which cannot be accounted for on the basis of the sound systems of Luganda and Kiswahili.

One has also to remember that even in those instances where native speakers of the source languages presented the material for Lugandanization, such speakers came from different dialectal areas. Phonological Lugandanization will involve: Tone/Stress, Vowels, and Consonants, and it is to these that attention will now turn.

Tone/Stress

Whereas Kiswahili and English are essentially stress languages, Luganda is primarily a tone language, although it has two types of stress, namely emphatic stress and a word-building stress, which occurs on the first syllable of the stem. In Kiswahili stress placement is normally on the penultimate syllable of the word, while in English it is less easily predicted.

The aim here is to examine what happens to stress when Kiswahili and English words are borrowed into Luganda. For example, does primary stress in English or penultimate stress in Kiswahili correlate with a specific incidence of stress or tone in Luganda?

Kiswahili Stress

Words borrowed from Kiswahili into Luganda have stress on the syllable which Luganda recognizes as the first in the stem. Examples:

Lugandanized Form (The first syllables of the stems are underlined)			*Kiswahili Form* (Stress is on the penultimate syllable)		
23. *ˋppos*ˋ*o* or *ˋppoʃˋo*	Cl. 1/2	'maize flour'	*poʃo*	Cl. 9/10	'ration'
24. *wuzˋi*	Cl. 9/10	'thread'	*uzi*	Cl. 9/10	
25. *wˆe:mbe*	Cl. 9/10	'razor'	*wembe*	Cl. 9/10	
26. *ˋomˋuka:fˆi:ri*	Cl. 1/2	'heathen'	*mkafiri*	Cl. 1/2	
27. *ˋomˋutarˋisi*	Cl. 1/2	'messenger'	*tariʃi*	Cl. 5/6	
28. *ˋeˋddaki:ka*	Cl. 9/10	'minute'	*dakika*	Cl. 9/10	
29. *ˋokˋusumˋama*	Cl. 15	'to wait at table'	*kusimama*	Cl. 15	'to stand up'

As to whether or not there is a correlation between stress in Kiswahili and tone in Luganda, the data analysed showed no correlation between stress in Kiswahili and a given tone in Luganda. Any tone seems capable of corresponding to penultimate stress in Kiswahili, although high and falling tones tended to occur here more often than low tone. There was also a tendency for vowel lengthening to correspond to Kiswahili stress (examples 26, 28, and 29).

English Stress

The principles involved in the Lugandanization of Kiswahili loan-words hold true too for loans from English. Thus stress falls on the first syllable of the stem of the Lugandanized form, while no correlation occurs between a given tone in Luganda and primary, secondary, etc., stress in English. Examples:

Lugandanized Form		*English Form*	
30. *\`ddom\`esitiki*	Cl. 1/2	'domestic science'	*douˈmestik* or *dəˈmestik*
31. *\`ggav\`ana*	Cl. 1/2	'governor'	*ˈgʌvənə*
32. *\`ss\`em˄eːnti*	Cl. 1/2	'cement'	*siˈment*

Kiswahili Vowels

The vowel system of Kiswahili consists of five vowels, namely, *i e a o u*, the qualities of which have practically the same values as those of the corresponding Luganda vowels *i e a o u*. Phonologically, however, the Luganda vowels differ from those of Kiswahili in three main respects: (i) Vowel length in Luganda is phonemic, while in Kiswahili it is not. (ii) In Luganda one vowel cannot follow or precede another except in interjections, while in Kiswahili sequences such as *ia*, *oa*, *oe*, *ua*, *ue*, *aa*, *ee*, and so on are very common, with each vowel belonging to a separate syllable. (iii) In Kiswahili vowels that occur before nasal compounds or after semi-vowel compounds are not lengthened as in most cases in Luganda.

Were it not for these three differences, it seems likely that loan-words from Kiswahili would have vowels that were phonologically identical to those of the corresponding Kiswahili forms. There are, however, differences that are not accountable for on the basis of these three factors. For example, it is difficult to see why Kiswahili *i*, as in *kusimama*, should have *o* or *u* as its correspondence in Luganda: *'ku'usom'aːma* or *'ok'usum'aːma*, 'to wait at table', particularly since Luganda has *'ok'usim'a*, 'to dig up'. Compare also:

Lugandanized Form			*Kiswahili Form*	
33. *'ekitabo*	Cl. 7/8	'a book'	*kitabu*	Cl. 7/8
34. *'om'urim^aːwa*	Cl. 3/4	'the lemon tree'	*mlimau* or *mlimao*	Cl. 3/4
35. *'e'ɲɲoːndo*	Cl. 9/10	'a hammer'	*ɲundo*	Cl. 9/10
36. *'e'kkuf'uru*	Cl. 9/10	'a padlock'	*kufuli*	Cl. 9/10

Probably these and others like them are cases of mispronunciation. Apart from such instances, vowel divergences are due to the above factors. That is: (*a*) Lugandanized forms from Kiswahili show vowel length where Kiswahili does not because a given vowel occurs before a nasal compound or after a semi-vowel compound, which is not followed by a long consonant; (*b*) Lugandanized words from Kiswahili may contain long vowels where Kiswahili does not because of Kiswahili stress and concomitant lengthening of the stressed syllable; and (*c*) Lugandanized words from Kiswahili may show length where Kiswahili has a sequence of vowels, e.g. *ee*, etc. Examples:

Lugandanized Form			*Kiswahili Form*	
37. *'e'bbeːnder'a*	Cl. 9/10	'flag'	*bendera*	Cl. 9/10
38. *'om'uswaːyir'i*	Cl. 1/2	'native of the E. African coast'	*mswahili*	Cl. 1/2
39. *'e'nn^eːma*	Cl. 9/10	'grace, blessing'	*neema*	Cl. 9/10

Note that in examples 37 and 38 above the Lugandanized forms do not exhibit vowel lengthening that corresponds to the Kiswahili stressed syllables.

Furthermore, not all Kiswahili vowel sequences Lugandanize into long vowels in Luganda as shown in example 39. It seems that only sequences of like Kiswahili vowels Lugandanize into long vowels belonging to different syllables (as in Kiswahili) by the insertion of a consonant (usually *r*, *w*, or *y*) between the two vowels. In the case of like vowels in Kiswahili that occur in word-final position, the process of Lugandanization treats the sequence as a long vowel and adds an extra syllable after it. For example, Kiswahili *aa* as in *mʃumaa* (which is syllabically *m-ʃu-ma-a*) Lugandanizes into *'om'usum^aːwa*, 'candle'. Another way of treating this is to assume that Lugandanization inserts *r*, *w*, or *y* between the like vowels of Kiswahili and lengthens the vowel preceding such a consonant. Examples:

Lugandanized Form			*Kiswahili Form*	
40. *\`e\`tta:ra*	Cl. 9/10	'lantern'	*taa*	Cl. 9/10
41. *\`e\`ppa:p^a:ri*	Cl. 5/6	'pawpaw'	*papai*	Cl. 5/6
42. *\`e\`aa^a:wa*	Cl. 9/10	'hour, watch, clock'	*saa*	Cl. 9/10
43. *\`ek\`irawur\`i*	Cl. 7/8	'tumbler, glass'	*bilauri*	Cl. 9/10
44. *\`cc^a:yi*	Cl. 1/2	'tea'	*cai*	Cl. 9/10
45. *\`e\`gg\`uniy\`a*	Cl. 9/10	'sack'	*gunia*	Cl. 9/10

There seems to be no system governing the choice of the consonant to be used, although in most cases *w* and *y* occur before or after *u* and *i* respectively.

English Vowels

A comparison of the English and Luganda vowel systems shows that there is very little similarity between them. Thus whereas Kiswahili vowel articulations and phonology display great similarity with those of Luganda, English vowel articulations and phonological function show great divergence. This, of course, was to be expected, inasmuch as English and Luganda belong to two historically unrelated language families (IE and Bantu respectively), while Kiswahili and Luganda are members of the same family.

The five short and long vowels of Luganda represent very few phonetic and phonological contrasts, in comparison with the more than twenty phonemic contrasts of the English system of 'pure' vowels and diphthongs. A complete Lugandanization of English forms inevitably reduces the contrasts in English. Lugandanization of 'pure' vowels equates several of them with one Luganda vowel, the determining factors being: (*a*) Frontness versus Backness of vowel; (*b*) Degree of opening; and (*c*) Speech sounds of teachers and others from whom English was learnt or heard.

Thus back vowels in English tend to be equated with back vowels in Luganda; front vowels in English with front vowels in Luganda; and central vowels in English with open vowels in Luganda. As will be seen presently, there are cases where the above principle does not hold true.

English *i* and *iː* tend to Lugandanize into Luganda *i* and *iː*; English *e* into Luganda *e* and *eː*; English æ, *ɑː*, ^, ə, and əː into Luganda *a* and *aː*; English ɔ and ɔː into Luganda *o* and *oː*; and

English *u* and *uː* into Luganda *u* and *uː*. However, there need not be a correspondence in length. A long English vowel may Lugandanize into a short or long vowel, just as a short English vowel may Lugandanize into a short or long vowel. Moreover, there are cases where, for example, the English central vowel ə Lugandanizes into Luganda *i* or *iː*; *e* or *eː*; *o* or *oː*; *u* or *uː*. English *i* may also Lugandanize into Luganda *e*. The following data will illustrate some of these points.

Lugandanized Form			*English Form*
46. *'e'kkaːmp'uni*	Cl. 9/10	'company'	*ˈkʌmpəni* or *ˈkʌmpni*
47. *riːg'eːnti*	Cl. 1/2	'Regent'	*ˈriːʤənt*
48. *'ffedereːs'oni*	Cl. 9/10	'federation'	*fedeˈreiʃən* or *fedəˈreiʃn*
49. *'ggav'ana*	Cl. 1/2	'governor'	*ˈgʌvənə*
50. *'vvaːŋg'aːda*	Cl. 9/10	'Vanguard (car)'	*ˈvængɑːd*
51. *'e'ss'ik'aːti*	Cl. 9/10	'skirt'	*skəːt*
52. *'e'ttip^oːta*	Cl. 9/10	'tea-pot'	*ˈtiːpɔt*
53. *'e'ccoːk^a*	Cl. 1/2	'chalk'	*ʧɔːk*
54. *'e'ffuːti*	Cl. 9/10	'foot (measurement)'	*fut*

In example 47 above, English orthographic 'g' is probably responsible for the use of Luganda *g*, since 'Regent' also Lugandanizes into *riːʤ'eːnti* or *riːʤ'eːnta*. Note also that all Lugandanized forms end in a vowel—usually either *a* or *i*.

Lugandanization treats English diphthongs, including sequences such as *aiə*, in a way similar to that in which it treats Kiswahili vowel sequences. The main points are: (i) a long or short Luganda vowel may correspond to an English vowel sequence or diphthong; (ii) a consonant may be inserted between the vowel elements; and (iii) one of the vowel elements may be dropped, especially in word-final position. Usually, it is the second element of a diphthong or third of a sequence such as *iou* that is dropped. Examples:

Lugandanized Form			*English Form*
55. *reːrw'e*	Cl. 9/10	'railway'	*ˈreilwei*
56. *way'a*	Cl. 9/10	'wire'	*ˈwaiə*
57. *ray'iti*	Cl. 9/10	'light, e.g. lamp's'	*lait*
58. *'ttaw'uro*	Cl. 9/10	'towel'	*ˈtauəl* or *ˈtaul*

Kiswahili Consonants

Unlike the vowel system, the Kiswahili consonantal system has several sounds that do not occur in Luganda. Phonemically (and according to the writer's dialect of Kiswahili), Kiswahili has twenty-six segmental phonemes compared with Luganda's nineteen (without counting long consonants). Kiswahili also has phonemic aspiration for some speakers.

1. Kiswahili *p t k b d g* Lugandanize into Luganda *p t k b d g*. The implosive allophones of Kiswahili *b d g*, like the explosive ones, Lugandanize into explosive allophones of Luganda *b d g*. But in several cases lengthening of the Luganda consonant occurs.

2. Kiswahili *c j* Lugandanize respectively into Luganda *c j*, with the implosive allophone of Kiswahili *j* being treated in a way similar to that of the implosive allophones of Kiswahili *b d g*.

3. Kiswahili *f s v z* Lugandanize into Luganda *f s v z* respectively.

4. Kiswahili θ ʃ Lugandanize into Luganda *s*, while Kiswahili ð Lugandanizes into Luganda *z*.

5. Kiswahili *h* Lugandanizes into Luganda *w* or *y*, or it is dropped. Although Luganda has *h* as in *h^a* versus *p^a* and ŋ^*a*, phonologically one may regard *h* as an alien unit in Luganda. This is because *h* occurs in Luganda only in several interjectives. The glottal stop occurs in both languages in more or less similar contexts.

6. Kiswahili *x* ɣ Lugandanize into Luganda *k g* respectively.

7. Kiswahili *r l* Lugandanize into Luganda *r*.

8. Kiswahili *w y* Lugandanize into Luganda *w y* respectively.

9. Kiswahili *m n* ɲ ɲ Lugandanize into Luganda *m n* ɲ ɲ respectively. Examples:

Lugandanized Form			*Kiswahili Form*	
59. `e`ccup`a	Cl. 9/10	'bottle'	*cupa*	Cl. 9/10
60. `om`uzabbib`u	Cl. 3/4	'grapevine'	*mzabibu*	Cl. 3/4
61. `ek`idu:k^a	Cl. 7/8	'small shop'	*kiduka*	Cl. 7/8
62. `e`kk`ar^a:mu	Cl. 9/10	'pencil, pen'	*kalamu*	Cl. 9/10
63. `om`up^u:ŋga	Cl. 3/4	'rice (in any form)'	*mpuŋga*	Cl. 3/4 (unhusked rice)
64. `ek`igun`iya	Cl. 7/8	'small sack'	*kiguniya*	Cl. 7/8
65. `om`uc^i:ɲja:ji	Cl. 1/2	'butcher'	*mciɲjaji*	Cl. 1/2
66. `om`ufere`jje	Cl. 3/4	'furrow, drain'	*mfereji*	Cl. 3/4
67. `sser`ugi	Cl. 9/10	'snow'	θ*eluji*	Cl. 9/10
68. `e`ffe:z`a	Cl. 9/10	'silver, money'	*fe*ð*a*	Cl. 9/10
69. `ewe:m`a	Cl. 9/10	'tent'	*hema*	Cl. 9/10
70. `gg`oro:f`a	Cl. 9/10	'storey'	ɣ*orofa*	Cl. 9/10

Kiswahili sequences *mb*, *nd*, *nz*, *bw*, *by*, *sw*, and so on, which correspond to nasal and semi-vowel compounds in Luganda present no problem in Lugandanization. Other sequences

Lugandanize by the insertion of a vowel between the elements of the cluster. Examples:

Lugandanized Form			*Kiswahili Form*	
71. *ˋbbafˋuta*	Cl. 9/10	'bleached calico'	*bafta*	Cl. 9/10
72. *ˋffˋura:sira*	Cl. 9/10	'measure of weight'	*frasila*	Cl. 9/10
73. *ˋeˋnnukˋuta*	Cl. 9/10	'letter of the alphabet'	*nukta*	Cl. 9/10 'dot point, mark'
74. *ˋddakitˆa:ri*	Cl. 1/2	'doctor'	*daktari*	Cl. 1/2

Note that these clusters are foreign even in Kiswahili and that there are dialects of Kiswahili in which these would be treated as in Luganda. The phonetic characteristics of the members of the cluster with or without those of the vowel they precede or follow seem to influence the choice of the vowel to be used. In examples 71 and 72 the choice of *u* is determined by Luganda *f*, which for many speakers is labio-velarized. In 73 the choice is influenced by the preceding vowel *u* and the voiceless velar stop *k*, while in 74 it would appear that it is the absence of back rounded vowels that leads to the selection of *i*.

English Consonants

The principles employed in the Lugandanization of English consonants are basically the same as those applied to Kiswahili consonants. The following English consonants have no counterparts in Luganda θ ð ʃ ʒ *h l*. Of these θ and ʃ Lugandanize into Luganda *s*, but the former also into *t*, probably because of the influence of English orthography. English ð and ʒ Lugandanize into *z*, while English *l* Lugandanizes into Luganda *r*. English *h* is dropped. The other English consonants Lugandanize into the corresponding Luganda ones.

English *mp*, *nt*, *tw*, *sw*, and so on Lugandanize into Luganda *mp*, *nt*, *tw*, etc. On the other hand, English clusters which do not involve nasals as the first member or semi-vowels are Lugandanized either by the insertion of a vowel between the elements of the cluster so that the resulting forms are made up of open syllables, or by the dropping of one of the members of the cluster. But the former method preponderates. Examples:

Lugandanized Form			*English Form*
75. *ˋssa:zˋidˆe*	Cl. 9/10	'Thursday'	ˈθə:*zdei*
76. *ˋmmezame:nti*	Cl. 9/10	'measurement'	ˈ*meʒəmənt*
77. *ˋeˋmmayˋiro*	Cl. 9/10	'mile'	*mail*
78. *ˋssepˋurˆi:ɲgi*	Cl. 9/10	'spring'	*spriŋ*
79. *wˋodˋuro:bu*	Cl. 9/10	'wardrobe'	ˈ*wɔ:droub*
80. *ˋeˋbbe:nsˋeni*	Cl. 9/10	'basin'	*beisn*
81. *ˋssˋuku:rˋu*	Cl. 9/10	'school'	*sku:l*

It is probable that English orthography influenced Lugandanization in example 78 since ŋ occurs in Luganda. In example 80 Lugandanization introduces pre-nasalization, but this was met only in connection with *s* and ʃ in the source language.

CONCLUSION

In this paper an attempt has been made to examine the principles and factors involved in the borrowing of words into Luganda and how such words are assimilated into the phonetic, phonological, morphological, and lexical systems of Luganda. On the whole, phonetic, phonological, and morphological Lugandanization typically forces loan-words into the Luganda patterns.

Consequently, Luganda, unlike English and Kiswahili, seems to have hardly any new sounds or morphological units except the introduction of the empty morph *-iŋg-* and roots longer than -CVC-. However, it is probable that foreign sounds and sequences may still, with time and increased education coupled with general development, be acquired by Luganda to an extent which will make them worth notice. This is because at present full Lugandanization characterizes speakers who are either fairly old or who are young but illiterate, whereas partial Lugandanization characterizes those with some education, and particularly those working in specialized fields where English is constantly used.

Lexically, Lugandanization mostly carries over into Luganda the meaning of the loan in the source language. There are, however, instances: (*a*) where the meaning of the loan covers a semantic field wider than that in the lending language, and (*b*) where the meaning is different from that of the loan in the source language. But of what relevance is all this to the adaptation of African languages to modern conditions?

On the grounds that each language handles loan-words on the basis of its internal structures and systems just as Luganda does, then it is reasonable to conclude that in a planned adaptation of any African language to modern needs one stands to benefit from an examination of the ways in which loans are treated by the given language. Of equal importance is a study of socio-linguistic factors, such as attitudes, conscious loyalty, etc., towards loans, the languages involved and their communities and sub-groups.

It is hoped that if this approach is used those responsible for the adaptation of a particular language to modern conditions will be more and better equipped to tackle the problem than without it. The approach will make them aware of the factors that are likely to hinder the achievement of their objectives while at the same time highlighting features that will enhance and maximize their effort.

REFERENCES

Ashton, E. O.
(1962) *Swahili Grammar.* London: Longmans, Green and Co.

Ashton, E. O., Mulira, E. M. K. Ndawula, E. G. G., and Tucker, A. N.
(1954) *A Luganda Grammar.* London: Longmans, Green and Co.

Chesswas, J. D.
(1959) *The Essentials of Luganda.* Kampala: The Eagle Press.

Cole, D. T.
(1967) *Some Features of Ganda Linguistic Structure.* Johannesburg: Witwatersrand University Press.

Fallers, L. A. (ed.)
(1964) *The King's Men.* London: Oxford University Press.

International Phonetic Association.
(1961) *The Principles of the International Phonetic Association.*

Inter-Territorial Language Committee for East African Dependencies.
(1939) *A Standard Swahili–English Dictionary.* London: Oxford University Press.

Jones, D.
(1960a) *An Outline of English Phonetics.* Cambridge: W. Heffer and Sons Ltd.
(1960) *English Pronouncing Dictionary.* London: J. M. Dent and Sons Ltd.

Kirwan, B. E. R., and Gore, P. A.
(1951) *Elementary Luganda.* Kampala: Uganda Bookshop.

Knappert, J.
(1964) 'Language Unites and Divides', *EAISR Conference Papers.* Kampala: Makerere University College, January 1964.

Mosha, M.
(1966) 'Secret Language and Puberty: The Significance of Secret Language During the Pubertal Period in Two Traditional East African Societies', *Puberty and Joking Conference*, Department of Sociology, Makerere University College, Kampala. December 1966.
(1967) 'The Role of Language in Nation Building', East African Institute of Social and Cultural Affairs and East African Academy Conference on *Mass Media and Linguistic Communication in East Africa*, Makerere University College, Kampala. 31 March—3 April 1967.
Nsimbi, M. B.
(1962) *Olulimi Oluganda*. Kampala: Longmans, Green and Co.
Roscoe, J.
(1965 [1st ed. 1911]) *The Baganda: an Account of their Native Beliefs and Customs*. London: Cass.
Tucker, A. N.
(1962) 'The Syllable in Luganda: A Prosodic Approach', *Journal of African Languages*, I, 2, 122–66.
Tucker, A. N., and Ashton, E. O.
(1942) 'Swahili Phonetics', *African Studies* I, 2/3, 77–103, 162–82.
Weinreich, U.
(1953) *Languages in Contact*. New York: The Linguistic Circle of New York.
Whiteley, W. H.
(1963) 'Loan-Words in Kamba: A Preliminary Survey', *African Language Studies*, IV, 146–65.

XVII. Problems of Terminology

HAILU FULASS

A number of developing nations in Africa have started to use one or several of their vernaculars as the official language(s) of their societies and as a medium of instruction in the schools, at least in the elementary grades. Ethiopia is one of these countries, and its official vernacular (= OV) is Amharic; all subjects in the public elementary schools are taught in Amharic. Ethiopia, along with those African countries that use OV in schools, hopes to use only OV for teaching all subjects in the secondary schools in the not too far distant future, and eventually in universities.

Such a language policy is very significant, and will certainly have far-reaching consequences for the overall development of these countries—particularly in the area of work on mass literacy. The preparation of textbooks in OV and its use by the media are only a partial implementation of such a language policy. It is extremely necessary for the success of this policy that the policy-makers and their advisers clearly realize the present limits and inadequacies in terminology of OV for the communication of modern scientific, aesthetic, and philosophical ideas. Of course, the limits and deficiencies are due to historical accidents and not to any inherent defects in OV; none the less, awareness of them is most crucial, for it indicates the need for careful and rigorous study of the problems and the use of scientific methods for the effective and efficient manipulation of OV to help it overcome its present limits and deficiencies in terminology. For, today, a language such as Amharic cannot be left to its own devices to cope with the plethora of new foreign terms and the proliferation of indiscriminately coined ones.

This could be done in the past, because for millennia, contact between peoples of different cultural and linguistic backgrounds was infrequent; consequently, the rate of cultural and linguistic borrowings was exceedingly slow; the need for cultural and linguistic innovations was very slight. Societies had centuries in which to assimilate, diffuse, and 'indigenize' what was borrowed and innovated. Thus items that were foreign or new in the language and culture gradually became among the characteristic elements of the language and culture environment in which a member was born, grew up, and, in the process, acted in and reacted to his various social roles.

In the last eighty years or so, however, the situation has radically changed. Now the rate of interaction between peoples of diverse cultural backgrounds has fantastically accelerated. Foreign influences—primarily those of the industrialized western nations—act upon the languages and cultures of (developing) peoples everywhere. The influences are reciprocal, but the influences of the industrialized (western) peoples on others are much stronger than the influences of the developing countries on the west. In spite of the clamour for a return to and a development of the ancestral heritage by the articulate segments of the peoples of developing African countries, the models that are actually followed and have decisively influenced the nature of development aspirations, the outlook on life and the social norms of conduct are the cultures of the industrialized, western nations. One instance of the extent of the influence of these nations on the societies of the developing countries is illustrated by the number of loan-words from the languages of the industrialized nations (henceforth IL) in the languages of the developing countries. The presence of loan-words in OV from IL is not important in itself; but when the number of loan-words is large, the frequency of borrowing (and coining) high, and the variety of the concepts great, then the effectiveness of OV as a means of communication is seriously threatened.

In the case of Amharic, this instance is most revealingly exemplified by the mass of loan-words and newly coined terms that one finds in reading books, essays, and newspaper columns, or in listening over the radio to discussions on such topics as economics, child-care, science, philosophy, and sports. The reader or listener is bewildered by his inability to understand texts or speeches in Amharic.[1] This is primarily a result of indiscriminate borrowing and coining of terms and using these

[1] This is not because of little education. Even university-educated speakers of Amharic have such complaints.

in OV to signify the same concepts found in IL. Writers and speakers seem unaware of the fact that this obstructs effective communication.

The OV writer or speaker owes it to his audience and to himself to communicate his messages in the clearest way possible. Therefore, if he is communicating new ideas and concepts from IL he should try to formulate them in terms of ideas and concepts found in OV. If such formulations could be done, then we have in effect definitions of the concepts and ideas from IL in OV. This would make coining a relatively easy and fruitful task. If, on the other hand, it is practically impossible to do a formulation of some concept C in IL in terms of concepts available in the linguistic and conceptual repertoire of OV speakers, borrowing the necessary term(s) from IL may be seriously entertained. For this would mean that certain elements of the cognitive, aesthetic, religious, philosophic, etc., aspects of the culture in which IL is spoken are absent from the culture in which OV is spoken. We can now speak of the existence of a terminological—and conceptual—gap between the societies in which IL and OV are spoken.

The present crisis in the effectiveness of OV as a means of communication in the mass media and as a medium of instruction in the schools is due to—among other factors—lack of proper appreciation of the linguistic and conceptual problems involved in terminology. In Ethiopia, and probably in the other African countries that have recently started using OV in the schools, there does not seem to be any awareness of the necessity of tackling this language problem in a scientific and organized way. Writers, teachers, and radio commentators unnecessarily borrow terms from IL; they coin terms that do not have formal or conceptual motivation in OV. This situation is also compounded by the lack of uniformity in the usage of the loan and coined terms.[1] For example, an OV writer may use a term X to signify the same concept as that signified by the term Q in IL; whereas the radio commentator and the teacher may use terms Y and Z respectively, where—as is commonly the case—X, Y, and Z differ both in morphemic shape and signification.

[1] For lack of phonetic uniformity of loan-words see Abraham Demoz, 'European Loan Words in an Amharic Daily Newspaper', in John Spencer (ed.), *Language in Africa* (Cambridge University Press, 1963).

It is factors such as the above that preserve the terminological and conceptual gaps between OV and IL. This gap may be defined as the difference between IL and OV measured in terms of their performance in distinctively and adequately labelling the elements of the cognitive, aesthetic, material, religious, etc., aspects of one another's culture and each of its own. There is no doubt that, on the whole, the performance of OV will be far less than that of IL. However, this limitation imposed on OV by the paucity in the variety of the constituents of the cognitive, aesthetic, material, etc., aspects of the culture in which it is spoken is not insurmountable. For there is a potential in any human language that transcends the bounds of the particular social environment in which it is spoken.

The problems of terminology, therefore, are in part a consequence of the ignorance of this inherent potential of language by language policy-makers and users of OV and the resulting failure to exploit this potential rationally, efficiently, and systematically. In this context, to exploit the language's potential rationally means to use one of the sources available for introducing new terms (e.g. borrowing, coining, or using existing terms in a new sense) only after careful consideration of the contributions of each to the clarity and effectiveness of the communication of the new concept(s) in OV. To exploit this potential systematically means to use to the greatest extent possible the existing formal, semantic, and structural patterns of OV in coining a new term. By efficient exploitation is meant the use of all possible ways and means for the quick spread of new terms, at the same time ensuring maximum uniformity in their usage.

Before a decision is taken to coin a term in OV for a concept (represented by the term T in IL), procedures such as the following should be followed.

I. Determination of the semantic domain of the reference of the term T; e.g. whether the reference is abstract or concrete.

II. Determination of the category of the semantic domain of the reference of the term T; i.e. whether the term's reference is an entity, an event, a relation, etc.

III. Determination of the existence of any concept(s) in

OV to which the concept represented by T in IL may be related and/or compared. If this can be done, then it may be possible to coin a term in OV to represent the concept C with a high degree of communicative effectiveness.

Two terms, one in IL and the other in OV, representing the same concept may correspond in one of the following ways:

(*a*) lexically, formally and conceptually
(*b*) lexically and conceptually
(*c*) formally and conceptually
(*d*) conceptually

Lexical correspondence refers to the similarity in the meanings of the roots from which the two terms are derived. Formal correspondence refers to the similarity in the 'internal grammars' of the two terms; that is to say, the correspondence in derivation, for instance, by affixing abstract-noun forming or adjectivizing morphemes. Conceptual correspondence refers to the sameness of the references of the two terms.

Let us illustrate each type of correspondence with one example.

(*a*) Suppose we were asked to coin a term in Amharic for the English term 'existence'. Let us assume that we have followed procedures I–III. We find that there is a lexical item in Amharic whose root has approximately the same meaning as the root from which 'existence' is derived.

(1) *norə* 'to exist (he existed; he lived)'
(2) *massəb maləṭ mənor maləṭ nəw*
To think means to exist
(3) *Cɨraq mənoru* / *yəCɨraq nurət* } *altərəgaggəTəm*
The existence of C^raq (Cyclopes?) has not been proved.
(4) *nurət kəbahrɨy qədami nəw*
Existence precedes essence.

The nominal *nurət* is not (yet) part of the Amharic vocabulary. It is most probable that it has not been used at all except by this writer. Notice, however, *nurət* has the same form as *qumət*, 'height', from the root *qomə*, 'to stand up',[1] and *šumət*, 'appointment to an office', from the root *šomə*, 'to appoint to an office'. Hence, as a nominal pattern *nurət* is naturally motivated, since the root *norə*, 'to exist; to live' belongs to the class of Amharic verbs whose root has the form *1o2ə*. Moreover, the root *norə* with its various derivations is the only one that can render into Amharic most approximately the root 'to exist' and its derivations. We see, therefore, that the derived noun *nurət*, 'existence', is a formally and semantically motivated coinage. It has also a lexical, formal, and conceptual correspondence to the term 'existence'.

(*b*) The Amharic work *wəsən* means 'a limit, a boundary'. We may consider it as derived from *wəssənə*, 'to limit, to bound, to restrict'. I have heard a number of Amharic speakers use *wəsən*, 'a limit, a boundary', with another item to represent the concept 'infinity'. E.g.

(5) *wəsən yəlləš*, 'limitless, infinite, infinity'

The internal grammar of the term *wəsən yəlləš* is sentential. The referential meaning of *wəsən yəlləš* as a sentence is 'you (f. sg.) don't have a limit'. Note that *wəsən yəlləš* and 'infinity' have only lexical and conceptual correspondence.

(*c*) Consider the word 'universal' in its non-technical senses. There is no morpheme (or word) in Amharic that corresponds to it in meaning. Take, for instance, the English sentence.

(i) Marriage is universal. Its Amharic equivalent may be
(ia) *gabicca hullu agər all.*

The Amharic sentence (ia) also means the same as the English sentence

(ii) Marriage is found in every place.

No doubt, the English sentences (i) and (ii) can be used interchangeably in many contexts. So, the notion 'found in

[1] In Amharic it is customary to give the third person singular, masculine perfect form of the verb as the root. For this brief discussion I will adhere to the traditional presentation.

every place' can sometimes be equivalent to the notion 'universal'. Consider, however, the sentence

(iii) He is a universal genius.

The phrase 'found in every place' cannot be substituted for 'universal' in sentence (iii). The Amharic equivalent of (iii) may be

(iiia) *yəssu ɨwqət kəməTən bəlay səffi nəw.*

The Amharic sentence (iiia) can very well be a good translation of

(iv) His knowledge is exceedingly wide.

Although the two instances of the word universal in sentences (i) and (iii) have different meanings, none the less they have many features in common, such as phonetic identity, the semantic features [exhaustive (i.e. complete), all-embracing . . .], and both belong to the grammatical category adjective. We cannot say the same for any two (groups of) items in the Amharic sentences (ia) and (iiia). There is practically nothing similar in the meanings of these two Amharic sentences.

Although the two instances of 'universal' differ in reference from the philosophical term 'universal', all three share common basic semantic features. Without going into detail, we may say that the philosophical term 'universal' is related to the common word 'universal' in some of its basic semantic features. Hence, knowing the common word 'universal', it should not be too difficult for the English speaker to grasp the meaning(s) of the philosophical term 'universal'.

In the case of Amharic the situation is more complicated, as the Amharic equivalents of sentences (i) and (iii) have demonstrated. Thus if we want to coin a term in Amharic for the English philosophical term 'universal' we may very well abandon the search for a lexically correspondent root. We may, however, be successful in finding or coining a formally and conceptually correspondent word. For example, we may decide to use the root *Təqəllələ*, 'to roll up (tr.), to fold (tr.)'. We find that there is an already existing derived form *T^q^ll*, 'rolled up; folded', and it is used in Amharic grammars to mean 'collective'. E.g.

(6) (*yə*) *Tiqɨll sɨm*, 'a collective noun, (a general name)'.

In Amharic almost any adjective can be used nominally. It is perfectly acceptable, therefore, to use *Tɨqɨll* as a noun. As such it would signify something that has generality, something that pertains to all things, something universal—and hence a *universal.*

This very brief illustration shows that although *Tɨqɨll* and the philosophical term universal do not have corresponding lexical roots that have similar meanings, still *Tɨqɨll* can be linguistically manipulated in such a way that it can represent the same—at least very similar—concept(s) as the term 'universal', without violating the syntactic or semantic rules of the language.

(*d*) One of the best illustrations of an Amharic term that has only conceptual correspondence to an English term is

(7) *səw sərraš*—'artificial, synthetic, man-made'.
(8) *səw sərrašɨnnət*,[1] 'artificiality'.

The Amharic term *səw sərraš* is a perfectly well-formed sentence, and its sentential equivalent in English is 'Human beings made you (f. sg.)'. The use of phrases that have the internal grammar of well-formed and acceptable sentences is one of the commonest means that Amharic uses for coining new terminology.

CONCLUSION

This brief and general discussion is merely an outline of the analysis of some of the factors that are responsible for the problems of terminology. The coining of the term *nurət* or the use of *Tɨqɨll* to mean 'a universal' are illustrations of procedures rather than actual proposals. Moreover, I am not advocating the keeping of the national languages 'uncontaminated' with foreign ways. Contamination is inevitable and, in fact, desirable. However, the contamination, so to speak, should be so controlled that it has a dynamic influence on OV without straining its communicative effectiveness and without destroying its characteristics.

I am suggesting, however, that this problem needs to be carefully studied, and if practical solutions can be found, then the Government and other relevant institutions must spare no

[1] -(*ɨ*)*nnət* is a bound suffix morpheme affixed to adjectives: (*a*) to form abstract nouns, and (*b*) to any morpheme (or phoneme) X whatever to mean '(the fact of) being X'.

effort to apply these solutions quickly. One way of tackling the problems of terminology is the establishment of a national OV institute whose membership includes scholars in other fields of study as well as in language. This body of people would then coin new terms, evaluate new coinages, determine the necessity of borrowing, and issue at frequent intervals what it considers is an acceptable list of new terms, with a clear description of each of the references of the terms. It must try to get the co-operation of writers, the mass media, and all public and private institutions. It must try to win the confidence of the people so that they may respect it, give a high regard to its pronouncements, and readily accept its suggestions.

REFERENCES

Bram, Joseph
(1955) *Language and Society*. New York: Random House, Inc.
Capell, A.
(1966) *Studies in Socio-linguistics*. The Hague: Mouton and Co.
Fishman, J. A., Ferguson, C. A., and Das Gupta, J. (eds.)
(1968) *Language Problems of Developing Nations*. New York: John Wiley & Sons, Inc.
Fodor, I.
(1965) *The Rate of Linguistic Change*. The Hague: Mouton and Co.
Halliday, M. A. K., Angus McIntosh and Peter Strevens.
(1965) *The Linguistic Science and Language Teaching*. Bloomington: Indiana University Press.
Henle, P.
(1958) *Language, Thought & Culture*. Ann Arbor: The University of Michigan Press.
Le Page, R. B.
(1964) *The National Language Question: Linguistic Problems of Newly Independent States*. London: Oxford University Press.
Ray, P. S.
(1963) *Language Standardization*. The Hague: Mouton and Co.
Rice, F. A. (eds.)
(1962) *Study of the Role of Second Languages in Asia, Africa and Latin America*. Washington D.C.: Center for Applied Linguistic of the Modern Language Association of America.
Spencer, John (ed.)
(1963) *Language in Africa*. Cambridge: Cambridge University Press.

XVIII. The Madina Project, Ghana (Language Attitudes in Madina)

JACK BERRY

Madina is a fast-developing suburban settlement situated on the Accra plains some ten miles north-east of Accra on the old Accra–Dodowah Road and some two miles north of the University of Ghana, Legon. The historical background to the founding of Madina in 1959 by Muslims from Northern Ghana and elsewhere, and its subsequent development as a 'mixed' suburb with residents of many different ethnic and widely different occupational and educational backgrounds, is described in a recent publication of the Institute of African Studies, University of Ghana, to which readers of this paper are directed: *Madina Survey*, Quarcoo, Addo, Peil, Legon, 1967.

The Madina Project of my title is, however, a second, socio-linguistic survey undertaken jointly by the Institute of African Studies of the University of Ghana and the Department of Linguistics, Northwestern University. Its field director is Dr. Gilbert Ansre, a Senior Research Fellow of the Institute and a leading Ghanaian Linguist.

The original decision to conduct a socio-linguistic survey of Madina, taken by Professor J. H. Nketia and myself in discussions held at Legon late in 1966, was influenced largely by evidence presented in the Quarcoo–Addo–Peil report which seemed to guarantee from the outset a situation of some considerable interest, specifically because of its cultural, social, and linguistic heterogeneity (See Tables 1–4).

For some time the Department of Linguistics at Northwestern had been seeking an opportunity to experiment in a meaningful way with such surveys, especially to acquire experience in organizational matters for which there were no precedents, such as training of personnel to administer questionnaires and field

Table 1

Occupational Structure of Tribes by Sex (i.e. Persons 16+)—Madina, 1966

Tribe	*Sex*	*Unemploy-ment*	*Farmer*	*Labourer*	*Craft*	*Shopkeeper Trader*	*Clerical*	*Teacher*	*Profes-sional*	*Army**	*House-wife*	*Total*
Ga-Adangbe	M	6·9	1·7	5·3	44·8	5·2	13·8	8·6	1·7	1·7	10·4	100·0
	F	6·3	4·2	2·5	4·6	49·3	—	4·6	—	1·5	29·2	100·0
Ewe and Related	M	4·1	1·8	8·8	58·5	2·8	11·5	2·3	—	3·7	6·5	100·0
Togos	F	9·5	1·6	6·3	4·7	27·9	1·6	2·1	0·5	2·1	43·7	100·0
Kwahu/Akwapim	M	7·4	—	5·6	40·6	9·3	9·3	3·7	3·7	—	20·4	100·0
	F	2·1	—	2·1	10·4	33·3	2·1	4·2	—	—	45·8	100·0
Other Akan	M	6·7	1·5	10·4	42·2	0·7	10·4	4·4	2·2	5·9	15·6	100·0
	F	5·3	1·1	2·1	9·6	10·6	1·1	—	—	1·1	69·1	100·0
Dahomeys/Kotokoli	M	2·1	6·3	47·9	29·2	4·1	6·3	—	—	—	4·1	100·0
	F	6·0	—	4·0	4·0	36·0	—	—	—	—	50·0	100·0
Moshi and other	M	14·8	3·7	40·8	22·2	7·4	—	3·7	—	3·7	3·7	100·0
U.V., Niger	F	—	—	—	—	23·1	—	—	—	7·7	69·2	100·0
Northern Ghana	M	6·3	6·3	46·9	15·5	9·4	3·1	—	—	3·1	6·3	100·0
	F	—	4·8	—	—	33·3	—	—	—	—	61·9	100·0
Other Ghana	M	4·7	2·3	34·9	30·2	2·3	—	11·6	—	—	14·0	100·0
	F	3·2	—	—	3·2	48·4	3·2	—	—	5·2	38·7	100·0
Hausa/Fulani	M	—	—	—	100·0	—	—	—	—	—	—	100·0
	F	—	—	—	—	—	—	—	—	—	—	—
Nigeria (non-Hausa)	M	—	—	38·9	27·8	22·1	5·6	—	—	—	5·6	100·0
	F	—	—	—	—	40·1	—	—	—	—	60·0	100·0

* Mainly Builders Brigade.

Table 2

Population by Sex, by Birthplace and by Former Place of Residence—Madina 1966

				Former place of residence									
Birthplace	*Sex*	*Total*		*Madina*	*Accra*	*Eastern Region*	*Western and Central*	*Volta Region*	*Ach. and B.A.*	*North Ghana and U.R.*	*Togo*	*Upper Volta*	*Other Ghana*
		Abs	%	%	%	%	%	%	%	%	%	%	%
Madina	M	57	100	93·0	7·0	—	—	—	—	—	—	—	—
	F	56	100	89·3	7·2	—	—	3·5	—	—	—	—	—
Accra	M	184	100	—	91·3	3·8	2·1	1·5	—	1·2	—	—	—
	F	167	100	—	89·2	5·4	3·0	1·2	0·6	—	0·6	—	—
Eastern Region	M	342	100	—	40·5	49·6	2·7	1·2	1·7	4·1	—	—	—
	F	242	100	—	47·5	41·3	3·3	2·9	1·7	2·1	1·2	—	—
Western and C.R.	M	98	100	—	39·2	10·2	43·3	2·1	3·2	—	—	—	—
	F	53	100	—	50·9	9·4	30·2	3·3	5·7	—	—	—	—
Volta Region	M	183	100	—	45·1	11·4	2·7	36·4	2·7	1·1	0·6	—	—
	F	170	100	—	47·7	11·1	3·5	31·4	4·7	0·6	—	—	—
Ach. and B.A.	M	35	100	—	38·2	10·9	10·9	—	40·0	—	—	—	—
	F	36	100	—	28·7	5·6	8·3	8·3	50·0	—	—	—	—
N./U.R. Ghana	M	46	100	—	76·1	4·3	2·2	2·2	—	16·2	—	—	—
	F	29	100	—	75·9	—	3·4	3·4	—	17·3	—	—	—
Togo	M	153	100	—	43·5	19·1	0·9	7·0	4·3	—	25·2	—	—
	F	103	100	—	46·6	16·5	1·9	5·8	7·8	—	21·4	—	—
Upper Volta	M	17	100	—	70·6	17·6	—	—	5·9	—	—	6·9	—
	F	6	100	—	50·0	16·7	—	—	—	—	—	33·3	—
Other Ghana	M	51	100	—	72·4	5·9	2·0	5·9	—	2·0	—	—	11·8
	F	31	100	—	72·3	3·6	3·6	14·3	—	2·6	—	—	3·6

Table 3

Distribution of Tribes by Type of Education—Madina 1966 (Percentage)

Tribe	*Sex*	*Total*		*None*	*Literate*	*Muslim*	*Primary*	*Senior Primary*	*Secondary*	*Technical and Teacher Coll.*	*University*
		Abs.	%								
Ga-Adangbe/Krobo	M	61	100·0	29·5	6·6	—	11·5	29·5	9·8	11·5	1·6
	F	55	100·0	59·1	1·5	1·5	9·1	22·8	4·5	1·5	—
Ewe	M	219	100·0	36·5	4·6	—	12·8	35·6	5·5	1·4	3·5
	F	192	100·0	71·4	2·1	—	4·7	18·2	1·6	1·0	1·0
Kwahu/Akwapim	M	58	100·0	17·2	5·2	—	8·6	53·4	10·4	—	5·2
	F	48	100·0	52·1	4·2	—	4·1	29·5	—	4·2	5·3
Other Akan	M	137	100·0	27·8	2·9	—	8·8	35·0	8·0	2·9	14·6
	F	75	100·0	50·7	6·7	—	16·0	20·0	4·0	—	2·6
Northern Ghanaian	M	32	100·0	65·6	3·1	18·8	6·3	—	3·1	—	3·1
	F	20	100·0	95·0	—	—	—	—	—	—	5·0
Nigeria (other)	M	16	100·0	62·5	6·3	12·5	—	18·7	—	—	—
	F	10	100·0	80·0	—	10·0	—	10·0	—	—	—
Hausa/Fulani	M	2	100·0	—	—	50·0	—	50·0	—	—	—
	F	—	—	—	—	—	—	—	—	—	—
Dahomeyan/Kotokoli and other Togo	M	48	100·0	45·8	2·1	45·8	—	6·3	—	—	—
	F	53	100·0	83·0	—	17·0	—	—	—	—	—
Moshi/other Upper Volta	M	26	100·0	61·5	—	34·6	—	3·9	—	—	—
	F	13	100·0	92·3	—	7·7	—	—	—	—	—

Table 4

Distribution of Tribes by Type of Education (Absolute Figures)

Tribe	*Sex*	*None*	*Literate*	*Muslim*	*Primary*	*Senior Primary*	*Secondary*	*Technical and Teacher Training*	*University*	*Total*
Ga-Adangbe/Krobo	M	18	4	—	7	18	6	7	1	61
	F	39	1	1	6	15	3	1	—	55
Ewe	M	80	10	—	28	78	12	3	3	219
	F	137	4	—	9	35	3	2	3	192
Kwahu/Akwapim	M	10	3	—	5	31	6	—	3	58
	F	25	2	—	2	14	—	2	3	48
Other Akan	M	38	4	—	23	48	11	4	20	137
	F	38	5	—	12	15	3	—	3	75
Northern Ghana	M	21	1	6	2	—	1	—	1	32
	F	19	—	—	—	—	—	—	1	20
Nigeria (non Hausa)	M	10	1	2	—	3	—	—	—	16
	F	8	—	1	—	1	—	—	—	10
Hausa/Fulani	M	—	—	1	—	1	—	—	—	2
	F	—	—	—	—	—	—	—	—	—
Dahomey/Kotokoli and other Togo	M	22	1	22	—	3	—	—	—	48
	F	44	—	9	—	—	—	—	—	53
Moshi/other Upper Volta	M	16	—	9	—	1	—	—	—	26
	F	12	—	1	—	—	—	—	—	13

tests, budgeting, etc. The Ghanaian linguists, for their part, were acutely aware of the urgent need for such surveys in view of the new interest in local languages which was being expressed on all sides but, especially, by educationists, in demands for an official statement of language policy at the national level. (These demands have since been formalized in the 15 resolutions of the recent planning conference held in Legon in May, 1968.)

At the October 1966 meeting it was agreed that rather than seek outside support a beginning could be made using the limited financial resources available to fund a small pilot socio-linguistic survey. The survey could, presumably, be justified later not only in terms of the data collected but also on the grounds that it had provided valuable experience for mounting such surveys in the future and had created a trained cadre to administer them. And should increased funds become available it might well serve as the prototype of a series of similar smaller-and larger-scale surveys in different parts of Ghana that could be useful for comparative purposes.

The choice of Madina for the pilot survey was determined largely by the need for economy. In the case of Madina a survey in depth at reasonable cost was feasible because of the small size of settlement (total population was around 2,000) and its proximity to Legon (2 miles), which made for easy access and low transport costs in conducting the survey and maintaining effective control and supervision of it. Further, the real possibility that Madina could be resurveyed easily at regular intervals proved very attractive.

The Madina project is still very much a matter of research in progress; Phase I has only recently been completed. The following notes, however, may have some interest as a preliminary report on the project itself and the data so far collected.

The immediate goal of the survey as it is defined in the records of the preliminary discussions between Professor Nketia and myself is quite simply a description of the 'language situation' in Madina, using the term 'language situation' as is now the common practice to refer to the total configuration of language use, including such data as: how many and what kinds of languages are currently spoken in Madina, by how many people and under what circumstances; and the attitudes and beliefs about languages held by the residents of Madina. We have assumed from the start that a full-scale description of the language situation in Madina along these lines will have intrinsic interest for linguists and other social scientists working in Ghana.

As to overall research design, I have described this in some detail in a paper delivered to the Twentieth Anniversary Conference of the Program of African Studies, Northwestern University, in September of this year. It is hoped this paper will shortly be available in published form as part of the Proceedings of the Conference; meanwhile duplicated copies may be had on demand.

Briefly, the survey is phased as follows. A first questionnaire has already been administered to nearly all residents of Madina (2,000 + respondents). From this questionnaire, which was essentially in the nature of a 'fishing expedition', the basic linguistic–demographic information we were seeking has been obtained. In addition, however, the few, open-ended questions on language attitudes included in the questionnaire have elicited responses of considerable interest, suggesting areas for future intensive investigation.

1. Is there any language which you do not know which you would like to know? Why?

2. Is there any language you know which you would like to know better? Why?

3. Are there any languages you speak which you do not like to speak on certain occasions? Why?

4. What language(s) do you like? Why?
What language(s) do you dislike? Why?

5. What do you think will be the main language spoken in the future in Madina? Accra–Tema? Ghana?

At this time of writing the results of the computerization of the data are not available, but it is possible to make certain observations with some assurance. These represent views arrived at independently by three investigators during the preliminary examination of the questionnaires in the coding process.

The survey clearly established that:

(1) Over 80 different languages are spoken natively by the residents of Madina.

(2) There are very few monolinguals in Madina (less than 4 per cent of all respondents admit to knowing only one language).

(3) The majority (over 70 per cent) of respondents claim competence in three or more languages. Respondents' claims of competence in second and third languages seem *prima facie* reasonably conservative. This statement, though purely impressionistic, is based, *inter alia*, on the evidence of the frequency of responses indicating a desire to improve knowledge of some language; responses indicating reluctance to speak a language for fear of ridicule by native speakers, and responses indicating awareness that the mother tongue is the only one properly understood. It is intended in Phase II to test the respondent's own assessment of his proficiency in second and other languages by the usual methods.

(4) There is little evidence of language shift in individuals. For nearly every respondent, the mother tongue is still the first language. There is strong loyalty to it. In no case was the mother tongue listed as a language disliked, and very frequently it was cited as the one preferred, often explicitly because it was the mother tongue. ('It is simply sweet and besides it is my mother tongue and anyway it is the only one I understand properly.')

(5) Nevertheless, there appears to be an 'acceptance' of the multilingual situation. Only a very few respondents indicated an unwillingness to learn new languages ('I don't have time to learn other languages'). The majority expressed a desire not only to learn new languages but to improve their knowledge of others in which they already had some competence.

(6) The languages which by far the most respondents wish to learn or to improve their partial knowledge of are Twi, English, and Hausa. These languages are most often mentioned as being 'liked' and least often cited as 'unpleasant' or 'disliked'. Twi, English, and Hausa were also considered the most likely to become the main languages of Madina and of Ghana.

The languages evaluated positively and negatively, and the reasons given for these evaluations pattern significantly. Only a few languages were disapproved of by a significant number of respondents: Ga (in almost every instance on grounds of 'profanity'); Nzema (for widely different reasons); Kotokoli and, less frequently, some of the languages of Northern Ghana, especially Dagbani (on 'aesthetic' grounds and 'manner of greeting'); and others as cited in the following table. Conversely, certain languages received almost universal approbation: English, French, Arabic, Hausa, and with somewhat more exceptions, Twi and Ewe.

The reasons given for wishing to learn or to improve performance in various languages also pattern, e.g. for economic and social advancement, for use in business, for purposes of travel, for religious reasons, and for more effective communication. A number of respondents stated that they wished to learn a language so as to know when its speakers were insulting or plotting against them.

The responses elicited by the questions about language attitudes were grouped for coding purposes as shown in the following tables. Typical answers are cited for each category.

TABLE I

	I like X because . . .	I dislike X because . . .
A	(1) 'I don't know—I just like it.'	(1) 'I just hate that language.' (Brong)
	(2) 'I like to hear it.'	(2) 'I just hate to hear it.' (Twi)
	(3) 'I want to learn it.'	(3) 'I feel irritated when I hear it, even on the radio.' (Dagbani)
B	(1) 'It is my mother tongue and sounds the most sweet to me.'	
	(2) 'It is my own language.'	
C	(1) 'It is beautiful when the old men speak it, with nice rhythm and intonation.' (Adangme)	(1) 'It disturbs my ears.' (Kru)
	(2) 'It sounds sweet.'	(2) 'These languages prick my ears; they will be hard to learn on account of their sounds.' (Nigerian languages/Nzema)
	(3) 'I like the way it is spoken.'	(3) 'It is *just horrible* to listen to it.' (Nzema)
	(4) 'The intonation is sweet.'	(4) 'It sounds ugly.' (Nzema)
	(5) 'It is spoken rapidly.' (French)	(5) 'It sounds hard.' (Nzema)
	(6) 'It is interesting and sounds nice.'	(6) 'It sounds queer; it doesn't look like any language.' (Nzema)
	(7) 'It is rich in idiom and dialects.'	(7) 'It doesn't sound nice at all; in fact it confuses me.' (Dagbani)
	(8) 'It is sweet in the ear.' (French)	(8) 'I don't like the tone.' (Dagbani)
		(9) 'It sounds like howling.' (Frafra)
		(10) 'Nigerian languages are noisy.' (Nigerian languages)
		(11) 'They speak on the tongue.' (Kabre)

TABLE 1—*continued*

I like X because . . .	I dislike X because . . .
C	(12) 'The words don't sound clearly.' (Kabre)
	(13) 'They always sound like quarrelling.' (Kotokoli)
	(14) 'It is spoken with too much violence.' (Ga)
D	(1) 'A lot of words are used to convey little meaning.' (Guang)
	(2) 'They have long words and they are ugly too.' (Ijaw/Kru)
	(3) 'They prolong the words too unnecessarily, especially when they are greeting themselves.' (Dagbani)
E	(1) 'They are too ceremonious.' (Kotokoli)
	(2) 'Their way of greeting is crude.' (Kotokoli)
	(3) 'Their greetings are too long.' (Kotokoli)
	(4) 'Their way of greeting offends me.' (Kotokoli)
	(5) See 'D' (3)
F	(1) 'They like abusive expressions too much.' (Ga)
	(2) 'Even the children use profane expressions publicly.' (Ga)
G (1) 'I know it best.'	(1) 'All languages I can't understand are crude.'
(2) 'It can be easily handled.' (Twi)	(2) 'Ewe is crude; it is too difficult to learn.' (Ewe)
(3) 'I know all the intricacies of it and have grown to like it more.' (Ga)	(3) 'It is so crude that I couldn't pick it up after many attempts when I was in public service.' (Nzema)
(4) 'I understand it better than any other language.'	(4) 'It is difficult to understand even after my two years among Kru-speaking people.' (Kru)
	(5) See 'C' (2)
	(6) See 'C' (7)
H (1) 'It is a widely spoken and popular language.' (English/Twi/Hausa)	(1) 'I don't like it at all and it is not widely spoken too.' (Nzema)
(2) 'I can speak to many people.' (English)	(2) 'It is irritating/crude; besides it is not widely spoken.' (Nzema/Dagbani)
I (1) 'I like the people.'	(1) 'Basari people are untidy/dirty, so their language doesn't interest me.' (Basari)
(2) 'I enjoy Twi music.' (Twi)	
J (1)	(1) 'Guang is a bad luck language, even Okomfo Anokye said it.' (Guang)
Y	

TABLE 2

I want to learn X because . . .	Although I know X I don't speak it because . . .
A (1) 'I just want to know it.'	
(2) 'I want to be able to speak it.'	
(3) 'I just find it interesting.'	
B (1) 'I like the way it is spoken.'	
(2) 'It sounds pleasant.'	
(3) 'I like it. I find it sweet.'	
(4) 'It is an international language and also polished.' (French)	
C (1) 'People who speak English are respected.' (English)	
(2) 'To impress people.' (English)	
D (1) 'To get a better job.' (English)	
(2) 'To write reports and sign papers.' (English)	
(3) 'To be able to speak more easily to my employer and customers.'	
(4) 'Ewes are many at my place of work and I must be able to communicate with them.' (Ewe)	
(5) 'To transact my business; to help in my trade.'	
E (1) 'To pass exams; for academic reasons.' (English/French)	
F (1) 'Arabic is used in my religion.' (Arabic)	
G (1) 'It is widely spoken in Madina/Ghana.' (English/Twi/Hausa)	
(2) 'It is an international language.' (French)	
(3) 'It is widely spoken and popular.' (English)	
H (1) 'So I can communicate with people who speak it.'	
(2) 'So I can communicate with many people; so I can express myself.'	
(3) 'So I will have no language problems when travelling; so my movements won't be restricted.'	
(4) 'I am surrounded by Ewes.' (Ewe)	
(5) 'After all, Ga is the language of this place.' (Ga)	
(6) 'Most people speak Hausa in Madina.' (Hausa)	
(7) 'So I can understand my children if they speak it.' (English/French)	

TABLE 2—*continued*

	I want to learn X because . . .	Although I know X I don't speak it because . . .
I	(1) 'I may one day visit a French-speaking country.' (French) (2) 'I might go to East Africa some day.' (Swahili)	
J	(1) 'I want to add it to the languages I know.' (2) 'There is nothing wrong in knowing many languages.'	
K	(1) 'So I can know what people think and say about me or detect when I am being insulted.' (Ewe) (2) 'So that when an Ewe talks about me I can check her.'	(1) 'To know people who are speaking ill of me.' (Ga) (2) 'I am a traveller. Ashantis are renowned for killing strangers. I may be able to escape if I overhear any danger pertaining to my life.' (Twi; also Ewe)
L		(1) 'I fear to speak Ewe in public because I may mispronounce and be laughed at.' (Ewe) (2) 'I don't speak it in front of Twis because I am not confident of my ability.' (Twi) (3) 'People laugh (when I speak Larteh)' (said by a native Larteh speaker)

It is hoped to implement Phase II of the survey in the near future. In this phase the investigators will address themselves in greater depth to the socio-cultural aspects of the language situation in Madina. The interview schedule prepared by Miss Minkus of Northwestern University (a copy of which is appended to this paper) will be administered to a sample of the population of Madina. In selected cases it is intended that this questionnaire be supplemented by intensive interviewing which will introduce other questions as appropriate. Also included in this phase will be testing of language competence; differential ability in various languages will be assessed both impressionistically by native speakers and, for smaller samples, more rigorously by the use of standardized language proficiency tests.

Phase III as it is envisaged at present is essentially one which provides for studies of language use by situation along the normal lines of anthropological investigation by participant-observation techniques. But these and other follow-up studies already being planned are better treated as the subject of another separate paper.

QUESTIONNAIRE—INTERVIEW SCHEDULE

1. What language did you first speak as a child?
2. Is this still the language you speak best? (*a*) Yes
(*b*) No

If No, (*i*) what language(s) do you speak better?
(*ii*) can you speak well now the language you first spoke as a child? (*a*) Yes
(*b*) No

3. What other languages do you know?
For each language:

I. How well do you speak Language X?
(*a*) Can you greet in it?
(*b*) Can you buy in the market in it?
(*c*) Can you carry on an ordinary conversation in it?
(*d*) Can you give a speech in it?
(*e*) Can you discuss any subject in it—are there things you're able to talk about in your own language that you're not able to in X?
(*f*) Do native X speakers mistake you for a native X speaker?

II. How well do you understand X?
(*a*) Do you understand greetings?
(*b*) Do you understand ordinary conversation?
(*c*) Do you understand the old men when they speak it?
(*d*) Do you understand it when spoken on radio?
(*e*) Do you understand speeches and sermon in X?
(*f*) Do you understand jokes in X—i.e. do you know what people are laughing about?
(*g*) Are there any situations in which you don't understand X or don't understand it as well as a native speaker?

III. (*a*) Do you count in X?
(*b*) Do you dream in X?
(*c*) Do you ever talk to yourself in X?
(*d*) Do you pray in X?

IV. (*a*) Can you read X?
(*b*) What do you read in X?
(*c*) Do you read in X more often than in any other language?
(*d*) Do you read X better than you read other languages?

V. (*a*) Can you write X?
(*b*) What do you write in X and to whom do you write in it?
(*c*) Do you write in X more often than in any other language?
(*d*) Do you write X better than you write other languages?

VI. (*a*) When did you first learn X?
(*b*) From whom did you learn it?
(*c*) Where did you learn it?
(*d*) How did you learn it?
(*e*) Why did you learn it?

VII. (*a*) When you were first learning X, to whom did you speak it?
(*b*) Whom do you speak it to now?
(*c*) How often do you speak it?
(*d*) Where do you speak X?
(*e*) When was the last time you spoke X? To whom did you speak it? Why did you speak X rather than some other language?

VIII. (*a*) Are there times you would rather speak X than your native language? Why?
(*b*) Are there times you would rather speak X than any other language? Why?
(*c*) Are there times you pretend not to understand X? Why?
(*d*) Are there times you don't like to speak X?

(*e*) Do you speak X to your children?
(*f*) Do you want your children to learn X? Why?
(*g*) Do you like X? Why?
Are there things you don't like about X?
(*h*) Do you think X should be used in broadcasts on the radio? Should it be taught in the schools?
(*i*) Do people generally like X?
Are there some who don't?
Why don't they?

4. Are there other languages you don't speak but which you know a bit—e.g. know a few words of?
5. Are you now learning any other languages?
   For each language: (*a*) From whom are you learning it?
   (*b*) How are you learning it?
   (*c*) How often do you speak it?
   (*d*) Why do you want to learn it?
6. Are there any other languages you do not know but would like to know?
   For each language: (*a*) Why do you want to know it?
   (*b*) Do you plan to learn it?
   (1) soon
   (2) someday
7. (*a*) Are there any languages you know which you are trying to improve your knowledge of?
   (*b*) How are you doing it?
   (*c*) Why do you want to?
8. Are there any languages which you would not want to know? Why?
9. What language(s) do you like best? Why?
10. What language(s) do you like least? Why?
11. What language(s) do you enjoy speaking most?
12. (*a*) What language(s) would you like your sons to know. Why?
    (*b*) What language(s) would you like your daughters to know? Why?
13. What languages do you speak to your spouse? What is your spouse's native language.
14. (*a*) Are you teaching your own language to anybody?
    (*b*) Have you taught it to anybody?

15. (*a*) Do you want other people to learn your language?
    (*b*) Would you want it to become the national language or one of the major languages of Ghana?
16. Are there people who don't like your language? Why don't they?
17. (*a*) Are you proud that you know Y number of languages?
    (*b*) Do people praise you for knowing more than one?
18. Of all the languages spoken in Ghana which would you least like to know? Why?

Name, sex, age, occupation, residence, marital status, how long in Madina, places of residence before Madina and period of time in each, years of schooling, religion.

The interview is to be conducted in the native language of the respondent using standardized questionnaire schedules printed in the major Ghanaian languages.

The interviewer should write down all responses verbatim in the language of the interview. He should add his own comments concerning the respondent's hesitance or enthusiasm about answering any specific question, whether questions were answered quickly or after a pause, if the respondent had difficulty understanding specific questions, who else was present during the interview, where the interview took place, the respondent's general attitude towards the interview and the interviewer, etc.

(Prepared by: Helaine Minkus,
Northwestern University,
Evanston, Illinois, U.S.A.)

XIX. Asians in Nairobi: A Preliminary Survey

BARBARA NEALE

This paper is a preliminary survey of the Asian (or Indian) population of Nairobi with special reference to the distribution and use of languages in the Asian community. My fieldwork to date has largely confirmed the findings of others, notably those who contributed to Dharam Ghai's *Portrait of a Minority*,[1] so much of what follows will be familiar ground to some.

Any study of the Indian community is an exercise in componential analysis, where language, caste, religion, and other cultural characteristics are used to define the individual, or subgroup, in much the same way as distinctive features are used in phonological studies to define the phoneme. The situation in Kenya is no exception: the Asian community is not a community in any academic sense of the word, but Bharati is probably exaggerating when he says, 'There is virtually nothing of sociological significance about the minority which would hold for all its constituent parts.'[2]

Asians in Nairobi are all, or almost all, North Indians, and the population is therefore more homogeneous than, for example, the Asian population of South Africa, where North Indians speaking Indo-Aryan languages and South Indians speaking Dravidian languages are found in roughly equal numbers.[3] There are a few scattered South Indians in East Africa, but the bulk of the Asian population has come from three North Indian areas—Gujerat, Punjab, and Goa—where the regional languages—Gujerati, Punjabi, and Konkani—are ultimately derived from Sanskrit, the language of the Indo-Aryan invaders from Persia and points west.

[1] Ghai, D. P. (1965). [2] Bharati, A. (1965), p. 15. [3] Kuper, H. (1960).

Indians first came to East Africa to settle in the Arab towns along the coast nearly 2,000 years ago, and they have been coming in increasing numbers ever since. Gujerati traders were settled on the coast and actively participating in the Indian Ocean trade as early as the seventh century A.D. Trading patterns shifted with the arrival of Portuguese adventurers, and the Goans came as clerks and accountants with the Portuguese, who garrisoned and governed the coastal towns in the sixteenth century. Punjabis came as railway coolies, troops, and artisans with the British in the late nineteenth century, when famine in Gujerat brought still more Gujeratis from British India to British East Africa.

The railway labourers from Punjab were contract workers where other Indian migrants were so-called 'passengers', that is, people who were able to pay their own fares. Most of the Punjabis returned to India when their contracts expired; 6,000 stayed out of the 32,000 who came. Two thousand continued to work for the railway, and the rest found work as traders and artisans.[1]

The Kenya Asian population is drawn largely from the middle levels of Indian society. There are a few Brahmins from the highest Hindu caste and a few Harijans (or untouchables) from the lowest, but the Asian population in East Africa is not a representative cross-section of the larger community in India. Many left their traditional occupations, especially the Gujerati and Punjabi farmers, when they came to Africa, where most are now engaged in trade. Caste restrictions in general, and ritual pollution in particular, are de-emphasized in Kenya, where caste ranking is difficult because people from different parts of a region like Gujerat have no way of equating caste divisions here with caste divisions in India, where caste rankings may vary from village to village. Caste endogamy is still important in East Africa; cross-community marriages may occur, but they are never arranged, and caste (or subcaste) is still the boundary of the endogamous group.

[1] Delf, G. (1963), p. 11.

ASIAN COMMUNITIES: THE CONTEMPORARY SITUATION

Nairobi had, in 1962, a total population of 266,794, including 155,388 Africans, 21,476 Europeans, and 86,454 Asians.[1] These proportions (roughly 60 per cent African, 10 per cent European, and 30 per cent Asian) cannot be generalized for Kenya as a whole because the Asian population is highly urbanized, and they should not be assumed for 1968, because they have been outdated by a large influx of Africans into Nairobi and by the recent Asian exodus from Kenya.

The Asian population was subdivided by political affiliation as Indians, Pakistanis, and Goans in a survey based on 1962 City Council figures,[2] and surveyed again by religious affiliation as Hindus, Moslems, Sikhs, Christians, and Others in the 1962 Census Report.[3]

When Asians were surveyed politically the total Nairobi Asian population of 86,454 included 5,250 Goans, 69,492 Indians, and 11,712 Pakistanis. When Asians were surveyed by religion in the 1962 Census the total Kenya Asian population of 176,613 included a Nairobi Asian population of 86,453 (not including the peri-urban areas), which was composed of 42,284 Hindus, 15,752 Muslims, 14,387 Sikhs, 9,577 Christians, and 453 Others.

Political affiliation is, of course, largely ideological. The census takers of 1962 also attempted a survey by national origin but abandoned the attempt as it:

> became clear that the distinctions between Goans, Indians and Pakistanis had become increasingly meaningless . . . some two-thirds of the Asian community in Kenya in 1962 were born in East Africa, while many of the older generation migrated to Kenya before the partition of India and Pakistan in 1947. Furthermore, since the occupation of Goa by India, many persons of Goan origin had become citizens of India. On the Census schedules a substantial number of persons were shown as "Ismaili" under race, and their classification as either Indians or Pakistanis was largely a matter of guesswork. Thus, it became clear that sociologically the most important subdivision of the Asian community is by religion.[4]

[1] Halliman, D. M., and Morgan, W. T. W. (1967), p. 107.

[2] Ibid., pp. 107–8.

[3] *Kenya Population Census* (1962). [4] Ibid., p. 2.

No one has so far attempted a linguistic survey of the Asian population, but Gujerati-speaking Hindus have been estimated at 70 per cent of the total Asian population of East Africa.[1] Nairobi Asians say that Gujeratis are the largest group, Punjabis the next largest group, and Goans the smallest group. A few families from other areas in India are currently living in Nairobi, but here again most are speakers of Indo-Aryan languages—Bengali, Hindi, Maharastrian, and Singhalese—rather than Dravidian languages. The Nairobi Asian community also includes, besides Hindus, Jains, Sikhs, Muslims, and Goans, a small but influential community of Parsees from Bombay.

Regional and religious differences in India are reflected in the major divisions in the Nairobi Asian community, where there are clear distinctions between Goan Christians, Gujerati Hindus, Gujerati Jains, Gujerati Muslims, Punjabi Hindus, Punjabi Sikhs, and Punjabi Muslims. Where religion is associated with a single region, the descriptions may be simplified: Goan Christians are defined by region alone as Goans; Gujerati Jains and Punjabi Sikhs are defined by religion alone as Jains and Sikhs. Where surname largely coincides with sect, the sect may be described by surname, as in Nairobi, where Singhs and Shahs are local synonyms for Sikhs and Jains respectively. Where Hindu sects are also endogamous, and this is true only of the Sikhs and Jains, they may be reinterpreted as castes.

Members of the other four groups—Gujerati Hindus and Muslims and Punjabi Hindus and Muslims—are identified by Hindu caste and/or sect and Muslim sect. Gujerati Hindus are Patels, Lohanas, etc., by caste, Swami Narayans, Mahakalis, etc., by sect. The larger castes, the Lohanas and Patels, have associations of their own, and some of the sects have temples of their own. Separate temples are not essential for most, because the Gujerati Hindu sects are all within the main stream of the Bhakti religion.

Punjabi Hindus are typically described by sect alone as Arya Samajists or members of the Sanatan Dharm Sabha. The Arya Samaj is a reform sect where the Sanatan Dharm Sabha is, like the Gujerati sects, part of the traditional Bhakti religion.

Gujerati Muslims are identified by endogamous subsect as Ismailis, Bohoras, or Ithnasheris. All are subdivisions of the

[1] Bharati, A., op. cit., p. 17.

larger Shia sect, which is predominantly Gujerati as the Sunni sect is predominantly Punjabi.

Punjabi Muslims and Christian Goans are exceptional because their religions are not exclusively Asian. Sunni mosques have Asian, Arab, and African members, and Christian churches have Goan, European, and African congregations.

THE LINGUISTIC SITUATION

Linguistic diversity is a common phenomenon in India, and the situation in Nairobi, where many Asians have four or five functionally distinct languages, is no exception. Language choice depends largely upon social context, which is private when all concerned are members of the same linguistic subgroup, public when they are not. Lingua francas are used in public contexts, other languages in private contexts. Here one has to be careful, because the languages one thinks of as lingua francas—Hindustani, English, and Swahili—may be used in public contexts by some groups, private contexts by others.

Hindustani (or Hindi-Urdu) is commonly used as a linguistic bridge between Gujeratis and Punjabis in public contexts like shops, and gatherings that are open to all, but it is also used in contexts which are private in fact, public in theory. The Gujerati-speaking membership of the Seva Dal, a social service organization, and the Punjabi-speaking membership of the Arya Samaj, a religious sect, use Hindi in their meetings. Both are local branches of larger Hindi-speaking organizations based in India, and the Seva Dal was founded by Gandhiji, who was committed to Hindi as the national language of India.

Language naming is somewhat confusing in Nairobi, where Hindi-Urdu is variously called Hindi, Urdu, and Hindustani. Individual Asians regard all three as versions of the same language, which is called Hindustani when it is spoken in public contexts, Hindi or Urdu when it is spoken in private contexts. Linguists typically describe Hindi and Urdu as twin literary idioms of the same language, Hindi-Urdu or Hindustani. Hindi is associated with Hinduism as Urdu is associated with Islam and differences in script and vocabulary have contributed to the popular belief that they are separate languages. Nairobi Asians prefer the neutral term, Hindustani, because it lacks the Hindu bias of Hindi and the Muslim bias of Urdu.

Gujerati and Punjabi speakers use English as a linguistic bridge with English speakers, and here an English speaker is anyone who speaks English as a first or second language. When English-speaking Gujeratis are in contact with English-speaking Punjabis they use Hindustani or English or both. When they are in contact with Europeans and Goans they speak English. When they are in contact with English-speaking Africans they use either Swahili or English or both.

English is also used in private contexts, notably in Goan households. The Goans have been exposed to European models through the Portuguese and through the Catholic Church for a much longer period than any other Asian group, and they are the most Westernized section of the Asian community. Westernization in general, and the English language in particular, distinguish the Goans from non-Christian Hindus and Muslims, on the one hand, and Indian Christians (i.e. non-Goans), on the other. Konkani is spoken in the homes of Goan craftsmen, especially tailors, who are housed in one of the poorer sections of the city. Social distance between the tailors and other Goans is reinforced by the shift from Konkani to English in the homes of the well-to-do, where Konkani is spoken by old people and visitors from Goa, but otherwise largely forgotten.

Gujeratis and Punjabis sometimes use English in their homes, but there is no evidence of a shift from Gujerati and Punjabi to English as a first language.[1] Schoolchildren talk to their older brothers and sisters in Gujerati (or Punjabi) and English, but parents and grandparents are typically addressed in Gujerati (or Punjabi). The Ismailis use English in private contexts outside the home when messages from their leader, the Aga Khan, are read first in English and then in Gujerati in the mosques, and when their marriage services are conducted in English.

Swahili is used as a bridge between Asians and Africans, but, here again, if both are English speakers English may be used instead of Swahili or both may be used simultaneously. Most Asians learn Swahili informally, and the Swahili they speak is heavily influenced by their own languages. They are aware of this, and some prefer to use English when they are addressing educated Africans. Swahili is used privately as a home language

[1] Unpublished survey data gathered by T. Gorman, Department of English, University College, Nairobi.

by some Ismailis and Ithnasheris whose forebears have lived in East Africa for several generations. Families of this sort are said to be fairly common in Zanzibar, rare in Nairobi.

Inter-Asian contacts do not, as a rule, take place in the home, since Gujeratis, Punjabis, and Goans do not intermarry, and most Asian home life revolves around the activities of the larger joint family. Gujerati Hindus meet Punjabi Hindus in some temples, in public gatherings addressed by visiting celebrities, at social service organizations organized on Indian models, and sometimes at social clubs. Hindus meet other Hindus, Jains, Sikhs, Goans, Muslims, and Europeans in offices and shops, in schools and university, in some social clubs, in sports clubs, and in social service organizations organized on European models like the Kenya Women's Society and the Lions Club. Nairobi Asians also have extensive contacts with the English-speaking world, and especially with the United Kingdom. Asians meet Africans in their homes as servants, in their shops as customers and employees, in schools and university as fellow students, and in offices as colleagues. Students have wider and more intimate contacts with the larger community than many adults. Schools are now integrated where they were formerly segregated on racial lines as European, Asian, and African schools.

The discussion so far has dealt with primary regional languages and secondary lingua francas. Primary languages are defined in functional, not chronological terms, and where the two do not coincide, a distinction is made between the language a person learns first, which is his first language, and the language he uses most, which is his primary language. For most Asians in Nairobi there is no separation between first and primary language, but there are some Cutchi Gujeratis who know Cutchi a dialect of Gujerati, as a first language and use Gujerati as a primary language, and there are also some Goans who know Konkani (or Portuguese) as a first language and use English as a primary language. Language shifts of this kind can be used to express social distance from others with the same first language and reinforce social nearness with others with the same primary language. Indian anthropologists have coined a term, 'Sanskritization', for similar shifts in non-linguistic behaviour. It would be rash to assume that this is the case in Nairobi at this stage of the survey, but it is a notion which should be investigated. Cutchi is said to be the first language of Ismaili Muslims, Swami Narayan and/or lower class Hindus, and some upper-class Hindus. Many upper-class Hindus use Gujerati as a primary language where other Hindus retain Cutchi. Some Hindus have therefore 'forgotten' Cutchi as many Goans have 'forgotten' Konkani.

Chavarria-Aguilar's division of secondary languages into complementary languages which are useful as, for example, lingua francas and supplementary languages which are largely ornamental is particularly interesting because it provides a means of coping with the languages of religion.[1] Nairobi Asians hear, and sometimes recite or read, prayers in languages which they do not, themselves, understand. Gujerati Hindus pray in Sanskrit, Gujerati Jains in Prakrit. Punjabi Hindus pray in Sanskrit if they are orthodox, in Vedic if they are Arya Samajists. Gujerati and Punjabi Muslims pray in Arabic. Sikhs and Goans are exceptions, because both use their first languages, Punjabi and English, for prayer, but, even here, the picture is confused, because Sikh Prayers are written in the Gurumukhi script, which is used only by Sikhs, and Goans have recently shifted from Church Latin to English. At least one church in Nairobi, the Consolata Mission, has retained Church Latin for weekday services and shifted to English for Sunday services.

Prayers in supplementary languages are read or recited by priests, and sometimes by the congregation. Gujerati Jains have prayer books where Prakrit prayers are followed by Gujerati explanations, and Ismailis read Arabic prayers from books with parallel texts in Gujerati and English. Goans read, or follow, Latin prayers from books. Hindu ladies have weekly, or bi-weekly, Satsangs where they gather to sing and pray in classical languages, and the languages of religion are also taught in some of the private, 'community' schools.

Classical languages are used only for prayer; other languages are used for sermons, explanations, announcements, and other business of the mosques and temples. Gujeratis, Goans, and Punjabi Sikhs use their primary languages—Gujerati, English, and Punjabi—where Punjabi Hindus and Muslims use their secondary languages—Hindi and Urdu.

[1] Chavarria-Aguilar, O. L. (1966), p. 3.

CONCLUSION

Language distribution and function have been stressed in this paper, which is essentially a description of the linguistic community. Subgroups have been defined by region and religion, and each has been further associated with a characteristic combination of languages used in private contexts—at home and in religious gatherings. Regional languages are widely used as home languages, but two language shifts are currently taking place, so language is not always predictable by region. Gujeratis speak Cutchi or Gujerati, and both are found in some households where Cutchi speakers are shifting to Gujerati. Goans speak Konkani or English and, here again, both languages are found in households where Konkani speakers are shifting to English.

Both shifts are spontaneous and both are partial, because upper-class Hindus and Goans are shifting where the lower classes—the Hindu masons and the Goan tailors—are not. Age and sex are also important because parents shift more readily than grandparents, men more readily than women. The Cutchi to Gujerati shift is particularly interesting because it involves only Hindus; Cutchi- and Gujerati-speaking Ismailis often marry, and both languages are spoken and sometimes mixed in Ismaili households on all social levels.

Asian children are a special case because they are involved in another kind of language change, a legislated shift from home languages to English as the medium of instruction in the schools. Spontaneous shifts in home languages and legislative shifts in school languages are different in kind and scope, and Asians are concerned about the school shift because their children are being exposed to English on a scale which has no precedent in India. Goans are exceptional because they use English in church and many also speak English at home, but other Asians, who want their children to do well in school and also want them to 'keep their religion' and to be able to communicate respectfully with non-English-speaking elders, have a real dilemma. Asian children who attend government schools are typically fluent but illiterate in Gujerati or Punjabi, which they learn as home languages, competent but illiterate in Hindustani (or Hindi–Urdu), which they know as the language of the Asian cinema and vernacular radio broadcast. Many parents, who see illiteracy in Asian languages as a threat to religion, send their children to community schools where Asian languages are still taught as subjects or used as the medium of religious instruction as Gujerati is used in the Hindu and Jain schools, Punjabi in the Sikh schools, Hindi in the Arya Samaj schools, and Urdu in the Muslim schools.

Language teaching of this kind is only a partial solution, because many children, especially boys, are not exposed to it at the secondary-school level. Most subgroups maintain co-educational primary schools and secondary girls' schools and some, like the Jains, also maintain secondary schools for boys; others, like the Arya Samaj and Punjabi Muslims, who provide only for girls, have extracurricular classes where Asian language teaching is a by-product of religious instruction. Even the Ismailis, who shifted voluntarily to English as a school language in 1960, are having second thoughts and are, this year, reinstating Gujerati as a subject in some schools and expanding their existing programme of extracurricular evening classes.

Concern for traditional patterns of authority is apparent in informal decisions about language choice in Asian homes and other private contexts. English, or a combination of Gujerati (or Punjabi) and English, may be used with English-speaking parents, typically fathers, and with siblings, but bilingual children and young people are expected to observe the conventions of language switching and avoid using English wherever it may be construed as disrespectful or exclusive behaviour. Acceptable usage is illustrated below in excerpts from language diaries by female undergraduates at University College, Nairobi. Most move in familiar networks, socializing largely with other students and with relatives whose language preferences are well known, but where it is necessary to make snap judgements about the competence or preference of other speakers, they use linguistic and non-linguistic signals—greeting, introductions, age, dress, and sex—as contexual clues.

1. 'In the morning, I helped my sister Kiran to make breakfast. Our whole conversation was in Punjabi except for the work "radio" . . . my conversation with my mum was in Punjabi. My mum understands English though she cannot read or understand English of higher standards.

Before noon we went to Siri Guru Singh Sabha temple. . . . The conversation I had with the ladies was in Punjabi exclusively, for even though I am used to resorting to English . . . when I can't think of the Punjabi alternative, I managed to avoid this on this particular instant. While having lunch after having finished with the serving, I spoke in Punjabi but again resorted to English in between. I was in the company of one primary school teacher and a nurse who are sisters-in-law. . . . A relative of theirs who was . . . interested in my jokes asked me to explain as she couldn't understand . . . towards evening, I went to my second maternal uncle's place and my first cousins and myself had a get-together party. Because my aunties were present, the conversation was exclusively in Punjabi . . . I chatted over breakfast with my dad. My conversation with my dad is full of English words and phrases. They happen to be convenient in understanding. . . . Whenever English phrases and words happened to be a short-cut I used them subconsciously.'

2. 'Breakfast: Mother, father and rest of family—all greeted each other in Hindi, but the conversation was all in Punjabi with a little English used only for better comprehension. . . . Lunch: at home with family spoke in English and Punjabi. . . . Evening: went for dinner to my auntie's house. Spoke most of the time in English and Hindi to the Parsee guests. In the kitchen I spoke to my mother and my auntie in Punjabi.

English is considered to be a very formal language, and it is used whenever two people meet for the first time, provided they both know it. On Saturday night, there was a party at one of my uncle's house. All my relatives were there, and so were many other teenagers. I found that among the teenagers, English was mostly used, whereas among the elder people, no matter what they were talking about, Punjabi was mainly used, although a few ideas were expressed in English. And I saw that it came naturally to me to greet my elder relatives with "Namaste" whereas I called out "Hi" or "Hello" to the teenagers there. It's perhaps a mark of respect or reverence that we talk to our elders in Punjabi rather than English. . . .

After a lecture in English, I proceeded to talk to an Indian (Sikh) professor in the college. Our talk . . . was entirely in English. The reason for this was that our relation was not informal enough for us to speak in a language which is our mother tongue. An attempt on my part to speak in Punjabi was not met half-way, because we could not speak in Punjabi, having a sense of oddness about it. . . .

In the morning I remained at home, talking in Punjabi to mum, taking care not to use too difficult English words in between, because she understands only a few English words. But to the rest of my family, I talked in Punjabi as well as English. . . . For lunch I went to my uncle's place. The elderly relatives (women) talked among themselves in Punjabi, but amongst the men (elderly) the language varied—sometimes English and sometimes Punjabi. . . . In the evening, a Sikh girl-friend came to see me at home. We spoke in Punjabi . . . but also using English. She spoke to my mum in Punjabi but when I introduced her to my sister the two of them talked together in English. Later in the evening, two of my aunts and their families came over. They spoke to my parents in Punjabi, but to my sisters and me in English. I noticed that they spoke to their children in English (the children being between the ages of five and seven), and the children seemed to know very little Punjabi.'

3. 'At work—to start with there is an Ismaili colleague with whom I talk in English as he prefers it that way. . . . With Miss Chandaria (Jain) the choice of language to be spoken is at random. Gujarati and English are randomly selected on majority of our meetings. With another Shah girl who is in charge of all staff members, I talk in English. Not that I prefer it but she always starts that way and it remains quite formal. . . . I talk with my uncle in Gujarati as speaking in English I think would seem to be arrogance and rudeness on my part. . . . At coffee time there were six of us . . . the majority of us spoke Gujarati but Miss Taneja could not understand so all general discussions were held in English whereas individual chatter went on in Gujarati (softly of course). . . . In the afternoon I went shopping. I fired my tailor who is an uneducated Gujarati. I spoke in Gujarati. . . . I also met a Goan girl with whom I talked in proper English. No mixing of words. No switching off and on from one language to another. I also met Miss Chandaria's sister (Gujarati) and she talked to me in Gujarati (We were complete strangers, never introduced but as I was talking to Miss Chandaria, her sister joined in the conversation and it was reciprocated.). I went into a shop and talked in Gujarati again as I know those people are also Gujarati, not very educated and would resent any conversation in English or laugh behind my back. . . .'

The school shift is relatively recent, and the full impact has not yet been felt; it will therefore be appreciated that the Asian population of Nairobi is currently a community in transition, and the picture presented above is subject to sudden change. School integration has broadened the contacts of Asian children, and Africanization in government offices and private business has changed the patterns of Asian–African contacts, and prompted many Kenya Asians to emigrate, or consider emigrating, to India, Pakistan, Britain, or Canada. All subgroups, with the notable exception of the Ismailis, who are mostly Kenya citizens, are subject to Africanization, but some are more immediately vulnerable than others. Most of the 16,000–18,000 who left in the 1968 exodus to Britain were Punjabi-speaking government servants, artisans, and craftsmen, and most of those currently planning to leave are Gujerati-speaking traders—Shahs and Patels. Many have gone, and more will go, but some will stay. A decision to stay will, for some, be a decision to assimilate, and Asians cannot assimilate to Western models without drastic revisions in social and linguistic patterns.

REFERENCES

Bharati, A.

(1965) 'A Social Survey', in D. P. Ghai (ed.) *Portrait of a Minority*, Nairobi: Oxford University Press.

Chavarria-Aguilar, O. L.

(1966) *English and Hindi in India: their Respective Roles*. Unpublished paper prepared for Conference on Language Problems in Developing Nations.

Delf, G.

(1963) *Asians in East Africa*. London: Oxford University Press.

Ghai, D. P. (ed.)

(1965) *Portrait of a Minority: Asians in East Africa*. Nairobi: Oxford University Press.

Halliman, D. M., and Morgan, W. T. W.

(1967) 'The City of Nairobi', in W. T. W. Morgan (ed.) *Nairobi: City and Region*. Nairobi: Oxford University Press.

——

(1962) *Kenya Population Census*. Vol. IV, Part. 1.

Kuper, H.

(1960) *Indians in Natal*. Natal: University Press.

XX. Language Choice in Two Kampala Housing Estates

DAVID J. PARKIN

The purpose of this paper is to explore from a social anthropological viewpoint some problems of language choice in a multilingual urban community. The community is of 1,468 households in two municipal housing estates in Kampala East, Uganda. Kampala, the capital of Uganda, was extended in late 1967 to include Mengo municipality, until recently the capital of the former kingdom of Buganda. My data is based on the situation preceding this when Kampala and Mengo were administered separately yet were each part of a single urban complex. I refer especially to the situation as I observed it from the middle of 1962 until early 1964. During this period Uganda's independence was formally declared in October 1962.

I call the period shortly before and after independence the political context of situation. A second context is that of residential area or neighbourhood. A third is that of tribe or ethnic group. Though no relationship is set exclusively in one or other context, I shall try to show that, for certain interactions, norms deriving from one context have primacy as a determinant of language choice. My examples will be those of 'apt and isolated illustration' (Gluckman, 1965) which, though obviously purposively selected, are most convenient for a short paper. First, I describe each of the contexts.

THE POLITICAL CONTEXT

Proportionally few of the local ethnic group, the Ganda, live in the housing estates, most preferring to live in Mengo. The non-Ganda who prefer to live in the estates, and out of the jurisdiction of Mengo, include townsmen from many different tribes, such as the Kenya Luo, Luhya, and Kisii, the northern

Uganda Acholi, Lango, Alur, Jonam, and Lugbara, and small numbers of people from the former kingdoms of the Great Lakes and from elsewhere (Southall and Gutkind, 1956).

With the approach of Uganda's independence, Kenyans felt uneasy at what they believed were likely prospects of being dismissed from their jobs. Earlier fears were that Ganda would be most likely to cause this dismissal when Uganda became independent. Later many Kenyans feared that it would be not just Ganda but Ugandans generally who would seek to reduce the number of Kenyans employed in Kampala and other Ugandan towns. Kenyans were conspicuous because they constituted a relatively large proportion of the labour force and were active in trade unions. They felt exposed to any changes which independence might bring. A few constitutional developments and public announcements gave rise to this impression. These need not be dealt with here. In the end, Kenyans' fears that they would be dismissed from their jobs and sent back to their home country did not materialize (Parkin, 1969). The relevance of the widespread anxiety is its effect on language choice in a number of social situations.

THE RESIDENTIAL AND NEIGHBOURHOOD CONTEXT

The transitionary period of Uganda's independence is thus the political context of situation. The housing estates of Kampala East have significance in this context because they include a large proportion of Kampala's expatriate Kenyan workers. But the estates also have distinct significance as dwelling areas *per se*.

The two estates are ranked according to the prestige of residence in them. Objectively, people with more secure and better-paid jobs live at Naguru, the higher-status estate, while less well-paid workers live in Nakawa, the lower-status estate. House rents at Naguru are higher than at Nakawa. Even within Nakawa one part of the estate has dearer houses than the other. People recognize that these geographical divisions coincide with socio-economic ones. There is a steady movement by tenants from 'lower' to 'higher' areas. The situation is complicated by the long waiting list for a house of two or three years. A relatively prosperous and educated senior clerk may have to 'tolerate' residence in a cheaper house in a 'lower' area until a dearer one more befitting his status becomes available.

In conventional terms, therefore, Naguru can be said to be of higher status than Nakawa. But within Nakawa there is a similar ranking of its 'lower' and 'upper' areas. People who otherwise know no English refer to 'Upper' Nakawa (or the 'up groups') and 'Lower' Nakawa (or the 'down groups'). Tenants associate a different lingua franca with each area. Thus, Lower Nakawa is exclusively a Swahili area, Upper Nakawa more of an English one, and Naguru an English and Luganda area. These folk designations are, of course, no more than approximations to the truth. They are used also at the level of public meetings, such as those of the tenants' associations. Thus, Naguru tenants' association uses English and Luganda at its meetings, while the Nakawa association uses English and Swahili. Ganda are, as mentioned above, few in the estates compared with their proportions in Kampala-Mengo. At Nakawa they provide only 4 per cent of the household heads, though at Naguru they are the second largest group at 20 per cent. Their higher proportion at Naguru explains the additional use of Luganda at public meetings there.

These three languages are lingua francas in a restricted and perhaps incorrect sense. English is the most widely spoken in the estates. The relatively high level of education and, again, the undeniably high prestige attached to a knowledge of this language make it the most widely used. A type of Swahili which ignores the grammars but is rich in vocabulary and expression is used mostly by Kenyans and Muslim Nubi, but over the years has come to be accepted by an increasing number of Ugandans, with the general exception of Ganda, many of whom feel that the use of Swahili would in some way undermine the nationally and culturally important position held by their vernacular. Luganda is itself understood and spoken at varying levels of fluency by a remarkably large number of non-Ganda. Related peoples from the other Interlacustrine Bantu kingdoms obviously find little difficulty after even a few months in Kampala-Mengo in learning Luganda. But even a number of Nilotic Luo men, who have been in Kampala for some years, acquire a very useful smattering. Kenya Bantu, such as Luhya and Kisii, acquire even more. Only northern Ugandans, who include Nilotic and Sudanic speakers, seem not to have learned more than a few words of Luganda.

Each housing estate can be said to be made up of small neighbourhoods. Houses are allocated not according to tribal membership but according to socio-economic status. Neighbourhoods are therefore multi-tribal and each set within a system of socio-economic grading. A result of these factors, which lack of space prevents me from elaborating, is that the residential context emphasizes the values of 'non-tribalism' and of individualistic competition for prestige and socio-economic status (Parkin, 1969). Within this context English is associated with higher-status people of some education. Luganda is largely ethnically confined. Swahili is the lingua franca seemingly most used by socially distant socio-economic and tribal categories, and so most likely to express their unity in the face of impending divisiveness.

THE TRIBAL AND ETHNIC CONTEXT

Nilotes form about 40 per cent of the two estates' population. The most numerous are the Kenya Luo. Though there appears to be considerable dialectal variation, there is sufficient mutal intelligibility to allow some limited casual conversation. For townsmen from Nilotic tribes who have stayed for some years in Kampala any marked differences among them of vocabulary and expression are quickly learned. The Nilotes in the housing estates also include Acholi, Lango, Alur, Jonam (singular Janam), and Padhola, who are Ugandans. They are thus linked linguistically and culturally but split nationally.

The two main Bantu-speaking groups on the estates are, first, those of the Interlacustrine societies, such as Ganda, Nyoro, Toro, Soga, Ankole, and Kiga. Of these, Lunyoro and Lutoro are the most obviously mutally intelligible, as are Ruciga (Kiga) and Runyankore (Ankole). Secondly, there are those from Kenya, such as Luhya and Kisii, and from East Uganda, the Gisu, Gwe, and Samia. The Samia are usually regarded as a sub-tribe of Luhya. During the political transition period, however, many Kenya Samia claimed that they were Ugandans in an attempt to escape what they thought would be discrimination directed against Kenyans working in Uganda. Kenya

Luhya are divided into a number of sub-tribal groups, sharing mutually intelligible dialects.

The Muslim Nubi are originally from different tribes in the Sudan. A small but significant proportion of them marry Ganda Muslim women. They speak a type of Arabic but also use Swahili for wider communication. Finally, there are small numbers of Nilo-Hamitic Teso and a larger number on the estates of Sudanic-speaking Lugbara and Madi.

This linguistic heterogeneity fosters the use of common media of communication. Whether a speaker uses Swahili, English, or Luganda as the common medium in any particular context obviously depends, firstly, on his linguistic competence in each of these languages. If he knows insufficient Luganda he can hardly communicate in it. It is worthwhile, therefore, to be selective and concentrate on speakers who have at least a smattering in all three languages and to see what social rather than linguistic factors influence their choice of language in particular relationships and situations.

The cases I now present are, I believe on impressionistic grounds, 'typical' enough on which to base generalizations, while being far from exhaustive of all possible cases.

Case 1. An example of instrumental aspects of language choice in the political context (partly observed and partly reported).

Jason is a Kenya Kisii living in Upper Nakawa. He is studying part-time in Kampala under the care and guidance of his elder full brother, with whom he lodges. Jason hopes to finish his course of typing and shorthand within another six months. He came to Kampala two years ago, but his course has been occasionally interrupted by various family crises which required him to return home to Kisii. Uganda's independence is due in a few weeks. Rumours have been circulating that Kenyans may have to leave Uganda in order to make way for the many young Ugandans who have no employment. During the preceding year the number of jobs declined considerably, and this and other factors have given rise to Kenyans' anxiety.

Jason was strolling by his house one evening when he met a young Luo, also in his early twenties, who lives a few doors from him. Jason is a Kisii whose vernacular is Bantu, while his Luo neighbour is a Nilotic speaker. But they use Swahili as their common language. Their conversation always starts with a greeting which includes the Swahili word 'ndugu', or brother. They have known each other well for a few months, during which time their conversation has revolved around the problem of Kenyans' future in Uganda. The Luo has recently lost his job, due, he claims, to his Ganda supervisor's prejudice against Luo. Together the Luo and Jason then blamed the Ganda for what they felt to be discrimination against Kenyans in employment in Uganda.

They bade farewell. Jason continued his stroll and later returned to his house in Upper Nakawa. He noticed that another neighbour, a Soga, had just come home from work, and decided to go and speak with him about a matter which had been on his mind for some time. The Soga is a senior clerk working for the head Post Office in Kampala city. He has School Certificate education, is now nearly thirty, and has been working in Jinja for a number of years before coming to Kampala. He is so obviously high status that it is widely assumed that he has applied for a house at Naguru. This is in fact the case. As a Soga he is also Bantu, or more specifically a member of the Interlacustrine Bantu group. All his life he has mixed with Ganda and speaks the language fluently. Nevertheless, he preserves a strong sense of Soga patriotism and is no blind admirer of Ganda institutions. He does, however, have a Ganda mistress, whom he met in Kampala and with whom he has established a good relationship.

Jason greeted him in Luganda and, for a little while, they spoke in this language. But Jason has not yet acquired great fluency in Luganda, and his Soga neighbour broke into English for easier communication. The Soga's English is, of course, excellent, while Jason's is certainly competent and better than his Luganda.

The purpose of Jason's visit was to ask the Soga to find him a job as an office messenger in the Post Office. With a job, he explained, he would be less of a burden to his brother and, with peace of mind, would pursue his studies more diligently. The request, which was granted, was actually made in Luganda, though by this time the two men were talking in English. The most remarkable aspect of the request was that Jason made an explicit appeal to the Soga: Jason claimed that because he himself was a Muntu (singular of Bantu) like the Soga, the Soga should regard this element of affinity as more important than his not being a Ugandan.

Analysis

Jason was in fact asking the Soga to overlook the difference in national origins or citizenship between them and to help Jason on the basis not of *cultural* but of general *linguistic* affinity.

There are many examples of men appealing to similarities of custom or culture, as distinct from language, as the basis of a relationship. The Kisii, and more particularly the Luhya, do so with the Luo. Both these groups in Kampala recognize that, compared to the Ganda, Soga and other people organized into kingdoms and possessing different customs, they have much in common. The Luo, like the Luhya and Kisii, are traditionally politically uncentralized. They all emphasize the significance of local descent groups in the allocation of land and property. They pay very high bridewealth for their wives and regard this bridewealth as giving them the rights over any children produced by the woman, even if begotten by another man. This cultural affinity is frequently the basis of relationships between Luo and Luhya or Kisii in spite of the fact that they are linguistically quite unconnected. The contrasting example of Jason and his Soga neighbour is of an appeal to disregard national and cultural difference and to consider only linguistic affinity of a general kind.

This is not to suggest that, simply because Jason and his Soga neighbour were both Bantu, Jason was given a job. Affinities of language, culture, or nationhood may separately be used simply as an idiom for confirming, strengthening, or utilizing a relationship. The underlying strength of the relationship is based both on personal factors of compatibility and on reciprocal advantage. Jason and the Soga neighbour certainly got on well with each other. One might speculate that the Soga was gratified at the approach made to him and might even have seen personal advantage in securing a type of client relationship with the Kisii. Urban patron–client relationships in the sphere of job-getting and other aid are not uncommon in Kampala, though they do tend to be among persons of the same tribe.

There are other socio-linguistically significant aspects of

Jason's case. He used Swahili with his fellow-Kenyan, the Luo, even though they both knew English well and could easily have communicated in it. This they might have done in what I call a 'conversational arena of prestige competition', an example of which I shall give below. But they chose Swahili, mainly, I suggest, because the relationship was situationally one of commiseration. The Luo had lost his job, and both expressed uneasiness as Kenyans regarding their futures in Uganda. They made frequent use of '*ndugu*' or 'brother' in addressing each other. Jason's relationship with his Soga neighbour was of status inferior to superior. English and Luganda, more formal languages from Jason's viewpoint, were used. But Jason's relationship with the Luo was of status equals in what seemed to them to be a common predicament as expatriates. The more 'brotherly' Swahili was used.

Jason's interactions with both the Luo and Soga were set in two of the three contexts described above, namely those of neighbourhood and political change. All three were neighbours. Both the Luo and Soga included in their conversations with Jason some discussion of the problems facing Kenyans. There can be little doubt that the choice of language used in each interaction was determined not by the norms of neighbourhood but by concern with these political problems. In other words, the prevailing political context had primacy in determining language choice in Jason's two interactions.

Politics involves a struggle for power or influence, or at least an attempt to make use of them. It is not surprising, therefore, that language choice in this case was manipulated almost deviously to forge cross-cutting alliances and divisions, e.g. Jason and the Luo expressed in Swahili their unity and common distrust of Ganda; but Jason and the Soga used Luganda and English in order to establish the beginnings of a patron–client relationship which explicitly repudiated the Kenyan 'brotherhood' and unity which Jason and the Luo had earlier communicated to each other in Swahili.

The political or instrumental aspects of language choice suggested by this case may be summarized as follows:

(1) An appeal to linguistic affinity may constitute the idiom through which a dyadic relationship may be manipulated for certain ends.

(2) Structurally there is no difference between the use of linguistic affinity as an idiom for manipulating relationships and the use of cultural, national, and, one might suggest, religious affinity as idioms for similar purposes.

(3) If this is so, then language is being used to convey much more than the conventional 'meaning' resulting from the actual conversation: it can be articulated to express *either* a difference *or* an equivalence of status between two (and perhaps more) persons (or groups), e.g. Jason and the Soga as incipient 'client' and 'patron', as against Jason and the Luo as 'brothers'.

(4) The use and potential use of Luganda, English, and Swahili in this case by persons for whom none were native languages suggests a special usefulness of a multiplicity of restricted lingua francas: they may be used selectively to bridge and manipulate the different role-relationships which an ego has with persons who are linked to him in varied and conflicting ways.

Case 2. An example of expressive aspects of language choice in the residential context (observed)

At one of the well-attended general meetings of the Nakawa tenants' association a well-dressed young Ugandan of the Teso tribe (Nilo-Hamitic) stood up to speak on the problem under discussion, which was how to improve the poor condition of some of the Nakawa houses. He is a clerk with a good knowledge of English, which is required in his work. He has been in Kampala for four years, but has not yet acquired any more than a rough knowledge of Swahili, probably because most of his time has been spent in one of the Mengo suburbs where Swahili is used to a far lesser extent than in Kampala East, where there are many Kenyans. He certainly knows very little Luganda, which would not any way have been acceptable as a lingua franca at the Nakawa association's meetings, and so had little alternative but to use English.

Unfortunately for him, general meetings of the association are supposed to be conducted in Swahili, to enable a majority of tenants on the estate to follow and contribute to the discussion. On trivial issues English is occasionally used by a speaker from the floor, and its use is not challenged. On this occasion, however, the issue was an urgent one. The poor condition of a house had been responsible for the death of an unskilled Acholi's nephew. Poor and prosperous tenants alike shared a common concern in the matter, since many houses were in need of some kind of improvement. But, as explained, poorer people live in Lower Nakawa and, of the three lingua francas, tend to speak only Swahili. A number of these Swahili speakers from Lower Nakawa protested vehemently at the Teso's use of English, which they could not understand. They successfully demanded the arrangement of a running translation as the Teso spoke. More than this, they condemned the young Teso, who was obviously more educated and financially secure than themselves and who lived in Upper Nakawa, of acting 'proudly', or of trying to exhibit his 'affluence' and education through his use of English.

The association's chairman, a Nilote from northern Uganda, tried to reassure the Swahili speakers that the Teso had been unaware of the implications of speaking English at a general meeting of the association and had not intended to insult the Swahili speakers by 'showing them up'. After all, he said, the Teso had lived in Nakawa for barely more than a year and might be excused this ignorance of procedure. In time, no doubt, he would acquire a good knowledge of Swahili. The chairman recalled how he himself had come to Kampala many years before without any knowledge of Swahili, but that now here he was addressing a large gathering in the language.

In parenthesis, it should be noted that committee meetings of the association are held in English, a difference of usage which the association has written into its constitution and which is observed. Committee members, including the chairman, are almost all of Upper Nakawa and are all English speakers.

Analysis

In this case the use of English *expressed* or made known differences which were reflected in the special graded structure of the housing estate. I emphasize the word 'expressed' because there appeared to be no purposive manipulation of language by either the speaker, his accusers, or the mediator. That is to say, language was not an instrumental device for securing specific ends as it was in Case 1. Clearly, the distinction between instrumentality and expressiveness is not watertight. There are elements of both in many social interactions. But the general concern of people at this public meeting was that Swahili should replace English and be used to express the value of neighbourhood or residential harmony and that socio-economic status differences and antagonism based on them should be suppressed.

The ideal norms of residence derive from the fact, firstly, that neighbourhoods are multi-tribal and that frequent disputes along tribal lines are simply inexpedient, and second, that socio-economic differences among people are made more glaringly obvious as a basis for disputes by the graded housing system. While it is obvious that individuals occasionally depart from these ideal norms, the relevant point here is that the tenants' association is a forum in which the norms exhorting harmony may be publicized and that the use of language is determined by this factor.

Similar cases can be given for Naguru where a public concern with multi-tribal harmony is also expressed at tenants' association meetings. At Naguru, Luganda is additionally a lingua franca in public meetings, as the Ganda are the second largest group, and as there are more Interlacustrine Bantu than at Nakawa. But not all tenants know Luganda, though they may speak Swahili or English. Ganda, as is well known, frequently oppose the use of Swahili, with the result that English emerges as the most commonly acceptable language at Naguru. But the choice may vary according to the issue under discussion, and all three languages are used from time to time. The main point is that, as with Nakawa, the choice of language in any situation is determined by a common need to override tribal and cultural differences among an ethnically heterogeneous community.

Returning to the case itself we may summarize some suggested findings thus:

(1) In the residential context of situation, with its emphasis on multi-tribal harmony, there is a tendency to select from the multiplicity of lingua francas that which has the highest common value as a medium of communication.

(This point may seem to be too obvious to warrant special mention. But it may at least be contrasted with the way in which a person may manipulate a number of languages to his advantage as Jason did in Case 1.)

(2) In this process of selecting a commonly acceptable

lingua franca, convergent status differences are expressed: English-speaker and Swahili-speaker; rich and poor; educated and uneducated; clerk and unskilled worker; and Upper and Lower Nakawa, or Naguru and Nakawa.

(3) There is a loose structural parallel with the use made of religion: in small-scale, monolingual, rural societies public rituals may temporarily reconcile internal divisions by reference to commonly acknowledged symbols (Turner, 1957); in an urban, multi-tribal housing estate public meetings may temporarily reconcile internal status divisions by using the language which has greatest currency among both low and high status.

(This is not the same point as (1). In (1) I refer to the attempt to solve a problem of verbal communication. In (3) I refer to the attempt to play down publicly socio-economic status divisions, which are nevertheless recognized by people as inevitable features of everyday life.)

THE TRIBAL OR ETHNIC CONTEXT AND 'AFFECTIVE NEUTRALITY'

The preceding emphasis on 'non-tribalism' is not intended to suggest that 'tribal' disputes never occur. Indeed, they do. But, out of expedience, public 'leaders' discourage them and mark them out for special condemnation. Ordinary tenants share their condemnation of 'tribalist' behaviour and conflict. One or other of the three lingua francas is available to a person: to *express* a common interest with a person of another tribe, to bridge the social distance between them, or simply to initiate a dyadic relationship; or it may be used purposively or *instrumentally* to articulate a relationship for specific ends.

On the basis of two cases, I have suggested that in the residential or neighbourhood context the expressive aspects of the lingua francas are paramount, and that in the special political context their instrumental aspects are most significant. These are intended to be no more than very broad generalizations, and the converse may occur in other cases. I turn now away from the use made of lingua francas and describe very briefly one or two situations in which 'tribal exclusiveness' in the housing estates is acceptable, even though, in other situations, this conflicts with the value set on 'non-tribalism'.

A simple first proposition is that the use of a tribal vernacular by persons in conversation denotes their exclusiveness: those not of the tribe or unable to understand the language are excluded from the conversation, an exclusion which may or may not have been intended by the speakers. At this level of generality it is possible to distinguish a few observed social events at which tribal and vernacular exclusiveness is not condemned and arouses no resentment. That is to say, the speakers use their vernaculars with impunity because the activities fall into a zone of 'affective neutrality' as far as inter-tribal relations are concerned.

The events at which tribal exclusiveness is accepted are various family and individual urban rites of passage which mark the birth of a child, the welcoming of a new wife to her husband's house in town, and death. The events are celebrated or mourned by immediate kin in the early stages of the rite or ceremony, and by fellow tribesmen friends of the man or woman in its later stages. Intimate occasions such as these are most conveniently restricted to at least a core of relatives and friends who know the esoteric customs involved. The occasions tend, therefore, to be conducted in the vernacular. Those of the man or woman's friends who are of a different tribe and do not speak the vernacular are inevitably excluded from a central part in the activities and, I would suggest from observation, may discreetly and voluntarily withdraw to no more than peripheral participation in the event, especially if many of the subject's kin and fellow-tribesmen are present. In conventional terms they appreciate the intimacy of the occasion. Variables altering the degree of tribal privacy attaching to the event are the status and popularity of the subject, and the proportion of his friends from other tribes to his kin and friends from his own tribe.

Though the situation is nowhere near so clear-cut as this short summary suggests, there do seem to be these special events which are recognized by neighbours of other tribes to be 'morally' and 'ritually' private and at which exclusive use of a vernacular is permitted. Though the events are 'morally' private, they are physically public, in that beer parties or dances of celebration or mourning have to be conducted outside the small houses and in full view of the many nearby neighbours of different tribes.

In other social situations, as in a women's multi-tribal gossip group or among a group of men drinking together at a local bar, use of the vernacular by a few of them may invite jocular and sometimes serious accusations of 'secrecy' and a demand that they speak Swahili, or, among a group of high-status men, English, and in a few cases, Luganda.

I have touched here on the use of vernaculars as distinct from the use of the three lingua francas. Falling between these two as media of communication are the respective dialects of persons of the same wider ethnic and linguistic group, an instance being those of the various Nilotes of Uganda and Kenya and, to a lesser extent, some of the Interlacustrine Bantu. It should not be assumed, however, that a group of, say, Luo and Alur, whose Nilotic dialects are very close, will necessarily use their respective dialects in conversation.

Case 3. An example of expressive aspects of language choice in a single ethnic context (reported)

In an interesting 'conversational arena of prestige competition' in a bar near to Nakawa, two Alur, two Jonam, and two Kenya Luo spent the evening drinking together but became involved in an argument which nearly came to blows. They were all residents of either Upper Nakawa or Naguru and had prestigeful clerical jobs in which they were required to use English. Most of their conversation had been inundated with banter and boasting about their individual statuses and achievements. This is not an unusual leisure pursuit among friends of relatively high status. The conversation was strictly in English, and indeed much of the jocular competition for prestige was to acquire credit for fluency and expression in this language. Towards the end of an otherwise pleasant evening one of the Luo was clearly emerging as the most articulate speaker of English. His jokes were witty and his light-hearted insults were always to the point. His main contender, one of the Jonam, was rapidly losing the game to him and began to suffer the also light-hearted derision of his other companions. Suddenly, without notice and to the surprise of all, the Janam took genuine offence and turned on the Luo. He accused Luo and other Kenyans of being 'so poor, and of having so little land that they have to come here to Uganda to work, but that really

Kenyans are poor men'. It is the severest of insults to call a Luo a poor man and to refer to his home country in such disparaging terms, and the Luo was on the point of returning the insult with violence. The Luo's fellow-tribesman switched from English to their own dialect and succeeded in calming him. The Alur and remaining Janam did likewise with the inflamed Janam, again in the Alur/Janam dialect.

Analysis

English is a prestige lingua franca of the *élite*. A pastime among relatively high-status friends is to drink and joke, and to tease each other about their possessions, their jobs, their 'wealth' or lack of it, their girl-friends, and their places of residence. The banter usually involves nothing more than a verbal competition, even though, as in the case, the friends could have used, at least partially, their respective dialects, if straightforward, factual communication was their only aim. The respective dialects were only resorted to when the intended light-hearted level of communication broke down and constituted a crisis among the gathering.

Some suggested findings of this case and of the preceding discussion in this section are as follows:

(1) Vernaculars should not, if possible, be used in multi-tribal contexts, either public or private, except in crisis situations or structurally similar events, such as personal or family rites of passage.

(2) In normal everyday discourse the use of a vernacular in a multi-tribal context invokes mild or more serious accusations of exclusiveness, if the speaker is perfectly well able to use a lingua franca.

(3) Members of different tribes but of the same wider language group may use a lingua franca in preference to their respective mutually intelligible dialects. A lingua franca has a special quality in being linked to the status system (e.g. English), or in connoting 'brotherhood' (e.g. Swahili) or deference (e.g. sometimes Luganda when used by non-Ganda). A lingua franca may thus be used to communicate much more than the mere transmission of verbal statement. In this respect it shows yet another parallel with the communicative power of ritual symbolism.

CONCLUSION

This is a highly condensed attempt to suggest some factors behind language choice in a specific ethnographic situation. Many of the points touched on should, in a longer paper, have been illustrated by more case material. I believe that, as in intensive sociological research, problems of language choice may be analysed on the basis of considerable material of this type. My material was what has been called 'apt and isolated illustration'. Ideally it should include 'extended cases' also.

A second methodological suggestion is that the sociological use of language may be said to have parallels with the use of other social phenomena. Affinities of language may be manipulated in a way similar to that in which ties of common culture, nationality, and religion may be used. This is the instrumental aspect of language choice. The expressive aspect of language choice has, in my view, some parallels with the expressiveness of ritual symbolism in small-scale societies. Both fulfil a need to reconcile, if only temporarily, conflicts and divisions in the community.

To have this function, the language chosen must be at least a restricted lingua franca. A restricted lingua franca seems to be a contradiction in terms. But in a community which is ethnically and linguistically heterogeneous it is possible to have a number of restricted lingua francas, the usage of each of which varies quantitatively and overlaps, so that together they cover the whole community. While exposing oneself to the accusation of arguing falsely by analogy, one might venture the suggestion that in some respects ritual symbolism in the small-scale, monolingual community has 'functions' which in a complex, urban industrial, multilingual community are performed by public usage of lingua francas. Just as a process of ritual differentiation may be linked to a process of social differentiation, so the proliferation or delimitation of lingua francas may reflect the social shifts and movements of groups and persons. The central concern in this paper has certainly been the use made of lingua francas.

I have been unable in this paper to explore the implications of 'private' and 'public' languages, 'restricted' or 'elaborated' codes (Bernstein, 1965), which, in a multilingual community, are probably very complicated. I have looked at language choice, firstly, from the point of view of the individual in dyadic relations (Case 1), and secondly, as an expression of group activity (Cases 2 and 3). Though my particular cases dealt with the converse, it is, of course, possible to find the instrumental aspect of language choice in group activity, and the expressive aspect in dyadic relations. Dyadic and group relations, and instrumentality and expressiveness, are perhaps useful preliminary concepts in the the study of language choice in a multilingual community. The additional Parsonian notion of affective neutrality may perhaps be used conveniently to refer to zones of social activity in which vernaculars are used with impunity in multi-tribal contexts. Otherwise the choice of language used in social interactions between people who live near each other other but come from different tribes and sometimes, but not necessarily, from different linguistic groups, may be determined by norms deriving from the prevailing political context or from the residential context. These contexts, and others not discussed here, such as workplace, formally organized recreation, and others, are extremely arbitrarily defined and no more than conveniently abstracted spheres of social life, the boundaries of which are at best blurred. The norms of many or all of these contexts may be present in any interaction, group, or dyadic, but the cases suggest that the norms of one context emerge as dominant and so determine the choice of language in particular situations.

REFERENCES

Bernstein, B.
(1965) A Socio-Linguistic Approach to Social Learning, in *Penguin Survey of the Social Sciences 1965*. Penguin Books, London.

Gluckman, M.
(1955) *Politics, Law and Ritual in Tribal Society*. Blackwell, Oxford.

Parkin, D. J.
(1969) *Neighbours and Nationals in an African City Ward*. Routledge and Kegan Paul, London, and California University Press.

Southall, A., and Gutkind, P.
(1956) *Townsmen in the Making*. East African Studies No. 9. East African Institute of Social Research, Kampala.

Turner, V. W.
(1957) *Schism and Continuity in an African Society*. Manchester University Press, Manchester.

XXI. Multilingualism in an African Urban Centre: The Lubumbashi Case

EDGAR C. POLOMÉ

Multilingualism pre-dates Westernization in Central Africa. In pre-colonial days intertribal relations had already led to the development of various contact vernaculars which merely spread farther into the country with the European penetration, as they were adopted by the colonizers for economical and administrative purposes. A typical example of a pre-colonial multilingual community was the capital of the Garenganze kingdom of Msiri in the last quarter of the nineteenth century. Its population consisted of several thousand people from all parts of Central Africa: baSanga, baLamba, baUshi, baLunda, baBemba, baLuba, belonging to the areas the muYeke conqueror had cut out of the territory formerly governed by the *Kazembe* (governor) of the Mwato Yamvo (Lunda emperor) or taken over during his campaigns against the baLuba; Arabs, waNyamwezi, waSwahili traders and immigrants from across Lake Tanganyika, as well as oviMbundu and Luvale from Angola. The town was an important slave-market to which many traders came from all directions. At one time Msiri especially encouraged the prosperous commerce in ivory and slaves with the Portuguese on the West coast; he even took the daughter of a former Portuguese officer in Bihe as his *Ihanga* ('first wife'), and the Arab traders soon had to strive to neutralize her influence on Msiri. As a result of the constant flow of trade caravans from East and West, Portuguese could be heard in Katanga, beside the more common Swahili from the East Coast, in which Msiri was himself quite proficient. Another important source of revenue for Msiri beside slaves and ivory was copper; all the digging and processing was directly controlled by the Bayeke. This mineral wealth was one of the main sources of the competition of the colonial powers for control of Katanga, which ended with the occupation of the Garenganze kingdom by the Belgians. The centre of their administration was, however, shifted to the South, where the 'Mine de l'Etoile' became one of the first urban nuclei in the Katanga mining district. In 1906 the Union Minière du Haut-Katanga was created, one year after the first convoy of ox-carts brought heavy mining equipment from Benguela on the West coast to Katanga. A copper-processing plant was then built alongside the Lubumbashi river a few miles from the 'Mine d'Etoile'. Very soon, Emile Wangermée, the head of the Comité Spécial du Katanga, which was administering the territory, had plans laid out for building the first colonial town to be founded in Katanga. In September 1909 the Belgian Government approved them and decided to call the place Elisabethville and to develop it as the administrative and economic centre of Katanga. On 27 September the railroad from Rhodesia reached the new town and connected it with South Africa and, somewhat later, with Beira in Mozambique. From then on the city grew at a tremendous rate due to the immigration of thousands of Europeans and tens of thousands of Africans, though the process of growth was not always smooth: the great companies—the Union Minière and the Katanga railway—discouraged their European employees from staying in Katanga until the depression of the thirties, when they began hiring Europeans on the spot instead of bringing them over from Belgium on limited-term contracts; at that time improved public health conditions made it possible for the employees to have their families stay with them: secondary schools were opened for European children, and the demographic pattern of the European community changed drastically, with a considerable increase in the population under 20 and over 40, as many Belgian residents began to regard Elisabethville as their home. As a background to this transformation in the urban picture the successful development of rural enterprises supplying fresh milk and agricultural produce to the town under the sponsorship of the Comité Spécial du Katanga was of primary importance. The first cattle and the first colonists arrived in 1911–12 and experimental farms were established; after the First World War the whole enterprise was in jeopardy for lack of financial resources and because the local Africans competed with the settlers in the growing of vegetables for the urban market. By the thirties the major problems impeding a prosperous development of the agricultural areas around the town had been solved, and the farms were able to supply fresh vegetables and dairy products to the steadily growing numbers of African as well as European inhabitants of the city. Meanwhile, the settlement of African peasantry in newly cleared land was encouraged so that a lively marketing economy between town and country developed.

Thus, the growth of the mining industry, the development of the communication system, especially after the establishment of the railway links with Port-Francqui (1928) and with Lobito in Angola (1931), and the steady supply of the necessary goods for a modern city by a growing agricultural belt and the burgeoning of diversified secondary industries ensured the boom of Elisabethville after the Depression.

In order to understand its linguistic situation it is necessary to examine how its population grew. Fortunately, the recent studies of Bruce Fetter on immigrants to Elisabethville provide us with valuable data on this matter: here again the policies of the Union Minière determined the pattern of development; until the thirties the Africans lived in restricted workers' camps, and only those whose employers could not afford to provide such accommodation stayed in the 'cité indigène', where conditions were much worse. In 1931 the colonial administration constituted this 'cité' as a new political unit called 'Centre extra-coutumier', placing its inhabitants under a special legal status independent of traditional African law. Some amount of self-government was granted to them: they had special urban courts of law and even a town council under Belgian supervision. This 'Centre extra-coutumier' became the rallying point of Africans from all parts of Katanga and beyond and had a very diversified ethnic composition, in contrast with the camps where the workers came from the various areas in which the Union Minière had conducted its man-power recruiting campaigns. Until 1925 the population of these camps was merely transient: thousands of workers were supplied by British companies from Northern Rhodesia across the Luapula river, but they were under strict contracts preventing them from settling down in Katanga; their numbers were more than matched by

Congolese recruits who came mainly from the Haut-Luapula, Lomani, Tanganyika-Moëro, and Lulua districts of Katanga. Those from the Haut-Luapula were from the ethnic groups that constituted the core of the old Garenganze kingdom (baYeke, baLamba, baUshi, baSanga); from the Lomani came the Luba-Kasai, the Songye, and Kanyoka; the Tanganyika-Moëro area provided a multitude of tribal groups, among which the largest were the Luba-Katanga, the Tabwa, the Songye, and the Lunda Kazembe; the Lulua districts which constituted Western Katanga brought mostly baLunda and baCokwe. While, at first, the mining company also applied the non-resident status to them, the labour shortage of the middle twenties induced the personnel service to try and make experienced workers stay in the city; they were now offered longer contracts and encouraged to bring their wives and families to live with them. But even so, the whole Katangese territory within 300 miles of the city had been practically depleted of available man-power by previous recruitment, so that new, more distant, recruiting areas had to be set up in Maniema, the eastern Kasayi, and the trusteeship territories of Ruanda and Urundi. With the change in policy new services had to be provided for the African population, especially public health and social assistance centres and schools, which helped to integrate the stabilized labour force in the city. In the first half of the thirties the economic depression stopped this development rather abruptly; recruitment ceased in Rhodesia and was practically never resumed; the 'centre extra-coutumier' lost almost half its population, which declined from 11,399 in 1929 to 6,282 in 1934. Most of the Africans leaving town, nevertheless remained in the area, scratching a living as menial help in rural enterprises in the neighbouring villages or settling down temporarily in close-by chefferies. When the economic life returned to normal they came back to the city, whereas the Union Minière recruited increasing numbers of Kasaians via the Port-Francqui railway. By 1945 they constituted 60 per cent of the Union Minière camp, but only 29 per cent of the population of the 'centre extra-coutumier'. By then the basis for the further development of Elisabethville had been solidly laid: an increasing proportion of Africans were firmly settled down there, and the numbers of locally born children grew steadily on school enrolment rosters. In the meantime the Belgian population had also become more stabilized: after the Depression Belgian boys born in the Congo outnumbered the foreign born by about 2 to 1. A majority of these Belgians working in the mining industry came from the Walloon part of the country on account of experience gained in the Belgian mines in that area; the administration was also essentially French-speaking; however, especially after the Second World War, the percentage of Flemish-speaking Belgians increased so considerably that special sections with Dutch as the language of the curriculum could be created in the local schools. As regards the non-Belgian expatriate population, it consisted essentially of Ashkenazic and Sephardic Jews (from central and eastern Europe and from the Mediterranean respectively), Italians (mainly from three villages near Vercelli), and Greeks from the Dodecanese islands. The Jewish community played an extremely important part in the social and economic life of the city; the rabbi of Elisabethville had jurisdiction over the whole of Central Africa. The Greeks were also quite prosperous, and their church was also the main Greek Orthodox religious centre for the whole area. British and South Africans who had been numerous before the Depression mostly moved to the Zambian Copperbelt during those difficult years, while the other foreigners stayed on. Before Independence a considerable number of Belgian settlers liquidated their businesses and the European population experienced a sharp drop, from which it only partly recovered in the middle sixties after the turmoil of the Katanga rebellion. On the other hand, the African population has considerably increased; thus in the camps of the Union Minière alone the number of school-going children has trebled over the last fifteen years.

From the background of this historical sketch of the development of Elisabethville, to which the African name Lubumbashi has now been restored, it is easier to understand the linguistic situation prevailing in the town. From the Belgian administration Katanga has inherited French as the language of all official documents, in keeping with the Constitution of the Democratic Republic of the Congo. French is also the language of the curriculum in all the schools of the town, and the Katanga *élite* makes it a point of honour to display its command of the language in public. However, in spite of the prestige position of French, Swahili is used widely on various occasions: the original text of documents for the public is composed in French, but when posted it is always accompanied by a translation in a form of Swahili which strives to approach the standard written language of the East Coast, known to the older generation through schooling in the Catholic and Protestant missions, but which shows definite features of the local Swahili creole, as well as glaring examples of un-Swahili literal translations from the French. Official sign-plates, e.g. in the Post Office, are bilingual. While educated people will use French in the various offices of the public services, the bulk of the population will resort to the local variety of Swahili to conduct its business there. In the shops in the centre of the town French may often be used as a starter, but every shopkeeper or craftsman will readily use Swahili whenever the customer chooses to switch to this language. As a matter of fact, conversations with constant switching, but prevailing use of Swahili can often be heard in most places along the central avenue de l'Etoile. In primary schools, where French is used from the very start as the language of the curriculum, the teacher will give explanations in Swahili until the students become proficient enough to enable him to resort exclusively to French (which usually takes two to three years). Swahili is currently used in political speeches addressed to the bulk of the population, and political pamphlets were already written in this language under the colonial regime, e.g. the appeal of the voters to the Confederation of the Katangese Associations (CONAKAT), under the leadership of Moise Tshombe before Independence. During the elections to the town council in 1959 the local settlers' association also appealed to the African electorate in Swahili, and their pamphlets were distributed in three languages: French, Dutch, and Swahili. The Mouvement National Congolais of Patrice Lumumba, however, resorted to French in its propaganda, whereas Jason Sendwe's Balubakat, which appealed more specifically to the tribal solidarity of the baLuba and their associates used the Katangese variety of Luba. Swahili is also currently used over the radio, and programmes with local pop-singers are extremely popular over the whole of Central and East Africa. The Swahili Press is, however, very limited: a weekly paper *Uhaki* (Truth) is practically the only regular publication with extensive texts in the language; the Union Minière used to publish a monthly paper—*Mwana Shaba* (The Child of Copper)—with local information of interest to its workers, which was mainly written in Swahili, but contained items in other languages commonly used by its labour force; in the middle sixties it had the widest circulation of any African-language paper in the Congo, with a run of 36,000 copies. The daily Press is exclusively in French. Plays are sometimes performed in Swahili: at the end of the colonial period the governor of the province actually tried to promote original writing as well as the performance of dramatic works in the language, and some very interesting texts were produced, e.g. an adaptation of the French medieval play '*La Farce de Maître Pathelin*' to Katangese situations. As a religious language, Swahili is mainly used in Protestant missions, where the services are usually conducted in this language.

As regards current conversation, Swahili would be mostly heard in the African market; it would prevail in the laundry, baby-care, and sewing sections of the 'foyer social', especially when expatriates would help the African women in their various activities; the same would be true in the dispensary and the hospital. In general, whenever Lubumbashi town-dwellers come into contact with other people in buses, small shops, cafés, and other public places Swahili is the language they naturally resort to, unless they meet fellow-tribesmen.

Tribal languages are indeed used essentially within the family group and wider tribal community, but with the growing rate of intertribal marriage among the younger generation this situation is changing rapidly, since Lubumbashi townspeople of different tribal origin will normally resort to Swahili or, at a higher level of education, maybe also to French. Accordingly, children born of such marriages will be raised in Swahili or, possibly, partly at least, in French, and will sometimes have no more than a passive knowledge of the respective tribal languages of their parents' family. The statistics on pages 372–73, covering a fairly substantial set of students in a teachers' training college and secondary school in the African suburb of Katuba in 1963, may illustrate the situation in the African community with the rising generation.

However, the Swahili spoken by the Lubumbashi townspeople is not the East Coast Swahili but a creolized form resulting from the adaption of the Swahili lingua franca introduced in the days of Msiri by the trading caravans from the East, and henceforth as a contact language with the local Africans by the Belgian colonial administration, as well as the foremen in the mining industry. This Swahili shows typical features of a pidginized language: phonological changes under the influence of the prevailing local Bantu languages, mainly Luba and Bemba; simplification of the morphology (especially disruption of the concord system and reduction of the conjugation to a few basic tenses); substantial reduction of the vocabulary. But, having been adopted as first language by a growing number of townsmen, it is being relexicalized with local Bantu words and borrowing from French. It also bears traces of the various language contacts typical of the area, e.g. a few Portuguese loans like *manteka* for 'butter' and a considerable number of technical terms from English, due to the influence of Rhodesian labour during the early period of development of the mining industry. The Flemish is extremely limited (e.g. *pazopo* 'pay attention'), but the influence of French is all-pervasive.

Thus, the linguistic situation in Lubumbashi is a clear reflection of the historical growth of the town under the colonial regime. The agglomeration of considerable masses of Africans of various origins has made the use of a lingua franca imperative: the obvious language for this was Swahili, and as a consequence of progressive detribalization in the urban context, it is gradually becoming the first language of an increasing number of townspeople. The local dialects are, however, still very much alive, and only loss of contact with the family back in the villages and more general intertribal marriage instead of the still prevailing habit of seeking a wife in the home region of the parents will threaten them seriously. The persistence of French as the prestige language may ultimately lead to the formation of a predominantly French-speaking *élite*, but in view of the frequent association between the various social levels, bilingualism with Swahili as the second language will undoubtedly be maintained by such a group. In view of the ousting of Swahili from the curriculum, it is to be feared that the knowledge of standard Swahili, to which some of the younger generation were at least

Language spoken	No. of students	At home				With friends				With strangers			
Tribal origin	475	*French*	*Swahili*	*Tribal language*	*Other*	*French*	*Swahili*	*Tribal language*	*Other*	*French*	*Swahili*	*Tribal anguage*	*Other*
Luba and Related Language Groups	303												
Luba (Katanga)	19	3	6	15	—	17	9	3	1	11	11	3	1
Luba (Kasayi)	80	7	16	75	—	60	49	4	5	59	44	—	5
Kanyoka	8	—	5	3	—	8	3	—	—	2	5	—	1
Kete	1	—	—	1	—	—	1	—	—	1	1	—	—
Samba (baZela)	10	1	5	6	5	7	5	1	2	7	5	—	1
Sanga	9	—	3	6	—	7	9	—	—	5	4	—	—
Songye	12	2	8	4	—	10	6	—	—	10	6	—	—
Kabinda	13	1	6	8	1	12	7	—	—	6	7	1	2
Hemba	75	7	50	34	—	63	27	1	1	49	39	—	1
(no further specification)	76	9	20	50	—	60	44	5	—	49	46	2	1
Bemba and Related Groups	56												
Lamba	1	—	—	1	—	1	—	—	—	—	1	—	—
Aushi	2	—	—	2	1	1	1	—	—	1	1	—	—
Tabwa	19	—	11	13	—	16	13	—	2	10	11	—	—
Kaonde	1	—	—	1	—	—	1	—	—	1	—	—	—
(no further specification)	33	1	17	25	—	26	18	—	1	18	24	1	1

Lunda and Related Groups	105												
Cokwe	12	2	4	10	—	9	6	—	—	7	8	—	—
Ndembo	5	1	1	4	—	4	2	—	—	3	3	—	—
Minungo	2	—	—	2	—	1	2	—	—	1	1	—	—
(no further specification)	86	9	32	64	—	63	53	7	6	60	54	6	9
Lesser Groups	9												
kaBwari	1	1	1	—	—	1	1	—	—	1	—	—	—
baYeke	3	1	1	2	—	3	2	—	—	1	1	—	—
Mambwe	1	—	1	—	—	1	—	—	—	—	1	—	—
Kalanga (Rega)	1	1	1	—	—	1	—	—	—	—	1	—	—
Bangu-Bangu	1	—	—	—	—	1	—	—	—	—	1	—	—
BaNgala	1	—	—	1	—	—	1	—	—	1	—	—	—
WaGenya	1	—	1	1	—	1	1	—	—	1	1	—	—
From Outside the Congo	2												
Ruanda	1	—	—	1	—	1	1	—	—	—	1	—	—
Malawi	1	—	—	1	1	1	1	—	—	1	1	—	—

Notes to the Table of Statistics

1. The higher totals of the languages actually spoken reflect the fact that several students list two or more languages as currently spoken in the social context under reference. Lower totals indicate that some students left one of the questions unanswered.

2. The other language spoken with strangers or friends is usually English, but occasionally also another Congolese language, e.g. liNgala, kiKongo.

temporarily exposed in primary schools, may deteriorate even further, in view of the fact that very little literature remains available in the language, and that the means of mass communication do not strive at all to conform systematically with the East Coast standard. A study in more depth of the Lubumbashi situation would, however, be required to assess to what degree the 'mother tongue' regresses among the younger generation, who still, as a rule, identify themselves with the tribe of their father, even if they no longer speak his language. A detailed study would have to be made of the use of the various languages (French, Swahili, tribal languages) according to the age groups, the economic and social background, the personality of the people to whom one speaks, and the circumstances in which the conversation takes place. For Swahili speakers, variations of style would also have to be examined according to the person or persons addressed in private or in public, and the contrast between the spoken and written forms would require careful investigation. Besides, the specific competence of the speakers in the various languages should be measured by adequate testing. With such data, a better assessment of multilingualism in Lubumbashi should be achieved.

BIBLIOGRAPHICAL NOTE

An extensive survey of the sources for the history of Lubumbashi is to be found in the note of Bruce Fetter: 'Elisabethville'—Bibliographical Supplement No. 7, to *African Urban Notes* (June 1968), 33 pages (mimeographed).

On the history of Elisabethville (Lubumbashi), see especially Bruce S. Fetter, *Elisabethville and Lubumbashi: the segmentary growth of a colonial city* (Ph. Diss., University of Wisconsin, 1968, 332 pages). Further important sources on the development of the town and the African settlement are: Jacques Denis, *Le phénomène urbain en Afrique centrale* (Brussels: Académie Royale des Sciences Coloniales, 1958); J. Benoît, *La population Africaine à Elisabethville à la fin de 1957* (Elisabethville: Centre d'Étude des Problèmes Sociaux Indigènes, 1958); Marc Richelle, *Aspects psychologiques de l'acculturation* (Elisabethville: Centre d'Étude des Problèmes Sociaux Indigènes, 1960); Paul Minon, *Katuba. Étude quantitative d'une communanté urbaine africaine* (Elisabethville: Centre d'Étude des Problèmes Sociaux Indigènes, 1960); Marcel Anselin, *De inlandse middenstand te Elizabethstad* (Elisabethville: Centre d'Étude des Problèmes Sociaux Indigènes, 1960); Bruce Fetter, 'Immigrants to Elisabethville: Their Origins and Aims', in *African Urban Notes.* Vol. III, No. 2 (August 1968), pp. 17–34.

On precolonial and early Katanga, see especially Auguste Verbeken, *Msiri. Roi du Garenganze* (Bruxelles: Louis Cuypers, 1956); *** *Comité Spécial du Katanga 1900–1950* (Bruxelles: Louis Cuypers, 1950).

On the linguistic situation in Katanga, cf. Maria Leblanc, 'Evolution Linguistique et Relations Humaines', in *Zaïre*, Vol. IX, No. 8 (1954), pp. 787–99; my articles: 'Cultural Languages and Contact Vernaculars in the Republic of the Congo', in *Texas Studies in Literature and Language*, Vol. IV, No. 4 (Winter 1963), pp. 499–511; 'The Choice of an Official Language in the Democratic Republic of the Congo', in J. A. Fishman, C. A. Ferguson, and J. Das Gupta (ed.), *Language Problems of Developing Nations* (New York: John Wiley & Sons, 1968), pp. 295–311; 'The Position of Swahili and Other Bantu Languages in Katanga', to appear in *Texas Studies in Literature and Language* (1969); 'Lubumbashi Swahili', to appear in the *Journal of African Languages* (1969).

XXII. Cross Cultural Meanings and Multilingualism

AIDAN SOUTHALL

Despite the amount of effort which anthropologists have put into ethnographic studies, there can be no question that they have conveyed to the informed public a very unfortunate and erroneous impression of the nature of cultural differences in African countries. They have allowed continued use of the concept of tribe in a falsely reified sense and have failed to make it sufficiently known that many of the units so referred to are actually of recent, colonial, and administrative origin rather than primeval traditional entities.[1] As an antidote, I would stress the importance of studying cultural borderlands and transition zones within nations, recognizing that they have no long-term unity. The borderland or transition zone to be explored by way of illustration here is that between Bantu and Nilotic speakers; the Alur and their Nilotic neighbours, with extensions to the Sudanic Madi and Lugbara, on the one hand, and the Nyoro and their Bantu neighbours, on the other.

The concept of *Jok Rubanga*[2] is symbolic of the marriage of Nilotic and Bantu culture. Forms of the term *jok* (*jwok*, *juok*), are common to nearly all the Lwoo-speaking peoples (Alur, Junam, Acholi, Lang'o, Palwo, Padhola, Kenya Luo, Sudan Luo) and even the Anuak, Shilluk, Nuer (*joagh*), and Lotuko (*ajyok*). On the other hand, *Rubanga* appears in Alur, Acholi, Madi, Lugbara, Bunyoro, Ankole, and in phonetically modified form in Buganda.

Most of the literature interprets *jok* as having the general meaning of spirit, including both single and multiple mani-

[1] Southall (1970). 'The Illusion of Tribe', *Journal of Asian and African Studies*, V, 1 and 2, January–April, deals with this matter in detail.

[2] For these and other terms see Table 1.

Schematic Map: Uganda and its Neighbours

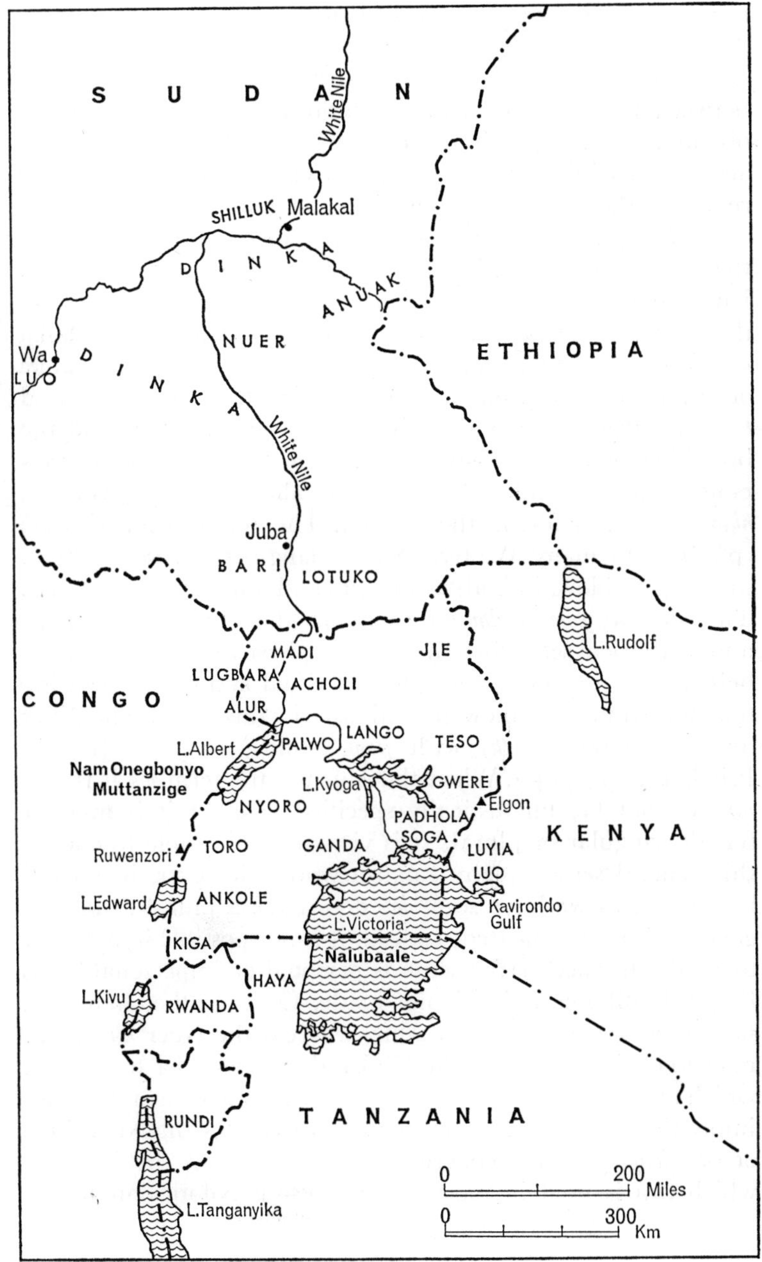

festations (Evans-Pritchard, 1956, p. 160). It is by far the most important religious term common to all Western Nilotes. Among several of these peoples a particular manifestation of *jok* is more prominent than others. Sometimes the connection between such prominent manifestations and *jok* is ambiguous, obscure, and impossible to define with certainty. Thus, in his account of Dinka religion Lienhardt uses the word Divinity to represent the Dinka *nhialic*, which is actually the locative form of *nhial* (sky).[1] It is clear that for the Dinka, *nhialic* falls within the compass of *jok*, which Lienhardt translates as 'Power'. All Dinka divinities and powers are *jok* (pl. *jaak*). On the other hand, the Nuer use *kwoth* (pl. *kuth*) as the equivalent of the Dinka *nhialic*, or highest form of divinity, and also for the whole range of *jok*. *Kwoth* is compared by Evans-Pritchard to *spiritus* and *pneuma*, suggesting 'both the intangible quality of air and the breathing or blowing out of air'.[2] The form of *kwoth* corresponding to the Dinka *nhialic* ('in the above, or sky'), is *kwoth nhial* ('spirit, or air, in the above'). The verbal form of *kwoth* (pl. *kuth*) in many Western Nilotic languages is *kudhu* (*kuto*), meaning to blow, in both a concrete and a metaphorical sense. The Alur say *yamu kudhu ber*, meaning 'the wind blows well' in a metaphorical sense for spiritual and physical health and well-being. They devote a great deal of ritual activity to ensuring that the wind does blow propitiously in this sense. The Nuer also link God (*kwoth*) with *jiom* (wind), cf. *yamu* (Evans-Pritchard, 1956, (4)). When the Alur use the term *jok* it is not, and cannot be, linguistically specified whether it is male or female, singular or plural. It is virtually impossible to convey this general sense by any English word. However, in related languages, as we have seen, *jok* does have a plural form, but gender is never indicated. Indeed, it is not possible in any way to establish whether the sense is personal or impersonal. This linguistic differentiation is not made. On the other hand, *jok* has no concrete referent in Alur, whereas the Nuer *kwoth* can refer to ordinary air and the Dinka *nhialic* can refer to the sky, which appears visible to men, though its locative form does also imply the presence of something else there. But the Nuer form of *jok* (*joagh*) has the concrete meaning of 'back, behind', for which *cien* is used in most other Western Nilotic languages.

[1] (1961, p. 29). [2] (1956, p. 1).

There is a symbolic correspondence between the fact that in Nuer *joagh* means both 'ghost' and 'back', while it is believed that ghosts ought to keep their backs to the living, i.e. stay away. *Cien* has the same double meaning in Dinka and Alur. 'Behind' is further associated with the ghosts in the Nuer euphemism 'to go behind', meaning to die (op. cit., p. 161).

We must now turn to the context of *Rubanga*. The term stands out from the Nilotic speech of the Alur as non-Nilotic in sound and seemingly Bantu in form. Among the Acholi neighbours of the Alur the form is usually *Lubang'a*. Both Wright (1940) and Crazzolara (1938) held that *Lubang'a* was brought to Acholi from Bunyoro by the early missionaries and became a substitute for *Jok*. But Boccassino (1939) found the usual attributes of *Jok* authentically attached to *Lubang'a*. Indeed, Crazzolara (1950, 62) says that 'mother elephant' in the famous myth of lost spear and bead, which accounts for the primary division between the major Alur, Acholi, and Nyoro Bito dynasties, 'was a kind of *Rubang'a* or *Jok*'. As I have described elsewhere (1969, 255–6) *Jok Rubanga* is the supreme ritual embodiment of a number of major Alur chiefdoms. It is believed to take the form of earth from the Alur homeland, contained in a pot with twin necks. There is a further strong association with the mythical twins who stand at the apex of the common genealogy of these Alur chiefdoms. If *Jok Rubanga* is the embodiment of the political structure of chiefdoms, *Jok Matar* (White Jok) (cf. V. W. Turner, 1962) is the embodiment of the lineage structure.

It is necessary to stress again that we are here all the time dealing with elements which transcend conventional cultural and linguistic boundaries and which are in this sense fundamentally trans-cultural, multilingual elements. This phenomenon is familiar enough in historically written languages, as in the derivation of concepts in Anglo-Saxon and Germanic languages from Greek or Latin roots, or the circulation of certain concepts between Hindi, Persian, Arabic, and other Semitic languages. But hardly any systematic work has been done on comparable phenomena among languages until recently unwritten. The result is that their mutual exclusiveness as vehicles of thought is greatly exaggerated. It is easy to jump to the conclusion that *Rubanga* (*Lubang'a*, *Lubanga*) is a Nyoro Bantu word, yet there is widespread evidence for its ancient occurrence among scattered groups whose linguistic antecedents were either Nilotic Lwoo or Sudanic Madi. Thus it appears as a personal name in genealogies of the Alur of Acer from six to eight or more generations ago (Crazzolara, 1954, p. 413). It appears as the most remote primal ancestor of the Logo people of Agooro in North Acholi, whose oral tradition derives them from farther north in the Sudan (Crazzolara, 1954, p. 513). It appears again as a clan name among the Paboo of North Acholi (Crazzolara, 1954, p. 477) and (in the form *Nyarubanga*) as the name of the spirit shrine of the Palabek chiefdom of north-eastern Acholi (Girling, 1960, p. 226).

More remarkably, Williams (1949, p. 203) records that among the north-eastern Madi of Moyo *Rabanga* is the name both of their principal divinity and of the earth. Further confirmation comes from Middleton's statement (1960, p. 69) that the Lugbara lineage shrines for the ghosts of more distant ancestors are usually called *rogbo*, but also *ridi* or *rudu* and that in some areas *ridi* is also called *orubangi*, which he relates to the Madi word *Rubangi*, God, while *rudu* is used for ordinary ghost shrines in Madi. Male sorcerers are said to be a recent introduction in Lugbara and are called *elojua*, which Middleton derives from 'the Alur *lojwok*, a magician' (op. cit., pp. 245–6). Actually the cognates are Alur *jajok* (pl. *jojogi*), Acholi *lajok* (pl. *lojogi*), Kenya Luo *jajuok* (pl. *jojuogi*). The *elojua* use poison from an onion or lily-like bulb *ojoo*, which seems to be the bulb which the Alur call *lenga*. Alur chiefs smear its juice on their stools to summon all sorcerers into their presence so that they may be identified and controlled. Crazzolara (1960, p. 305) gives the Lugbara form *ɔ̀dzɔ́* for the lily bulb, together with the Terego (East Lugbara) form *torobangi* (*toro-bángì*), while the form *ɔ́dzɔ́ɔ* is translated diviner, magician, medicine-man, and midwife. *ɔ̀dzɔ́-ɔ̀dzɔɔá* (op. cit., p. 306) are *ɔ̀dzɔ́* leaves and mysterious or magic charms in the form of fruits or crushed leaves thrown at a person and causing magic disease and initiation to sorcery itself. *ɔ̀dzɔ̀* is the craft of divination, and with so many varied forms one wonders whether the whole complex can be of such recent introduction. With *dzɔ̀dzɔ̀kì* meaning phantom, spectre, ghostly appearance, we are recognizably back to the Nilotic form *jajok*, and indeed Crazzolara quotes a Lugbara phrase incorporating the term which he glosses 'it is the Aluur (and some other people are believed to have this capacity) who can transform themselves into phantoms (i.e. by night)' (loc. cit., p. 225). A complementary borrowing by the Alur seems to be the incorporation into their *Jok* cult of the Lugbara *orindi* (the soul). 'Linguistically it is a compound of the words *ori*, ghost, and the intensive particle, *-ndi*: so that it means "the essence of the ghost"' (Middleton, 1960, p. 30). '*Ava* (breath) and *orindi* leave the body together at death, but are distinct' (ibid.). The Alur *Jok Rindi* is believed to be a powerful medicine kept by chiefs and capable of curing ear infections (Southall, 1956, p. 374).

Can this distribution be explained by the intermittent movement of refugee or splinter groups from among the Lwoo or Madi and Lugbara between one another and into the sphere of Nyoro cultural influence and back again, or, on the other hand, by the settling among the distant Lwoo or Madi of prestigeful yet refugee or splinter groups from within the Nyoro sphere? The ethnographic and linguistic record remains too incomplete to permit any reliable conclusions. It is true that many historical movements of this sort are referred to in the rich, but unsystematic account of the oral traditions of these peoples by Crazzolara (1950–54) and elsewhere. In any case we are forced to accept a cross-cultural, multilingual circulation, exchange and metamorphosis of terms and concepts which it seems highly unsatisfactory to dismiss as merely fortuitous. Are we to regard such exchanges as simply the product of particular historical circumstances in which splinter groups have moved to and fro across linguistic and cultural boundaries? Or should we rather see such exchanges as a necessary product of the juxtaposition and interaction of societies of a certain structural type? I incline to the latter view, but it requires further demonstration.

Accepting the widespread and ancient occurrence of various forms of the *Rubanga* concept among Lwoo- and Madi-speaking peoples, we must return to its position among the Bantu speakers. The axis of contact between the Lwoo and Madi, on the one hand, and the Bantu, on the other, lies principally between the Nyoro and the Alur. This is partly because my evidence for the Alur is best. They were the immediate neighbours of the Nyoro across Lake Albert and were in communication with them along the Nile through the Junam, who appear to have regarded themselves as Alur until the present century. The Palwo groups in North Bunyoro and South Acholi form an equally important bridge, but they were severely disturbed by the sleeping-sickness epidemic early this century, and adequate information for them is lacking.

While *Rubanga* occupies a very prominent position in the religious system of the Alur, this is certainly not the impression conveyed by the accounts we have of the Nyoro religious system. The meaning of *Rubanga* is given as 'the *omucwezi* of twins' (Davis, 1952, p. 147). This connection is quite clear in Roscoe's account, although he himself seems unaware of it. '*Lubanga*, the god of healing, was the god to whom the pastoral and agricultural people resorted for help in any sickness. His temple had a strong stockade of growing trees. When a suppliant went he took a pot of beer in which was a drinking-tube. The medium sucked a little of the beer from the tube and squirted it from his mouth on each side of the temple' (Roscoe, 1923, p. 24). At the great festival for the removing of twins from seclusion 'the chief medicine-man' (*Kibandwa Lubanga*) (op. cit., p. 169) must plant four branches of the sacred trees at the place where the twins are laid between the rival parties of their paternal and maternal relatives. This place is called *Ekibare kya Lubanga* (op. cit., p. 254). Since *Kibandwa* is a nominal form of the verb *kubandwa*, which means 'to practice divination, be possessed' (Davis, 1952, p. 4), we are forced to identify *Kibandwa Lubanga*, 'the chief medicine-man', as the medium referred to in the previous passage describing the temple of *Lubanga*. In conformation of this Beattie (1962, p. 2) refers to 'the *mbandwa* spirit *Rubanga*, one of the most powerful of the traditional *cwezi* spirits, and especially concerned with twin birth'. The *-bandwa* root is consciously echoed by the Alur. They refer to the acolytes and assistants of a medium, who have themselves been possessed and who enjoy participating, dancing, and even going into trance at subsequent séances—*mon abende*. *Mon* is the irregular plural of *dhako*, meaning woman, or wife. However, the sense here seems to be figurative, suggesting 'wives of *Jok* (God)' without necessarily being female in sex, though in fact many of them are. *Abende* does not seem to have other forms in Alur and is more likely a modified form of the Nyoro *-bandwa*, as was clearly implied by an Alur who said in discussing the matter with me: '*mon abende, gin abende, gi-bandwa*', thus straddling the two languages: '*mon abende*, they are *abende*, they become possessed'.[1]

Strangely enough, Roscoe does not include *Rubanga* in his list of the nineteen *Cwezi* (op. cit., p. 22).[2] He represents *Ruhanga* as the supreme deity, creator, and father of mankind. The *Cwezi*, 'though regarded as immortal and almost divine, were completely subordinate to *Ruhanga*, whose immediate descendants they were. After living as men in the country for many years these *Bachwezi* suddenly departed, leaving behind them their priests, who could communicate with them and obtain blessing and favours from them' (op. cit., p. 21). 'Each of the *Bachwezi* had one or more representatives who were the *Bandwa* (sing. *Mandwa*) or priests of the nation, and either claimed to be themselves mediums for the *Bachwezi* or were accompanied by mediums whose utterances they communicated to the people. A clan had always one particular *Muchwezi* to whom its members applied in difficulties through his priest. Though a shrine might be built to a *Muchwezi* in any part of the country where offerings were made to him, each had a principal shrine where his priest dwelt' (op. cit., p. 22).[3] On the other hand, *Ruhanga* had no priesthood and no temple, he was 'regarded as having retired from active participation in the affairs of the world which he had created' (ibid.). However, *Ruhanga* 'and, more frequently, *Enkya* were called upon by the people in distress or need; prayers were made to them in the open, with hands and eyes raised upwards' (op. cit., p. 21). So also the head of a Nuer household may pray to God (*kwoth*) 'standing or squatting with his eyes turned towards heaven and his arms outstretched from

[1] *Ekibare* appears as *kibali*, e-, n., spirit shrine (Davis, 1952, p. 65). The better spelling would probably be *kibaale*. Thus *ekibaare kya Rubanga* means 'the shrine of *Rubanga*'. In the Gwere language, which resembles Nyoro in some ways and Ganda in others, *kibaale* has the same sense, with *malubaale* meaning 'diviners', also called *baswezi*. The place of the shrine of Kibuka in Mawokota is Mbale (sc. *mbaale*), and there was actually a god of this name according to Roscoe (1911, p. 316), 'the god Mbale had his temple at Mbale in Buddu'.

[2] According to others there were only nine *Cwezi* (Needham, 1967, p. 435). There is great inconsistency in the various lists of names given.

[3] Cf. Fallers, M.C. (1960, p. 69), where the relation of *balubaale* to former heroes, to their clans, shrines, and mediums (*bandwa*) is described for Buganda in very similar terms.

the elbows, moving his hands, palms uppermost, up and down' (Evans-Pritchard, 1956, p. 22).

Evans-Pritchard has insisted with great delicacy that the Nuer do not think that God is air, simply because they address God by a term which has the meaning of air, but rather that they think God is in the air and manifests himself through it

Table 1

Language Data

The order follows the order of relevance in the text as far as possible. Most Nyoro words are taken from Davis (1952) and Maddox (1902), Ganda words from Kitching and Blackledge (1925) or from the other references cited. Crazzolara (1938, 1960) and Savage (1955) are also used. Miss Rebecca Nyonyintono helped me with some points in Luganda, which is her first language.

Nyoro:	*-kya*, v.i., be over, pass (rain or darkness), clear up (rain); dawn; *obu-ire bu-kire*, day has dawned, the sky is clear.
Ganda:	*-kya*, v.i. (pf. *kedde*), dawn, clear up (rain); (*obu-dde bu-kedde*), day has dawned).
Nyoro:	*E-nkya*, n., God.
Ganda:	*e-nkya*, n., morning; as adv., in the morning.
Nyoro:	'*h*' — Ganda '*w*', e.g. Nyoro *hano*, Ganda *wano*, — here.
Nyoro:	*-hanga*, v. tr., create, fix in handle, mortise, dig deep, plough.
Ganda:	*-wanga*, v. tr., injure, fix in handle, mortise, treat badly.
Ganda:	*-banga*, v. tr., found (city), cut notch in, mortise, begin at.
Nyoro:	*-hangahanga*, v. tr., invent.
Nyoro:	*-hanga*, v.i., to shine at midday (sun).
Ganda:	*-wanga*, v.i., to be sharp.
Nyoro:	*-banga*, v.tr., cut notch in, mortise.
Acholi:	*bang'*i, n., twins.
Teso:	*ibangin*, n., twins.
Nyoro:	*Ru-hanga* (class I) God.
Nyoro:	*ru-hanga* (class VI) a skull.
Ganda:	*lu-wanga*, a skull (esp. of dead notable).
Ganda:	*eki-wanga*, a skull (ordinary living).
Nyoro:	*Nya-mu-hanga*, same as *Ruhanga*.
Ganda:	*Mu-wanga*, n., a god (*lubaale*).
Ganda:	*-Wanga*, n., the oldest of the gods.
Nyoro:	*Ru-banga*, n., the *omu-cwezi* of twins.
Ganda:	*Lu-banga*, n., a god (*lubaale*), thwart or seat of canoe (which is *mortised* in).
Madi:	*Rabanga*, n., the earth, God (Williams).
Madi:	*Rubangi*, n., God (Middleton).
Lugbara:	*orubangi*, n., shrine.
Ganda:	*Lubaale* (pl. *balubaale*), n., god, deity, spirit.
Nyoro:	*rubaale*, n., red bull with tiny white spots (significantly not, apparently in *ru*-class, just as *Lubaale* is not in *lu*-class).
Nyoro:	*omu-iru rubaale*, n., bondslave.
Ganda:	*Ka-ddu-lubaale*, n., chief wife of King.
	(Nyoro *omu-iru*, Ganda *omu-ddu*, slave.
	Nyoro *ka-iru*, Ganda *ka-ddu*, slave (diminutive).
Ganda:	*Na-lubaale*, n., Lake Victoria (implies female, mother or source of gods).
Nyoro:	*Kibaale*, n., spirit shrine.
Ganda:	*Mbaale*, n., name of a number of sites associated with important shrines of deities.

Table 2

Cognate forms of *jok*: Nuer (*joagh*), Shilluk (*juok*), Dinka (s. *jok*, pl. *jaak*, possessive *jong'*), Lotuko (*ajyok*), Alur (s. *jok*, pl. *jogi*) Kenya Luo (s. *juok*, pl. *juogi*).

Permutations

Nuer	Dinka	Alur	Acholi	Luo
joagh adv. behind, n. ghost	*jok* spirit, power	*jok* spirit	*jok* spirit	*juok* spirit
	cien behind ghost	*cien* behind ghost	*ceen* behind ghost (vengeful)	*chien*, *Jachien* behind, 'devil'[1]
s. *kwoth* pl. *kutho* v. *kutho* air, spirit blow		v. *kudhu* blow	*kuto* blow	*kudho* blow
jiom wind		*yamu* wind	*yamo* wind	*yamo* wind
nhial up, sky	*nhial* up, sky *nhialic* in sky	*malo* up, sky	*malo* up, sky	*malo* up, sky
Kwoth nhial Sky spirit, Divinity	*Jok nhialic* do.	*Jok malo* (*Rubanga*) do.	*Jok malo* do.	
Kuth nhial/piny Spirits of the above/below	*jong'nhial/piny* do.	*jok malo/piny* do.		

(op. cit., pp. 1–3). The same argument applies to the Dinka use of the locative form *nhiálic* ('in the sky'). Indeed, the principle has wide application. Thus, in the Nyoro case above *enkya* is used like *Ruhanga* to address God in prayer. There can be no doubt that *enkya* contains the meaning 'dawn', but it does not follow that the Nyoro worship the dawn.

If *Ruhanga* was the supreme if otiose deity of Bunyoro, and *Rubanga* was only one of nineteen or nine *Bacwezi*, about whom comparatively little is recorded, we may well ask why it was *Rubanga*, rather than *Ruhanga*, who became the highest manifestation of *Jok* in major Alur chiefdoms. Further investigation of the relevant roots suggests the strange conclusion that *Ruhanga* and *Rubanga* are structurally the same.

If the evidence of the dictionaries is to be relied upon, the verbs -*hanga* and -*banga* in Nyoro have an important overlap in

[1] St. Joseph's Society (1935), *Dholuo Grammar*, Kisumu Stores, Kisumu, Kenya, 140.

meanings. The idea of making a joint (mortise) or of fitting a handle into its socket is very closely connected with that of creation and of divinity in many languages and thought systems. Since Nyoro '*h*' corresponds to Ganda '*w*', Maddox (1902, p. 104) puts *Ruhanga* in the sense of God in the first (personal) class, whereas the same word in the sense of skull is in the sixth class. Therefore *Ruhanga* (God) corresponds to *Muwanga* in Ganda, and *ruhanga* (skull) to *eki-wanga* in Ganda. *Rubanga* in Nyoro is *Lubanga* in Ganda. Its concrete sense of canoe thwart is an intriguing insistence upon the marine and island associations of the gods (*ba-lubaale*) in Ganda, who were nearly all supposed to have come from the Sesse Islands in Lake Victoria (*Na-lubaale*). Even more intriguing is Roscoe's (1911, p. 313) tantalizing mention of the fact that *Wanga* was believed by the Ganda to be one of the oldest of the gods, the father of *Musisi* (the *lubaale* associated with earthquakes), who was himself the father of *Mukasa* (in practice, the most important of the Ganda pantheon and very closely associated with Lake Victoria -*Nalubaale*). In fact, according to Roscoe (1911, pp. 64–5), Ganda twins were due to the direct intervention of the god *Mukasa*, and were always called after him *Mukasa* (male) and *Namukasa* (female). When the sun fell from its place in the heavens, and there was total darkness for some days, the King (Kabaka) in his distress sent to Wanga (in the Sesse Islands) for help. Wanga consented, came to Buganda, and restored the sun to its place. Wanga was consulted in reference to sickness and disease, and he also foretold in what manner common evils might be averted. He had a temple, medium, and priests in Busiro just like Mukasa.

Wanga's control of the sun (presumably on the occasion of the eclipses) recalls the intransitive meaning of the Nyoro verb -*hanga* 'to shine at midday'. Several of the names of the *Bacwezi* spirits in Bunyoro are connected with the shining of the sun, for example, *Ka-zoba*, or *Ka-zoba wa Ndahura*. (Nyoro, *Ka-zoba*, title given to the Creator, and *Izoba*, sun, a day; Ganda *njuba e-*, n., the sun). We remember also that *Ruhanga* is prayed to by raising palms and eyes towards heaven. The Ganda *Wanga* recalls the Nyoro *Rubanga* somewhat in function, since both are accredited with a special concern for sickness and healing. On the other hand, *Wanga* is clearly superseded in prominence by his grandson *Mukasa*, and to this extent has become somewhat otiose like the Nyoro *Ruhanga*, to whom he is more certainly cognate linguistically.

We have seen that the concrete and figurative meanings denoted by a single stem may be treated in various ways. In the stem *-hanga* the abstract idea of creation is not differentiated in any way from the concrete notion of fitting a handle into its socket. Nor are these transitive senses distinguished phonetically from the intransitive sense 'to shine at midday'. *Ruhanga* (God) is not distinguished phonetically from *ruhanga* (skull), but they are grammatically distinguished by the agreement of the former with the first class and the latter with the sixth class of concords. Sometimes the concrete denotation of a stem is preserved in one language, while the figurative denotation is retained by its cognate in a neighbouring language. Thus, we have in Nyoro *Rubanga* (the *omucwezi*-spirit of twins) and in Ganda *Lubanga* (a *lubaale*—spirit, and also the thwart of a canoe). Or again, more significantly, we have *e-nkya* (dawn, morning) in Ganda and *E-nkya* (Divinity) in Nyoro; in Ganda *lubaale* (spirit, god, divinity), and in Nyoro its cognate *rubaale* (a red bull with tiny white spots). It may be seriously doubted whether the full range of meanings has been recorded for Nyoro. However, there is very widespread evidence for the fact that red and white is the auspicious colour combination associated with divinity. Black, red, and white are the primary symbolic colours over much of Eastern Africa and beyond. 'Nothing black must ever be offered to the Bacwezi' (Fisher, 1911, p. 59). When the Nyoro King Dubongoza was fleeing from Buganda he was unable to drink the milk of a black cow to save himself from starvation until the cow had been rendered red and white by being smeared with red earth and having white chalk rubbed on to its horns (Fisher, 1911, p. 150).

We find a closely similar set of associated ideas among the Dinka, one of whose most important divinities is *Garang'*. *Garang'* was the name of the first man in the myth of the separation of earth and sky, and is also a 'Power of the sky which enters the bodies of some men by falling on them from above, and thereafter becomes their divinity' (Lienhardt, 1961, p. 84). The emblem and association of *Garang'* is a snake. 'Its colours, which are the significant feature, are red and white' (loc. cit.,

p. 85). *Garang'* is associated with red-brown and red-and-white combinations wherever they appear in cattle, sheep, and goats. 'For the Dinka there is an imaginative connexion between the colours red, or red and white, and tawny and the sun, and between *Garang'* and the sun. A red and white bull (cf. *Rubaale*) with a red-brown body and a flash of white on the belly is called *makol*, and *akol* is the Dinka word for "sun"' (ibid.). When the Shilluk king is chosen 'the pebble representing the king-elect turns red, or white, or red and white. Red stands for prosperity in cattle, white for good crops' (Lienhardt, 1954, p. 157). Such specific interpretations are more variable than the basic general meaning of the colour combination.

It might be supposed that the reason why it is *Rubanga* and not *Ruhanga* which assumes a prominent position in the Alur religious system is purely phonetic, since the sound '*h*' does not appear in Alur and other neighbouring Nilotic languages. Both terms contain the same semantic aspects of the idea of creation, and *Ruhanga* might well appear as *Rubanga* in Alur speech. However, it seems more plausible to attribute the presence of *Rubanga* to the importance of twinship or duality in the Alur representation of chiefship and more fundamentally in their metaphysical and cosmological system as a whole. Twin birth is perhaps the most human and the most social representation of metaphysical and cosmological duality.

The Alur *Rubanga* is associated with the most sacred embodiment of Alur chiefship, with the earth of their homeland carried in a twin-necked pot and with the twin origin of their major ruling dynasties (Southall, 1956, pp. 371–2 fn.). These dynasties claim descent from the daughter of a local ruler who was impregnated by a mysterious stranger and gave birth to twins (Crazzolara, 1951, pp. 179–83). If we take the three formal components of this myth, change of male line, illegitimate parentage, and twin birth we have them all repeated in the myth of the founding of the Bito dynasty of Bunyoro. In Alur, *Ucak*[1] *Upodho* (the 'Starter, he who fell'—presumably from the sky) finds *Nyilak* (*Kilak*), the daughter of *Kwong'a* ('the Beginning') herding in the pasture, and eventually she bears him twin boys, *Upiyo Lavor* (the quick one, the lion) and *Udongo*

[1] *Cako* also means to name and hence to create (cf. Evans-Pritchard, 1956, pp. 4–5).

Utira (the slow one, the erect). In some versions *Upiyo* the Lion seems to stand for the animal kingdom, while *Udongo* the Erect stands for the human race.

Their grandfather *Kwong'a* orders the bastard twins to be put to death, but as usual in such cases they survive and are ultimately recognized by *Kwong'a*. *Upiyo* the Lion is the favourite and on his deathbed *Kwong'a* calls him to receive his inheritance. But as in the myth of Jacob and Esau, *Udongo* the Erect simulates the hairy arms and growling voice of his elder brother, deceives his grandfather, and succeeds in running away with the kingdom. This ritual testament is irrevocable and *Upiyo* the Lion goes off into eternal exile as lord of the animal kingdom (cf. Crazzolara, 1951, p. 179).

In the Bunyoro version it is the elder twin, *Isengoma Mpuga Rukidi Nyabongo*, who usurps the throne, while his younger brother, *Kato Kimera*, usurps that of Buganda. *Rukidi* is an unusual name, and the only other instance I know of is as the name of the great shrine established in Alurland at the place where *Rubanga*, carried with them by the earliest Alur chiefs at their entry to the country, in the form of the homeland earth in the twin-necked pot, vanished into an anthill in the chief's wife's hut and refused to budge further (Southall, 1956, pp. 372–3). In Nyoro twin ceremonies the twins' placentae are sealed up in small anthill cones, garlanded with ritual plants (several of them the same as the Alur and other Lwoo use) at the spot called *ekibare kya lu-banga*. The kinsfolk of the twins' father and mother are stationed opposite one another by two fires called *bi-banga*, after the wood and grass torn from the twins' birth hut to kindle them. In Buganda also the placentae of twins are deposited in anthills (Roscoe, 1911, p. 70).

Many other Interlacustrine Bantu ruling dynasties participate in or reproduce to a greater or lesser extent the Nyoro version of this mythological framework. Many of the major Acholi dynasties, such as Payera, Koic, and Patiko, similarly share in the Nilotic version, with appropriate modifications. Interestingly enough, the Atyak ruling clan of North Acholi, which seems to have spoken Madi until recently, yet shares its clan name with the major ruling dynasty of the Alur (Southall, 1956, pp. 352–4), regards *Labong'o-lawiarut* as its founding ancestor. According to Crazzolara (1951, p. 297), *lawiarut* means 'the twin' or 'double-headed', because a slight depression on his head caused a front and back bump on it. Furthermore, *Labong'o* (*Nyabong'o*) is always the name of the twin or brother who leads one section of Lwoo to Bunyoro and is known there as *Isengoma Mpuga Rukidi*. *Labong'o-lawiarut*'s father was Kwac (leopard) and *Kwac's* brother was *Acut* (vulture). The Acholi actually use the term *bang'i* (twins), especially in the phrase *min bang'i* (mother of twins). As both Acholi and Alur have the term *rut* (pl. *rudi*) for twin, which seems Nilotic, and *bang'i* has no singular form or other permutations, it may rather be connected with the *-banga* stem in Nyoro and Ganda. Furthermore, the Teso use *ibangin* for twins (Lawrance, 1957, p. 80).

The most widespread recorded incidence of twin-birth mythology as a symbolic representation of the unity and difference of human and animal nature is among the Dinka. Thus the crocodile is the divinity of the Patek clan because its founding ancestor was born as a twin with a crocodile (Lienhardt, 1961, pp. 118–19). The same is true of the relation claimed between man and lion, and man and hippopotamus, in the case of other clans. This is among the Western Dinka, and farther east such twin birth explanations are actually said to be usual (Seligman, 1932, p. 149). These cases are among the 'warrior' clans. Among the 'spearmaster' clans the theme of illegitimate and actually incestuous birth appears, but not that of twinship. Among the Shilluk also, the twinship theme is not explicit, but almost the same effect is produced by the half-human, half-crocodile nature of *Nyakaya*, who bears the founder hero *Nyikang'* not to her husband but to a mysterious river spirit. Both these expressions of duality are combined in *Isengoma Mpuga Rukidi*, who not only was a twin himself but had a double nature, with one side dark and one side light. (*Mpuga* is the name for a piebald cow.) Furthermore, the Shilluk *Nyikang'*, of part human and part animal mystical descent, himself provides for the orderly differentiation of the human and animal worlds which the twin theme accomplishes in Dinka and Alur.

This borders on the general problem of dualism, in which we cannot become involved. The Lugbara neighbours of the Alur, whose culture is very different, begin their oral tradition with a series of paired siblings, brother and sister, who reproduce a further pair incestuously in each generation, culminating in the pair of male siblings *Jaki* and *Dribidu*, from one or other of whom the present Lugbara clans claim descent. This dualism is continued in the approximate but overlapping pairs of the High People (*Urule'ba*) and Low People (*Andrale'ba*), the high speech (*uruleti*) and low speech (*andraleti*), and in the wider paired ethnic identities of Madi and Lu (Middleton, 1960, p. 231; 1965, pp. 16–18). We have noted, however incompletely, the considerable interpenetration between these Sudanic-speaking peoples and the Nilotic Alur, despite the apparently firm linguistic and cultural barrier between them, centring upon exchanges round the terms *Jok*, *Rubanga*, and *Rindi*. This adds some weight to the tentative idea that such cross-cultural exchanges of sounds and meanings, naturally involving considerable metamorphoses of both, seem a necessary concomitant of cultural juxtaposition rather than haphazard historical accidents.

We have left unanswered the question as to whether borrowing was mainly from Bunyoro or in the other direction. We have perhaps shown that the situation is more complex than has usually been indicated, and both directions of influence, and others, may have been important in different instances. There are many other indications of apparent Lwoo influence in Bonyoro, of which we can only mention a few. The Nilotic Lwoo drum names of the Babito kings of Bunyoro are a well-known example, as also are the Bunyoro *mpako* names (Alur *pak*, *pako*, 'praise', 'to praise'). All these names have meanings in Lwoo but not in Bantu speech. The word *ki-kali* (Nyoro, king's or chief's enclosure) is not commonly used in Ganda—where the King's enclosure is *Kisakate* and an ordinary enclosure *lukomera*—nor in other Bantu languages. It is derived from *kal*, meaning fence or chief's enclosure in Alur and Acholi. *Jo-kal* are the chief's courtiers in Alur. *Lo-kal* are the members of the chief's clan in Acholi. *Ekal* in the Nilo-hamitic language of the Jie is the fenced yard of each wife in a homestead and by extension the group of people living in it (Gulliver, 1955, p. 49). The above examples might be explained by the entry of the Babito into Bunyoro as an initially Lwoo-speaking ruling dynasty. More fundamental is *eki-rwara* (Nyoro, red earth), not found in Ganda and other Bantu languages, but with cognates in Alur,

Acholi, and Kenya Luo (*lwala*, 'red earth') and Dinka (*ma-lual*, 'red').

I have addressed myself to the problem of cross-cultural semantics on a rather narrow front, through a single set of closely related themes, which none the less showed a marked tendency to splay out in all directions. This was the point I wished to stress. There is a far more profound and widespread semantic sharing between the Nilotic Alur and the Bantu Nyoro, and between the whole cluster of Nilotic and Interlacustrine Bantu peoples than has ever been recognized. I have no space to develop other comparable sets of themes and can only insist that many others await development and could certainly be treated with much fuller detail, much greater documentation of usage, and much greater precision and refinement. The analytical study of single languages, or even of single-language clusters, tends to obscure this sharing.

It is as though there is a certain stock or pool of sounds and concepts or archetypes, lurking in the constitution of every cultural group. Not only does the pool itself ebb and flow, as population groups expand and contract, migrate and intermingle. But different draughts are taken from time to time out of the stock of archetypes which lie in the pool. One facet is emphasized here, another there. In course of time the archetype itself goes through a process of transformation and metamorphosis. Yet there are certain identities which may retain continuity and consistency over large reaches of space and time. But there are often apparent gaps and discontinuities. Perhaps they are puzzling only because the story is always incomplete. Such archetypal identities must always have both semantic and phonetic expression, and here, again, the two strands may run together or apart; intertwined, then separate, and later converging once more. Such themes have been celebrated most vividly in literature by Thomas Mann,[1] by Carl Jung[2] in analytical psychology, Mircea Eliade[3] in comparative religion, and so on. But the great ubiquitous archetypes are will o' the wisps, which seem to lead the ethnographer floundering deeper into an endless morass. There are more limited cultural archetypes, whose temporal and spatial range is more restricted and manageable, such as the theme of the elephant, the spear,

[1] (1963). [2] (1964, etc.). [3] (1954, 1960, 1961).

and the bead, among the Lwoo and their neighbours. Even these limited archetypes constantly echo elements of wider themes.

The argument here takes off from the classical anthropological principle of beginning from a firm and specific concrete base in a particular culture, but then establishing several such bases in neighbouring and cognate cultures and, above all, refusing to accept the conventional barriers of language and culture as a mere initial framework, rather insisting on continuous lines of communication from one base to another, and preferably transcending the central, standardized focus, recognizing that centre and periphery are highly relative and often need to be reversed, so that intensive study of what previously appeared as marginal contact areas may give a more balanced view of the ebb and flow through time and space of themes which bind sounds and meaning together. At the practical level I would reiterate that the kind of cross-cultural semantics I have advocated would, if improved and refined, provide not only a fascinating field of research for East African scholarship but a highly motivated classroom method for teaching East Africans about themselves and the richness of their cultural heritage, not dividing them from one another as usual through the emphasis on misleading linguistic and cultural boundaries but uniting them by establishing firm bridges of conceptual sharing and participation between the varieties of the cultural background.

The modern technology of the mass media, the printing press, radio and television, the whole process of education, necessitate standardization through selection of certain dialects and the neglect of others. But this process of standardization, and the whole effort to demarcate linguistic boundaries, do create discontinuities and barriers that were not there before. The enrichment of language through the incorporation of new words and ideas is accompanied by an impoverishment through the loss of many vivid and varied modes of rich traditional expression. Any attempt to turn the clock back is futile, but if the teaching of cross-cultural semantics could be brought right into the educational process these linguistic riches of the past would not be wholly lost, and pride in the national and cultural heritage would be greatly stimulated.

REFERENCES

Beattie, J. H. M.
(1962) 'Twin Ceremonies in Bunyoro', XCII, pp. 1–12.

Beidelman, T. O.
(1961) 'Right and Left Hand among the Kaguru: a Note on Symbolic Classification', *Africa*, XXXI, pp. 250–7.
(1964) 'Pig (Guluwe): an Essay on Ngulu Sexual Symbolism', *South Western J. Anthrop.*, pp. 359–92.

Boccassino, R.
(1939) 'Characteristics of the Supreme Being of the Acholi of Uganda', *Uganda Journal* VI, 4.

Butt, A.
(1952) *The Nilotes of the Sudan and Uganda*. London: International African Institute.

Crazzolara, J. P.
(1938) *A Study of the Acholi Language*. London: Oxford University Press for the International African Institute.
(1950, 1951, 1954) *The Lwoo*. Pts. I, II, III, Museum Combonianum No. 3, No. 6, No. 8, Verona.
(1960) *A Study of the Logbara (Ma'di) Language*. London:

Davis, M. B.
(1952) *A Lunyoro–Lunyankole–English and English–Lunyoro–Lunyankole Dictionary*. London: Macmillan.

Eliade, Mircea
(1954) *The Myth of the Eternal Return*. New York: Bollingen-Pantheon.
(1960) *Myths, Dreams and Mysteries*. London: Harvill.
(1961) *Images and Symbols*. London: Harvill.

Evans-Pritchard, E. E.
(1956) *Nuer Religion*. Oxford University Press.

Fallers, M. C.
(1960) *The Eastern Lacustrine Bantu*. London: International African Institute.

Fisher, Mrs. A. B.
(1911) *Twilight Tales of the Black Baganda*. London: Marshall.

Girling, F. K.
(1960) *The Acholi of Uganda*. Colonial Research Studies No. 30. London: H.M.S.O.

Greenberg, J. H.
(1963) 'The Languages of Africa,' *Int. J. of Comparative Linguistics*, XXIX, 1, Pt. II.

Gulliver, P. H.
(1955) *The Family Herds: A Study of two Pastoral Tribes in East Africa, the Jie and Turkana*. London: Routledge.

Helm, June
(1968) *Essays on the Problem of Tribe*. Proceedings of the 1967 Annual Spring Meeting, American Ethnological Society. Seattle: University of Washington Press.

Jung, Carl G.
(1964) *Man and his Symbols*. London: Aldus; New York: Doubleday.

Kitching, A. L., and Blackledge, G. R.
(1925) *A Luganda–English and English–Luganda Dictionary*. Kampala: The Uganda Bookshop; London: SPCK.

Lawrance, J. C. D.
(1957) *The Iteso*. Oxford University Press.

Lienhardt, G.
(1954) 'The Shilluk of the Upper Nile,' in Daryll Forde (ed.), *African Worlds, Studies in the Cosmological Ideas and Social Values of African Peoples*. London: Oxford University Press for the International African Institute.
(1961) *Divinity and Experience, the Religion of the Dinka*. Oxford University Press.

Maddox, H. E.
(1902) *An Elementary Lunyoro Grammar*. London: S.P.C.K.

Mann, Thomas
(1963) *Joseph and His Brothers*, trans. H. T. Lowe-Porter, London: Secker and Warburg (Berlin, Vienna, Stockholm, 1933–43).

Middleton, John
(1960) *Lugbara Religion*. London: Oxford University Press for the International African Institute.
(1965) *The Lugbara of Uganda*. New York: Holt, Rinehart and Winston.

Needham, R.
(1960) 'The Left Hand of the Mugwe, An Analytical Note on the Structure of Meru Symbolism', *Africa*, XXX, pp. 20–33.
(1967) 'Right and Left in Nyoro Symbolic Classification', *Africa*, XXXVII, pp. 425–51.

Ogot, B. A.
(1961) 'The Concept of Jok', *African Studies*, XXVII, p. 2.

Okot p'Bitek
(MS) 'Is Jok God?' Unpublished MS.
(1963) 'The Concept of *jok* among the Acholi and Lang'o', *Uganda Journal*, XXVII, 1, pp. 15–29.

Rigby, P. J.
(1966) 'Dual Symbolic Classification among the Gogo of Central Tanzania', *Africa*, XXXVI, pp. 1–17.
Roscoe, J.
(1911) *The Baganda*. London: Macmillan.
(1923) *The Bakitara or Banyoro*. Cambridge University Press.
Savage, G. A. R.
(1955) *A Short Acoli–English and English–Acoli Vocabulary*. Kampala: Eagle Press.
Seligman, C. G., and B. Z.
(1932) *Pagan Tribes of the Nilotic Sudan*. London: Routledge.
Southall, A. W.
(1956) *Alur Society, a Study in Processes and Types of Domination*. Cambridge: Heffer, for E. African Institute of Social Research.
(1969) '*Spirit Possession and Mediumship Among The Alur*', in Beattie, J. H. M. and Middleton, J. (eds.) *Spirit Mediumship and Society in Africa*. London: Routledge & Kegan Paul.
(1970) 'The Illusion of Tribe', *J. African and Asian Studies*, V, 1/2, January–April.
Taylor, B. K.
(1962) *The Western Lacustrine Bantu*. London: International African Institute.
Turner, V. W.
(1962) *Chihamba, the White Spirit*. Manchester: Rhodes–Livingstone Institute Papers, No. 33.
Williams, F. R. J.
(1949) 'The Pagan Religion of the Madi', *Uganda Journal*, XIII, 2.
Willis, R. G.
(1967) 'The Head and the Loins: Levi-Strauss and Beyond', *Man*, n.s. II, 4, p. 519.
Wright, A. C. A.
(1940) 'The Supreme Being Among the Acholi of Uganda—Another Viewpoint', *Uganda Journal*, VII, p. 130.

Index